Classics of British Literature

John Sutherland, Ph.D., D.Litt., FRSL

THE
GREAT
COURSES

PUBLISHED BY:

THE GREAT COURSES
Corporate Headquarters
4840 Westfields Boulevard, Suite 500
Chantilly, Virginia 20151-2299
Phone: 1-800-832-2412
Fax: 703-378-3819
www.thegreatcourses.com

John Sutherland, Ph.D., D.Litt., FRSL

UCL Emeritus Lord Northcliffe
Professor of Modern English Literature
University College London
Visiting Professor of Literature
California Institute of Technology

Professor John Sutherland is UCL Emeritus Lord Northcliffe Professor of Modern English Literature at University College London and Visiting Professor of Literature at the California Institute of Technology (Caltech). Professor Sutherland received his B.A. and M.A. from the University of Leicester and earned his Ph.D. from The University of Edinburgh while teaching there as a junior lecturer. He also has received honorary doctorates from the University of Surrey and the University of Leicester and is a Fellow of the Royal Society of Literature.

After 10 years at The University of Edinburgh, Professor Sutherland moved to a post at University College London, the first institution in England to admit Nonconformist, Jewish, and female students, and the first institution to pioneer, in 1830, what is taken to be the first university English department in England. After a decade at University College London, he was appointed Visiting Professor of Literature at Caltech, where he won teaching excellence awards instructing a predominantly scientific undergraduate community in his own unscientific field.

In 1992, Professor Sutherland was appointed to the Lord Northcliffe Chair at University College London. He maintained a split appointment until 1994, when he retired from active teaching at University College London.

Over the course of his career, Professor Sutherland has had visiting appointments at Dartmouth College, the University of Münster, and The University of Western Ontario, teaching students at every level in a variety of academic contexts. He has received numerous awards and honors, including the Associated Student Body of Caltech Excellence in Teaching Award

(1992 and 2003) and the Sherman Fairchild Distinguished Scholar Award from Caltech (1993).

Professor Sutherland is the author of more than 30 scholarly editions (mostly of classic Victorian fiction) and scores of articles in learned journals. Starting in 1992, he wrote a weekly column in *The Guardian* newspaper for seven years. As a result of his journalism and broadcast work, he is one of the best-known academics outside of academia.

Professor Sutherland's books range from close examinations of manuscript materials (*Thackeray at Work*) and publishing history (*Victorian Novelists and Publishers*; *Fiction and the Fiction Industry*) to biography (*Mrs. Humphry Ward: Eminent Victorian, Pre-eminent Edwardian*; *The Life of Walter Scott: A Critical Biography*; *Stephen Spender: A Literary Life*) and *The Longman Companion to Victorian Fiction* (*The Stanford Companion to Victorian Fiction* in the United States), a massive encyclopedia of one of English literature's major genres. This last work took a decade to complete, and he regards it as his major effort in scholarship.

In 1996, Professor Sutherland embarked on a series of literary "puzzle books" with Oxford University Press, beginning with *Is Heathcliff a Murderer? Puzzles in 19th-Century Fiction*; the work was extraordinarily popular, even appearing—for a glorious week or two—on *The Sunday Times* bestseller list. Five more puzzle books followed, culminating with *Henry V, War Criminal? and Other Shakespeare Puzzles* (with Cedric Watts).

Professor Sutherland continues to publish prolifically. Since 2005, in addition to a wealth of journalism and reviewing, he has written *Victorian Fiction: Novelists, Publishers, Readers*; *Inside Bleak House: A Guide for the Modern Dickensian* (a companion to the BBC TV dramatization of Dickens's novel); *So You Think You Know Jane Austen? A Literary Quizbook* (with Deirdre Le Faye); *So You Think You Know Thomas Hardy? A Literary Quizbook*; *Bestsellers: A Very Short Introduction*; *The Boy Who Loved Books: A Memoir*; *How to Read a Novel: A User's Guide*; and has edited an edition of Robert Louis Stevenson's *The Black Arrow*. ■

Table of Contents

Table of Contents

Table of Contents

SUPPLEMENTAL MATERIAL

Classics of British Literature

Scope:

This course could as properly be titled *A History of British Literature*, in that it is sequential and essentially "historical"—historical, that is, in two senses. It follows the trajectory of literary achievement from earliest to latest times in a progressive line, and its basic presupposition is that literature cannot be (and *should* not be) examined outside the historical circumstances in which it came into being. Of course, great literature is timeless. That is one of the main connotations of the word *classic*. Shakespeare, for example, is "for all ages." But it is vital, while appreciating that universal, transcendent, and classic quality of literature, to appreciate, as fully as one can, the conditions that gave birth to these works of literature, to reinsert them, that is, back into history. This is one of the principal aims of this "historical" course.

Literature, as an object of study, is dependent on texts—vehicles that give the literary work permanence. We can understand oral literature, the pre-textual literary universe, only insofar as it has been preserved through time and ultimately inscribed. English literature (a deceptively simple term) begins with the transcription (three centuries or so after its composition) of the great Anglo-Germanic epic *Beowulf*. This magnificent poem (authorless, from our perspective) exemplifies one of the foundational principles of this course: namely, that we can find "classic" quality at any point along the 1,300-year arc from *Beowulf* to the present day.

The dawn of British literature is obstructed by Anglo-Saxon—the early English dialect in which *Beowulf* is written. Nonetheless, enough of the essence of the work comes through in translation for us to appreciate it. There is no such obstruction with the true father of English literature (it will, alas, be some centuries before a mother appears), Geoffrey Chaucer. With Chaucer, a keynote is struck: the idea that great literature is supremely enjoyable, indeed, laugh-out-loud enjoyable, even after half a millennium. But how, given the cultural, social, and national turbulence of the 14th century could such a masterwork as *The Canterbury Tales* happen? To ask the question and investigate the issue is to enrich still further one's appreciation of the work.

Edmund Spenser, it is fair to say, could never have written his great chauvinistic epic *The Faerie Queene* did he not have Chaucer on which to build. Likewise, Shakespeare could not have created the plays that are commonly regarded as the highest ever achievement of British literature did he not have Chaucer, Spenser, the early "Miracle" street drama, and above all, Christopher Marlowe from which to work.

Classic literature will always strike us as unique, but it has its roots in earlier literature, and it responds, livingly, to the world around it. Shakespeare's drama, for example, is as much a product of London, the London stage, and the extraordinary florescence of the English language as it is the sole creation of a glover's son in the provincial town of Stratford.

The early modern period, a period in which England (an insignificant, small, cold island off mainland Europe) was establishing itself as a world power, saw the birth (or renaissance) of a world-significant literature. The creators of this literature fondly believed that it could rival the achievements of ancient Rome and Greece and excel the current achievements of Italy and France.

Jewels in the English Renaissance literary crown feature the King James Bible (to this day, the most read work of English literature); the work of the so-called Metaphysical poets, who raised wit to hitherto unscaled heights; and Milton's supreme religious epic, justifying the "ways of God to men," *Paradise Lost*. For this poem, Milton created a diction that is both idiosyncratic and artistically necessary. *Paradise Lost* exemplifies another basic tenet of the course, that we must labor (pleasurable labor that is) to read these works on their own terms. ■

Anglo-Saxon Roots—Pessimism and Comradeship
Lecture 1

We begin this course with a brief look at some of the ideas embodied in the phrase "English literature." Of course, literature existed long before England did and before printing. The texts we will read in this lecture largely come from a tradition of oral poetry.

The phrase "English literature" is so familiar that we rarely feel impelled to unpack it. But if we pause to consider what we mean by English literature, it's anything but simple. Of course, literature existed before England. Literature also existed in the form of oral epics, elegies, and ballads before these things were printed in books. English literature is not the same thing as literature in English. American literature, for example, is not simply English literature written and published in the United States.

In 2005, the listeners of the BBC radio program *Today* voted William Shakespeare the greatest Briton who had ever lived. It was believed that he most embodied the soul of Britain. Linguists have said that a language is a dialect with an army behind it, and one might adapt that quip by defining literature as writing with a national state behind it. More importantly, literature is embedded in the nation, as the heart is embedded in the body. In the wide-ranging remarks found in these lectures, it is not merely the words on the page that we shall be considering, but the United Kingdom itself in its most revealing aspect, its inner self, its soul.

In *The Poetics*, Aristotle, our first great literary critic, makes the claim that literature is truer than history. History, the chronicle of events that actually happened, is shackled to the accidental and incidental. Literature, however, can penetrate to the heart of the human condition. It can generalize. It can extract the truth.

Our course will begin with the first milestones on the long, winding path of English literature—primarily the Anglo-Saxon epic *Beowulf*, but also some other works of poetry. Most people coming to *Beowulf* wonder how such a complex and, in its own terms, perfect work of literary art could be produced by a primitive tribal community. Similarly, Karl Marx wondered how a society as primitive as Periclean Athens could produce literature as sophisticated as *Oedipus Rex*. By way of explanation, Marx offered his law of uneven development. According to this law, primitive, preindustrial communities can produce perfect works of art, as perfect as anything we can produce.

Much ancient English literature has been lost or exists only in fragments, but we can recover some aspects of how it was put together. The greatest work of the early period of English literature was the creation of minstrels or *scops*. Early literature was sung, recited, or spoken, not written or printed. Oral literature is fragile, and it presumes a different author-audience relationship. It is literature of the ear as much as the eye. It also is typically a communal, not a private, experience.

Karl Marx.

The first text on which the structure of English literature rests—*Beowulf*—dates from around the 6th century, during the Dark Age that fell after the exodus of the Romans from the British Isles. This period was not an ideal one for the development of literature, which requires a certain stability. The Romans left, however, one monument behind them, the Latin language, used by the one beacon of light and learning in these dark times, the church. The church was tolerant, although not entirely sympathetic, to pagan literature. During this same time, England was under invasion by the Angles, Saxons, Jutes, Danes, and Vikings. These newcomers brought with them a tribal, oral literature. Of course, the Christian missionaries who came to England brought with them the Bible, and inevitably, long-rooted pagan traditions collided with Christian orthodoxies. The result was a kind of clash of civilizations that would energize and cross-fertilize language and literature up until 1066, when the Normans came to England.

The church was the foundational institution in these early centuries, based on monasteries and abbeys. These communities encompassed farms, schools, and vineyards and were supported by taxes or tithes. Within their walls, monasteries were sites of higher learning. Above all, these communities were, until the bureaucratic Normans came in the 11th century, the nation's chroniclers.

The institutional language of the church was Latin; nonetheless, the primal text in English literature, *Caedmon's Hymn*, is in the vernacular. The Venerable Bede (672/73–735), a monk at the Northumbrian monastery of Saint Peter in the 8th century, tells us about Caedmon in his *Ecclesiastical History*. Caedmon was an Anglo-Saxon herdsman, working in the fields around the monastery at Whitby. He was illiterate and ignorant of the art of song. After supper, when the harp was passed around among the herdsmen to entertain one another, Caedmon would slink away. According to Bede, Caedmon was given the art of song in a dream. He went on to become a zealous monk and an inspirational religious poet in his own Anglo-Saxon tongue. The hymn we have is his only surviving work.

How could the Dark Ages produce something so impressively literary as this hymn? Further, how could it be produced, not from the mouth of some privileged noble or prince of the church, but by an ordinary laboring man, who had no claim to education at all?

Anglo-Saxon literature is principally poetic, largely because its continuity depended on the *scop* or the singer. This poetry does not use rhyme, nor does it obey the complicated metrics of Latin prosody. It is composed in half-lines, units that make memorization easier, and these half-lines are divided by a silent pause or *caesura*, a "cut." The poetry is alliterative, meaning that the first letter or consonant of every word matches the next consonant of the next word. Additionally, it is organized around stress, not syllables. To understand this type of organization, begin by considering the line "This is the *house* that *Jack* built" from an English nursery rhyme. In reciting the line, an English speaker will stress two words and understress the rest: "This

5

is the house that Jack built." A lengthier line of 10 syllables (pentameter), as spoken in English, will divide naturally into two half-lines, each containing two stresses. For example: "To *be* or not to *be, that* is the *question*." Half-lines and organization by two stresses per half-line are found in both English and American poetry to the present day. These features give the poetry its "Englishness."

> **In the wide-ranging remarks found in these lectures, it is not merely the words on the page that we shall be considering, but the United Kingdom itself in its most revealing aspect, its inner self, its soul.**

The poetry of Anglo-Saxon England, the period roughly from the 8th to the 11th centuries, falls into distinct genres, or styles, including hymns or secular songs; elegies, that is, short poems of poignant loss; riddles and other minor works; and of course, epics, such as *Beowulf*.

Elegies are less heroic than stoic. They celebrate suffering nobly borne. In two of the greatest of them, *The Wanderer* and *The Seafarer*, the singers are men who have lost their ring-giver (*thegn*, or chief), and with that, their communities. The great modernist poet Ezra Pound gave us a beautiful translation of *The Seafarer* that is true to both the alliteration and the two-stress half-line of the original. In this translation, note the compound "bitter breast-cares," which are examples of a form called a *kenning*. As we'll see, *kennings* are a prime feature of Anglo-Saxon poetry.

As the lines from these poems testify, the invaders who came from Friesland and northern Germany brought, along with their swords and chain mail, a somber view of life, a kind of tough pessimism. A line in *Beowulf* sums up this overriding mood: "*Wyrd bith full aread*," "Fate will be fulfilled." For these pioneers, life was a constant battle against the elements, monsters, their fellow men, and nature. But in that battle, it was believed, the greatness of humanity would shine brightest. We see this view in the late heroic Anglo-Saxon poem, *The Battle of Maldon*, which recounts an 11th-century invasion by the Viking heathens. The English are defeated in this battle, but they go down with defiance and courage.

On the other hand, not all Anglo-Saxon verse was somber. We have a whole library of verse riddles from what must have been an Anglo-Saxon joke book. Riddle 82, written in verse, asks readers to identify a creature with one eye, two feet, 1,200 heads, a back and a belly, two hands, two arms, two shoulders, one neck, and two sides. What was this strange creature? A one-eyed garlic seller.

As our discussion suggests, this poetry had more than one mood. The strongest moods are found in the epic narratives, which also convey an overwhelming sense of the virtue of comradeship, based on the sword.

As a result of an almost miraculous series of accidents, we have *Beowulf*, the only surviving Anglo-Saxon or Germanic epic, in something like the form in which it was first recited. *Beowulf* was composed for recitation, probably in the 6th century, by pagan newcomers from the northeast. It was handed down through generations of minstrels until it was transcribed by a monk, who couldn't resist interpolating Christian doctrine at various points.

The 3,000-line narrative is divided into two parts; the first part is twice as long as the second. In the poem, the titular Beowulf is a Geat, a member of a tribe in what is now Sweden. He is a mighty warrior, not yet a king but destined to be one. In the first part of the epic, Beowulf comes to Denmark to help Hrothgar, king of the Scyldings, whose great hall has been terrorized by a monster, Grendel, for 12 years. Beowulf defeats both Grendel and the monster's mother, and there follows feasting, drinking, and treasure giving before Beowulf sails back to his own people. In the second part of the epic, which takes place many years later, Beowulf is king of the Geats, but now his kingdom is being terrorized by a dragon. Beowulf slays the dragon but is mortally wounded, and the poem ends with Beowulf's burial.

Readers who come to Beowulf for the first time usually have two very different reactions. The first is incomprehension; the language is so foreign that it jars. The second reaction is just the opposite. Even for someone who has not read the poem, it seems familiar, largely because of the echoes of the work we see in the writing of J. R. R. Tolkien.

The opening three lines of the poem appear below, first in Anglo-Saxon English, then in Seamus Heaney's 2002 translation. Keep in mind the features of Anglo-Saxon poetry discussed earlier: half-lines, alliteration, and the four stresses per line.

> Hwæt! We Gardena / In geardagum,
> þeodcyninga, / Þrym gefrunon,
> hu ða æþelingas / ellen fremedon.

> So. The Spear Danes, in Days gone by
> And the kings who ruled them, had courage and greatness.
> We have heard of those princes' heroic campaigns.

The first word in the Anglo-Saxon, *Hwæt*, is our word "what," used here to attract attention and impose silence. In the modern translation, the "Spear Danes" tells listeners what tribes are involved in the story, which in turn makes them aware that this will be a historical chronicle, recounting great deeds in the past, among a society known, if only by reputation. From these lines in both versions, we also know that the audience is upper class—from the reference in the original to *æþelingas*, "princes," and in the recent translation to their "heroic campaigns."

Most impressive in these lines is the poetry itself. In the first line, the word *geardagum* (meaning "yore-days" or "days of yore") contains the essence of Anglo-Saxon verse. Anglo-Saxon compresses into one compound noun, or *kenning*, a concept that Heaney must translate into four words. The rugged economy of Anglo-Saxon represents its highest linguistic achievement, along with its ability to create new words, neologisms. The creative writer, we may say, remakes language. And in so doing, he or she serves a vital function for society as a whole. It is thanks to such writers that language lives in its best and most precious form.

Clearly, the *Beowulf* poet, whoever he was, was talking to people who were part of his own community. There was common ground between them—just as there is for us, to some extent, in reading the poem hundreds of years later. In this way, literature is a time machine. It can take us back and connect us with people who are no longer here. It is, in the best sense, a conversation with the dead. In fact, this is the reason we read and study literature and the reason that it lives for us. This living quality of literature—the fact that it is still animated over centuries—makes it worth our time and effort and makes a historical approach to literature valuable. ■

Suggested Reading

Anonymous, *The Seafarer*.

Aristotle, *Poetics*.

Baugh and Cable, *A History of the English Language*, chapters 1–3.

Chickering, *Beowulf: A Dual-Language Edition*.

Crystal, *The Stories of English*, chapters 1–4.

Drabble, ed., *The Oxford Companion to English Literature* (for all lectures).

Heaney, *Beowulf*.

Stenton, *Anglo-Saxon England*.

Questions to Consider

1. In what sense can literature be said to have a "history," and what value to us, as modern readers, is the reading or study of "old literature"?

2. We think of early society as, in many ways, "undeveloped," even "primitive." Is early literature similarly "primitive"?

Anglo-Saxon Roots—Pessimism and Comradeship
Lecture 1—Transcript

The subject of these lectures is English literature. It's a familiar term, so familiar indeed that we rarely feel impelled to unpack it, to look at what's inside it. But if we do pause to look inside what we mean when we use the term "English literature," it's anything but simple. There was, of course, literature before there was an England. There was, if we want to be precise, not to say pedantic on the matter, literature, by which we mean oral epics, elegies and ballads, before there was literature in its modern sense of written or printed texts—books.

English literature is not—and I want to be emphatic here—it is not the same thing as literature in English. It's a very important distinction. Any school or college curriculum in North America or Australia will demonstrate the falsity of that idea. Is American literature English literature written and published in the United States? No, it's not. You could start another Boston Tea Party with that proposition.

In 2005, the BBC program *Today* conducted a poll to establish who was the greatest Briton who'd ever walked our green and pleasant land. The *Today* program has an audience of 2 million. In fact, I sometimes appear on the program, and it's a wonderful feeling. You are addressing the nation. The result of that poll, Great Britain's great Briton—the shortlist included such obvious giants as Winston Churchill, Good Queen Bess, and the Lady with the Lamp, Florence Nightingale—but the clear outright winner was William Shakespeare.

As it emerged in the post-result analysis, the Swan of Avon—of course, Shakespeare—was voted for by *Today*'s millions of listeners not merely because of his literary genius, but because it was felt by these voters that he embodied what one might call the soul of Britain, or, as Shakespeare himself put it in an immortal quotation, which is much repeated, "This precious stone set in the silver sea … This blessed plot, this earth, this realm, this England." Is it any wonder that the author of those inspiring words should be considered the greatest Englishman ever?

Linguists like to say that a language is a dialect with an army behind it, and one might adapt that quip by defining literature as writing with a national state behind it. And, more importantly, the literature is embedded in the nation, as the heart is embedded in the body.

In the wide-ranging remarks which follow over the lectures which I'm going to give as I follow the millennium-long track of English literature from *Beowulf* to Virginia Woolf and beyond, it is not merely words on the pages that we shall be considering, and I stress, enjoying. It is, in a very real sense, the United Kingdom, as we now call it, in its most revealing aspect, its inner self, its soul.

I want to switch ground quite radically by going back 2,000 years to Classical Greece. In *The Poetics*, Aristotle makes the grandest of claims for literature. Aristotle is our first great literary critic, possibly our first great philosopher. The Athenian philosopher asserted 2,000 years ago, as I say, before Shakespeare put quill to paper, that literature is truer than history. Why is it truer than history? Because in history, the chronicle of what actually happened is shackled to the accidental and incidental. It has to record what really happened. Literature, and Aristotle was thinking particularly of Sophoclean tragedy, could penetrate to the heart of the human condition. It could generalize. It could extract the truth.

I want to look at the first milestones on the long, winding path of English literature. Principally, I'll be looking at the Anglo-Saxon epic, *Beowulf*. Before doing so, I must point to another paradox, something which vexed another great philosopher, Karl Marx. How was it, Marx wondered, that a society as primitive as Periclean Athens could produce literature as sophisticated as *Oedipus Rex*, which, as Aristotle thought, was the greatest work of literature ever produced? And we might well agree with that. Marx offered by way of explanation his law of uneven development. Primitive, pre-industrial communities can produce perfect works of art, as perfect as anything we can do.

In my experience, everyone coming to *Beowulf*, that dragon standing at the mouth of English literature, has the same reaction: wonder. Wonder that such complex and, in its own terms, a perfect work of literary art could be produced by a tribal community with none of the things that we consider essential to a modern functioning society. It was primitive.

There was, as I have said, an English literature before there was an England, but most of that literature, alas, is forever lost. We'll never know what it was. Only fragments have survived. Some aspects of the sociology—the way in which it was put together—of that early literature we do know. We know, for example, that the greatest work of the early period was the creation of minstrels or *scops*. These were very different from our poets, but you can see a genetic link. We know that early literature was sung, recited, or spoken. It was not written and certainly not printed. Its circulation was oral, not scriptive.

Oral literature is notoriously fragile, and it presumes a different author-audience relationship. It is a literature of the ear as much as of the eye. And, typically, it is a communal not a private experience. That is to say, oral literature is experienced in a group. The audience is there en masse.

The first text on which the mighty structure of English literature rests, *Beowulf*, dates from around the 6th century, as we can best make out. This Dark Age, the night that fell after the Romans went home to their own dark age, was not propitious for literature. It was too chaotic and literature requires stability. The Romans left, however, one mighty monument behind them: Latin, the Latin language. The one beacon of light and learning in these dark times was the Church. The Church was not entirely sympathetic to pagan literature. How could it be? Although it was often less censorious than one might expect. It was tolerant, but not entirely welcoming to what was going on, as it were, among the people in their own tongue.

The language of the parish was quite important, though, and thoughtful clerics were very judicious about this. They had to be because, in fact, at this period, England was in such an, upheaval. The great invasions by the Angles, the Saxons, the Jutes, the Danes, on which Anglo-Saxon rests, had happened in the 5th and 6th centuries.

As much immigrants as invaders, unlike the later, more predatory Vikings, these newcomers from across the North Sea brought with them in their little boats a tribal, oral literature. Christianity was also a relatively new arrival, and the missionaries, who also came across the sea to the same parts of England, actually, the northeast coast, brought a great book with them: the Bible.

Inevitably, long-rooted pagan traditions collided with Christian orthodoxies. There was a kind of clash of civilization, which would energize and cross-fertilize literature and spill blood for centuries. Until 1066, when the Normans came to England—they came in force, I have to say—there would be a linguistic maelstrom. Dialects warring, fusing, amalgamating until English, my language, your language, finally emerged.

The Church was the foundational institution in these early centuries. Monasteries and abbeys were the Church's headquarters. They were communities. They were small cities almost. Farms, schools and vineyards were part of their domain. They were supported by taxes or tithes. Within their walls, monasteries were sites of higher learning. The commencement hat and gown, monastic garb, are witness of that heritage on every campus every summer in America. That is to say, it goes straight back, hundreds and hundreds of years to those ancient churches.

The churches formulated laws, and in English courts, the lawyers wear gowns and wigs, which again pay tribute or witness to that connection with the early churches of England. And above all, these churches were, until the bureaucratic Normans came in the 11th century, the nation's chroniclers. They kept the records. And their physical structures took decades to build. Their fortifications were huge and they were intended to last for centuries, till doomsday, the end of the world, when, in fact, the final judgment would come in.

The church's institutional language was Latin, the great linguistic bond which glued together the parts of what we now call Europe, and glued together also the present with the past. It went all the way back to the times when the Romans brought the first civilization to the shores of England. Nonetheless, the primal text in English literature, our first work of literature, *Caedmon's Hymn*, as it's called, is in the vernacular. It's in the language of the people or the folk, not of the clerics. That's very important.

We know the author, Caedmon, and have the work, thanks to another founder figure, the Venerable Bede, as he's called. Bede was a monk at the Northumbrian monastery of St. Peter in the 8th century. Bede was also a great scholar and, by report, although we don't have any of his poetry, he was himself a poet.

Bede tells us about Caedmon in his *Ecclesiastical History*, which is the first great work of history in the English language, by the way. Caedmon was an Anglo-Saxon herdsman, working in the fields around the monastery at Whitby. Caedmon was illiterate and, as Bede tells us, entirely ignorant of the art of song. One has to go back, as I've said earlier, to the sociology of this. After supper, when the harp passed around the table and all present would be invited to do their turn, Caedmon would slink away and find refuge among his uncritical cows because he couldn't sing.

Then something wonderful happened. One night, in a dream, this is what Bede tells us, Caedmon was given the art of song. He went to sleep a keeper of cattle and he woke up a poet. Caedmon went on to become a zealous monk and an inspirational religious poet in his own Anglo-Saxon tongue, the vernacular.

Sadly, only one of Caedmon's works survives to us, thanks again to Bede, who meaningfully calls it a *carmen*, which is Latin for a song, not a hymn. Here's what Caedmon's fellows heard as they sat at table in the middle of the 8th century, 1,300 years ago, drinking their mead and relaxing and wanting to be entertained, and at the same time, uplifted by literature.

I'll read the first two lines in Anglo-Saxon and then the translation. Imagine, if you will, in your ear the tuneful twanging of the harp and the clank of the drinking vessels and the silence as people begin to listen carefully to what Caedmon is singing.

> Nu scylun hergan hefaenricaes uard
> metudæs maecti end his modgidanc

I'll do it now in English, and I'll do the whole hymn. It's very short.

Now let me praise the keeper of Heaven's kingdom ...
He first created for the sons of men
Heaven as a roof, the holy Creator,
then Middle-earth the keeper of mankind,
the Eternal Lord, afterwards made
the earth for men.

He was indeed Almighty.

It's a very fine poem. But how, one wonders, could the Dark Ages produce something so impressively literary? It does, in fact, strike us as a poem. And how could it be produced, not from the mouth of some privileged noble or prince of the Church, but an ordinary laboring man, who had no claim to education at all?

Anglo-Saxon literature, the foundation block of English literature, is principally poetic, largely because its continuity depended on, as I said earlier, the *scop* or the singer. Anglo-Saxon poetry has features which may initially be strange and even repugnant to us, such as those two lines of Caedmon which I read.

It doesn't use rhyme, nor does it obey the complicated metrics of Latin prosody. It is composed in half lines, units that make memorization easier, and these half lines are divided by a silent pause or *caesura*, a "cut," as it's called. It is alliterative, and that means the first letter or consonant of every word matches the next consonant of the next word. And, most importantly, the poetry is organized around stress not syllables. Let me explain, then, what that means.

Think, if you would, of the English nursery rhyme, "This is the house that Jack built." Every child knows it in England. Ask a French person to say it and they will produce something like "*This is the house that Jack built*," giving an equal stress to each syllable. That's how French works. An English speaker will, by contrast, stress two words and understress the rest. "This is the *house* that *Jack* built."

Even in a pentameter, that's a 10-syllable line, such as the most famous in English literature, "To be or not to be, that is the question." As spoken by a native English speaker, the line will divide naturally into two half lines, each containing two stresses. For example, "To *be* or not to *be, that* is the *question.*"

Half lines and organization by two stresses per half line will be found in English poetry to the present day, and in American poetry as well. It's a main aspect of the "Englishness" of it, the English language.

Like all bodies of poetry, that of Anglo-Saxon England, the period roughly from the 8th to the 11th century, falls into distinct genres, or styles. There are hymns and secular songs, like Caedmon's, which I've just been talking about. There are elegies, which are short poems of poignant loss. There are minor works, like riddles, which are there only to entertain. And most impressively, there is a 3,000-line epic, the earliest we have from the Germanic peoples, *Beowulf.*

Before coming onto *Beowulf,* let me say a word or two about the elegies. They're less heroic than stoic. They celebrate suffering nobly borne. In two of the greatest of them, *The Wanderer* and *The Seafarer,* the singers are men who have, for reasons which we never know, lost their ring-giver or their *thegn,* their chief, and with that, they have lost their community. They're rootless. They belong nowhere. They have nothing to live for, but they decide to live on nonetheless.

Now, let me recite the first few lines of *The Seafarer* in translation by the great modernist poet, Ezra Pound. It's very beautiful.

> May I for my own self song's truth reckon,
> Journey's jargon, how I in harsh days
> Hardship endured oft.
> Bitter breast-cares have I abided,
> Known on my keel many a care's hold,
> And dire sea-surge,

You have to imagine *The Seafarer* rather like Kate Winslett in *Titanic* at the front of his vessel, bearing nobly the harshness of the weather. It's a fine translation, Ezra Pound's, and it's true to both alliteration and the two-stress half line, which, in fact, as I say, jangles a bit on the ear, except he's being faithful to the original.

And, if you would, bear in mind, until we come to *Beowulf*, one striking aspect of the diction: namely, compounds such as Pound's "bitter breast-cares." The technical term of these is *kennings* and they're a prime feature of Anglo-Saxon poetry. I'll say more about them later, but effectively, they're a lot of words compressed into a small area.

As these lines testify, those invaders, who came in small boats from what we now know as Friesland and Northern Germany, brought, along with their swords and chain mail, a somber view of life, a kind of tough pessimism.

There's a line in *Beowulf* which sums up the overriding mood and itself it's a wonderful Anglo-Saxon word, "*Wyrd bith full aread.*" What that means is "fate will be fulfilled." It's going to happen, *que sera sera*. And *wyrd*, incidentally, is the etymological ancestor of *weird*, which is still a powerful word in our modern tongue. It's used by teenagers because it has this strange kind of power to it.

For these pioneers, life was a constant battle against the elements, against monsters, against their fellow men, against nature. It was a hard life. But in that battle, the greatness of humanity shines brightest, or so they thought.

The finest late heroic Anglo-Saxon poem is *The Battle of Maldon*, and it recounts an 11th century invasion by the Viking heathens, who were very different from the Anglo-Saxons. The English in this battle are defeated, but as they go down, an old warrior, Byrhtwold, stands defiantly over the body of his dead king, and he brandishes his ash spear and he shouts, "Mind must be the firmer, heart the more fierce / Courage the greater, as our strength diminishes." And he will, he says, "fall where his king fell: fighting to the end." And he does just that. The British, as they will later become, are famously good losers. Being on the losing side, they think, brings out the mettle in them. It brings out the best in them.

Anglo-Saxon verse is not, as we have it, entirely somber. The Anglo-Saxons could laugh as the harp and mead cup passed round, and if we doubt that, we should look at a whole library of verse riddles, which have survived very happily, in what must have been an Anglo-Saxon joke book.

For example, let me just give you Riddle 82, and I'll translate it.

A weird creature came to where men were altogether, and this weird creature hauled itself up to the high company of these people who were there, and they thought they were very clever. This weird creature lurched with one eye. It had two feet, 1,200 heads, a back and a belly, two hands, arms, shoulders, one neck, two sides. Now, think hard. What was this? What was this strange creature? It's done in verse, by the way. And what is the answer? The answer is a one-eyed garlic seller, and if you got it, another pot of mead for you. But in fact, obviously the Anglo-Saxons liked fun as much as we did. In fact, there probably wasn't as much comedy and fun in their life as we're privileged to have.

There is, the point I'm making, more than one mood, but the strongest moods are found in the epic narratives, and they also convey an overwhelming sense of the virtue of comradeship, comradeship which is based on the sword. Like the gun in the Wild West, the sword is the instrument of civilization and of terror. It is power.

Women make a marginal and dignified appearance in the ale hall, where warriors, after the day's battle, boast and drink communally until, having drunk too much, they slide off the ale bench in wassail. And if you go into an English pub today, a unique national institution, you'll feel a connection to the ale hall in *Beowulf*. In the pub, you'll notice the men still drink in rounds, like their Anglo-Saxon ancestors, and, if truth be told, they also boast rather more than they should, as the Anglo-Saxons did when they relaxed in their ale halls.

That we have *Beowulf*, the first, and, indeed, the only surviving Anglo-Saxon or Germanic epic in something like the form in which it was first recited is the result of an almost miraculous series of accidents. It was composed for recitation, probably in the 6th century, by those pagan newcomers from the northeast, and the epic was handed down through generations of minstrels until, at the point that it would certainly have disappeared, a monk, we don't know who he was, transcribed it.

He evidently took the text down faithfully, but he couldn't resist interpolating some pious Christian doctrine at various places. It's very easy to see where and it doesn't damage the poem at all. The 3,000-line narrative is divided into two parts, and the first is twice as long as the second part.

Beowulf is a Geat, a tribe in what we call Sweden now. Think of Gothenburg. He's a mighty warrior. He's not yet a king, but destined to be one. He comes to Denmark to help Hrothgar, King of the Scyldings, whose great hall has been terrorized by a monster from the nearby marsh, Grendel, for 12 years. Beowulf defeats Grendel in single combat. Then when Grendel's mother comes to take revenge, he drives her back to her watery lair and dives in to kill her underwater, and there follows feasting, drinking, and treasure-giving before Beowulf sails back to his own people.

In the second part of the epic, now many years later, Beowulf is himself King of the Geats, a great man. And it is now his kingdom which is terrorized by a great dragon. Beowulf slays the dragon, but is himself mortally wounded, and the poem ends with his ceremonial burial.

In my experience, readers who come to *Beowulf* for the first time have two very different reactions. The first is incomprehension. The language is so foreign, it jars. The second reaction is just the opposite. Why, even if we have not read it, does the poem seem so familiar? We seem to know it. We seem to know what's happening in it, and the reason can be traced back to J. R. R. Tolkien.

Tolkien is a household name today for his *Lord of the Rings* saga, but Tolkien was also the greatest *Beowulf* scholar of the 20th century, and his view on the poem was uncompromising. It was a fantasy, the monsters, the dragons and the epic battles which made *Beowulf* great. And the best preparation, I would argue, for a reading of *Beowulf* is to go to the cinema and watch one of the Peter Jackson adaptations of Tolkien's narratives. Look around at the enraptured audience. That, I suspect, is how the first listeners of *Beowulf* looked 1,500 years ago.

I want to finish by looking at two small sections of the poem to give a flavor of the whole. The first is the opening three lines. Remember what I said earlier about half lines, alliteration and the four stresses per line.

> Hwæt! We Gardena / in geardagum,
> þeodcyninga, / þrym gefrunon,
> hu ða æþelingas / ellen fremedon.

This is how Seamus Heaney translates it, in his magnificent 2002 modernization of the poem:

> So. The Spear Danes, in Days gone by
> And the kings who ruled them, had courage and greatness.
> We have heard of those princes' heroic campaigns.

Note the first word in the Anglo-Saxon; *Hwæt* is our word "what" and it's designed to attract attention and impose silence. "Listen up" might be our equivalent. And then note *Gardena*, "Spear Danes," as Heaney translates it. Exactly what tribes will be involved is very important information for the original audience, and they are, remember, listeners.

This will be a historical chronicle, recounting great deeds in the past, among a society known, if only by reputation. And the audience is, as with most heroic literature, upper class, aristocratic, hence the reference to *æþelingas*, "princes," and their "heroic campaigns" in the third line.

But most impressive to me is the poetry, not the historical allusions. In the first line, one word, *geardagum*, contains the essence of Anglo-Saxon verse. Literally, it means "yore-days" or "days of yore," long ago. Anglo-Saxon can compress it into one compound noun or *kenning*. Heaney, who translates it, "In days gone by," is obliged by modern language to use a preposition, a noun, a past participle and a preposition.

The rugged economy of Anglo-Saxon represents its highest linguistic achievement, that and the ability to create new words, neologisms, as they are called. It's a quality we'll encounter time and again in English literature. The creative writer, we may say, remakes language. And in so doing, he or she serves a vital function for society as a whole. It is thanks to poets, to writers, that language lives in its best and its most precious form to us.

The point I've been trying to make in this lecture is that clearly, the *Beowulf* poet, whoever he was, was talking to his own people. He was talking to people, in fact, who were part of his community. There was common ground between them. What is wonderful about literature, it seems to me, and is one of the reasons why we dedicate our lives either to reading it and sometimes some of us talking about it, is that it gives us, to some extent, a connection across many hundreds of years. That is to say, *Beowulf* is not merely talking to those, as it were, contemporaries, and we can only imagine what it was like to be sitting in a rush-lit hall, drinking ale, listening to some *scop* jangling away in his half lines and with all the kind of rugged Anglo-Saxon. We can only imagine what it was like, but *Beowulf* is also talking to us, and that is wonderful.

Literature, not to make too much of it, is a time machine. It can take us back. It can connect us with people who are no longer here. It is in the best sense a conversation with the dead and a great conversation with our predecessors. And that, in fact, is the reason why we read it. It's the reason why we study it and it's a reason why, even though the makers are long dead, and in the case of *Beowulf*, we don't even know who the makers were, it lives for us.

And that living quality of literature, the fact that it's not, as it were, a museum, it's not a graveyard, it is, in fact, something which still vibrates. It's still animated. That is what makes it worth, as it were, spending time and effort. And it's hard work. Reading Anglo-Saxon is not easy, even if one reads it in Seamus Heaney's wonderful translation, *Beowulf* is a hard poem, but it's worth the effort. And that, I think, is what makes a historical approach to literature worthwhile, which is what this course is. It's the history of literature as we know it, English literature.

And, with this lofty sentiment in mind, I want to move on in the next lecture to one of the greatest makers and re-makers of language in English literature, Geoffrey Chaucer.

Chaucer—Social Diversity
Lecture 2

In the opening lecture, we covered some six centuries of literature, as that literature ... has descended to us very imperfectly in fragments and rewritings. ... Much changed in the regional kingdoms and fiefdoms of Britain during the half millennium which separates *Beowulf* from *The Canterbury Tales*, and that's the text we'll be mainly looking at in this lecture and the next.

In the years between the transcription of *Beowulf* and the writing of *The Canterbury Tales*, the kingdoms of Britain experienced repeated attacks by Vikings, followed by the invasion known as the Norman Conquest. The Scandinavian language infiltrated English with the Viking incursions but never fully took hold. As late as the 11th century, Anglo-Saxon, that alien tongue that we encountered in Beowulf, was still the language of literature.

By the 1390s, however, in the wake of the Norman Conquest, the English language had changed significantly, to the point where modern readers can generally understand the famous opening lines from the *Prologue* of *The Canterbury Tales*:

> When that Aprilis, with his showers swoot,
> The drought of March hath pierced to the root,
> And bathed every vein in such licour,
> Of which virtue engender'd is the flower;

Chaucer is essentially speaking our language here. We are also familiar with this verse form, rhymed iambic pentameter.

Such changes were the result of the invasion of England by the Norman French in 1066 and the defeat of the Saxon king, Harold, at Hastings on the English coast. The Normans brought with them a unifying mission—to bind into national unity the tribal and ethnic enclaves that had, to this point, made up Britain. The Normans unified Britain, installing a language and a system of law, a class system, Parliament, and other institutions. The Normans also conducted a vast census of the country, the results of which are recorded in the *Domesday Boke*.

The Normans also brought with them an organic connection to Europe, which included the rich Latin heritages of Italy and France. Part of this cultural baggage also included rhyme and syllabic verse. Nevertheless, we can still hear the stress systems of Anglo-Saxon literature underneath the syllabic superstructure of Chaucer's lines.

A close look at the *Prologue* to *The Canterbury Tales* tells us something about Chaucer's audience. The poem opens with an *apostrophe* to spring, a direct address to the moment in the year when the world is reborn. This was also a favorite theme of the Italian poet Petrarch and of many Romantic poets since. Chaucer's audience, we assume, was cultivated. His readers probably knew Petrarch and were acquainted with the 14th-century science of astrology. Chaucer's poetry draws on the kind of institutional learning that would eventually become concentrated in universities. Some knowledge of Latin is implied in these opening lines by the reference to Zephyrus, the Roman god of wind. We also find some French: *corage* ("courage") and *pilgrimage*.

The tone of the verse is civilized, imbued with what Chaucer would have called *gentilesse*. There are urban, cosmopolitan forces at work here, with none of the primitivism that we saw in Anglo-Saxon verse. In Chaucer's work, nature, an important element in English literature, is not cruel as it was in *The Seafarer*. Here, the rain is sweet, not harsh. A new worldview emerges through this poetry, and the poetry itself emerges from this worldview.

Despite the poem's title (given later, not by Chaucer himself), the action is not set in Canterbury, the site of the cathedral of Thomas à Becket in Kent. We don't know, in fact, if the pilgrims ever actually reached Canterbury. The poem opens in London in April 1389. The pilgrims, including Chaucer himself, are gathered at the Tabard Inn on the south bank of the Thames, across the river from Saint Paul's Cathedral. (*Tabard* is a French word meaning "drum," as one would beat a drum to gather a group of people.) The pilgrims' guide is Harry Bailey.

This band of pilgrims intends to travel by horse the 100-odd miles to Canterbury to the tomb of Thomas à Becket, martyred in his cathedral. The purpose of the trip is as much social as religious. The pilgrims travel in a party for safety because brigands and highwaymen lurk outside London. The journey to Kent will probably take them about four days.

Harry Bailey decrees that each of the 29 pilgrims shall tell two tales on the way to Kent and two on the return trip. The best storyteller shall win a prize. This framework recalls Boccaccio's *Decameron*, a similarly bundled collection of tales with which Chaucer was obviously familiar.

Chaucer's London is still recognizable under the surface of modern-day London. By Chaucer's time, London had become the engine of a thriving England. It was located on a great tidal river that served as the country's main port. Chaucer spent a large part of his working life in the port and met people there from throughout Europe. London was also the site of the monarchic court, the legal courts, Parliament, and the great cathedral at Westminster. All the main components of a modern state were in place.

The dialect of London was inexorably becoming the national standard, although literature was still being produced in other anachronistic or regional dialects. The poet of *Sir Gawain and the Green Knight* wrote his Arthurian romance in an Anglo-Saxon dialect. *Piers Plowman*, an epic of working-class life written in the dialect of the west of England, is almost incomprehensible to us. Many languages existed in England, but they were gradually being subordinated to the English of London, and Chaucer was a main actor in this standardization process.

For modern readers, the most striking feature of the pilgrims of *The Canterbury Tales* is their social diversity. Anglo-Saxon poetry was generally restricted to three classes: thains, warriors, and peasants. Women were largely invisible. These three classes are represented in Chaucer's pilgrims, along with others. Moreover, we perceive in Chaucer's pilgrims a stratified class system or hierarchy that is similar to our own.

The person of highest status in Chaucer's company and the first tale-teller is the knight. He is of a noble class and possesses gentle manners. His tale is told in high literary style, permeated with the subtle codes of courtly love and the stoical Boethian philosophy. Courtly love decrees that love is not merely an emotion but a set of moves by either party to bring the game to some conclusion, perhaps marriage or adultery. These moves were codified, refined, and popularized in medieval romance. Boethius was a 5th-century Christian Roman philosopher, who enjoined an acceptance of the fickleness of fortune. According to his *The Consolation of Philosophy*, to know that fortune was fickle was the best defense against its fickleness. Chaucer translated this work of Boethius, which explains the tone of worldly gloom we often encounter in his writing.

For modern readers, the most striking feature of the pilgrims of *The Canterbury Tales* is their social diversity.

At the bottom of the social ladder within *The Canterbury Tales* are the cook, the reeve (a land agent), the miller, and a shipman. A notch above them are the merchant and the franklin, members of the emergent bourgeoisie. Of the same class are the doctor of physic and sergeant at law.

Also among the 29 are a host of ecclesiastics and churchmen, and women, friars, monks, nun-priests, nuns, summoners, pardoners (whom Chaucer despises), and a parson. The parson offers what may be the least interesting tale in the set, a series of sermon-like biblical precepts, and the monk's tale offers a catalogue of great people who have fallen from fortune. Generally speaking, the best tales come from the least interesting people or the worst people in the company.

Some would say that the most interesting pilgrim is the businesswoman, Alisoun, the Wife of Bath, owner of a denim factory. She has had a string of husbands and profited by all of them.

The academic in the company, the clerk, possesses 20 books, a huge library. He can read and write and has mastered the arts of rhetoric and logic. He is meek in character but formidable in intellect, and he will cross swords with the Wife of Bath on the subject of a woman's place.

Each of these pilgrims is identified by his or her trade, profession, or station in life and, thus, socially stereotyped. But in each case, the social stereotype is shot through with ironies and individualizing touches that run against the grain. The nun-prioress is a good example of this cross-grained quality. She has a senior position in her holy order and is described as very devout, but Chaucer slyly subverts that description with a portrait of a woman who possesses some qualities that may be at odds with her nun's vocation. She wears, for example, a bracelet with the inscription "Love conquers all." Chaucer does not voice any criticism in his description. The unspoken verdict is clear but affectionate: The nun-prioress is, like the reader, human.

In bringing these people together, Chaucer is making a point about the social inclusiveness and elasticity of the Christian religion. It can contain all types, even those who are not excessively Christian. Chaucer is also giving us a sense of the dynamism and complexity of English society. The pilgrims' tales reflect the pilgrims and, in the process, offer a microcosm of a complex but familiar world to us.

The 18th-century poet John Dryden said of *The Canterbury Tales*, "Here is God's plenty," by which he meant that the poem offered readers the world. It seems almost miraculous that Chaucer can make these connections with us across time and, in the process of writing about his world, reflect our own. ■

Suggested Reading

Chaucer, *The Canterbury Tales* (original-spelling edition).

———, *The Riverside Chaucer*.

Pearsall, *The Life of Chaucer*.

1. In what ways can we consider Chaucer the first "modern" writer, in "modern" English?

2. We know little of Chaucer's life, and never will know much. What can we reconstruct about him from his writings?

Chaucer—Social Diversity
Lecture 2—Transcript

In the opening lecture, we covered some six centuries of literature, as that literature, so to call it, has descended to us very imperfectly in fragments and rewritings. And sometimes, working at this depth, one feels more like an archaeologist than a student or a literature lover. Reading those surviving Anglo-Saxon works, *Caedmon's Hymn*, for example, it's almost as if one were hearing indistinct echoes from a long way off. They're fascinating, but one can't always make out what's being said.

Much changed in the regional kingdoms and fiefdoms of Britain during the half millennium which separates *Beowulf* from *The Canterbury Tales*, and that's the text we'll be mainly looking at in this lecture and the next. I want to deal in this lecture with the poem, and in the next lecture with the man who made the poem, Chaucer.

There was continual and exhausting invasion by the Vikings, invasion which eventually led to the accession of a Viking king, Cnut or Canute, the monarch who demonstrated his only human powers at the seashore. He tried to command the waves, not because he believed he could, but to demonstrate that he couldn't. And he proved to his subjects that a king's power was limited. Canute, we may guess, had a great sense of humor, unlike many kings of the time, unlike kings of all time, I think.

Scandinavian, which is what the Vikings were, although it infiltrated English, and can still be heard in the Geordie accent of English speakers in the northeast of England, never took hold. As late as the 11th century, Anglo-Saxon, that alien tongue that we encountered in *Beowulf*, was still the language of literature.

But what happens if we jump 200 years to the 1390s? Listen, if you would, to the opening lines of what can still claim to be the greatest narrative poem in English. It's from the *Prologue* or introduction to Geoffrey Chaucer's *The Canterbury Tales*.

When that Aprilis, with his showers swoot,
The drought of March hath pierced to the root,
And bathed every vein in such licour,
Of which virtue engender'd is the flower;
When Zephyrus eke with his swoote breath
Inspired hath in every holt and heath
The tender croppes and the younge sun
Hath in the Ram his halfe course y-run,
And smalle fowles make melody,
That sleepen all the night with open eye,
(So pricketh them nature in their corages);
Then longe folk to go on pilgrimages,
And palmers for to seeke strange strands,
To ferne hallows couth in sundry lands;
And specially, from every shire's end
Of Engleland, to Canterbury they wend,
The holy blissful Martyr for to seek,
That them hath holpen, when that they were sick.

There's no problem in hearing this, and I think, obviously, the unenlightened reader or listener is baffled by the occasional word. We're listening to Chaucer across seven centuries, after all. But the gist of what is being said is quite clear. Spring is lovely. The world wakes up again, joyously. The birds sing, the flowers spring, and, of course, the people want to go on a pilgrimage. They want to travel. They want to have a spring break.

Something has happened, something very significant. Chaucer, even though there are these, as it were, awkwardnesses to our ear, is talking our language and saying things that are familiar to us. Moreover, the verse form, which is rhymed and iambic pentameter (dee-*dum*, dee-*dum*, dee-*dum*, dee-*dum*, dee-*dum*) falls easily on our ears. We can, as we say, make sense of it. It sounds right.

How did this great change happen, and how did it happen so suddenly? The answer to those questions is 1066, the epochal date of the Norman Conquest and the defeat of the Saxon king, Harold, at Hastings on the English coast.

These French invaders, and distantly they too were gallicized Vikings, men from the north—that's what Norman means—brought with them a unifying mission, to bind into national unity the little kingdoms, tribal and ethnic enclaves that had, up to this point, made up Britain. They unified the country. They installed what we would call a national infrastructure, a language and a system of law, a hierarchy of nobility and commoners, that is to say, the British class system, and with it parliament, the French or the Norman means "talking place," which, in fact, is really what they do. They talk more than they act, but, nonetheless, that great institution came with the Normans.

The greatest document of the Norman period is the *Domesday Boke*, a hugely comprehensive register of every town and village and hamlet in the country. It's a vast census exercise. What the Normans created after they'd taken over the country was not merely a unification of what is today called the United Kingdom, and Chaucer calls Engeland, and the Angles, of course, gave us that word, land of the Angles, a Germanic people, but they also brought with them unification or an organic connection with Europe as well. It's fair to say they kept one foot in where they came from, Normandy, and the other foot in England, the country they conquered.

With them came the rich Latin heritages of Italy and France; this was their cultural baggage. Among that cultural baggage, the Normans brought with them rhyme and syllabic verse. Nonetheless, beneath these poetic forms that the Normans brought with them, even in the passage I quoted from Chaucer, "When that Aprilis, with his showers swoot," you will have heard the stress systems of old Anglo-Saxon literature throbbing away under the syllabic superstructure. That is to say, "When that *Aprilis* with his showers *swoot*" not the jog, jog of "*When that Aprilis with his showers swoot*" which, as I say, is how the French would say it.

Let's look, then, more closely at some of the active ingredients in those opening lines of Chaucer's *Prologue* to *The Canterbury Tales*. It opens with an *apostrophe*, or rhapsody, to spring, an address, as it were, to the moment in the year when the world is reborn. Now, this was significantly, and it's not hard to see why, a favorite theme of the Italian poet Petrarch, as of many romantic poets since. It's, to use the word which is so often used in poetry, conventional, a thing of conventions.

What Chaucer wrote, we assume, and may safely assume, is poetry for people who knew poetry. They were cultivated people. They probably read Petrarch as well as they read Chaucer. Chaucer's reference in that passage I read to Zephyrus and the Ram indicates a nodding acquaintance with astrology, and that, in fact, was 14th-century science. So, in fact, this is not just, as it were, poetry which alludes to poetry. It is also poetry which draws on learning, on knowledge, on the kind of bodies of institutional learning, which eventually became concentrated in universities. So an educational system lies behind this poetry, as well as, as it were, a tradition of poetry itself.

More specifically, a knowledge of Latin is implied. Zephyrus is the Roman god of wind, so to some extent, there's an allusion right the way back to the classical Romans. There's also, among the familiar medley of English words, some French as well: *corage, pilgrimage*. *Corage* is the French word "courage," and Chaucer I think would have pronounced that with a long final syllable, pilgrim*age*, not pilgrimage. We bite it off, but that's something that's happened over the succeeding centuries.

Chaucer probably used certain words with what we would think of as a French accent. There are good reasons for that. As I've said, the fact is that French was, in fact, part of the living fabric of English at this time. Now, from this, we apprehend, Chaucer is a poet with a variety of linguistic resources at his disposal, some from outside his own country. And above all, I think we must feel the tone of the verse is civilized. It belongs to a civilization. It's imbued with what Chaucer himself would have called *gentilesse*. Again, it's a word of French origin and it's a word for which, unfortunately, we have no exact equivalent. Our genteel is a very sort of, I think, inadequate descendant. *Gentilesse* means something like "of good breeding."

There are urban, cosmopolitan forces at work here, and there's none of the savagery or primitivism, much as we may admire it, or tribalism evident in Anglo-Saxon verse. This, in fact, belongs to a different universe. Most strikingly, nature, that hugely important element in English literature, is not the frost-ridden, cruel thing that we saw in *The Seafarer*. The rain is sweet, not harsh: April showers are "swoot." This, we may say, is not merely a new world, but as I say, a new universe. It's a new worldview, which is emerging through the poetry, and out of which the poetry itself is emerging.

Now, briefly, I want to say something about the setting of *The Canterbury Tales*. This is not Chaucer's title, by the way. Because we like titles, we've given it a label. He, in fact, would have not seen it as necessary to entitle his poem. But despite being called *The Canterbury Tales*, it's not set in Canterbury, which is the cathedral town in Kent. It's still there and the cathedral is still there, the same cathedral that Thomas à Becket and Chaucer knew.

Now, in fact, the poem might have reached Canterbury—it doesn't actually reach Canterbury—had he finished the work, and I'll say more of the reasons that he didn't finish it later. The setting as the poem opens is London, April 1389. It's a fine spring day in the capital. Remember, medieval England is still enjoying what's called the Medieval Warm Period. There were various kinds of climatic change, which meant that England was a much warmer place when Chaucer lived there than it is now. Lucky him.

We're on the south bank of the Thames as the poem opens, across the river from St. Paul's Cathedral, a couple of hundred yards from where Shakespeare's Globe Theatre will erect itself 200 years later. And a group of pilgrims, one of them Geoffrey Chaucer—he inserts himself into the poem, a rather nice touch—are gathered at the Tabard Inn, under the bluff supervision of their guide, Harry Bailey. *Tabard* is a French word, which means "drum," and you beat a drum when you want people to come to join you.

Now, this band of pilgrims intends to go by horse the 100-odd miles to Canterbury, and the tomb of Thomas à Becket, martyred in his cathedral by the king for being difficult. The purpose of the trip is as much social as religious. That is to say, it's, as I said earlier, a spring break. It's a holiday, in the modern sense, as well as the antique sense of holy day. These pilgrims intend to enjoy themselves. They will stop at taverns along the way. They will eat and drink well. They will get to know each other. There might even be romance, who knows? It is, after all, a voyage, in their sense.

The pilgrims travel in a party for safety. Outside London, on Blackheath, as they find their way towards Kent and Canterbury, there are brigands and highwaymen, and, therefore, they have to go, as it were, in a band for protection. The journey to Kent—there are women and old people present in the company—will take them probably about four days, perhaps longer. That is to say, doing 25 miles a day by horse is just about what you can comfortably manage. And, as any frequent flyer today knows, long trips can be boring, and some in-flight entertainment is in order. Harry Bailey, who is an old hand—he's a professional who knows his job well—decrees that there shall be four tales from each of the 29 pilgrims, among whom is a silently observing Geoffrey Chaucer.

This makes 116 tales in all, coming and going, and there'll be a prize for the winner. That is to say, the person who can tell the best tale will get, I don't know, some small award, and also, of course, the glory of being the best tale-teller. This was a time when, in fact, being able to tell a good story was a social skill.

Now, one inevitably recalls, and Chaucer certainly knew, Boccaccio's *Decameron*, which had a similarly bundled collection of tales from different mouths, so Chaucer is not entirely original, but nonetheless he's joining, as it were, a library, already quite a distinguished library, of European literature with *The Canterbury Tales*.

Nonetheless, Chaucer's London is recognizably there under the surface of present-day London. It's, in fact, very much an English poem, however many Italian influences we like to find in it. By Chaucer's time, London had become the engine room of a commercially thriving England. It was now less a city than a metropolis. It had grown. It had, in fact, a number of functions, which we would recognize as being wholly modern. It was located on the great tidal river, the Thames, and this was the country's main port. And, of course, it was the main connection to the world outside. And Chaucer, as we'll see in the next lecture, was, for a large part of his working life, employed in the port. And it meant that he met people from all over the place.

And London was also where England's monarchal court, where the king or queen, but usually the king, was, and where the legal courts were set up, not to mention Parliament and the great cathedral at Westminster. There's this large nexus. All the main parts of a modern state are there, almost within a few 100 yards of each other.

But more important for this poem, it is the dialect of London, English, that is inexorably becoming the national tongue. That is to say, London, to some extent, is standardizing the language. It's important, nonetheless, to stress that the conquest of England, begun in 1066, is not yet quite complete. Masterpieces are still being produced in other anachronistic or regional dialects.

There is, for instance, the Gawain poet, who is still using Anglo-Saxon in the wonderful Arthurian romance, *Gawain and the Green Knight*. Let me just read the opening of that poem.

> SIÞEN þe sege and þe assaut watz sesed at Troye,
> Þe bor3 brittened and brent to bronde3 and askez,
> Þe tulk þat þe trammes of tresoun þer wro3t
> Watz tried for his tricherie, þe trewest on erþe.

It's baffling, of course. You can't understand it. You can't read it without assistance. It isn't English as we know it. Chaucer is, but the Gawain poet, he's writing at the same time and writing a very important poem.

There's another great poem that emerges at this period, *Piers Plowman*. It's an epic of working-class life, and it's a very important and very wonderful poem, but it's in another incomprehensible regional dialect, the dialect of the west of England, the Malverns. Let me just read the first two lines. "What this mountaigne bymeneth and the merke dale / And the feld ful of folk, I shal yow faire shewe."

It's meaningless to us. As I say, the student can penetrate it, but not the general reader. There are also Welsh and Gaelic songs, which I won't attempt to read to you. The point I'm making is that there are lots of languages in England, which are gradually being subordinated to the English of London, and Chaucer is a main actor in this standardization process.

There are those who would argue that *Gawain* and *Piers Plowman* are fully as great literature as *The Canterbury Tales*, or Chaucer's other great poem, *Troilus and Criseyde*. That may be so, but the fact remains that since they are not in what we recognize as English, they are lost to us in ways that Chaucer's poetry is not. Chaucer talks to us because he's using our language.

To the contemporary eye, the striking feature of the dramatis personae, the pilgrims, of *The Canterbury Tales*, Chaucer's 29 people, is their social diversity. They are indeed what he calls them, "sundry folk"—different people, very different.

Now, effectively, Anglo-Saxon poetry, as we saw it, is restricted to three classes: thanes, warriors, and peasants. Women, one must point out, are largely invisible and wholly insignificant. Knights, soldiers and peasantry are represented in Chaucer's crew; but there's much more besides, including powerful women. Moreover, we perceive a stratified class system or hierarchy, which is similar to our own.

The first person, the top person in Chaucer's company and the first tale-teller, because, in fact, he leads the way, is the knight. Now, the knight is a veteran of the Crusades, in which, it has been suggested, he may have done some brutal things in the Holy Land for his religion, but the important thing is he is no working man, nor a professional, nor a cleric, but noble, and he's noble in both senses. The knight is high born and he's also of gentle manners. He is *gentilesse* and courtliness personified. And appropriately, his tale is in the high literary style, permeated with the subtle codes of courtly love and of the stoical Boethian philosophy which Chaucer favored. I'll say more of that later on.

Courtly love decrees that love is not merely an emotion, a surge of the heart and of the loins, but a set of moves on either part to bring the game to its conclusion: marriage, adultery, or no result. These moves were codified, refined and popularized in medieval romance. Romance, of course, is one of those double-edged words that means a kind of literature and also love, and the knight's tale is one such romance. Courtliness, along with the skills of courtship, which, again, is the business of love, were honed in the courts and castles of the leisure class, where young men and women had time for love, and also time to actually refine the ways in which they made love to each other.

Boethius, of whom I'll say a lot more later, was a 5th-century Christian Roman philosopher, who wrote his major work in prison. And he enjoined an acceptance of the fickleness of fortune. To know that fortune was fickle was the best defense against its fickleness. This was what Boethius called *The Consolation of Philosophy*. It is, to be honest, not much of a consolation, but to know it is at least better than not to know it. Chaucer translated this work on *The Consolation of Philosophy* and it's an essential companion, I think, to his poetry and explains the tone of worldly gloom that we regularly encounter in his writing.

Let's return to the company gathering in the Tabard pub, that April morning in 1389. At the bottom of the social heap, and already, we suspect, drinking heavily, are the cook, the reeve, the reeve being a land agent, the miller—and the miller and the reeve hate each other—and the shipman. They're what we call regular working guys.

A notch above them are the merchant and the franklin. They're members of the emergent bourgeoisie, burgers Chaucer would have called them, middle-class people. Of the same class, professionals, as we would say, are the doctor of physic and sergeant at law. And among the 29 are a whole gaggle of ecclesiastics and churchmen and women, friars, monks, nun-priests, nuns, summoners, pardoners, pardoners Chaucer despises certainly most of all, and, most admired, a parson, someone who really worked with people, as opposed to the pardoner, who merely takes money from them.

The last of these, the parson, offers the least interesting tale in the set, I think, a series of sermon-like biblical precepts, and the monk's tale, the monk is another good ecclesiastic, offers a catalogue of great people who have fallen from fortune. Generally speaking, the best tales come from the least interesting people or the worst people in the company.

Some would say the most interesting person in the company is a businesswoman, Alisoun, the Wife of Bath, who runs her own denim factory in that cathedral town of Bath and has had a string of husbands and profited by all of them. She's a gold digger, but an admirable survivor in a world where the chances of success are biased against her sex, in which a woman needs to be twice as tough as a man to make it in the man's world, and Alisoun is twice as tough as a man.

There's also an academic in the company, the clerk, who possesses all of 20 books, a huge library. It's awe-inspiring that a man could have so many books. He can read, write, and has mastered the arts of rhetoric and logic. He's meek by character, but he's formidable in intellect and he thinks women should know their place, and he's going to cross swords with the Wife of Bath on this subject.

Each of these pilgrims, along with a score of others, is identified by their trade, their profession or their rank in life, and thus socially stereotyped. Knights are knightly, parsons are pious and so on, but in each case, the social stereotype is shot through with ironies and individualizing touches, which run against the grain.

Now, the nun-prioress is a good example of what I call the cross-grained quality. The prioress tag indicates that she had a senior position in her holy order and she's described as very devout, as anyone in her line of work should be. But that devoutness is subverted slyly in the portrait which Chaucer goes on to paint of her. She is, we understand, a woman as well as being a nun-prioress, and that womanliness may be at odds with her nun's vocation. Let me just read the introduction to her.

> There was also a Nun, a Prioress,
> That of her smiling was full simple and coy;
> Her greatest oathe was but by Saint Loy;
> And she was cleped Madame Eglantine.

Cleped means called. What is this? Call me Madame? This is a nun? Eglantine, moreover, sings well and she speaks French "full fair" and this is still an indication, even 200 years later, that the Norman victory at Hastings left a heritage, that it was useful to have powerful friends, and the fact that she speaks French means that she does, in fact, have useful contacts. She eats delicately, we are told. She is tenderhearted.

She was so charitable and so pitous,
She woulde weep if that she saw a mouse
Caught in a trap, if it were dead or bled.
Of smalle houndes had she, that she fed
With roasted flesh, and milk, and wastel bread.

What, we may ask, is a Benedictine nun doing with lap dogs, dogs who dine better than the majority of the country's population, most of whom would count themselves lucky to have roast meat once a week on Sunday? Should not that tender heart be reserved for the poor, the sick, the maimed? Forget Mickey Mouse. Eglantine, we learn, has fine features.

But sickerly she had a fair forehead.
It was almost a spanne broad I trow;

I trow means "I vouch."

She has a finely tailored cloak and
Of small coral about her arm she bare
A pair of beades, gauded all with green;
And thereon hung a brooch of gold full sheen,
On which was first y-written a crown'd A,
And after, "*Amor vincit omnia.*"

That fine forehead, as broad as a man's hand, should, of course, be modestly hidden by her wimple. She's displaying it. It's like showing her leg, in fact, in a modern situation. And a bride of Christ like her should never have personal jewelry on display, particularly a bracelet with the unholy inscription "Love conquers all." That is to say, it should be religion which conquers all, surely.

Chaucer voices not a word of criticism, but the unspoken verdict is clear, if affectionate. The nun-prioress is, we understand, a human being. Do we despise her as a hypocrite? No, we smile and we forgive. We, too, are human. We're just like her.

By bringing together this motley crew, Chaucer is making a point about the social inclusiveness of the Christian religion and its elasticity. It can contain all types, even those who are not excessively Christian. Chaucer is also giving us a sense of the complexity of the English society. These 29 sundry folk live in a world which is like ours and very complex. There is nothing monolithic about this society. It is dynamic, fluid, socially mobile. It's moving forward progressively through history. It's not static.

The pilgrims' tales will reflect the pilgrims, and offer in the process a microcosm of a complex, but very familiar world to us. If you go to London today and you cross Tower Bridge, look at the pedestrians, stand outside the Tabard, close your eyes, and, as it were, take a mental time trip back 700 years. Then walk along the south bank to Southwark Cathedral, where Chaucer's great friend in poetry, John Gower, has his tomb. Chaucer himself is buried as the first occupant of Poets' Corner in Westminster Abbey, just up river on the other side. Our world we see as his world, and few have painted that world as well.

It was the 18th-century poet, John Dryden, who said, "Here is God's plenty." What he meant by that was that if you go into Chaucer's *Canterbury Tales*, and that's the poem he was principally thinking of, you're not just going into literature. You're going into a world. You're finding, in fact, as it were, all sorts of things there, which ring bells with your own world. It seems to me almost miraculous that somehow Chaucer can put out these connections to us across all this time, and that even though he was writing for his own context, his own people, he was writing for people that he knew, he was writing for people of his own class, principally. Nonetheless, he talks to us as an equal and he reflects our world, as well as reflecting his own world. It is, as I say, one of the wonderful features of this poem.

And in the next lecture, what I want to do is to talk about Chaucer himself, what we know of this man, this kind of genius. If there is one figure who, above all, stands head and shoulders above every great writer in England, it is Geoffrey Chaucer, and it is, I would say, through him that we must enter this huge edifice of English literature.

Chaucer—A Man of Unusual Cultivation
Lecture 3

> In the last lecture, we looked at *The Canterbury Tales*, and the stress was on what a wonderful poem it is, but who was the author of *The Canterbury Tales*? What kind of man was he? ... How did he come by his extraordinary knowledge of human nature, not to say his skill as a writer?

The poet we know as Chaucer was born Geoffroy de Chaucer (c. 1342/43–1400). His family name is derived from the French word for "shoemaker," *chausseur*. The Chaucer family had risen well above the level of cobblers and moved away from their French origins. In Geoffrey's lifetime, they had connections with, and received favors from, the court.

The literature he left shows us that Chaucer was a man of unusual cultivation. He had a phenomenally busy career as a businessman, soldier, government official, scholar, and author. He was also the father of English verse, called by later poets *Dan*, Spanish for "Don" or lord.

Chaucer was born in London. His prosperous family, as members of the middle class, saw the value in education in order to rise higher in rank. Chaucer's father was in the import/export wine trade. This profession involved intimate connection with France, which was, then as now, the center of the world of wine. We may assume that the Chaucer family's lifestyle was cosmopolitan and cultivated.

Geoffrey was lucky to pass the formative years of his life in the reign of Edward III. England was experiencing a period of climatic warming and was more or less at peace, despite such uprisings as the Peasants' Revolt and the never-ending hostility with France. England was also poised to achieve a leading role among Western European states.

We know very little of Chaucer's youth. He may have attended one of the two great universities at Oxford or Cambridge, or he may have received his higher education from house tutors. In any event, he was highly educated, bookish, and well read in several languages.

Chaucer did not follow the scholar's path into the church or academia. He seems to have wanted more from life than the monk's cell or the study. He may have toyed with the idea of going into law, but from his father, he probably inherited a propensity for business. Little is known about the dates and sequence of Chaucer's various works, other than the fact that *The Canterbury Tales* is a late creation. He probably wrote from an early age, but as a young man he also craved adventure; thus, he embarked on a military career in 1359.

In that same year, Edward III invaded France for the third time in a campaign that went disastrously wrong. Chaucer was taken prisoner by the French and ransomed. This incident may have resulted in his affection for the imprisoned philosopher Boethius, whose stoical theories of life he would popularize, notably in Troilus and Criseyde.

The Teaching Company Collection.

Equestrian portrait of Chaucer.

On his return from France, Chaucer married and settled down; his wife, Philippa, was nobly born and, presumably, well dowered. Chaucer's sex life is a matter of debate. A charge of rape was later brought against him, but we do not know if he was guilty. From his more erotic and bawdy writings, however, we can assume that Chaucer was no celibate.

Chaucer had powerful friends and patrons, including Edward III, who in 1367, settled upon Chaucer a life pension of 20 marks for his service as "our beloved Valet." Today, we would call Chaucer essentially a civil servant. In the early 1370s, he was employed in the king's service abroad, traveling to Genoa and Florence. He may have met Petrarch in Padua. Italy, at this point, was the literary capital of the Western world, and Chaucer brought what he learned there back with him to England.

In 1374, Chaucer was appointed controller of the customs in the port of London for the lucrative imports of wools, skins, and tanned hides. These were good years for Chaucer; he lived well, traveled widely, and hobnobbed with interesting people. *Troilus and Criseyde*, a courtly love epic shot through with Boethian gloom and set during the siege of Troy, dates from this period. Unlike *The Canterbury Tales*, it is written in stanzas in a stylized, difficult poetic idiom.

In the 1380s, Chaucer, now a widower, fell into difficult circumstances. His patrons were temporarily out of power, and he was pressed for money and short of favors from the court. In this slack period, he retired to Kent and devoted his time to writing *The Canterbury Tales*.

Chaucer died in 1400, probably around the age of 70 or 71. As a mark of his literary eminence, he was buried in the Poets' Corner of Westminster Abbey.

The Canterbury Tales has come down to us in manuscript form. We do not have a full text of the poem, and the portion we have has been reconstructed from various versions, none of which is in Chaucer's hand. Chaucer's original design called for 116 tales, two from each of the 29 pilgrims on the way to Canterbury and two on the return trip. What survives is only about 29 tales, some of which are fragmentary. *The Canterbury Tales* was written and transcribed in scriptoria or copy shops some 100 years before printing was introduced. The poem was initially written for recitation and, undoubtedly, was learned imperfectly by some reciters who passed on their corrupted renderings. Manuscript versions would have been available, but very expensive to purchase. The poem was widely circulated and had a significant effect on the emergence of standard English. The language we speak today owes a good deal to Chaucer, perhaps most of all to *The Canterbury Tales*.

The tales we have play against each other in interesting ways. To understand how the tales interact, imagine the tellers in a candlelit tavern, raptly attentive, eager for some after-dinner entertainment. The sequence opens with the knight's tale. He is the pilgrim of highest standing and embodies "truth, honor, generousness, and courtesy." His tale is one of courtly love and fraternal rivalry. It is high literature, set in ancient Greece, with a tournament and appearances from the gods. The opening of the knight's tale stresses high estate, warfare, and love. One of its main characters is Theseus, a duke, a warrior, and a great lover. None too subtly, the knight is holding up a flattering mirror to himself in his description of Theseus.

The poem was widely circulated and had a significant effect on the emergence of standard English.

The knight's noble romance is followed almost immediately by a *fabliau*, or bawdy tale, told by the miller. The miller is drunk and convinced that he, too, has a noble tale to tell. Harry Bailey tries in vain to stop him, but the miller launches ahead with his story of bawdy sex. The vulgar tale ends hilariously, with a couple of the characters sticking their bottoms out of windows to be kissed by an unwitting lover on a ladder, who expects to kiss his beloved's sweet lips.

Chaucer describes Alisoun, the young wife of an old carpenter, whose prettiness provokes the comic mayhem. The fact that she is as "supple as a weasel" hints at trouble to come.

The miller and the reeve, who follows as the next storyteller, share a mutual animosity. The reeve maliciously tells a story of a doltish miller who is cuckolded and whose daughter is "swyved," that is, seduced, by two students from Cambridge. The reeve is not nearly as nice as the miller, and his is a very unpleasant narrative.

Chaucer varies the tone of this collection of tales wonderfully; the tales themselves modulate according to the status and character of the teller. Chaucer sets up each of the stories with a prologue, usually delivered in the pilgrim's own voice and character.

The longest, most garrulous, and most interesting of the prologues is that of the Wife of Bath, Alisoun. She is more interesting as a character than for the story she tells. Alisoun is what Chaucer and Shakespeare would have called a shrew. She has been married five times and has used marriage to gain the property of her husbands, who die suspiciously often. She has no children but has focused her energy on making pilgrimages and profiting from her textile business. She manufacturers *toile de Nîmes*, denim, and has made her industry quite profitable in Bath. Alisoun has been on three pilgrimages to Jerusalem, perhaps seeking divine intervention to cure her infertility or perhaps simply as a mark of her status. In her prologue, she tells us that she has learned from life, not books. She has had a difficult life, marrying first at the age of 12 and burying five husbands. She has certainly been beaten by one or more of her violent husbands and, as a result, has lost her hearing in one ear. She directs her comments of finding woe in marriage to the gentlemen in her audience, not the ladies.

Alisoun's theme in her prologue and tale is a central one in *The Canterbury Tales*: *maistrie*. The meaning of this word can be summed up in the proverbial question: Who wears the pants in your house? When the woman is being wooed, she has the power in a relationship, but once she is wed, she must become obedient. The Wife of Bath, from the depth of her experience in the politics of marriage, asks why this should be so. The wife takes the privilege of telling a tale as more than just entertaining the company; she challenges her fellow pilgrims.

In his own day, Chaucer's listeners probably got the most out of "The Parson's Tale," which is full of advice about how to live a good Christian life. But for us, the poem has different resonances, and Chaucer, in fact, seems to be speaking, not just to his own time, but to all time.

As Dryden said, all life is here; every generation can get something new out of Chaucer. In writing *The Canterbury Tales*, Chaucer established literature in the middle level of society; after him, literature would become an important element in the emergence and progress of what we know as England. ■

Suggested Reading

Cooper, *Oxford Guides to Chaucer: The Canterbury Tales*.

Pearsall, *The Canterbury Tales*.

Questions to Consider

1. *The Canterbury Tales* is constructed around a pilgrimage to a holy shrine. Does that make it a "religious" poem?

2. Does Chaucer, as evidenced in his major poetry, have a problem with his women characters?

Chaucer—A Man of Unusual Cultivation
Lecture 3—Transcript

In the last lecture, we looked at *The Canterbury Tales*, and the stress was on what a wonderful poem it is, but who was the author of *The Canterbury Tales*? What kind of man was he? How could he have done it? How did he come by his extraordinary knowledge of human nature, not to say his skill as a writer?

The poet who we know as Chaucer was born Geoffroy de Chaucer. As my pronunciation indicates, it is in origin a French name. *Chausseur* means "shoemaker" in French. But Chaucer's language, which was obviously English, and his family had risen well above the level of cobblers and workers in leather, and well above their French origins. The Chaucers had connections and received favors from court, as would Geoffrey himself throughout his adult years. And the Chaucers had risen so high in the world that they even had a heraldic coat of arms. "Per Pale Argent and Gules a Bend Countercharged" is what the College of Heralds called it.

We don't know anywhere near as much as we'd like to about Geoffrey Chaucer, but we do know from the literature he's left us that he was, as I said, a man of unusual cultivation. He would be, in the course of a phenomenally busy career, a businessman, a soldier, a high and trusted government official, far-ranging traveler, a scholar and, above all, an author. And he was also the father of English verse. "Dan" Chaucer, the poets who followed him called him. Now, *Dan* is the Spanish "Don" or lord. What they meant was that he was the most important poet in the history of the language, and from him, as Edmund Spenser put it, springs "the well of English undefiled," a lovely tribute.

Chaucer was born in London. Dates of birth were less carefully recorded in those days because so many newborn infants died before they lived, it was not worth recording. Survival into adult life, not birth, was the memorable thing. Now, young Geoffrey, thank heaven, did survive to pass his childhood in a prosperous family, a notch or so, as I say, beneath titled nobility, in the rank, which, it happens, most English literature has been created in. That is to say, in the middle part of society, where people are educated and where they want to rise higher. The upper classes tend not to worry too much about being educated because they've already got the good things in life and the lower classes will never get it, but in the middle, this is where literature usually happens.

Chaucer's father was in the import/export wine trade, and this was, at the time, a very dignified line of commerce. It still is, as it happens. And apart from anything else, it involved intimate connection with France. France, then as now, was the center of the wine world, but also, as the French then and now think, the most civilized country on earth. Some English would disagree with that, but they do have a very good claim.

The Chaucer family's lifestyle was cosmopolitan and cultivated. That we may assume. Young Geoffrey was lucky to pass the formative years of his life in the reign also of Edward III. These were good years for England, which was basking in the Medieval Warm Period and more or less at peace, despite uprisings like the Peasants' Revolt and the never-ending hostility with France. England was achieving a leading role among western European emergent states. It was, we are told by a historian, "an age of elaborate courtesy, of high-paced gallantry, of courageous venture, of noble disdain for mean tranquility." It was a good time to be alive, in other words, and a good time to be writing literature. One should recall that key word that I was talking about earlier in the other lecture, *gentilesse*. England was going through a civilizing process, and Chaucer's literature would play a part in that process.

We know very little of Chaucer's youth. He may have attended one of the two great universities at Oxford and Cambridge or, conceivably, he could have had his higher education from house tutors. I think that's more likely. He may have finished that education in France, but one thing we do know, he was highly educated, he was bookish and he was well-read in several languages. He didn't follow the scholar's path into the church. That was one thing that you could do if you were well educated, but Geoffrey Chaucer wouldn't do that. Nor would he, like his clerk in *The Canterbury Tales*, live the monastic self-denying life of the academic. He didn't want hair shirts. He wanted to live.

This is one of the endearing things about Chaucer, one of the things we can deduce about what we do know about him, that he wanted more out of life than, as it were, the study or the cell. I mean, of course, the monk's cell. Nor, although he may have toyed with the idea and even tentatively tried it out, did he go into the law. Making money was, we can deduce, more important to Chaucer. Now, I suspect he inherited that propensity from his businessman father. He wanted things out of life that only money could get.

Chaucer is described in his youth as being "of a fair beautiful complexion," and we're also told that "his lips were red and full" and his size was of "just medium, and his port and air graceful and majestic." He was a fine figure of a man. Now, we know little else about him, physically. There are no reliable portraits other than one in late age. Little too is positively known about the dates and sequence of his various works, other than the fact that *The Canterbury Tales* is a late creation, the masterpiece of his maturity as a writer. I think that's obvious to anyone that comes to it. It's written by a man who's seen the world and lived. And I suspect the man who wrote it probably looked like the only, as it were, likely portrait that we have of him.

We can assume that Chaucer wrote from an early age, whether or not it was a hobby, but on the side, he probably wrote from his youth, from his adolescence onward. Now, as a young man, however, Chaucer clearly craved adventure. He wanted more out of life than writing poetry, and he entered on his military career in 1359. In that same year, Edward III invaded France for the third time and that campaign went disastrously wrong.

Chaucer was taken prisoner by the French and ransomed, and I suspect the period of imprisonment may have formed the lifelong affection he had, that I mentioned earlier, for the imprisoned philosopher, Boethius, whose great work, *The Consolation of Philosophy*, Chaucer would later translate or "English," as the phrase was, and whose stoical theories of life he would popularize, notably in *Troilus and Criseyde*, which is a very Boethian poem.

On his return from France, Chaucer demobilized, put down his arms, married and settled down, and his wife, Philippa, of whom we know very little, was nobly born—we do know that—and presumably well dowered. She brought money with her to the marriage. That presumably was one of her attractions.

Chaucer's sex life is a matter of debate. A charge of rape was later brought against him. Whether or not he was guilty of that crime is disputed and will never be known now, but what we can deduce, what we can assume, supported by the more erotic and bawdy of his writings—a lot of them are extremely bawdy—is that he was no celibate. In fact, that was one part of his life that was fully lived.

Chaucer, by now the married Chaucer, had powerful friends and patrons. People knew him, liked him and wanted to do things for him. He was also building a reputation as a poet and the authorities smiled on him. The authority, of course, who was in charge of other authorities, was the king, and Edward III, in 1367, settled upon Chaucer a life pension of 20 marks "for the good service which our beloved Valet, Geoffrey Chaucer has rendered, and will render in time to come." This was the statement that went with the pension.

Valet does not mean that Chaucer parked the royal coach—grooms did that— or handed the king his shirt in the morning. Chaucer was what we would today call a civil servant. He was an administrator, and in this capacity in the early 1370s, Chaucer was employed in the king's service abroad. He traveled to Genoa and Florence. He may have met Petrarch at Padua. He clearly knew that poet's work intimately, along with the writings of Dante and Boccaccio.

And Italy, at this point, was the literary capital of the Western world. Chaucer brought what he learned there back with him to his windswept, rainy, northern island, and his career continued its upward trajectory. That's his career outside literature. In 1374, Chaucer was appointed controller of the customs in the port of London for the lucrative imports of wools, skins and tanned hides. Now, these were very good years for Chaucer. He lived well, traveled widely and hobnobbed with interesting people.

Troilus and Criseyde, a courtly love epic, shot through with Boethian gloom, set during the Siege of Troy, dates from this period, this high point of Chaucer's life. Unlike *The Canterbury Tales*, it's written in stanzas in a very stylized idiom. It's a poem which is full of artifice. Just to give a taste of it, this is the stanza describing the heroine, Criseyde, or Cressida, the beautiful, faithless woman on her first appearance.

Criseyde was this lady name a-right;
As to my dome, in al Troyes citee
Nas noon so fair, for passing every wight
So aungellyk was hir natyf beautee,
That lyk a thing immortal semed she,
As doth an hevenish parfit creature,
That doun were sent in scorning of nature.

It's a much more difficult poetic idiom than we encounter in *The Canterbury Tales*. In this description, the emphasis is on her beauty, and Troilus falls in love with Criseyde on the spot. It's love of the eye, something Chaucer was very interested in, as opposed to love of the heart. She's a widow with children, but that doesn't matter. Love conquers all, but it doesn't, as it happens. The poem ends very badly, but, as Boethius would say, what else can you expect in this life? And the poem ends with a very Boethian conclusion.

To go back to Chaucer's life, in the 1380s, now a widower—his wife had died quite early—Chaucer's circumstances became rather difficult, and his patrons were temporarily out of power. In fact, he didn't have people behind him to help him. He was not exactly poor—he still had his pension—but he was clearly somewhat pressed for money and short of favors from the court. The sun wasn't shining on him any more and he retired to Kent. Canterbury is the county town there, which is one reason, I think, that *The Canterbury Tales* comes out of this period of his life.

He was living on pensions, living on money he'd saved and money that he was still getting from what he'd earned earlier. And it's lucky for posterity that Chaucer did fall out of favor, I think, because in this slack period, he devoted his time to writing *The Canterbury Tales*. And we're also lucky that Chaucer enjoyed a full lifespan, which wasn't something that was guaranteed, even to middle classes in the 14th century. Chaucer died probably around age 71. We're not certain of his birth date, but we know when he died, and 70 was a good age. It still is a good age.

And, as a mark of his literary eminence, Chaucer was buried in Westminster Abbey, Poets' Corner, where his tomb is visited to this day by reverent lovers of English literature. That, in fact, is one of our pilgrimages. Now, very sadly, we don't have a full text of *The Canterbury Tales*, and the portion we have has to be reconstructed from various other versions, which are not in Chaucer's hand. It came down in manuscript form and some of those manuscript forms may be slightly corrupted.

But what survives for posterity to admire is a narrative which, if it doesn't quite follow Harry Bailey's initial plan as they set out from the Tabard Inn, it still makes up a poem which is longer than most others in the English language. What Chaucer originally designed was 116 tales. That is to say, each of the pilgrims produced two going and two coming back, and since there are 29 pilgrims, that's what it would have worked out to be. But we don't have anything like that. We have only about 20-odd, and some of those are fragmentary.

The Canterbury Tales was written and transcribed in scriptoria or copy shops some 100 years before printing was introduced, which came in with William Caxton in the 15th century. As it happens, Chaucer's works were very high on Caxton's first list of published volumes. He was still a best-seller. The poem was designed initially as Chaucer wrote it for recitation, and, indeed, if you read it, it rolls off the tongue. It does actually almost speak itself. And it was designed for circulation, if, in fact, anyone wanted to buy it, in very expensive manuscript versions, which would have been illuminated. They would have had very fine illustrations and only a very few people would have been able to afford such luxuries, so most people heard it. They didn't read it.

And doubtless too, reciters learned it and they may have actually learned it imperfectly. They may have corrupted it slightly and then circulated it on. It's a Chinese whispered effect, one knows it well, but nonetheless we do still have the essence of the poem. And the poem, we may assume, was very widely circulated and it had a huge effect on the emergence of standard English. That is to say, the language we speak owes an awful lot to Chaucer, and I think it owes most of all to *The Canterbury Tales*.

It's a very long poem, and one can't do it all, but I want to make a very small exploration of the contents of *The Canterbury Tales*. The 29 tales that we have play against each other very interestingly. First of all, in order to understand how it is they sort of interact, we must imagine the tale-tellers in some candlelit tavern, raptly attentive. They've eaten and they've drunk and they're about to go to bed, and they want some entertainment before they do so. You know, we turn on the TV at nine o'clock and watch. They want to be told a story.

And the sequence opens, as I said earlier, with "The Knight's Tale", which is appropriate. He is the pilgrim of highest standing. He's the one that everyone admires and he embodies "truth, honor, generousness and courtesy." These are the phrases which are applied to him. And, of course, Chaucer means these compliments. It's unlike the slier remarks he made about the nun-prioress, which we looked at.

The knight is, in a word, knightly, but he's also very modest in his attire. This is how he's described by Chaucer in the Prologue, the general description:

> But for to tellen yow of his array,
> His hors were goode, but he was nat gay.
> Of fustian [a cheap cloth] he wered a gypon [a smock]
> Al bismotered with his habergeon [his work],
> For he was late ycome from his viage [he had just come back from
> his travels],
> And wente for to doon his pilgrymage.

The first thing he does when he comes back—and he's been abroad, fighting for his country—is to go on a pilgrimage to the shrine of Thomas à Becket in Canterbury. And he's wearing his overalls. He's still wearing his work clothes. Now, we have to admire him for that. He's a knight, but he's very modest in his attire.

And the tale is similarly knightly. It's high tone. It's a tale of courtly love, fraternal rivalry, and a climactic tournament set in ancient Greece, the gods making a prominent appearance. It's, in fact, very high literature. This is how the knight's tale begins, and I'll read it in translation.

Once, as old histories tell us,
There was a duke who was called Theseus;
He was lord and governor of Athens,
And in his time such a conqueror
That there was no one greater under the sun.
Very many a powerful country had he won;
What with his wisdom and his chivalry,
He conquered all the land of the Amazons,
That once was called Scithia,
And wedded the queen Ypolita,
And brought her home with him into his country.

That is the opening of the knight's tale, and you'll notice the stress on high estate, on warfare, and on love. Theseus is a duke, a great warrior in foreign lands, and a great lover. And none too subtly, what the knight is holding up is a flattering mirror to himself. He's a modest man, but he's also aware of his status in society.

There are, indeed, many other mirrors in *The Canterbury Tales* and many characters, very different from the knight. The knight's noble romance is followed almost immediately by what is called technically a *fabliau* or bawdy tale, and this is given us by the miller. The miller is drunk, but he's convinced that he too has a noble tale to tell. There's some very comic business as Harry Bailey tries vainly to stop the miller, but he can't because the miller has got his head down, and he's got to tell a tale. No one can stop him. And what the tipsy miller offers is a story which is all sex and comic knockabout. It's not romance. It is bawdy sex and it's less courtly love than Benny Hill, if you know the English comedian. It's very naughty.

Now, the story ends hilariously and it's the acme of vulgarity, but it's done very well, with a couple of characters sticking their bottoms out of windows to be kissed by an unwitting lover on a ladder, who expects his beloved's sweet lips and gets something very different. And pantomime mayhem ensues.

I'm not going to read that part, but let me read another portion, first in Chaucerian English, then in translation. It's not improper but is, rather, the description of the old carpenter's young wife, Alisoun, whose prettiness provokes all the comic business. This is how it goes, first the Chaucerian version, and then the translation.

Fair was this yonge wyf, and therwithal
As any wezele hir body gent and smal.
A ceynt she werede, barred al of silk,
A barmclooth as whit as morne milk
Upon hir lendes, ful of many a goore.
Whit was hir smok, and broyden al bifoore
And eek bihynde, on hir coler aboute,
Of col-blak silk, withinne and eek withoute.
With coal-black silk, within and also
The tapes of hir white voluper
Were of the same suyte of hir coler;
Hir filet brood of silk, and set ful hye.
And sikerly she hadde a likerous ye;
Ful smale ypulled were hire browes two,
And tho were bent and blake as any sloo.

This is the translation.

Fair was this young wife, and moreover
As any weasel was her body graceful and slender.
A belt she wore, with decorative strips all of silk,
An apron as white as morning milk
Upon her loins, full of many a flounce.
White was her smock, and embroidered all in front
And also behind, around her collar, without.
The ribbons of her white cap
Were of the same color as her collar;
Her headband broad of silk, and set very high.
And surely she had a wanton eye;
Her two eyebrows were plucked very thin,
And those were bent and black as any sloe.

Sloe is a fruit that grows in English hedgerows. It's very bitter, but it has a lovely velvety touch to the tongue. I personally wish the word *gent*—"supple as a weasel"—was still in our vocabulary, and doesn't that simile "weasel" hint broadly at trouble to come?

"The Miller's Tale," which is, as I say, very funny and very knockabout, is followed by "The Reeve's Tale," and it's a grudge tale. These two men, the reeve and the miller, hate each other. And the reeve maliciously tells a story of a doltish miller, who is cuckolded, that is to say his wife is seduced, and whose daughter is "swyved," that is to say, made love to by two randy students from Cambridge. It's, I think, a very unpleasant narrative. The reeve is nowhere near as nice as the miller, and one wouldn't really want him riding alongside one as one went down the Old Kent Road toward Canterbury.

But Chaucer, in fact, is actually varying the tone of this collection of tales wonderfully, and they modulate according to the status of the teller and the character of the teller. Chaucer sets up each of the stories with a prologue, which is not to be confused with the general prologue, which actually, as it were, describes the characters to us as a company. And these prologues are usually delivered in the pilgrim's own voice and character.

Now, the longest and most garrulous and most interesting of the prologues is that of the Wife of Bath, and by comparison, her tale is something of anticlimax. The interesting thing about the Wife of Bath is what we know about her, rather than the tale she tells, although the tale itself is about rape and the violence which men do to women, which, in fact, fits in quite well with her prologue.

Alisoun, who is the wife, and that just means married woman, is what Chaucer and Shakespeare would have called a shrew. She talks too much. She also does other things more exuberantly than most of us. She's been a wife many times over. She's, in fact, been married five times, and marriage was one of the few ways that a woman like her could get rich. More specifically, a widow, since, in fact, the married women's property was their husband's while he lived. If he dies, then she inherits, and the wife of Bath's husbands die suspiciously often.

She's a wife, but she's no mother, and, in fact, one feels the slight kind of tragedy in her life. She has no children. This, I think, is why she's made so many pilgrimages, but she's also made a lot of money from her textile business. She's in, as I said earlier, the denim business, *toile de Nîmes*, which, in fact, is textile that comes from the French town of Nîmes. We know it as what we wear on our legs as denim jeans. But she's brought that kind of industry to Bath and she's made a lot of money out of it. We assume that she began by being very dexterous with her needle, but now, in fact, she has effectively a factory. She's a capitalist.

Canterbury is no big deal for the Wife of Bath. She's been to Jerusalem on pilgrimage three times. That would be a big deal today. Then it was kind of amazing. I suspect that she wants divine intervention to cure her infertility, or perhaps she undertakes these prestigious pilgrimages as a mark of her status. She is a woman who has made it in the man's world and that's very difficult. It's very difficult now. It was infinitely more difficult in the 14th century.

These are the opening lines of Alisoun's prologue. Again, I'll give the Chaucerian and the modern English versions.

> Experience, though noon auctoritee
> Were in this world, is right ynogh for me
> To speke of wo that is in mariage;
> For, lordynges, sith I twelve yeer was of age,
> Thonked be God that is eterne on lyve,
> Housbondes at chirche dore I have had five.

Let me translate that.

> Experience, though no written authority
> Were in this world, is good enough for me

She has lived—that's what she's learned. She's learned from what she's done in life, not from what she's read in books.

> to speak of the woe that is in marriage

That is what she is going to do.

> For, gentlemen, since I was twelve years of age,

She first got married at the age of 12.

> Thanked be God who is eternally alive,
> I have had five husbands at the church door.

So she's taken five husbands to the altar and she's the only person that's survived. The woe that is in marriage—she had her first marriage at 12. Five husbands, they're all dead. It hasn't been an easy life to be the Wife of Bath, and note that it is the gentlemen, not the ladies, in her audience whom she addresses.

Now, a question I've always wondered is "Can she read?" She may have picked it up from her husband, Jankin. She's certainly very smart, but what is certain is that she's been battered, beaten by one of her more violent husbands, so violently she's lost much of her hearing in one ear.

Her theme, in her prologue, and the tale is a central one in *The Canterbury Tales*: *maistrie*. Now, that word, which we no longer have, takes us not into the artifice of courtly love that the knight was talking about, but the real world of marital problems. It can be summed up in the proverbial question "Who wears the pants in your house?" As the franklin later observes, conventionally the man is "servant in love and lord in marriage." When she is being wooed, the woman has the power. Once the ceremony is performed, she is the obedient one. He wears the pants. Her power is simply in saying yes or no, but once she's said yes to him, then, in fact, the power returns to the man.

"Now, why should this be?" asks the Wife of Bath, and it's a very good question. She's a feminist before, in fact, we even had the word in English. And it's as pressing a question today as it was 700 years ago. Why should men have more power in marriage than women? This is the question that the Wife of Bath asks. She's a wife. She may not know much from reading, as she says, but her experience is she's had five husbands and she knows what it is to be married, and she knows the kind of power politics there are in marriage. She knows what sexual politics are.

And in the very long prologue she has, which is very exuberant, very aggressive, she takes the privilege of being able to tell a tale as being more than just entertaining the company. She challenges the company. In fact, as I said in the last lecture, the great thing about Chaucer is that he talks to us, as well as talking to his contemporaries. This is what makes the poem great.

The poem is full of good things. I mean everyone will choose their own. I suspect that, in his own day, Chaucer's listeners and those who read the manuscript got most out of "The Parson's Tale," which is full of good precepts. It's full of good advice, how to live your life, how to live a good Christian life by someone who, in fact, knows what it is to live. The parson is a very admirable man. But for us, the poem has different resonances, and Chaucer, in fact, is speaking, it seems to me, not just to his own time, but to all time. As I said in the earlier lecture, Dryden said, "All life is here," all life in all periods, every generation can get something out of Chaucer.

One of the wonderful things about literature is that we return to it. We return to writers like Chaucer and Shakespeare, and every generation that comes to them finds something different, but every generation that comes to them finds something. And, it seems to me, obviously one reads *The Canterbury Tales* and one admires, but most of all what Chaucer has done is he's set up literature in the middle of society. Literature after Chaucer is going to be a very important element in the emergence and progress of what we know as England. He is, as they say, Dan Chaucer, the lord of literature.

Spenser—*The Faerie Queene*
Lecture 4

Literature has many functions in society. That's one of the things that makes it so interesting to read and to study and to reread. Literature, good and bad, can instruct; it can entertain; it can educate. In some circumstances, literature can even corrupt us.

Given literature's dramatic power to influence readers, it perhaps isn't surprising that exactly which works of literature are corrupting has been much disputed throughout the centuries. A key example is Mark Twain's *Huckleberry Finn*, which has been both censored and prescribed at different times.

If literature can corrupt, it can also civilize or at least contribute to the civilizing process by articulating the elements that hold a society together. Literature defines the core values on which a civilization is founded.

This discussion brings us to Edmund Spenser's magnum opus, *The Faerie Queene*, arguably the greatest poem composed during the reign of Queen Elizabeth I. *The Faerie Queene* is dedicated to the monarch who inherited a reformed England and who, during her 45-year reign (1558–1603), transformed a small northern island into a world power.

Spenser (1552–1599) was a courtier, a soldier, a political player, and a poet, and the values that formed his sense of a civilized society descended hierarchically from the fount of England's honor, the queen. The English honor system runs throughout England to this day, but it was at its most dynamic during the reign of Elizabeth I, and it received its finest literary celebration in *The Faerie Queene*. Along with its stature as a great poem, Spenser's work is a literary gesture of devotion to the court, as we see in its dedication.

Spenser was not a professional writer; no one will be able to claim that description until many years later. His pen was not his main source of income in life, and it was not his main ambition in life to be a writer. He was the son of a prosperous cloth-maker and was educated at the Merchant Taylors' School and at Pembroke College, Cambridge. As a young man, he was an assistant to the provincial governor in Ireland. His job there was to enforce martial law and root out sedition and rebellion. He outlined his authoritarian views on governing the Irish in pamphlets and, as a reward for his services, was given an Irish estate. Spenser had ambitions to advance his career at court and, with that in mind, conceived *The Faerie Queene*. The poem won him a small pension but not the great favors he craved. Subsequently, his life was marked by disappointment.

His castle was burned down by Irish rebels in 1598. He may have lost his wife and children in that attack, and he certainly lost his status in the colony. In 1599, he moved back to London, where he died in distressed circumstances, at age 46. His career as a politician had been unsuccessful, but his reputation as a poet was outstanding. His tomb is next to that of Geoffrey Chaucer in Westminster Abbey.

The subject of *The Faerie Queene* is England itself. The epic was initially intended to run to 12 books, but Spenser completed only six. *The Faerie*

Edmund Spenser.

Queene addresses itself to six great virtues, which are anatomized in six books, arranged in 12 cantos per book, and made up of rhymed stanzas that came to be called "Spenserian stanzas." The number 12 is an apostolic number, and numerology underlies the work. The virtues that Spenser covers are holiness, temperance, chastity, friendship, justice, and courtesy.

These moral virtues are embodied in a band of knightly heroes. The knights in the poem include five men and one woman, all in armor and all on quests to set the world to rights. In Book III, the female knight, Britomart, is, like the

Virgin Queen, the embodiment of militant chastity. Knights are warriors, but they also hold values that go beyond merely slaughtering their adversaries. Their battles are battles for virtue as well as for victory. Spenser points out that life is often too complex for even the best-intentioned, purest knight.

The opening image of the first book, devoted to holiness, is stereotypical: A noble knight, wearing a red cross on his chest, gallops across the plain in search of "fierce encounters." This crusading young knight is called Red Crosse, named after the shape that serves as the basic constituent in the British national flag, as well as the symbol of Christianity. He will later be identified as Saint George, the patron saint of England, who conquers the dragon, representing paganism, and brings civilization to England.

Spenser was a major innovator in poetry, and the techniques he invented would be passed on to other poets. His "Faerie" land is anything but the happy world we might imagine; it is a dangerous realm of magic, a literary zone where the poet's imagination creates an alternative universe. The result is sometimes threatening and terrifying.

The "big three" literary devices that help us understand English literature are allegory, irony, and ambiguity. Allegory is, essentially, saying something by means of saying something quite different. A simple form of allegory is the simile: "My love is like a red, red rose." In general, allegory goes beyond simile into systematic parallelism. Consider, for example, Shakespeare's meditation on kingship in *Richard II*. Here, one gardener instructs another in the care of plants, but he is really talking about the running of a country. He allegorizes the state of England in terms of a garden, and by implication, the king becomes the grand gardener, appointed by God to keep the nation well tended.

Irony is saying one thing and meaning its opposite. Our example here comes from the most accomplished of literary ironists, Jonathan Swift. In 1729, Swift, then a clergyman resident in Ireland, penned a savage satire on English maladministration of the province entitled *A Modest Proposal*. The pamphlet purports to be written by an economist confronted with the contradiction that the Irish peasants were both starving and producing numerous children. To the economist's mind, the solution is easy: The peasants should eat babies.

Swift, of course, believed quite the opposite—that the English government should accept its responsibilities toward its colonial territory and stop starving the Irish people.

The last of the trio of literary devices key to understanding English literature is ambiguity (or polyvalence). Ambiguity is saying two things simultaneously. Shakespeare's Sonnet 129 contains the famously ambiguous line: "Th' expense of spirit in a waste of shame." On the surface, the line refers to the expenditure of one's talents to no good end. If we unpack the line, however, we get a sly double entendre: *Spirit* can mean liquid. *Waste* means garbage, but *waist* is a part of the body, below which, according to Lear, everything belongs to Satan. *Expense* means expenditure but can also mean expending effort. In short, while speaking abstractly about degradation, the sonnet also conveys a subversive sexual image, the sexual act with an unworthy partner.

The "big three" literary devices that help us understand English literature are allegory, irony, and ambiguity.

We'll encounter these three literary devices many times on our journey through English literature, but with Spenser, allegory is paramount. The cross on the chest of Red Crosse symbolizes Christianity, and it is red because it is by the blood of Christ that we are all redeemed. The other knights in the Spenserian troupe have new armor, but Red Crosse's armor is battered and beaten. Why? The fact that the metal is dented recalls the great battles of Christianity fought for us by our forefathers. We did not have to suffer persecution, martyrdom, deprivation, or crucifixion to assert our faith because those who came before us did so. The armor we inherit and that protects us has been worn in blood-spattered battle by our victorious predecessors.

The personal virtue that the Christian must cultivate is humility; hence, the opening passage notes that Red Crosse is "solemn sad." For the Christian, the principal adversary is oneself, one's pride. The enemy is inside. This will be a recurrent theme in Red Crosse's subsequent career in arms. He will almost come to grief in the House of Pride and in combat with the giant Orgoglio, which is Italian for "pride." The guiding principle of Red Crosse's quest is unity, which is embodied in his patroness, Una. His most seductive enemy is her look-alike, Duessa, or duplicity. There is, in other words, only one religious truth.

In the opening episode of Book I, Red Crosse thinks he has found his enemy, the dragon, inside the cave of Error. He finds, instead, a great worm that looks like a dragon. The description of the creature in the cave as half-monster/half-woman hints that sex may be a problem for those who are holy.

Red Crosse's "glistring armor," the light of religious teaching, gives him a little illumination but not enough. Error later catches the knight in his toils, vomiting books and papers, and Red Crosse can only escape when he heeds Una's advice to rely on faith and avoid trying to reason with error.

When we first meet Red Crosse, he is young; it is only when he becomes older, wiser, and wearier that he will meet and overcome his dragon, which is partly himself. In this way, the epic communicates the idea that we are baptized Christians, but that we only become Christians in our maturity. Red Crosse must learn in this early episode that one cannot engage with error on a rational level. Avoid the cave entirely, Una advises. Rely on faith, not reason.

In the fifth book of *The Faerie Queene*, the theme is justice. In this legalistic world, it is essential to engage in subtle logic chopping, rational discussion, and weighing of alternatives. Where religious faith is concerned, however, we must be single-minded. This is the first foundational virtue, which is why it's the first book in the poem.

Poetic diction is another feature of Spenser's work that is critically important in the evolution of English literature. Spenser established the principle that the language of poetry is not the language of ordinary people. It is elevated, or beautifully antique, or Latinate. The history of English literature has seen recurrent moves to return poetry to the language of everyday men and women. But these corrective initiatives never succeed. Poetry retains its own special language and subtly revitalizes the language of everyday speech.

Such poets as Spenser remake the English language for their own purposes, creating a distinct idiom. Spenser's personal tendency, like that of Sir Philip Sidney, is toward ornamentation. He describes, for example, the beautiful "bower of bliss" that tempts the knight who embodies temperance, Guyon. In this description, Spenser recycles the poetic truisms of mutability, vegetation, and decay. For this knight who requires self-control and discipline, the richness of Spenser's language makes the temptation of despair in the face of mutability almost irresistible.

Spenser's poetic diction is one of his great bequests to the poets who follow him. The Spenserian line—its richness, its poetic artificiality, its high diction—runs through the body of subsequent English fiction like a vein of gold. Other writers create works, but Spenser created a whole field of literary endeavor. He mapped out poetry, we may say, for 500 years of poets to follow. ■

Suggested Reading

Neale, *Elizabeth the First.*

Spenser, *The Faerie Queene.*

Questions to Consider

1. If *The Faerie Queene* is a great "national" epic, what vision, or "idea" of the English nation does the poem project?

2. Why did Spenser "invent" a poetic diction for his poem, and does that diction work?

Spenser—*The Faerie Queene*
Lecture 4—Transcript

One word, a rather antique word nowadays, sums up the literary subject matter of Edmund Spenser. That word is "gallantry." Literature has many functions in society. That's one of the things that makes it so interesting to read and to study and to reread. Literature, good and bad, can instruct, it can entertain, it can educate. In some circumstances, literature can even corrupt us.

Exactly which literature is corrupting has been much disputed through the centuries, and you think of a text, for instance, like *Huckleberry Finn*. At different times, *Huckleberry Finn* has been both censored and prescribed. Some generations have to read it, some generations are forbidden from reading it. This has happened ever since Mark Twain published it to the present day. Which party—the banners or the prescribers—was, or is, right? It's very hard to say. What happens is every generation makes up its own rules on this.

If one accepts, and I think one has to accept, that in certain circumstances, at certain times, literary works can corrupt, literature can also do the opposite. It can civilize, or at least it can contribute materially to the civilizing process by articulating in complex and subtle ways what it is that holds a society together. Literature, to pursue the point, can define, with a precision no other discourse can rival, those core values on which a civilization founds itself, which is why, I would suggest, there's been no great civilization, from the Greek to the American, which has not also had great literature.

Those literatures are not mere appendages or byproducts. In a very real way, they make civilization, which brings us by a roundabout route to Edmund Spenser's magnum opus, *The Faerie Queene*. It is, arguably, the greatest poem composed during the reign of the Virgin Queen, Elizabeth I. There's a lot of competition for that particular title, but I think most people, including myself, would back Spenser.

The Faerie Queene is, significantly enough, dedicated loyally toward the monarch who inherited a reformed England, reformed by her father, and who, during her 45-year reign from 1558 to 1603, transformed a small northern island into a world power. She did it by the force of its navy, largely, but that's another story.

Spenser was a courtier. He was a soldier. He was a political player for high stakes, and he was also a poet, and arguably, he was the greatest poet after Chaucer and until Shakespeare. And the values which formed Spenser's sense of what a civilized society was descended hierarchically from the fount of England's honor, the queen. Now, I think it's necessary, particularly for American readers, to understand the peculiar nature of the English honor system that I'm referring to.

It runs like the arteries in the body through England to this very day. My university chair, for example, is a Privy Council chair. I'm appointed not simply by my university and its trustees but by that committee of high-ranking political figures and dignitaries, the privy, or private council who advise the queen. I'm a professor of the queen.

England, even today, looks up to the throne to define the set of moral values which ultimately determine standards of acceptable conduct. Senior law officers are called Queen's Councils, QCs. The prime minister is the monarch's first minister. He's answerable to the queen primarily, not to parliament. This honor system, which had been modified over the centuries, was at its most dynamic during the reign of Elizabeth I, and it is this system which received its finest literary celebration in *The Faerie Queene*.

Spenser has written a great poem, but it is also a manual of courtesy, of good manners, and a literary gesture of devotion to the court. The court, of course, is shorthand for those courtiers privileged to be close or privy to the monarch. The word itself means those who bow or make themselves short physically in the presence of regal greatness.

Let me, for the purpose of illustration of the point I'm making here, read the title page of *The Faerie Queene*—read it out to you as well. This is as it was first published for the England publisher, William Ponsonby, in 1596.

THE FAERIE QVEENE.
Disposed into twelue bookes,
Fashioning
XII. Morall vertues
TO
THE MOST HIGH,
MIGHTIE
and
MAGNIFICENT
EMPRESSE RENOVV-
MED FOR PIETIE, VER-
TVE, AND ALL GRATIOVS
GOVERNMENT ELIZABETH BY
THE GRACE OF GOD QVEENE
OF ENGLAND FRAVNCE AND
IRELAND AND OF VIRGI-
NIA, DEFENDOVR OF THE
FAITH, &. HER MOST
HVMBLE SERVANT
EDMVND SPENSER
DOTH IN ALL HV-
MILITIE DEDI-
CATE, PRE-
SENT
AND CONSECRATE THESE
HIS LABOVRS TO LIVE
VVITH THE ETERNI-
TIE OF HER
FAME.

That, in fact, is a dedication. Now, let's stop at this title page for a moment. Let's move from that to the creator behind the poem, with a brief outline of Edmund Spenser's life.

He was not, one should begin by saying, a professional writer. No one will be able to claim that description until many years later. Let's say someone who lived by his pen. In fact, his pen was very important, but it was not his main source of income in life and not his main, as it were, ambition in life to be a writer. Although Spenser's work was printed by Ponsonby, he wrote principally for the admiration of a coterie, his coterie. Personally, Spenser was sufficiently noble himself not to need noble patrons or paymasters.

He was born in 1552—we're not quite sure of the date—the son of a prosperous cloth-maker. Young Edmund was educated in London at the Merchant Taylors' School. It was a guild establishment, and you'll notice the word tailor or cloth-maker. And he went on to be educated at Pembroke College, Cambridge.

As a young man, Spenser went then to Ireland, which at the time, in the 16th century, was a downtrodden English colonial possession. He doesn't mention it very prominently in his dedication, but it was like Virginia. And he went there as an assistant to one of that province's governors. And he did his official work in Ireland efficiently and promotions followed.

It was not, we should be aware, paperwork that Spenser did. He was instrumental, like other governors of English colonies and possessions, in the ruthless putting down of sedition and rebellion. He believed, like most of his class, in savage colonial discipline, martial law, with none of the rights for the Irish that English citizens enjoyed. Spenser outlined his authoritarian views in pamphlets, which did him no harm at court, although they may make us, and certainly the Irish, love him less.

He did his work well, as I say, and as a reward for his services to the English queen, Spenser was given an Irish estate. He was given a chunk of Ireland. And Sir Walter Raleigh was a fellow colonial governor. We know Walter Raleigh as a great explorer, also as a poet, but he too, in fact, had his properties in Ireland. And like Raleigh, Spenser hoped to figure in the top echelons of the royal court back in England, and it was with this in mind that he conceived *The Faerie Queene*. It was a poem which would advance his career.

He was, however, only partially successful in this ambition. The poem won him a small pension, but not the great favors he craved and had aimed at. And disappointment is the flavor of Spenser's subsequent, sadly short, life.

His castle was burned down by Irish rebels in 1598. He may have lost his wife and children in that attack, we don't know, but he certainly lost his status in the colony. And in 1599, he moved back to London, where he died in distressed circumstances, a mere 46 years old.

But already, his reputation as a poet was huge. He'd been writing on the side and that was doing well for him. And it was arranged on his death for his coffin to be carried by six other poets, and they threw pens and quills and scraps of poetry into his grave with many tears. And it was a wonderful death, but it indicated that he died a great poet, even, in fact, if he died an unsuccessful politician. Now, Spenser's tomb is situated next to that of Geoffrey Chaucer in Westminster Abbey. He is one of the fathers of English literature, and it's a fitting resting place for him.

The subject of *The Faerie Queene* is less the queen herself, who never appears, than the England she ruled over. The epic was initially intended to run to 12 books, but it only managed 6, and like *The Canterbury Tales*, there's a magnificent incompleteness about *The Faerie Queene*. The half work, the half *Faerie Queene* which we have, addresses itself to six great virtues, which are anatomized in six "books," all of them literally book length, arranged in 12 Cantos per book, made up of rhymed stanzas, that is to say, verses.

They came to be called "Spenserian stanzas" and were much imitated in subsequent literature. You'll hear one presently. Twelve is an apostolic number, and numerology underlines the work. It's like an inner frame. The virtues which Spenser anatomized are, to catalogue them: in Book I, holiness; in Book II, temperance; in Book III, chastity; in Book IV, friendship; in Book V, justice; and in Book VI, courtesy. We don't know what the other six would be, but you can fill in the gaps quite easily.

These moral virtues are embodied or incarnated in a band of knightly heroes, and the overall genre is that of Arthurian epic. And one gathers from the dedicatory letter to his fellow courtier and Irish comrade, Raleigh, King Arthur was to be introduced at the climax as the epitome of all 12 of the virtues. It was a poem which was designed as homage to kingship and queenship.

The knights in the poem as written are five men and one woman, all in armor, on horses, on quests to set the world to rights. The woman knight, Britomart, in the third book of *The Faerie Queene* is, like the Virgin Queen herself, the embodiment of militant chastity. Knights are, to put it at its simplest, warriors with values other than merely slaughtering their adversaries. Beowulf, for example, is not a knight. Attila the Hun's horsemen were not knights, but fearsome fighters.

Galahad, on the other hand, was a knight because, as the poet Tennyson put it, he was not merely invincible in battle, but pure in heart, and the two are indivisible. "My lance is strong, because my heart is pure." Were Galahad not pure in heart and high in morals, he would just be another brute on horseback.

The knight's battles are battles for virtue as well as for victory. They fight in good cause, or they intend to. And, as Spenser likes to point out, life is often too complex for even the best-intentioned, purest-hearted knight. It gets very difficult to be a knight. The code of knightliness is still with us. Officers in the British Army, for example, hold their rank by virtue of the Queen's Commission. I, at one period of my life, was a soldier of the queen, as well as a professor of the queen. That's another story altogether.

Another great writer of this period, Malory, in *Le Morte d'Arthur*, celebrated the Arthurian company of Knights of the Round Table. They've been revisited, right the way down to the musical *Camelot* and the mythology surrounding the court, so to call it, of President John F. Kennedy.

Let's move on to sample what I've been talking about abstractly. The following is the opening of Book I of *The Faerie Queene*, and if you're not familiar with Spenser's idiosyncratic technique, it will, I think, strike your ear as very strange indeed, but let me quote it.

> A gentle Knight was pricking on the plaine,
> Y cladd in mightie armes and siluer shielde,
> Wherein old dints of deepe wounds did remaine,
> The cruell markes of many' a bloudy fielde;
> Yet armes till that time did he neuer wield:

His angry steede did chide his foming bitt,
As much disdayning to the curbe to yield:
Full iolly knight he seemd, and faire did sitt,
As one for knightly giusts and fierce encounters fitt.

That, in fact, is the first stanza of *The Faerie Queene*, and very striking it is. He had a bloody cross, a red cross on his chest, which, we're told, is "The deare remembrance of his dying Lord, / For whose sweete sake that glorious badge he wore." This, remember, is the book which will be devoted to holiness, which, in fact, is the first, as Spenser sees it, of the great virtues. The opening image is, largely thanks to Spenser and Malory, stereotypical. A knight is galloping across the plain, looking for dragons to slay and maidens to rescue. And gentle means not soft in manner, but, as in Chaucer, high-born, of the gentility.

This knight, at this point, is called Red Crosse, which you remember is the basic constituent in the British national flag, as well as of Christianity. He's a knight errant. He's wandering, wandering through the world with the intention of righting wrong. He's a crusader. He is, we gather from his violent charging about, only newly knighted. The bit is between his teeth.

In fact, this knight will later be identified as St. George, the patron saint of England, and it will finally be the dragon whom he conquers, and England, which will, in fact, as it were, bring civilization to the country. The dragon, in fact, represents paganism quite clearly.

I think just in terms of listening, one can enjoy the music and the cunning poetic style, but we must move beyond that to get the full value and understand the techniques which this poet is using because, in fact, these techniques are passed on to other poets. Spenser, to some extent, is making poetry, not just a poem. He's a major innovator, a refiner of techniques, and he comes at things from odd angles sometimes.

First of all, consider that word in the title, "Faerie." Spenser's, we'll quickly appreciate, is not the cozy fairy land of *Peter Pan*. It's a dangerous realm of magic, a free literary zone where the poet's imagination is free to create an alternative universe. It's like science fiction, in a way. Spenser's Faerie is also terrifying. It's an awful place sometimes. It's terrifying and as threatening as anything imagined by Stephen King, whose *Dark Towers* saga, by the way, is a direct descendant of Edmund Spenser's work.

And closing in, even on that first stanza, we should note the striking poetic devices which the poet employs. Generally speaking, there are, in my judgment, three major literary devices which, when you've mastered them, will equip you to make sense of most of the great works of English literature. They're the three big wrenches, if you like, in the reader's literary toolbox, and they are allegory, irony and last but not least, ambiguity.

What, precisely, do the terms do? What do the devices do? Allegory, at its simplest, is saying something by means of saying something quite different, in a dimension beyond the literal. A very simple form of allegory is the simile, or the one-to-one comparison. For example, "My love is like a red, red rose." Now, in point of fact, my love isn't at all like a garden plant. She doesn't have petals, leaves, or roots sunk in the dirt. I don't stick her in a vase full of cold water. But for the purpose of literary appreciation, we can handle that doublethink, even if a Martian might find it tricky. That's allegory.

Now, allegory goes beyond simile into systematic parallelism. In keeping with the horticultural theme, think of the scene, if you know it, in *Richard II*, Shakespeare's great meditation on kingship. Two gardeners come onto the scene and they start talking about gardening. Now, what does that mean? This is what one says to the other:

> Go, bind thou up yon dangling apricocks,
> Which, like unruly children, make their sire
> Stoop with oppression of their prodigal weight:
> Give some supportance to the bending twigs.
> Go thou, and like an executioner,
> Cut off the heads of too fast growing sprays,
> That look too lofty in our commonwealth:
> All must be even in our government.
> You thus employ'd, I will go root away
> The noisome weeds, which without profit suck
> The soil's fertility from wholesome flowers.

Obviously on one level, they're talking about gardens, but on another level, they're talking about a more important thing, that is, how do you run a country? And just as you prune plants, you take their heads off when they become rebellious, so you have sometimes to kill people, in fact, who rebel against the state, who rebel against the kingship.

And so, in fact, what this gardener is doing is allegorizing the state of England in terms of a garden, and by implication, the king is the grand gardener appointed by God to keep the national garden well-ended. When Hamlet, for instance, says of Denmark, "fie upon it, 'tis an unweeded garden that grows to seed"—this is what happens under bad kings, and bad gardeners. The two are, to some extent, parallel, and allegory creates that parallelism in a very creative way.

Irony, to move onto the next of these devices, is, again, duplicitous or doubly meaningful in its literary operation. It is, at its simplest, saying one thing and meaning its opposite, or something quite different. Let me give an example from the most accomplished of literary ironists, Jonathan Swift.

In 1729, Swift, then a clergyman resident in Ireland, penned a savage satire on English maladministration of the province. He called his pamphlet *A Modest Proposal* and it purports to be written by an economist confronted with the contradiction that—one—the Irish peasantry were currently starving, and—two—they were producing children, lots of children. To the economist's mind, therefore, unclouded by any sentiment, the solution is easy: let them eat babies. This is the philanthropic and the rational policy. Moreover, it might also be good eating.

This is what Swift's economist says:

> I have been assured by a knowing American of my acquaintance that a young healthy child well nursed is at a year … a most delicious, nourishing and wholesome food, whether stewed, roasted, baked or boiled; and I make no doubt that it will equally serve in a fricasee or a ragout.

And so it goes on for the whole length of the pamphlet, arguing that the best way to solve Ireland's problems is cannibalism. Swift, of course, believed something quite contrary, that the English government should accept its responsibilities toward its colonial territory and stop starving Irish people. And in his modest proposal, he was being ironic, saying one thing and meaning another. That's what literature very often does, and we have to be aware of it.

Now, the third of the terms I mentioned, ambiguity, is a device by which you say two or more things simultaneously. In many varieties of human discourse, we aim strenuously to disambiguate. No one, for example, wants an ambiguous legal contract. "Look out," we say to someone sticking their head out of a train window. They do look out, and get their head knocked off by a tunnel wall. Now, of course, what we meant by "Look out" was "Look in." That's ambiguity.

Literature has a quite different priority from law. It loves ambiguity. It loads its discourse with ambiguity or polyvalence, as it's sometimes called. Take, for example, the famously ambiguous line from Shakespeare's Sonnet 129, "Th' expense of spirit in a waste of shame." It means the squalid expenditure of one's talents and abilities to no good end. On the surface, that's what it means, but supposing, with the ear not the eye, you hear "waist of shame"? The line then has a sly double meaning, or double entendre.

Spirit can mean liquid. *Waste* can mean garbage, but also a part of the body. "But to the waist do the Gods inherit," says Lear. "Everything below is Satan's." *Expense* means expenditure, but also the act of propelling or pushing, as in expending effort. It's a synonym for ejaculation. "Th' expense of spirit in a waste of shame." In short, while loftily talking abstractly about degradation, the sonnet also conveys a subversive sexual image, the sexual act with an unworthy partner. The line, we may say, is ambiguous, and much the richer for it.

We'll encounter allegory, irony, and ambiguity many times on our journey through English literature, but with Spenser, it is allegory which is paramount. Let's talk a bit about Spenser and allegory, Spenserian allegory. Focus, if you would, on the portraiture of Red Crosse which I read out a few minutes ago. The cross on his chest symbolizes, obviously, Christianity. He's a Christian knight. He will, in point of fact, end by divesting himself of his armor and taking on a monk's humble robes, having, that is, slain his dragon.

But why red? Because it is by the blood of Christ that he is redeemed, as are we. The other knights in the Spenserian troupe have glistening new armor, but Red Crosse's armor is battered. It's beaten. It has deep dents on it. "Wherein old dints of deepe wounds did remaine," says Spenser of his armor. Now, why is that? The metal is battered and dented because the great battles of Christianity have been fought for us by our forefathers, assuming we're Christian, but so too with all the great religions.

We did not have to suffer persecution, martyrdom, deprivation, or crucifixion to assert our faith. Those before us did it for us. The armor we inherit and that protects us has been worn in blood-spattered battle by our victorious predecessors, and their victory was hard won. Did we, like Lydgate [*sic*], burn at the stake so that we could read the Bible in English? No, he did, and he did it for us.

The personal virtue which the Christian must cultivate is humility, hence the stress in the opening passage on Red Crosse's being "solemn sad." For the Christian, the principal adversary is oneself, one's pride. The enemy is inside, and this will be the recurrent theme in Red Crosse's subsequent career in arms. It is himself, Red Crosse, whom he is combating. He will almost come to grief, as we read on, in the House of Pride, and in combat with the giant Orgoglio, which is Italian for "pride."

The guiding principle of his quest is singleness or unity, which is embodied in his patroness, Una. His most seductive enemy is her look-alike, Duessa or duplicity. That's to say, there is one religious truth. It's very hard to find and hold it, but it is very single. It is unified.

In the opening episode of Book I, Red Crosse thinks he has already found his great enemy, the dragon. He looks inside the cave of Error, and inside that cave of Error, he finds, in fact, a great worm, what looks like a dragon, but, in fact, it isn't.

But full of fire and greedy hardiment,
The youthfull knight could not for ought be staide,
But forth vnto the darksome hole [the cave] he went,
And looked in: his glistring armor made
A litle glooming light, much like a shade,
By which he saw the vgly monster plaine,
Halfe like a serpent horribly displaide,
But th'other halfe did womans shape retaine,
Most lothsom, filthie, foule, and full of vile disdaine.

Now, obviously, this, in fact, is not the real dragon, and I think Spenser is also hinting that sex may be a problem for the holy person, that's to say, his half-monster and half-woman. The religious teaching, which is the light from his "glistring armor," gives him a little illumination, but not enough. And what happens thereafter is error catches him in his toils, vomiting books and papers, and Red Crosse can only escape when he ceases to become entangled. And it's Una who gives him the necessary advice.

She tells him:

Add faith vnto your force, and be not faint:
Strangle her, else she sure will strangle thee.

What Spenser is saying here allegorically is you cannot reason with error. You must stop your ears and rely on faith. Best of all, as the lady originally advised him, is never to go near the cave of Error at all, but Red Crosse, we remember, is young. When we first meet him in that first stanza, he's "pricking," madly spurring his horse. It's only when, having lived, learned and become older, wiser, and wearier, that he can meet and overcome his dragon, which, as I say, is partly himself. We are baptized Christians, but we only become Christians in our maturity, if we're lucky.

What Red Crosse has to learn in this early episode in the cave of Error is that once you engage with error, on a rational level, you're lost. You must not go into the cave. Avoid it entirely, Una advises, and she's right. Rely on faith, not reason.

Now, a very different line is followed in the fifth book of *The Faerie Queene* on justice. In Artegall's legalistic world, subtle logic chopping and rational discussion and weighing up of alternatives is essential. Where religious faith is concerned, you must be single-minded. You have, as it were, to close your ears and go straight ahead. And it is the first foundational virtue, the rock on which all the others virtues depend, which is why it's the first book in the poem.

Now, in parenthesis, my favorite of the books is the sixth, Calidore, which is directed to the virtue of courtesy. I believe that courtesy had a particular place in Spenser's heart and in the England of his time, but, in fact, it is a rather late virtue.

There's another feature of Spenser's work, which is critically important in the evolution of English literature, namely, what's called poetic diction. No one ever actually spoke in the way that Spenser writes, at least not seriously. Spenser established the principle that the language of poetry is never, or never quite the language of ordinary people. It is elevated or beautifully antique or Latinate.

There are recurrent moves through the long history of English literature to return poetry to the language of everyday men and women, notably Wordsworth, who we'll be looking at later, and who tried to make poetry that would be like men speaking to men. But these corrective initiatives never succeed. Poetry retains its own special language, its own poetic diction, and, in the process, poetry subtly revitalizes our language, purifying the "language of our tribe," as another poet put it.

Poets like Spenser remake the English language for their own purposes, creating a distinct idiom. Spenser's personal tendency, like that of Sir Philip Sidney, is toward ornamentation. He loads "every rift with ore," as his great disciple, John Keats, put it. There's a wonderful description of the "bower of bliss," for instance, which tempts another knight, Guyon. He embodies temperance, and bliss is a great sort of temptation for him.

> So passeth, in the passing of a day,
> Of mortall life the leafe, the bud, the flowre,

Ne more doth flourish after first decay,
That earst was sought to decke both bed and bowre,
Of many a Ladie, and many a Paramowre:
Gather therefore the Rose, whilest yet is prime,
For soone comes age, that will her pride deflowre:
Gather the Rose of love, whilest yet is time,
Whilest loving thou mayest loved be with equall crime.

Carpe diem. What Spenser is doing in this particular bower of bliss thing is recycling the poetic truisms of mutability, vegetation, and decay. But it is very wrong in that book for Guyon, who, as I say, sort of allegorizes, as it were, self-restraint, to surrender. The knight, we learn from that book, requires self-control, discipline. Spenser makes the temptation of despair in the face of mutability almost irresistible by the richness of his language, but it must be resisted.

So poetic diction is used by Spenser and is one of the great bequests which he leaves other poets who follow him. The Spenserian line, its richness, its poetic artificiality, its high diction runs right the way through the body of subsequent English fiction like a golden vein. The Romantic Revival, notably the poetry of Keats, could never have happened without Edmund Spenser. Other writers create works. Spenser created a whole field of literary endeavor. He mapped out poetry, we may say, for others to follow, for 500 years of poets to follow, which is why it's worth going back and revisiting *The Faerie Queene*, one of the really great monuments of English literature.

Early Drama—Low Comedy and Religion
Lecture 5

Incredible as it seems, we're now 1,000 years into the history of English literature. Now, at some point between the 15th and 16th centuries, two big things have happened. One is the emergence of the printed book. ... The other ... was the emergence of the theater.

English drama, like drama in other countries and cultures, began on the streets of English towns, with townspeople for actors. It was open to all, not just to the few people who were literate. Drama, as Nietzsche pointed out in his work *The Birth of Tragedy*, is as universally human a practice as praying or, for that matter, playing. Drama originated in folk literature, coming up from below rather than trickling down from above.

Theater in England in its modern form began with the so-called mystery or miracle plays. In the medieval period, the most important story was the Bible itself. Playwrights and performers faced the challenge of communicating the narrative running from Genesis to Judgment Day as effectively as possible to a largely illiterate population.

England was undergoing urbanization during the late 15th and early 16th centuries, and in the growing towns, the guilds and craft associations were very powerful. The early industries that evolved in the medieval period, such as goldsmithing, glass-blowing, and so on, required mastery of tools and skills, but these abilities were kept as jealously guarded secrets and passed on only through a system of apprenticeship and guilds. In keeping with the secrecy surrounding the guilds and their professions, in the Middle Ages the word "mystery" was connected with the French word *metier*, which means "trade or profession," but had overtones of secrecy. The guilds, or *metiers*, became rich and powerful and took it upon themselves to spread the word of Christianity, the mysteries of the greatest story ever told.

Annually, usually at Easter, dramatic cycles would be staged, in which each of the guilds would sponsor a wagon or a float. Typically, each guild would choose an episode from the Bible that fit with its profession. The carpenters, for example, would tell the story of the crucifixion; the bargemen might tell the story of Noah.

The church was generally tolerant of this activity. Indeed, some clerics, who were usually the most literate members of society, may have helped write the scripts. At the same time, the church probably maintained an oversight function of the productions.

The mystery plays were extremely popular and probably influenced future dramatists, such as Shakespeare and Marlowe. Hamlet, for example, instructs the players who are visiting Elsinore not to "out-Herod Herod." This line is an allusion to the figure of Herod in the mystery plays, who was traditionally played to the gallery, with crowd-pleasing ranting and roaring. Noah's wife was usually played as a scold who nagged her husband constantly, a shrewish figure who serves as the model for characters in Shakespeare and Marlowe dramas.

The guilds kept lavish costumes, the inventories of which survive, along with certain business papers and scripts. Written copies of the plays were necessary when new actors came into the plays. We have the texts of a number of the major city-based cycles, including those of Coventry, Leicester, York, and Wakefield.

The *Second Shepherds' Play* comes from the Wakefield cycle. It's impossible to date the *Second Shepherds' Play* accurately, but it was probably composed around 1475 and performed with various elaborations for many years afterward.

Wakefield is a town in what is now Yorkshire that was prosperous in the 14th century. From earliest times, it was famous for two things: its wool production and its piety. Given the town's principal industry, shepherds were important and respected members of the community. The Wakefield cycle encompasses 30 plays, beginning with Creation and ending with the hanging of Judas. The cycle has two shepherds' plays, both of which are centered on the adoration of the newborn savior, Jesus.

In addition to being responsible for much of the wealth in Wakefield, shepherds also have a strong symbolic character in Christianity. Christ is allegorized as a shepherd with the Christian congregation as his flock. Pastors are Christ's deputies, and "pastor" means "shepherd" in Latin. As we will see, the *Second Shepherds' Play* undercuts this image to a degree with its irreverence and parody.

Historically speaking, the English theater has had a difficult career. It originated on the streets, under an uneasy license from the church.

The *Second Shepherds' Play* opens during the period of the nativity in the area around Bethlehem. Three shepherds are on the hills, watching their sheep by night, when they learn that the savior is about to be born. The first shepherd angrily bemoans the bitterly cold weather and the oppressions, including taxes, that poor folk like themselves must bear while the rich are snug, well-fed, and warm in their beds. He would prefer to trade in his current occupation for farming, which would generate more money, enable him to relax in the winter, and allow him some rest at night. Rebellions were fairly common in the medieval period (the most famous of which was led by Jack Straw), but the play doesn't continue along this radical line. The second and third shepherds are more patient with their lot in life. Their attitude is more one of Christian submission. The mystery plays were often didactic in this way, but they did give a voice to protest.

After this prologue, the character Mak enters; he is a rogue who steals one of the lambs that the other shepherds are guarding. He and his wife Gil then attempt to hide the lamb as a baby in a cradle so that no one will know what they've done. The other shepherds come to Mak's cottage to give the new baby a silver sixpenny piece. A humorous exchange follows, with Mak trying to keep his fellow shepherds away from the "baby." When the shepherds finally discover Mak's trick, they put him in a bag and beat him.

The play then reverts to familiar religious orthodoxy. The angel of the Lord appears and instructs the three good shepherds to worship the babe in Bethlehem, who is lying between two animals. We see now that the business with the lamb is a parody, verging on the blasphemous in its association of the newborn Christ with an animal of the field. Only the comedy of the scene ensures that we're not offended. Stealing a sheep or a lamb was a hanging offense, but given that the play revolves around Christmas, a time of forgiveness, and that Christ came into the world to forgive, Mak gets off with a beating. The lamb in the cradle also reminds us of the degradation of the savior's birthplace, in an animal manger. The audience members would not have been able to read the details of Christ's birth in the Bible, but they would have been open to learning them after they had laughed at the comic business taking place in front of them.

Above all, the *Second Shepherds' Play* is of and for the people. Although we will never know the name of the master who wrote it, he (or she) had a clear connection with the audience.

Historically speaking, the English theater has had a difficult career. It originated on the streets, under an uneasy license from the church. But the Puritans, who wanted to refine religious practice and became increasingly powerful, never approved of what they called "mummery" or "imitations." As Nietzsche pointed out, drama and paganism are close relatives. There was always the suspicion that drama was somehow pre-Christian and dangerous. Decent, "respectable folk" never approved of the theater or theater people, who were thought bohemian and immoral. As a result of Puritan pressure, English theater was controlled and censored from the 18th century onward for 200 years. Nervousness about drama has been built into the institutions of England almost to the present day. As late as 1960, every play produced on the English stage had to be approved for performance by the Lord Chamberlain, who rigorously excluded references to royalty, blasphemy, and sex.

This nervousness (in England and elsewhere) carries through to the current licensing and rating of films. We still have an anxiety about public performance. Even Shakespeare found himself in trouble when his play about deposing kings, *Richard II*, was performed during a rebellious period.

Nonetheless, the street theater we've explored in this lecture is the entryway to a golden period in English drama in the 16th and 17th centuries. The "unrespectability" of theater is part of that heritage. An important and entertaining cultural influence in the late medieval period, the mystery plays created the framework within which our next great talents, William Shakespeare and Christopher Marlowe, would write their masterpieces. ∎

Suggested Reading

Anonymous, *Everyman and Other Miracle and Morality Plays.*

Beadle, ed., *The Cambridge Companion to Medieval English Theatre.*

Woolf, *The English Mystery Plays.*

Questions to Consider

1. In what sense are the mystery plays genuinely "of the people"?

2. What, other than religious devotion, motivates the mystery plays?

Early Drama—Low Comedy and Religion
Lecture 5—Transcript

Incredible as it seems, we're now 1,000 years into the history of English literature. Now, at some point between the 15th and 16th centuries, two big things have happened. One is the emergence of the printed book. This, as it were, is invented and begins to come into the public domain at the end of the 15th, the beginning of the 16th century. It's some time before it dominates, but it's there and it's changing things. Shakespeare, for instance, we know existed in two forms: shortly after his life as printed books, but during his life, on the stage.

The other thing that happened about this period, at the end of the 15th, beginning of the 16th century, was the emergence of the theater, as we now know it formally. One says stage and theater, but what one means is drama. Of course, drama existed before there was a stage to play it on or theaters to play it in. English drama, like other dramas in other countries and other cultures, began on the streets of English towns, with townspeople for actors.

This is important because in order to read a book, you had to be literate, so you needed a great deal of education, which was in very short supply at this time. But the drama, in fact, offered a wide open gateway for the populace. You didn't need to be educated to see people on a stage talking and to understand what they were saying and, to some extent, participate at quite a high aesthetic level in what was going on.

In looking at the early drama, we're in the same world, the same England, but in another sense, a world away from Edmund Spenser, whom we looked at in the last lecture. Drama, playacting, as philosophers like Nietzsche in his work, *The Birth of Tragedy*, point out is as universally human a practice as praying, or come to that, as playing. If you look at children playing in the street, you'll see that they're playing games, but also they'll be staging a spectacle, "Look at me, only pretend," they'll say, and there may well be singing that goes along with it, nursery rhymes, the kind of little songs that children make up as they go through their kind of theater of the street.

So drama—like the ballad, which is street poetry—brings the people, as I say, en masse into literature. That, in fact, is sociologically one of the reasons why it's so important. And it is in origin a folk literature. It comes up from below. It doesn't trickle down from above. You don't need to know Latin, for instance.

Drama in England, theater in England in its modern form begins with the so-called mystery plays. They're also sometimes called the miracle plays. Both those terms will become clear as we go on, mystery and miracle. What were these, and why were they called mysteries? One can answer that by asking another question. What, in the medieval period, was the most important story? Well, it answers itself. It was the Bible, of course, the story of stories.

But if you had a population which was largely illiterate and could never afford books, even if they could read them, how did you get that story, the narrative that runs from Genesis to the Final Judgment, how do you get that story across? More so, if it was, until the late 16th century, in Latin? A lot of churchmen, who were educated, couldn't read the Bible very easily.

Enter, at this point, socially, the most prosperous members of urban society. Remember that England at this period is urbanizing, and in these great compressions of people and activity, all sorts of interesting things are happening. The country is being modified by its town life. In the towns, the guilds and craft associations were very, very powerful. To go back to that term mystery, which, in fact, is a bit of a poser, perhaps. In the Middle Ages, that word, "mystery," connected with the French word *metier*, which means "trade or profession," and which had overtones even then of secret history, which is what we mean by mystery and things like mystery novels. But craft and the skills of craft were the primary associations of mysteries, and that feeds into the mystery plays.

The early industries which evolved in the medieval, pre-modern period, in the hothouse of the medieval town were such things as goldsmithing, glass-blowing, farriery or horse care, shoemaking, glove-making, masonry, carpentry. These were not simple things. They required the mastery of tools and skills, and these jealously guarded skills were passed on by the guild system, a precursor, if you like, of the trade union. Only guild members were qualified to practice and tout for work. You couldn't actually get a contract unless you had, as it were, a guild membership behind you.

Masters of a trade would enroll apprentices and pass on the skills and the tricks of the trade, and apprentices too in time would become members and masters. The guilds were set up in every large town and every large city, cities being towns with cathedrals, by the way, and they became rich and powerful. If you go, for instance, today to the city of London and you look at the Guildhall, it is one of the city's most sumptuous structures and it goes right the way back to the medieval period we're talking about today.

The guilds, or *metiers*, took it on themselves to spread the word, the mysteries of the greatest story ever told. They'd made money and they had a social responsibility. Like the church, they felt it was their responsibility, to some extent, to do something for the people, the people, in fact, who supported them. In short, what they decided to do was to dramatize scripture, the stories of the Bible, for those who were incapable of reading the book itself.

And annually, usually at Easter, which, as you know, in the Christian calendar is the moment when the word of God is taken out into the larger world, there would be dramatic cycles, in which each of the guilds would sponsor a wagon or a float. In essence, it was rather like the annual Pasadena Rose Parade, except, just out of interest, that parade takes place at New Year and goes back to old vegetation myths, the renewal of the birth of growth in the natural world in January.

But the guilds, in fact, would actually take an episode from the Bible, and typically, they would take an appropriate episode, something that, in fact, fitted with their guild. The carpenters, for example, would do the crucifixion. Why? Because the cross was made of wood. The bargemen, for instance, might take the story of Noah because Noah built a ship.

The church was generally tolerant of what the guilds were doing. There was a kind of relationship, a kind of, as it were, give and take between the church and the guilds. They were both very powerful institutions, arguably, with the Crown, among the most powerful institutions in the country. And, indeed, some clerics, we may suspect, may have helped write the scripts and possibly, being the most literate and creative members of society, like Chaucer's clerk, they may have had a big input, but there was no authorship as such. That is to say, you can't identify who did anything in terms of creating these works.

But nonetheless, and we can deduce this, I think, quite fairly, the church was also suspicious of what the guilds were doing, and they probably kept a sort of, as it were, oversight function on the plays that were produced. There's always been, in British literary history, a Puritan objection to the stage. That's to say, moralists and church people generally are dubious and worried, and authorities generally are worried about what theater is doing. Now, there are good reasons for that, which we can perhaps look at a bit later.

The mystery plays were hugely popular and manifestly had an influence on juvenile future dramatists like Shakespeare and Marlowe, who we'll be looking to in the next lectures, when these young men, as boys at formative periods of their growth, were coming of age in provincial towns like Stratford and Canterbury.

When, as you'll remember in *Hamlet*, the Prince gives his instructions to the players who are visiting Elsinore, he firmly instructs them not to "out-Herod Herod." What does that mean? What he's alluding to is, traditionally, Herod was played to the gallery or the street audience, with crowd-pleasing ranting and roaring. It was one of the things that people looked forward to and expected every year. And Shakespeare, we can gather and presumably plausibly deduce, watched mystery plays as they trundled through the Stratford streets in the 1580s on these great wagons drawn by four, six horses, and in fact, he probably loved them as much as other Stratfordians did.

There were other much-loved stereotypes. We've been talking about Herod, but Noah's wife—which, as I say, the Noah's Ark story was probably sponsored by the shipbuilders or the bargemen—was routinely played as a scold, as a kind of woman who actually nagged her husband. "What are you building this boat for?" And that again was something that people looked forward to every year.

Lavish costumes would be kept by the guilds, and the inventories survive, as do the scripts, which is why we know as much as we do about these plays. Generally speaking, oral literature disappears, but there were good reasons why they had prompt copies, because, of course, every so often, you'd need a new actor to play Noah or Herod. People would do it year in, year out, but you know, *anno domini*, time would pass and you'd need to, as it were, get somebody else to do it. And certain business papers have survived as well, so we know quite a lot about these mystery plays, which, in fact, is really very lucky for us. We have the text of a number of the major city-based cycles. Those are Coventry, of Leicester, of York and Wakefield.

I want to look at one mystery play segment by way of illustration. It's the *Second Shepherds' Play* from the Wakefield cycle. Wakefield is a town in what is now Yorkshire, in the northeast of England. It's not a very big or very important place at the moment, but it was prosperous in the 14th century. The town had its own cathedral, which, in fact, is a very large church. It was a major player in terms of the urban ensemble in 15th-, 16th-century England.

From earliest times, Wakefield was famous for its wool production and its piety, two things. That's to say, they made very good textiles, and they were notably churchgoers. Given the town's principal manufacture, wool, shepherds were a prominent feature of Wakefield life. They were important and respected members of the community. It's impossible to date the *Second Shepherds' Play* accurately, but it was probably composed around 1475 and performed with various elaborations for many years afterward.

The Wakefield cycle, and the cycle, remember, is Genesis to the end, but in the Wakefield cycle, it begins with the Creation and ends with the hanging of Judas, what a wonderful climax, which is 30 plays later. There may have been some appendices, we don't know. But you've got these 30 plays, which, in fact, move chronologically through the Bible as narrative.

There are two shepherds plays, both, as in the New Testament, centered on the adoration by these humble men of the fields of the newborn savior, Jesus. In addition to being main creators of wealth in Wakefield, shepherds also have a strong symbolic character in Christianity. Christ himself is allegorized as a shepherd, and the Christian congregation is his flock. Pastors are Christ's deputies, and "pastor," of course, means in Latin "shepherd."

So you've got this kind of, as it were, dignity attaching to the idea and the title of shepherd, but working against this, which is a conventional sort of image of shepherding, the *Second Shepherds' Play* is notably irreverent and parodic. It subverts, it undercuts. This is one of the things that make it such a wonderful piece of, as we would say, drama. Though at the time, people in Wakefield must have seen it much more as a wonderful piece of religious instruction, as well as being entertaining.

The *Second Shepherds' Play* opens at the period of the nativity in the area around Bethlehem. A trio of shepherds are on the hills watching their sheep by night, as the traditional carol puts it, and they learn that their savior is about to be born. Now, it's biting cold, as it inevitably is in Yorkshire in winter. And the first shepherd, who's a much fiercer chap than his fellows, angrily bemoans the cruel weather and the oppressions, including tax, which poor folk, like themselves, had to put up with while the rich are snug, well fed and warm by their firesides or in their cozy beds. It's a powerful blast of raw, proletarian anger, which wouldn't come amiss, I think, from a 19th-century radical.

And I'll read it out and I'll modernize it. It's in Old English, in a sense, but also it's in dialect. It's not the easiest thing to understand.

> No wonder as it standys if we be poore,

It's not surprising we're poor—

> ffor the tylthe of oure landys lyys falow as the floore,

—because, in fact, no one's actually cultivating our land. Shepherds are grazers, and he wondered why, in fact, there isn't a bit more arable work, which would generate more money and they could, as it were, take it easy in winter, because everybody else in winter, of course, goes away until the crops start growing again.

As ye ken.
we ar so hamyd,

We're so hammered.

ffor-taxed and ramyd,

We're so oppressed and taxed.

We ar mayde hand tamyd,

We're beaten down. They tame us, they actually drive us down—

with thyse gentlery men.

—with these gentlemen, these people, in fact, who are above us in the social order.

Thus thay refe vs oure rest

Thus they take away our rest. We have to work at night to keep the wolves away.

oure lady theym wary!
These men that ar lord fest thay cause the ploghe tary.

These men who are resting now while we're working, they, in fact, make us work instead of actually tilling the fields and letting the fields work for them. He obviously wants to be a farmer for various reasons, apart from the fact that farmers often own land.

That men say is for the best we fynde it contrary;

We disagree with this. We protest.

Thus ar husbandys opprest

Thus are working men oppressed

> in pointe to myscary,
> On lyfe.

And so it goes on.

It's a very, very angry voice that one hears here. Rebellions were, as it happens, fairly common in the medieval period, and the most famous of them was led by Jack Straw. There was a lot of ferment. The church and the guilds, in fact, were the means of controlling sometimes these anarchic forces in society.

And the play doesn't continue along this radical line. It's just one speech. The second and third shepherds, the majority, are more patient with the hard lot they've drawn in life or that God has awarded them. They actually accept what they are and what they have to do. Their attitude is more one of Christian submission, and the mystery plays are often didactic in this way, but what's good is they do give a voice to the protest, as well as another voice to, as it were, Christian acceptance.

Nonetheless, like the first shepherd, the other two shepherds expatiate eloquently on the hardness of working in sleet, snow, hail, and fog, while others sleep in soft beds. Now, in its way, this is pure *Brokeback Mountain*, that modern morality play which also features shepherds. They've always drawn a very hard lot in life, one may think.

Now, after this prologue comes the action of the *Second Shepherds' Play*, and very powerful it is. Enter Mak. Mak is a rogue, and he steals one of the lambs which the other two shepherds are guarding. They're guarding them, of course, from predators. As I say, there were still wolves in England at this period. Mak makes off with his booty, and he and his wife Gil attempt then to hide the lamb as a newborn baby in a cradle so no one will know what they've done.

The other shepherds come to Mak's cottage, and they quite naturally want to cuddle what they think is a new human being born into the world, and they want to give it a silver sixpenny piece. Mak feverishly tries to stop them and change the subject.

This is the exchange. It's one of the high points of the comedy. The third pastor, third shepherd says:

> The child will it not grefe that lytyll day starne.
> Mak, with youre leyfe let me gyf youre barne,
> Bot sex pence.

This means "Don't worry, Mak. Let me just look at the child and give it sixpence," which is a lot of money. Mak says:

> Nay, do way: he slepys.

This means "Go away, he's fast asleep." The third shepherd says again:

> Me thynk he pepys.

This means "He's looking out." Mak:

> when he wakyns he wepys.
> I pray you go hence.

This means "If you wake him up, he'll start crying. Go away, please." And the third shepherd says:

> Gyf me lefe hym to kys

Of course, we know it's a lamb, so this is quite funny.

> and lyft vp the clowtt.

The clowtt means the clothes he's wearing, or perhaps even the blanket which is covering him.

> what the dewill is this? he has a long snowte.

He's got a long nose. Indeed, lambs do. The first pastor says:

> he is merkyd amys we wate ill abowte.

"He's a very strange looking baby." And the second pastor says:

> Ill spon weft, Iwys ay commys foull owte.
> Ay, so!
> he is lyke to oure shepe!

And of course, they realize what's happened. So they discover Mak's trick and they put him in a bag and they beat him. Now, after this knockabout, which I suspect had them laughing fit to die on the pavements of Wakefield every Easter, the action of the play reverts to familiar religious orthodoxy. We've laughed. Of course, you can't laugh in church very often. And now, in fact, we are to be devout. We are to be good Christians.

The angel of the Lord appears and instructs the three good shepherds, whom we feel very affectionate toward now. We don't feel affectionate toward Mak, though we may like him as a lovable rogue. The good angel comes and tells them to worship the newborn babe in Bethlehem.

This is what he says:

> At bedlem go se,
> Ther lygys that fre
> In a cryb full poorely,
> Betwyx two bestys.

There's a young child lying there between two animals. The business with the sheep, discovering a strange babe, is, of course, parody. It's a parody plot and it's daring. It verges on the blasphemous, because, in fact, to see the newborn Christ as an animal of the field, you know, you can see that they're on very, very thin ice here, but, in fact, they skate over it. The comedy, in fact, carries it across and we're not offended. I think probably not even churchmen would have been offended by the *Second Shepherds' Play*.

You have to also remember that the holy babe is a stolen sheep. This was a hanging offense. There's an English proverb "As well be hanged for a sheep as a lamb." If you stole a lamb, you were quite likely to find yourself dangling at the end of a rope, but Christmas, of course, is a time of forgiveness, and Christ came in the world to forgive, so Mak, in fact, is not hailed off into the local jail and put before a magistrate and strung up by his neck. He just gets off with a beating.

The holy babe rests in an animal manger, so all this business with the lamb, in fact, reminds us of, as it were, the degradation of that birthplace of our savior. And even after seven centuries, I think, the gradual discovery of what lies in Gil's cradle, building as it does to a comic climax, is irresistibly, laugh out loud funny, but it keys into the biblical story, and the mirth is what draws you in. And to some extent, what's happened at this point is people have laughed so much, they now, in fact, get the, I suppose, commercial message. They're now told what they could not read in the Bible, that is to say, the details of Christ's birth, which is very important in terms of the Christian narrative.

So you can say it's theater, but it's also religious instruction. But from our point of view, of course, it's the theatrical dimension which is most remarkable. That laughter, which we can imagine in the streets of Wakefield at Easter in the 15th century, will ring through the ages, from Shakespeare to Tom Stoppard. This, in fact, is what happens in theaters. People laugh in theaters and then they go very silent and they become very, as it were, sort of attentive. And you can see these things happening in the *Second Shepherds' Play*.

But above all, to go back to what I was saying at the beginning of this lecture, this play is of the people. It is for the people, and although we have no name for the Townley master who wrote it, it was clearly by one of the people. That is to say, someone, somewhere wrote a great work of literature. We'll never know how he, and possibly even she, was.

Historically speaking, the English theater has had a difficult career, much more difficult career in some ways than literature and books. It originated, as we've just been talking about, on the streets, under an uneasy license from the church. There's a plausible theory, though we can't test it, that it may have begun even earlier in Easter rituals within the precincts or consecrated ground of the church itself We don't know about that, but it's a good hypothesis.

As I said, the Puritans, that is to say, those who wanted to refine religious practice—and they were an increasingly powerful force in the land until the Civil War in the 17th century and beyond—never approved of what they called "mummery" or imitations, falsehoods, graven idols. They were inherently un-Christian. There was something, in fact, from their point of view, wrong about taking the Christian message and making it a matter of laughter in the streets.

And as Nietzsche, who I mentioned earlier, observed, drama and paganism are very close relatives. There was always that suspicion that drama was somehow pre-Christian and dangerous. And neither did decent, "respectable folk" approve of the theater. Theatrical people have always been thought bohemian and immoral. Who was the woman who tempted the monarch, Charles I? It was Nell Gwynn, the orange seller in the theater.

Dramatists have always had a rather dubious reputation and actors as well. And as a result of the Puritan pressure, English theater was licensed, that is to say, controlled and censored from the 18th century onwards for 200 years. When we come to Jane Austen, we'll see that one of her great novels, *Mansfield Park*, has at its center some domestic theatricals, which in fact, caused huge upheaval in the household. That is to say, it is highly disapproved of for people to act in plays, even in the middle of the 18th century, even in their own houses. There is this feeling that plays are, as I say, socially dangerous and morally corrupting.

A nervousness about drama has been built into the institutions of the country of England almost to the present day. As late as 1960, every play produced on the English stage had to be passed for performance by the Lord Chamberlain, and the Lord Chamberlain is a privy counselor of the Queen, who's charged with keeping public order in the realm. And he would scrutinize every line of a proposed dramatic performance. The Lord Chamberlain rigorously excluded language, references to royalty, blasphemy and sex, above all sex, and we're talking here about 1960, not 1560, and we're talking of the country with the strongest claim to have invented modern forms of liberal, parliamentary democracy.

And this nervousness carries right the way through to the current licensing of cinema, for instance, because in fact, it, like drama, is dangerous. That's why films have ratings, PG, R, or X. TV programs don't and novels certainly don't. We still have this, as it were, anxiety about public performance. And even Shakespeare had to be careful when his play about deposing kings, *Richard II*, was performed, at a period when, in fact, it was rather dangerous for Elizabeth because there could be rebellion about. Shakespeare himself found him and this theatrical company in very hot water.

Nonetheless, the street theater that we've been looking at in places like Wakefield is the gateway, the entry, to a period of English literature which we can truly call golden, that is to say, the drama of the 16th and 17th centuries. And we have to remember that this, as it were, "unrespectability" is also part of that heritage, which we have when we come to the 17th century. That is to say that Shakespeare's theater was cheek by jowl with the taverns and the brothels on the south bank of London. And even though the company had noble sponsors, they carried with them this sense that they were both dangerous and exciting and above all, popular.

So the importance of the mystery plays is not just that they're entertaining in themselves, not just that they were important in terms of their cultural influence on the late medieval period, the early Renaissance, but that they, as it were, create the framework within which our next great talents, that is to say, the son of a Stratford glover, who happened to be called William Shakespeare, and the son of a Canterbury shoemaker, who happened to be Christopher Marlowe, created their masterpieces.

And that is what we are looking forward to in the next lectures.

Marlowe—Controversy and Danger
Lecture 6

In the last lecture, we looked at the drama, which sprang up ... in provincial parts of England, but drama, as it evolved, took its present shape ... in the biggest ... city in England, indeed, probably the biggest city in Europe, London. And in London, drama was no longer the trundling provincial wagon, but the playhouse.

Drama began to take on its modern form in the playhouses of London in the 16th and 17th centuries. The Globe Theatre, the playhouse most closely associated with Shakespeare, encompassed all of life. As part of the mercantilist revolution that was taking place in London, there was now a price of admission. Such theaters as the Globe or the Rose were capable of containing thousands, mostly "groundlings."

The great London theaters of the late 16th and early 17th centuries are best understood in terms of the recently reconstructed Globe on the south bank of the Thames. The large, polygonal theater is constructed of timber planks and plaster. The raised stage, called a proscenium, comes forward into the audience, allowing the theatrical equivalent of a close-up for the actors. Behind the rudimentary scenery are flies and exits to the front and back. Overhead is the sky with stars painted on it. There is also a trapdoor for ghosts and devils to pop out of and villains to fall into.

Shakespeare and his contemporaries lacked the effects, the props, and the machinery of the modern stage, but they did have luxurious wardrobes, the inventories of which survive. The richest property of Elizabethan theater was neither furniture, nor dress, nor makeup, but language. The English language was undergoing an explosive expansion during this period. Examples of neologism can be found in almost every scene and speech of Shakespeare.

In 1593, a mysterious scuffle took place in a house on the south bank of the Thames, not far from the theater and brothel district, in which a 29-year-old man, probably Christopher Marlowe, was stabbed to death. Had Marlowe lived, he might have become an even greater poet than Shakespeare. In his short life, Marlowe (1564–1593) wrote four plays that changed literature and, more importantly, drama forever. He bequeathed to Shakespeare, Milton, Wordsworth, and writers to this very day English literature's great literary instrument known as blank verse.

Marlowe was born in Kent, the son of a shoemaker. Like Shakespeare, he was a descendant of the guild system. Those two facts alone tell us that literature was moving out of the upper classes to become the property of the lower classes as well.

Marlowe was university educated and seems to have had an ambivalent relationship with Catholicism. Religious uncertainty was dangerous: Recusants, those who did not accept the new Protestant regime that had been established by Henry VIII, were likely to be burned at the stake or hanged, drawn, and quartered for treason. We find a persistent hint of atheism in Marlowe's plays, a risky theme because atheists were dealt with as harshly as heretics.

If religion was a serious business in the late 17th century, so were politics and diplomacy. England was becoming a world power, and Marlowe probably served his country in France as a spy. Espionage was also a hanging offense, another dangerous game played by Marlowe.

Evidence points to the supposition that Marlowe was gay. His play *Edward II* strongly supports this notion, and he is quoted as having said, "All they that love not tobacco and boys are fools." Further, he remarked that Saint John the Baptist and Christ were lovers.

Everything about Marlowe was controversial and dangerous, including his death. For centuries, it was said that he was killed in a drunken brawl in a tavern over a woman of the streets. Only later has it emerged that he was probably assassinated because of some political intrigue.

In a theatrical career that spanned a mere five years, Marlowe left us four great tragedies, all of which share two features in common: They all deal with the theme of overreaching, that is, man's attempt to become greater than himself, and they were all written in blank verse.

Marlowe's first dramatic triumph, *Tamburlaine the Great*, was staged in the late 1580s. The hero of the play is a semi-mythic Asian shepherd, who, according to contemporary playbills, becomes a mighty emperor, defying almost death itself. We see the tinge of atheism in the playbills' description of Tamburlaine as the "scourge of God." The play introduced a repertoire of humanistic themes, linguistic creativity, and moral daring into the world of drama. The moment when royal ambition begins to stir in Tamburlaine serves as an example. He has been watching the Persian king Mycetes and wonders why he, too, should not be a king. He turns to his yes-men and asks, "Is it not *pass*ing *brave* to *be* a *king*, / And *ride* in *tri*umph *through* Per*sepolis*?" One sycophant answers that kings enjoy powers and pleasures even gods do not have. The message, a seditious one, is that even an illiterate peasant like Tamburlaine, unanointed by God, can usurp the powers of a king if he has the will to do so.

Everything about Marlowe was controversial and dangerous, including his death.

Even a short sample from the play reveals the suppleness and fluidity of Marlowe's blank verse. This is, essentially, the 10-syllable iambic pentameter that we encountered in Chaucer: "Is *it* not *pass*ing *brave* to *be* a *king*, And *ride* in *tri*umph *through* Per*sepolis*?" Blank verse is unrhymed, which suits English, a language that is poorer in rhyme endings than most European languages. The unrhymed quality also situates blank verse in a borderland between high poetry and conversational English. It allows a slightly elevated style of speech, but not one that is cramped and formal.

Tamburlaine the Great is Marlowe's first performed play and has the weaknesses of an opening effort. Principally, it lacks plot. It is the simplest form of tragedy, called *de casibus*: the irresistible rise, followed by the inevitable fall.

In his next plays, Marlowe became a more interesting playwright, one who could handle increasingly complex themes. In *The Jew of Malta*, for example, he explored Machiavellianism. That doctrine, also considered seditious at the time, asserted that rulers were political players in the fascinating game of statecraft. *Edward II*, one of Marlowe's later plays, is about a king who is destroyed by his homosexual love for a favorite courtier.

Marlowe's most famous work, however, is *Doctor Faustus*, whose tragic history is known to many who have never read the playwright's text. Marlowe's version subtly transforms the "overreacher" theme. The play opens with a magnificent soliloquy, a dramatic device perfected by Marlowe. Here, the hero lays out the main theme of the play: What, precisely, would you sell your soul for? For Faustus, the answer is easy: knowledge, that forbidden fruit that tempted Adam and Eve in the Garden of Eden. Knowledge is power and Faustus wants it. More importantly, Faustus wants an exciting new power, what we would call science and he calls necromancy.

The action opens with Faustus in his study at the University of Wittenberg. He has mastered rhetoric, philosophy, and theology, as well as law and medicine. He knows everything that a university can teach him, but he now seeks the knowledge contained in necromantic books, that is, books of the black art. He calls up Mephistopheles, who offers a warning of sorts to the doctor—"Why, this is hell, nor am I out of it"—but Faustus doesn't heed him. So voracious is Faustus for knowledge that he signs a contract in blood with Mephistopheles, by which he will get 24 years of service from the devil. No doors will be closed to him. He'll have power and knowledge that no mortal man has previously enjoyed, after which his soul will be forfeit to Satan.

Faustus wastes his omnipotent years on self-indulgence, most magnificently when Mephistopheles supplies him with Helen of Troy as a bed partner. The soliloquy that ensues when Faustus sees this beautiful woman is Marlowe's most famous. Ironically, the woman isn't Helen but a succubus, a soul-stealer. In the end, Faustus is betrayed, not by his intellect, but by his flesh. So powerful are Marlowe's verse and speeches, however, that one feels almost that the world, even one's soul, is "well lost" for such a sublime experience as a night of love with Helen of Troy.

Marlowe was, in many ways, still an apprentice dramatist while writing *Doctor Faustus*. Magnificent as the play is, it includes quite a bit of clumsy comic relief, and the author never tells us exactly what kind of knowledge it is that Faustus craves. We don't have a complete text of *Doctor Faustus*, but the play nonetheless has irresistible power.

Perhaps most powerful of all is Faustus's final soliloquy, delivered during his last hour on earth. In the soliloquy, Faustus commands the "spheres of heaven" to stop so that his doom will be postponed. He watches as sunset begins: "See, see, where Christ's blood streams in the firmament! / One drop would save my soul, half a drop: ah, my Christ!" Suddenly, a demon appears and tears at Faustus's flesh. He cries, "Ah, rend not my heart for naming of my Christ!" In fact, Christ probably could redeem him, even at this moment, if he truly repented and accepted the pains that the savior suffered on the cross, but he's too much of a fleshly man to do that. As night falls, Faustus is doomed. The fact that he speaks alone on the stage is a daring dramatic move on Marlowe's part, but the playwright's powerful language carries the scene. Faustus's last words are: "I'll burn my books!—Ah, Mephistophilis!" This message would have been particularly pertinent in a time when books had only recently become available. Books enabled people to teach themselves, as opposed to teaching coming from such institutions as universities or the church.

The larger theme is that overreachers must die. We do not feel any satisfaction from Faustus's eternal damnation; we admire his ambition, his God-defying rebellion against the sterile doctrines of old learning. Why, then, did Marlowe not celebrate Faustus's rebellion? Quite simply, Marlowe could not end the play atheistically. At most, he could make us admire Faustus, then fall into line and concur that such overreaching must surely be punished. An outright glorying in Faustus's antireligious, antiauthoritarian career would have brought down the apparatus of censorship to control Marlowe. Thus, he was obliged to end his play with the moralistic message that overreaching does not pay.

What might Christopher Marlowe have achieved had he not been killed so young? Shakespeare might well have had to tussle for the crown of England's greatest dramatist. What Marlowe left us is a small treasure trove of innovative early drama. He created some of the foundation stones on which the great edifice of Shakespearean drama would erect itself. ∎

Levin, *The Overreacher*.

Marlowe, *Complete Poems and Translations*.

Questions to Consider

1. What, in terms of prosody, or verse mechanics, did Marlowe bequeath to his successors in drama?

2. How heretical, blasphemous, or atheistical is Marlowe's drama, and how important is that element in our appreciation of his achievement?

Marlowe—Controversy and Danger
Lecture 6—Transcript

In the last lecture, we looked at the drama, which sprang up from the streets of middling to large towns in provincial parts of England, but drama, as it evolved, took its present shape, its most dynamic shape in the biggest town, the biggest city in England, indeed, probably the biggest city in Europe, London. And in London, drama was no longer the trundling provincial wagon, but the playhouse.

The playhouse was a large public building, and mercantilism, that is to say, early capitalism, business, entrepreneurship, by the end of the 16th century, had capitalized drama sufficiently for it to have an auditorium, a place of performance, as large as a town church in a place like Wakefield, as big as Wakefield's little cathedral.

The Globe, the theater most closely associated with Shakespeare, is a very meaningful name. All life was there. It was there if you could afford the entry price, because, as part of that mercantilist revolution I'm talking about, you had to pay to go in. You didn't have to pay to watch the mystery plays— they were given to you, but, in fact, now the cash nexus intervened.

Theaters like Shakespeare's Globe or the Rose were palatial in their size, particularly in the eyes of residents of London in the 16th and 17th century. They were capable of containing thousands, some seated, mostly "groundlings," as they were called, who stood. And this is a very interesting point: archaeologists have been digging up the Rose Theatre, the surviving parts of the Rose Theatre underground. They have discovered innumerable nutshells on the auditorium floor. This is the early version of popcorn. And we should remember the nutshells when we read playwrights like Shakespeare.

Literature needs institutions. We can't always see them when we read the texts as they come down to us in printed form, but we must know the institutions of literature, which were there, and how their frameworks affected the artistic product. The great London theaters of the late 16th, early 17th century are best understood in terms of the recently reconstructed Globe, the house of Shakespeare, on the south bank of the Thames. It's there. You can walk into it. You can watch plays there now. You stand up, as it happens.

It's large, it's polygonal, and it's got big columns, which are constructed of large timber planks and plaster. There's a box office outside, which is literally a box. There's a raised stage so everyone can see, which is called a proscenium, which comes forward to the audience, allowing the audience the theatrical equivalent of close up or, with the soliloquy, voiceover. So the actor can come right forward into the body of the audience and talk to them, almost person to person. There are flies behind for rudimentary scenery, and exits front and back. Overhead, there is a blue firmament—the sky—with stars painted on it. There's a trapdoor for ghosts and devils to pop out of and villains to fall into.

Now, Shakespeare and his contemporaries lacked the effects, the props and the stage machinery of the modern stage, but what they did have was luxurious wardrobe, and the inventories survive. And they were very expensive clothes that they wore on stage, which were magnificent, but the richest property was, as Shakespeare's choruses imply, neither stage furniture nor actor's dress nor makeup, but language.

The English language was going through an explosive expansion at this period. Shakespeare's vocabulary is huge, five times as large as that of the father of French theater, Racine. It's full of neologisms, words which never happened before in the language, and examples of those can be found in every scene and speech. I want to actually go a few years before Shakespeare in this lecture and to look at his great precursor, even though we tend, I think, unfairly to ignore him, Christopher Marlowe.

It's always interesting in literary history to play the "What if?" game, to indulge what I call counterfactual possibilities. Now, let me give an example. There's a mysterious scuffle in a house on the south bank of the Thames, not far from the theater and the brothel world, where, in fact, Shakespeare was working. A young man was stabbed to death. It's 1593. Now, the victim of this assault was only 29 years old. He may have been a government spy or a double agent. There are those who say he may even have been Shakespeare. That's to say, people say that Marlowe was Shakespeare. We'll go into that a bit later. His death was probably what in gangster fiction would be called a hit.

But supposing that young 29-year-old victim had dodged the dagger and lived another 20 years, as long, that is, as Shakespeare lived? How different would English literature have been, had Christopher Marlowe, as he was, been allowed those few decades? Now, that young man, Christopher Marlowe, Kit Marlowe, could, I think, have lived to be an even greater poet than the Swan of Avon, Shakespeare himself. We'll never know.

As it is, with his left hand, so to speak, Marlowe tossed off in his short adult life four plays which changed literature forever. More importantly, it changed drama forever. He bequeathed to Shakespeare, Milton, Wordsworth, right the way through to the present day, English literature's great literary instrument: blank verse.

I don't want to get into the niceties of prosody—we will get onto that eventually, but for the moment, just let's look at the outline of Marlowe's life. It was exciting, and an excitingly short life. Shakespeare was born the son of a glove-maker in Stratford. Marlowe, this other great tragedian of the age, was born a few years earlier, the son of a shoemaker in Kent, both descendants of the guild system I was talking about in the previous lecture. And those two facts alone tell you much about the things that are happening to literature at this period. That's to say, it's becoming, as it were, sort of a property of the lower classes, not an exclusive property of the upper classes.

Unlike Shakespeare, there was quite a bit of the possibility of social mobility at this time. Unlike Shakespeare, Marlowe was university educated, but like Shakespeare, he seems to have had an ambivalent relationship with Catholicism. Most thinking people did have this ambivalent relationship during Elizabeth's reign, but one needs to be careful. Recusants, as they were called, those who did not accept the new Protestant regime which had been set up by Henry VIII, Elizabeth's father, were likely to be burned at the stake or hung, drawn and quartered for treason. It was no light thing, the kind of religion that you followed.

In Marlowe's plays, there is a persistent hint of atheism. With the censorship which operated at that time, it was very dangerous. Playing this game that Marlowe played was dangerous because atheists were dealt with as harshly as heretics. Religion, as I say, was a very serious business in the late 17th century, and so were politics and diplomacy. England was becoming a world power.

And probably Marlowe served as an English spy abroad. We don't know much about this, but he does seem to have been in this very kind of murky business, a kind of James Bond before the time. He served, apparently, in that capacity in France. And these allegations have always sort of shrouded his reputation and added a kind of, as it were, atmosphere of mystique around him. Of course, espionage was something else for which you could find yourself dangling at the end of a rope. That, in fact, was another dangerous game that Marlowe was playing.

There was a third dangerous game he was playing. Marlowe is supposed, on very good grounds, to have been gay. His play, *Edward II*, strongly supports this supposition and he's quoted as having said, "all they that love not tobacco and boys are fools." And he also said, and this is quite an extraordinary remark, "St. John the Evangelist was bedfellow to Christ and leaned always in his bosom, that he used him as the sinners of Sodom," that St. John the Baptist and Christ were lovers. That too could have got someone into court and indeed, worse than court, could have got them into death row.

Everything about Marlowe, we may say, was controversial and dangerous, not least what happened in 1593 when he was killed. For centuries, his death was supposed to have been the result of a drunken brawl in a tavern over a woman with whom he was lewdly associated, a woman of the streets. Only later has it emerged that he was probably assassinated because of some political intrigue, whose details we shall never now know.

Well, what then do we know? Marlowe left four great plays in a theatrical career which spanned a mere five years. It was a wonderful literary blaze. These four tragedies all have two things in common. They all deal with what has been called the "overreacher" theme. That is, man's attempt to become greater than himself, vaulting ambition. The other shared feature of these four plays is the mighty line, and we come back to blank verse and prosody.

Blank verse had existed before Marlowe, but he supercharged it. But first of all, I want just to say a couple more words about overreaching. What, in detail, does that mean? Well, Marlowe's first dramatic triumph was staged in the late 1580s, about five years before the young William Shakespeare had made his way to London. That play of Marlowe's was called *Tamburlaine the Great*.

Now, the hero of the play, Tamburlaine, is a semi-mythic Asian shepherd, who, by sheer force of will, becomes a mighty emperor, defying almost death itself. This is how the contemporary playbill, which was posted throughout London, put it. Incidentally, these playbills would be fly-posted on walls all over the place, but also prominently on what were called pissing posts, that's to say, public urinals. So in fact, you stand there and you'd read it.

This is what it read, the description of the play:

> Tamburlaine the Great. Who, from a Scythian Shephearde by his rare and woonderfull Conquests, became a most puissant and mightye Monarque. And (for his tyranny, and terrour in Warre) was tearmed, The Scourge of God.

That last phrase, it could mean either he was God's scourge punishing men, or atheistically, and, as I say, the tinge of atheism is always there in Marlowe, that he, Tamburlaine, a mere man, had scourged God himself. The play was a huge hit. It introduced a whole gallery of humanistic themes into drama. It also introduced a new repertoire of linguistic creativity and moral daring.

Let me give just one example: the moment when royal ambition begins to stir in Tamburlaine. Remember, he's a shepherd, like in the Wakefield play we were looking at, but very different. He's been watching the Persian king Mycetes. "But why should he not too be a king?" thinks Tamburlaine. And he goes on to muse, why should not he "ride in triumph through Persepolis!—Is it not brave to be a king …?" Remember, he's walked down on the proscenium, right to the front of the stage here and he's talking to the audience. But he turns round and addresses the question to his companion brigands and yes-men, Techelles, Usumcasane, and Theridamas. Wonderful words, they roll off the tongue. "Is it not passing brave," asked Tamburlaine, "to be a king, / And ride in triumph through Persepolis?"

He's thinking of himself, riding in triumph through Persepolis. Why shouldn't he do it? And seeing which way his lord's mind is tending, Techelles replies, "O, my lord, it is sweet and full of pomp!" Terrible yesman. And the sycophantic Usumcasane adds, "To be a king is half to be a god." And Theridamas puts in his sort of ha'ppence as well and he puts what Tamburlaine is thinking into flattering words.

He says:

> A god is not so glorious as a king:
> I think the pleasure they enjoy in heaven,
> Cannot compare with kingly joys in earth;—
> To wear a crown enchas'd with pearl and gold,
> Whose virtues carry with it life and death;
> To ask and have, command and be obey'd;
> When looks breed love, with looks to gain the prize,—
> Such power attractive shines in princes' eyes.

This, one should say, is very seditious stuff. Killing kings, which is the main issue of Shakespeare's history plays, is the hottest potato in Elizabethan and Jacobean England. But Tamburlaine is going further than this. He's saying that anyone, even an illiterate peasant like himself, unanointed by God, can usurp the powers of a king. If, that is, he has himself the power and the will, as Tamburlaine's three companions prudently admit they have not. They, in fact, serve him because he was the willpower.

Even in this small sample, the suppleness and fluidity and magniloquence of the mighty line is evident. This, in fact, is the supercharged blank verse I was talking about. Essentially, it's our old friend, the 10-syllable iambic pentameter that we encountered in Chaucer (dee-*dum*, dee-*dum*, dee-*dum*, dee-*dum*, dee-*dum*). "Is *it* not *pass*ing *brave* to *be* a *king*, / And *ride* in *tri*umph *through* Per*sepolis*?" But, of course, one doesn't say it that way, in that rhythmic jog trot. That way, it sounds almost prosaic. What one says is, "Is it not passing *brave* to be a *king*, / And *ride* in *triumph* through Persepolis?"

Blank verse is unrhymed, and that's a very good thing too, since English is poorer in rhyme endings than most European languages. I mean how many rhyme words for love can you come up with? Glove, dove. You can't do very much with that poetically, but compare it, for example, to the Italian *amore*. I'm not an Italian speaker, but I do know that there's the word *cuore*, which is heart, and there's the word *onore*, which is honor. So you've got *amore, onore*. I could write a poem myself using heart, honor and love. But it's much harder in English.

And blank verse, because it's not rhymed, is able to occupy that borderland between high poetry and conversational English, which is where most writers like to be, it seems to me. They want a slightly elevated style of speech, but not one which is cramped and formal. One which speaks to you, but at the same time is more sort of noble than you could, as it were, utter yourself.

Tamburlaine is a first play, a first performed play, and has the weaknesses of an opening effort. Principally, it lacks plot. Plotwise, it's the same thing over and over again. Tamburlaine goes on to ever greater victories, stamping on more and more heads until, finally, he loses and dies, and death stamps on his head. Even he has met his match. It's the simplest form of tragedy, what's called *de casibus*: the irresistible rise, the inevitable fall.

In his next plays, Marlowe became a much more interesting playwright, one who could handle much more complex themes. In *The Jew of Malta*, for example, he explored Machiavellianism. That doctrine, which was considered very seditious at the time, asserted that kings and princes and rulers—you can take your pick—were political players in that most fascinating of power games, the game of statecraft.

Edward II, for instance, one of Marlowe's later plays, is about a king who is destroyed by what? His homosexual love for a favorite courtier, Gaveston. That's a play, which for obvious reasons, has attracted a lot of contemporary interest. But the work I want to concentrate on in the rest of this lecture is Marlowe's most famous, *Doctor Faustus*.

The themes of *Doctor Faustus* are known to many who have never seen or read Marlowe's texts. The tragical history of *Doctor Faustus* is part of the grain of our modern worldview and it takes the "overreacher" theme and makes it really rather subtle. The play opens with a magnificent soliloquy, which again is a dramatic device which, if Marlowe didn't quite invent, he perfected. It is the hero speaking to himself, but more, he's thinking as much as he's talking. And the soliloquy is a way of taking the audience inside the character's head.

The main theme of *Doctor Faustus*, which is laid out in this opening soliloquy, is simple enough. What precisely would you sell your soul for? Every man, as they say, has his price. For Faustus, the question is easy: knowledge, that forbidden fruit which tempted Adam and Eve in the Garden of Eden. Knowledge is power, and Faustus wants it. More importantly, Faustus wants an exciting new power, what we would call science and he calls necromancy.

The action opens with Faustus in his study. It's the University of Wittenberg, which, as you may remember, is Hamlet's alma mater. The scholar-hero, Faustus, has mastered the classic educational trivium. That's the three-part syllabus, rhetoric, philosophy, and theology. He's also an expert in law and medicine. He knows everything that a university can teach him. He's omniscient, but he feels there is something more he should know, and that is the knowledge contained in necromantic books. Necromancy is the black art.

And so he calls up Mephistopheles, who is the henchman of Satan, and there follows a famous exchange as Mephistopheles appears: "How comes it," asks Faustus, "then, that thou art out of hell?"

And Mephistopheles replies:

> Why, this is hell, nor am I out of it:
> Think'st thou that I, who saw the face of God,
> And tasted the eternal joys of heaven,
> Am not tormented with ten thousand hells,
> In being depriv'd of everlasting bliss?

Isn't that a wonderful line? "Why, this is hell, nor am I out of it." Faustus, at this point, should take warning, but, clever though he may be, he doesn't. He may be smart, but he's not very wise.

So voracious is he for knowledge, forbidden knowledge, that he signs a contract in blood with Mephistopheles, by which he will get 24 years of service from the devil. He'll get exactly what he wants. No doors will be closed to him. And thus, as he fondly anticipates, power and knowledge he'll get, more than any mortal man has previously enjoyed, after which his soul will be forfeit to Satan. That's the price he's paying. It's a good bargain, he thinks, at the beginning of his two dozen years, that is.

Ironically, Faustus wastes his two dozen omnipotent years on self-indulgence, most magnificently when Mephistopheles supplies him with Helen of Troy as his bed partner, an amazing conception. And the soliloquy which ensues when Faustus sees this beautiful woman, the woman over whom wars had been fought, is Marlowe's most famous soliloquy, and it's the most glorious example, I think, of his mighty line at its mightiest.

This is how it goes:

> Was this the face that launch'd a thousand ships,
> And burnt the topless towers of Ilium [that's Troy]—
> Sweet Helen, make me immortal with a kiss.

And he kisses her.

> Her lips suck forth my soul: see, where it flies!—
> Come, Helen, come, give me my soul again.

He is going to make love to her.

> Here will I dwell, for heaven is in these lips,
> And all is dross that is not Helena.

It's a man selling his soul, but we feel it might be worth it, at least as Marlowe presents it. And the irony, of course, this isn't Helen at all, but what's called a succubus, a soul-stealer. But in fact, Faustus believes that this is worth doing.

In the end, he's betrayed, and this is one of the complexities of the play: he's betrayed, not by his intellect, but by his flesh. But so powerful is Marlowe's verse and speeches like is "this the face that launch'd a thousand ships" that one feels almost that the world, even one's soul, is "well lost" for such a sublime experience as a night of love with Helen of Troy.

Marlowe was still in many ways an apprentice dramatist while writing *Doctor Faustus*, magnificent as that play is. There's a lot of clumsy comic relief, and he never quite gets into the question of exactly what kind of knowledge it is Faustus craves. That's to say, he doesn't define science as we would understand it. There were other people doing it at the time, Francis Bacon notably, who is the father of contemporary scientific method.

We don't have a complete text of *Doctor Faustus* unfortunately, but the play nonetheless has irresistible power. The conception and also, of course, the wonderful mighty lines and the soliloquies, which have come to us. And perhaps most powerful of all is Faustus's last soliloquy. It's delivered during his last hour on earth.

As the clock ticks—it's done in real time, practically—so the moment approaches in which his soul must be surrendered. His 24 years are up, and he will descend through that stage trapdoor to eternal torment. In fact, demons will come up and take him down.

And this is that last soliloquy:

> Ah, Faustus,

He's talking to himself, he's thinking, of course.

> Now hast thou but one bare hour to live,
> And then thou must be damn'd perpetually!
> Stand still, you ever-moving spheres of heaven,

He looks up into the sky. It's late afternoon and he wants the skies to stop so that his doom will be postponed.

> That time may cease, and midnight never come;
> Fair Nature's eye, rise, rise again, and make
> Perpetual day; or let this hour be but
> A year, a month, a week, a natural day,
> That Faustus may repent and save his soul!
> *O lente, lente currite, noctis equi!*

Even at this moment, he can't stop being the scholar, so he breaks into Latin, "Oh, go slowly, go slowly, you horses of heaven," thinking of Phoebus's chariot in classical mythology.

> The stars move still, time runs, the clock will strike,
> The devil will come, and Faustus must be damn'd.

He can't stop time.

> O, I'll leap up to my God!–Who pulls me down?–
> See, see, where Christ's blood streams in the firmament!

That most beautiful line. At sunset, the horizon goes red, red sky at night, shepherd's delight. He looks at it and realizes that night is coming, and with night, comes midnight, and at midnight, his soul is taken from him.

> See, see, where Christ's blood streams in the firmament!
> One drop would save my soul, half a drop: ah, my Christ!

And then suddenly, a demon comes up and tears his flesh. And as I say, flesh always betrays Faustus.

And he says:

> Ah, rend not my heart for naming of my Christ!

In fact, Christ probably could redeem him, even at this moment, if he truly repented and accepted the pains, the pains that Christ suffered on the cross, but he's too much of a fleshly man to do that. And then he's doomed. Night falls.

> Yet will I call on him: O, spare me, Lucifer!–
> Where is it now? 'tis gone:

He looks up and the red sky isn't there any more. Dark has fallen.

> and see, where God
> Stretcheth out his arm, and bends his ireful brows!
> Mountains and hills, come, come, and fall on me,
> And hide me from the heavy wrath of God!
> No, no!

So it goes on. It goes on for quite a while. It is very daring at this point in the drama not to have any action, but just to have a man speaking alone, just standing on stage. But in fact, so powerful is Marlowe's language that in the theater, it's a most extraordinarily potent moment in the play. If you go to the theater, what you find is the audience is still and it is so quiet as people pay attention as this man is now facing his ultimate destiny.

And then he does actually go on for several more lines, but then finally the devils come in and they want their payment:

> My God, my god, look not so fierce on me!

He looks up into the sky and there's nothing there but darkness.

> Adders and serpents, let me breathe a while!

These are, as it were, the demons whom he sees as snakes, and of course, the snake it was who destroyed Adam and Eve in the Garden of Eden.

> Ugly hell, gape not! come not, Lucifer!
> I'll burn my books!–Ah, Mephistophilis!

That's his last word. Isn't it wonderful? "I'll burn my books!" Was there ever a more poignant last word that a scholar uttered than "I'll burn my books!—Ah, Mephistophilis!"? He wants to revoke the contract.

It is important, of course, that books are now a part of the conventional landscape in literature. It's something that happened relatively recently. People were very nervous of the kinds of things which books could do. What would happen if anyone could pick up a book and teach themselves, as opposed to learning, being controlled by institutions like universities or the church?

That, in fact, is a sub-theme here, but the important thing is: so die all overreachers. That, if you like, is the commercial. That's the message that the play leaves us with. We do not, I think, feel any satisfaction in Faustus's punishment and eternal damnation. Rather, in the play, we admire his vaulting ambition. We admire his God-defying rebellion against the sterile doctrines of old learning. He's no less an adventurer or explorer than Sir Walter Raleigh sailing round the four quarters of the world.

Why, then, did Marlowe not celebrate Faustus's rebellion? Why didn't he actually, as it were, respond to his hero as we respond to his hero, with admiration, wholeheartedly? Why the moralistic ending? Well, the reason quite simply is Marlowe could not end the play atheistically, as he probably wanted to. The most he could do is to make us admire Faustus, and then fall into line and concur that such overreaching must surely be punished.

It was a tightrope that Marlowe was walking. Thank heavens he walked it so well. An outright glorying in Faustus's antireligious, antiauthoritarian career would have brought down the whole apparatus of censorship to control him. It might even have cost him his life, certainly his license to write any more plays. And so, like those makers of gangster movies in the 1930s, Marlowe was obliged to wind up with a crime that does not pay, overreaching, in his terms, does not pay, moralistic ending. But we can see through it to the subversive themes beneath.

And to go back to the original question: What, one has to wonder, might Christopher Marlowe have achieved, had he had another 20 years? Shakespeare, one may guess, might well have had to tussle for the crown of England's greatest ever dramatist, but that one blow from a dagger, why, in fact, that blow fell on his chest, we don't know, but that one blow from a dagger in 1593 made Marlowe's later career, that career we can only hypothesize about, impossible.

But what he's left us is a wonderful small treasure house of drama, early drama. I don't think there's been any more innovative dramatist and possibly any more innovative author in English literature than Christopher Marlowe. And the plays themselves, in fact, are still very good on the stage. And the other thing, of course, is that he created some of the foundation stones on which the great edifice of Shakespearean drama would erect itself, and that is what we shall be looking at in the next two lectures.

Shakespeare the Man—The Road to the Globe
Lecture 7

There's no question as to who was the greatest author in English literature: William Shakespeare. And the next two lectures will try and deal with his achievement. One hundred lectures wouldn't be enough, but so be it.

William Shakespeare (1564–1616) was born about six years into the reign of Queen Elizabeth. England was experiencing a period of stability under Elizabeth, although there were still echoes of the turmoil of the reign of Bloody Mary. Under Mary, it had been dangerous to be Protestant. Under Elizabeth, it was dangerous to be Catholic. Many English people, including Shakespeare's family, prudently kept both irons in the fire.

The late Tudor period, ushered in by Elizabeth, was one of growth and relative stability. There were no great foreign wars or invasions and no civil war to tear the country apart, although the memory of the Wars of the Roses remained frightening. During the years of Elizabeth's reign, there emerged a growing sense of national greatness, tempered only by the question of succession, given that Elizabeth was, famously, a virgin queen. In keeping with this national question, the most significant political question in Shakespeare's plays is: How is one king replaced with another? He explores regicide in *Macbeth*, usurpation in *Richard II*, and inheritance in *Henry IV* and *Henry V*. Shakespeare returns to this question up through his last play, *Henry VIII*, but he never comes up with a definitive answer.

Shakespeare's father was a prosperous glove-maker and an alderman in Stratford-on-Avon, a beautiful town in England's West Country, about 150 miles from London. His mother, Mary Arden, was higher born than her husband, and her son's aim in life was to rise to the condition of the gentry. He aimed to leave life at a higher social station than he had entered it. Young William attended grammar school, where he read Holinshed's English histories, Plutarch's classical histories, and Ovid (the latter two probably in translation). Ben Jonson, a fellow dramatist, would later observe that Shakespeare had little Latin and less Greek. By our standards, Shakespeare was highly educated.

On leaving school in his early teens, Shakespeare probably worked for his father, learning the techniques and tools of working with leather that would later appear in his plays. He may also have been arrested for poaching. At the age of 18, Shakespeare married a local woman, Anne Hathaway. She was older than he and three months pregnant. The marriage would produce two daughters and a son, Hamnet or Hamlet, who died in infancy. Many have speculated that the marriage was unhappy based on the fact that Shakespeare, in his will, left Anne his "second-best bed." The recurrence in the plays of difficult, cold, and domineering wives, such as Lady Macbeth, is also read as evidence of an unhappy marriage, but we have no real knowledge of the conditions of Shakespeare's married life.

Between 1585 and 1592, the formative years of his young manhood, we know nothing about Shakespeare's life. He may have left Stratford and found employment as a country schoolteacher. Another hypothesis offered for these "lost years" is that he was in the north of England, working as a private tutor to the children of a Catholic family. Access to a good library in a wealthy home might explain the otherwise mysterious intellectual sophistication of even his earliest work. Yet another theory is that Shakespeare joined a traveling group of players. His membership in such a group would explain the mature stagecraft displayed in his drama, even in his early works.

By 1592, Shakespeare had become a prominent figure in the London stage, writing plays and incurring resentment from rival playwrights. By 1594, he had risen to the top of the theatrical world; he was an actor and a shareholder in the Chamberlain's Men, as well as an author.

He would go on to live many years in London, dabbling at times in commerce and adding substantially to his net worth. In his 20-year career in London, he penned some 38 or 39 plays, as well as the sonnets and other poetry. The sonnets were written mainly in the 1590s; they offer insight into Shakespeare's mind and his sexuality. Many of the sonnets are clearly addressed as love poems to a young man, the fair lord; others, to a possibly married woman, the dark lady. It's possible that Shakespeare may have been bisexual, just as he was both Catholic and Protestant.

The sonnets can be dated with some degree of confidence, but it's much more difficult to establish the chronology of the composition and first performance of Shakespeare's plays. We can say, however, that his evolution moves through several easily identified phases.

Earliest in that evolutionary process is the first trilogy of *Henry VI* history plays, set during the Wars of the Roses. These are high-action works. Arguably, the first mature play is *Richard III*, to which the date 1593 has been assigned, when Shakespeare himself was not yet 30.

The opening soliloquy of *Richard III* is deservedly famous. Richard, the speaker, is physically malformed, but he has performed heroically in the civil wars that destroyed the house of Lancaster and brought the house of York to the throne. The Yorkist king, Edward IV, is weak, and Richard resolves to become king himself. Richard hates the peace but will occupy himself by killing the king. Richard proves himself a glorious villain, winning the crown by marriage to a woman whose husband he has killed and other acts of cold-blooded unscrupulousness. Remarkably, though, this first speech—indeed, the whole play—is shot through with humor. We can't help liking this seductive scoundrel, especially compared to the dullards, second-rate villains, and even some of the virtuous people whom he treads down. When he finally dies on the field at Bosworth, we feel regret at the loss of this antihero. The dramatic competence evident in this early play is breathtaking. We should note, however, that Shakespeare could not have written it without Marlowe's *The Jew of Malta*, with its seriocomic treatment of Machiavellian heroism, or *Tamburlaine the Great*.

> **We can't help liking this seductive scoundrel, [Richard III], especially compared to the dullards, second-rate villains, and even some of the virtuous people whom he treads down.**

The historical Richard III was nothing like Shakespeare's villain. His history here is pure Tudor propaganda, written partly to please Elizabeth and her court.

Shakespeare's plays have been grouped by critics into histories, comedies, tragedies, Roman plays, problem plays, and romances. The year after *Richard III*, he produced *The Taming of the Shrew*, a comedy perhaps best known to us in its musical version, *Kiss Me, Kate*. The play is set in Italy, a favorite location for Shakespearean comedy, as well as the site of the tragedy *Othello*. In this play, Petruchio, a well-born Italian gentleman, marries the daughter of a prosperous Paduan merchant, Katherine, who desires to be in charge in the marriage. Petruchio's motive in marrying Katherine is purely mercenary—he wants her dowry, and he wagers his male friends that he can tame her. After the marriage, he embarks on a systematic campaign of humiliation of Katherine. He starves her and doesn't allow her to sleep, all in the guise of caring for her well-being. Petruchio's strategy works and, in the final scene, he wins the wager. Not only does Kate submit to her lord, but she proudly philosophizes on the theme: "Thy husband is thy lord, thy life, thy keeper, / Thy head, thy sovereign; one that cares for thee." It's fair to assume that most modern audiences of either gender find uncomfortable both the speech in which Petruchio lays out his intentions and the speech in which Katherine submits. The Elizabethans, too, may have seen the irony in the fact that they were ruled by a woman of whom it was boasted that she had the heart of a man.

In another of Shakespeare's comedies, *Much Ado about Nothing*, the feisty Beatrice is triumphant. Other strong women in the plays include Lady Macbeth, Volumnia in *Coriolanus*, Regan and Goneril in *Lear*, and Cleopatra. Shakespeare is anything but rigid on the subject of gender.

Shakespeare was also fascinated with the Roman Republic. The first of his Roman plays was *Titus Andronicus*, a bloody story of revenge. The action in this play opens with Titus, a general, returning to Rome after 10 years campaigning for the empire. The emperor has died, and Rome is faced with a succession crisis. Titus has brought with him captives, the Goth queen Tamora and her lover, the Machiavellian Aaron, who is a Moor. In the succeeding scene, Tamora's sons meet the noble Roman maiden Lavinia in a wood and rape her over the body of her slain lover. They then cut out her tongue and cut off her arms so that she cannot identify her assailants by speech or writing. Improbably, Lavinia learns how to write holding a stake between the stumps of her arms and writes the names of her assailants. Incredibly, the play gets even more violent, culminating in a "Thyestean scene," as it's called, in which Tamora is tricked into eating a pie containing the meat of her two rapist sons.

Shakespeare did not pursue the level of violence in *Titus Andronicus* in his later drama, although we do find scenes of blood and horror in the tragedies. In this later work, Shakespeare is more interested in the process by which the tragedy unfolds, what Aristotle called the necessary and the probable, that creates the climactic effect of catharsis. *Titus* is a young dramatist's play, an exploration of just how far the dramatic art could go. Shakespeare's world was a violent one, and this work perhaps draws on the appetite of its audience for blood.

Shakespeare became a much more sophisticated dramatist as his career progressed. He never stayed in the same genre, moving through at least five or six kinds of mastery toward what is perhaps his greatest achievement, the tragedies. ■

Suggested Reading

Shapiro, *A Year in the Life of William Shakespeare, 1599.*

Weis, *Shakespeare Revealed.*

Wells, *Shakespeare and Co.*

Questions to Consider

1. How important is it that we know anything about Shakespeare, other than the plays he wrote?

2. How did Shakespeare "happen"?

Shakespeare the Man—The Road to the Globe
Lecture 7—Transcript

There's no question as to who was the greatest author in English literature: William Shakespeare. And the next two lectures will try and deal with his achievement. 100 lectures wouldn't be enough, but so be it.

Shakespeare was born in early 1564. The exact date we don't know. It's something that throws out anniversary celebrations a bit. He was born within a few months of Christopher Marlowe, the dramatist we were talking about in the last lecture, and about six years into the reign of Queen Elizabeth, The Faerie Queene. She was, of course, the Virgin Queen. And it's a good thing that he was born then, in many ways, but not least because the stability her reign brought to England would last four more decades. It was a good time to come into the world, but particularly good if you were going to build a career in literature.

Nonetheless, even though it was a stable reign, the turmoil of the previous reign, that of Bloody Mary, was still roiling the country, was still in a state of upheaval. Under Mary, it had been dangerous to be Protestant. Under Elizabeth, the reverse was the case: it was dangerous to be Catholic. And many English people prudently kept both irons in the fire. They'd been Catholic in their youth and had to be Protestant in their adulthood.

And it seems quite certain that Shakespeare's family was among that number, seesawing prudently in their religious affiliation, being very careful. Now, was Shakespeare himself a Catholic or a Protestant? He was probably both and probably neither, although there's a huge amount of critical debate on the subject to this day.

The late Tudor period, ushered in by Elizabeth, was one of growth and, as I say, of relative stability. There were no great foreign wars or invasions. The one, as it were, unlucky invasion for the Spanish, the Armada, was repelled in 1588, or, as the medal struck on that occasion recorded, "God Blew and they were Scattered." God blew a gale, the enemy was scattered and England was safe.

There was no civil war to tear the country apart, although, following the long conflict of the Wars of the Roses, such an event remained a traumatic and inexpugnable fear. Civil strife was the worst thing that could happen to a country, people of Shakespeare's time felt.

Marc Antony's speech in *Julius Caesar* outlines the horrors of civil war:

> Blood and destruction shall be so in use,
> And dreadful objects so familiar,
> That mothers shall but smile when they behold
> Their infants quarter'd with the hands of war;

And it has that wonderful phrase:

> Cry "Havoc!" and let slip the dogs of war.

So civil war was absent, but it was always there as something which was, as it were, a potential threat. And in fact, historically, civil war would be avoided in England until the 1640s, well after Shakespeare's death. So over the years of Elizabeth's reign, there emerged also a growing sense of national greatness.

The only fly in the ointment of the decades of Elizabeth's reign was the fact that she was famously a virgin queen and no parthenogenesis was possible. That's to say, she couldn't have an heir, a direct heir from her own body. It might be very well for poets like Edmund Spenser, concocting complimentary verse to celebrate the fact that she was a virgin, but as the century advanced, the question of succession loomed ominously.

You can't read a play like *Hamlet*, *Macbeth*, *King Lear* or any of the history plays of Shakespeare without recognizing that the big political question in his drama is "How do you replace one king with another king? Is regicide the answer?" That, in fact, is explored in *Macbeth*. Is a strong man usurping the throne from a weak man, as in *Richard II*, where Bolingbroke makes himself Henry IV, is that the answer? Is inheritance the answer, as in *Henry IV* and *Henry V*? That's to say, the bloodline?

Shakespeare nags at this question right the way through to his last written play, *Henry VIII*, and he never quite comes up with a definitive answer. And that anxiety was generated by the fact that there was no direct, obvious successor to Queen Elizabeth.

To return to Shakespeare's life, as best we know it: William Shakespeare was born the son of a prosperous glove-maker and an alderman in the town of Stratford-on-Avon, which is in England's west country, a very beautiful town. And of course, the beauty is infused into Shakespeare's own sense of natural landscape. It's about 150 miles from London, on one of the country's great inland rivers and, as I say, some of the most beautiful countryside in England, Warwickshire.

William's mother, Mary Arden, was rather higher born than her husband, and Shakespeare's aim in life, like his father, was to rise to the condition of the gentry. He wanted, in fact, to leave life at a higher social station than he had entered it. He wanted to be, as it were, upper middle class, and he was born in what you might call the kind of respectable lower middle class.

Young William attended grammar school, as they were called, where he received instruction from very good teachers. He was very lucky in that respect, although Ben Jonson, a university man and a fellow dramatist, would later observe that Shakespeare had little Latin and less Greek. It's clear that he could read the ancients, but his sources—Holinshed's English histories, Plutarch's classical histories, Ovid—were mainly in translation. But we should remember that, even though he was a son of a businessman, Shakespeare was, by our standards, extremely highly educated.

He seems, on leaving school in his early teens, to have worked for his father. There is, in his plays, a great deal of expertise about leather and the working of the material of leather and its tools. The mark of the glove-maker's son would be with him for life. Now, he may also, and this is, in fact, legendary, he may have been arrested for poaching.

But what we do know from church records is that, at the relatively young age of 18, William Shakespeare married a local woman, Anne Hathaway. She was older than he, and three months pregnant. Now, this wasn't unusual at the time. Very many pregnant women went respectably to the altar. And also the fact that she was slightly older, again, was not that unusual, though we know so little about her that a great deal has been read into that fact.

There would be two daughters to the marriage, and a son. The son was called Hamnet or Hamlet, and he died in infancy. That, in fact, is another fact which we can read back into the plays, into the tragedy of Hamlet. It's been speculated that the Shakespeares' marriage may not have been happy. They were separated for a long time. He was in London, she stayed in Stratford. Certainly, for the major part of their married lives, as I say, they were separate, but again, one shouldn't read too much into this, though, in fact, we know so little, and nature abhors a vacuum, that people have speculated.

And there's the famous business that in his will, he left Anne Hathaway, who survived him, the "second-best bed." There's a good reason for that because they slept in the second-best bed and the best bed was kept for guests. Now, again, you can actually pull this both ways. Either, in fact, it was a calculated post-mortem insult or, in fact, it was where they'd been closest and he wanted her to keep that and nobody else to sleep in it.

There is the fact, and again, much has been read into this, difficult and cold wives and domineering wives, Lady Macbeth, for instance, recur in the plays. And the plays are, as Keats memorably put it, the allegory of Shakespeare's life and the closest that now we shall ever get to him. So we read them and we do actually sort of try and get an impression of Shakespeare from them. To go back to the marriage, we can fill in the blanks of those married years as it pleases us. I think the marriage may, in fact, have been quite happy, but I don't know. It's just my feeling.

Between 1585, three years after his marriage, and 1592, when he begins to be mentioned in London theatrical circles, we know absolutely nothing about Shakespeare's life. These are what is called the "lost years." In anyone's life, these are very formative years. They're the years of young manhood. And was he living in Stratford at the time? Probably not, because his father's affairs were not going well at all. He might have worked as a country schoolteacher. He was certainly clever enough to do that.

Two more persuasive hypotheses have been offered for the lost years, these seven lost years. One hypothesis is that he was in the north of England with a Catholic family, to whose children he acted as a private or domestic tutor. Now, again, people have looked into this and speculated that there was a good library in the house and Shakespeare educated himself, as well as the children, over these years. This would explain the otherwise mysterious intellectual sophistication of his work, even his earliest work.

The other hypothesis, which is very attractive, is that he joined a traveling group of players or touring actors. One of the reasons that the mystery plays died out was that touring from the metropolis, from London, came more and more to, as it were, take the place which it previously had. If Shakespeare, in fact, joined a troupe of actors, it would explain the mature stagecraft that his drama displays from its early manifestations. He seems to have known the machinery of the stage very well.

But the simple fact is we'll never know. What we do know is that in 1592, William Shakespeare had become a prominent figure in the London stage, writing plays and incurring resentment from rival playwrights, whose work was already being eclipsed by his. He's called by one rival an "upstart crow." This, in fact, is an indication of the fact that he was very successful. He was going up like a meteor, almost from the moment he arrived in the early '90s.

By 1594, Shakespeare had risen to the top of the theatrical world. It's a very slippery pole, lots of competition, but he was there. He was a principal player. He seems to have acted quite a lot, and he was a shareholder in the Chamberlain's Men. This was named after the company patron, the Lord Chamberlain. And his name began to appear on playbills, as a crowd-drawing author. People wanted to see the latest Shakespeare.

He would go on to live many years in London, dabbling at times in commerce on the side, adding substantially to his net worth. He's a bit of a capitalist, Shakespeare, no fool. In his 20-year career in London, Shakespeare penned, as far as we can establish, some 38 or 39 plays. And when not so occupied, when, for instance, the plague closed the theaters, as it often did in summer, he turned out a quantity of wonderful poetry, notably the sonnets, which are the finest example of that genre, the 14-line poem that we have.

These were written mainly in the 1590s, and they offer us, I think, one of the closest insights that we have into Shakespeare's mind and, most interestingly, into his sexuality. Many of the sonnets are clearly addressed as love poems to a young man, the fair lord, others to a possibly married woman, the dark lady. Homosexuality and adultery were things that he could, to some extent, sort of play games with in these poems. We'll never know, but the chances are that Shakespeare may have been bisexual, as he was both Catholic and Protestant. But sexual politics were different in those days and there was less neurosis about it.

Did Shakespeare, for example, have a soft spot for the boy actors in the company, who played the women's parts? Women weren't allowed into the theatrical profession and the parts were played by boys whose voices hadn't broken. Did he have a soft spot for some of those boy actors? Some have thought he might have done, but again, these are areas of high speculation.

The sonnets we can more or less date, although they were not published until a decade later, with a title page reference to a "Mr. WH," which has always mystified critics. Now, it's much less easy to establish the chronology of the composition and first performance of Shakespeare's plays, although his evolution clearly moves through several large, easily identified phases.

Earliest in that evolutionary process is the first group or trilogy of *Henry VI* history plays, which are set during the Wars of the Roses, the civil wars that I was talking about earlier. These are high action works. Arguably, the first mature play, so to call it, is *Richard III*, to which we can provisionally assign the date 1593. Shakespeare, remember, is himself not yet 30. And the opening soliloquy is famous, deservedly so. And the play is a favorite star vehicle and many great actors over the centuries have played it, from Richard Burbage to Laurence Olivier.

As Richard III comes on stage, you must remember him coming right the way down the proscenium stage, right into the body of the audience. He's a physically malformed noble. He's got a hunched shoulder and he limps. He's performed heroically in the civil wars, which have brought the house of York to the throne. The house of Lancaster has been destroyed, and so, in fact, a Yorkist monarch is on the throne. But the king, Edward IV, is very weak and

Richard III resolves to play the Machiavellian. He himself will become king one day. It's a very Marlovian theme.

It's also a great Shakespearean theme. How do you replace one king with another? Let's actually just hear a little bit of that speech. It's very fine. In my lifetime, it's been immortalized by Laurence Olivier.

> Now is the Winter of our Discontent,
> Made glorious Summer by this Son of Yorke:
> And all the clouds that lowr'd vpon our house
> In the deepe bosome of the Ocean buried.
> Now are our browes bound with Victorious Wreathes,
> Our bruised armes hung vp for Monuments. ...

He says this very contemptuously. He hates the peace. And then he goes on to talk about himself.

> But I, that am not shap'd for sportiue trickes,
> Nor made to court an amorous Looking-glasse:
> I, that am Rudely stampt, and want loues Maiesty,
> To strut before a wonton ambling Nymph:

We imagine him limping, with his bad back.

> I, that am curtail'd of this faire Proportion,
> Cheated of Feature by dissembling Nature,
> Deform'd, vn-finish'd, sent before my time
> Into this breathing World, scarce halfe made vp,
> And that so lamely and vnfashionable,
> That dogges barke at me, as I halt by them.

What will he do in the time of peace? Well, what he's going to do in the time of peace, of course, is to kill the king and make himself king, which he does very successfully. It's a wonderful speech. It has high impact. I mean if you see this done in the theater, even today, it actually sort of grabs the audience by the throat.

And he goes on to prove a glorious villain, winning the crown by marriage to a woman whose husband he's killed, mass murder, including the princes in the tower, and cold-blooded unscrupulousness of a kind which even Machiavelli himself would have blanched at. But what is remarkable about that speech, and indeed the whole play, is the way in which it's shot through with humor. The dogs bark at him? That is what's called hyperbole. It's overstatement, but very funny.

And we can't help liking this seductive villain, this monster—he's a lovable monster—liking him more than the dullards, the placemen and the second-rate villains whom he treads down, and even some of the virtuous people in the play, who are very dull. And when he finally dies on the field at Bosworth, with his agonized "A horse, a horse, my kingdom for a horse" we feel something like, if not sorrow, regret that such an entertaining antihero should be no more.

The dramatic competence evident in this early play is breathtaking. Shakespeare could not, of course, have written it had Marlowe not bequeathed him *The Jew of Malta* with its seriocomic treatment of Machiavellian heroism and *Tamburlaine the Great* as well. But *Richard III* is streets ahead of Marlowe.

In passing, of course, we should note that the historical *Richard III* was nothing, absolutely nothing like Shakespeare's villain. Shakespeare's history, as historians will tell you, is pure travesty. It's Tudor propaganda, but he's written partly to please Elizabeth and her court. Her claim to the throne descended from the other party, from the Lancastrians, and she was quite pleased, and people around her were quite pleased, when dirt was done on the Yorkists, like *Richard III*. But, you know, great literature doesn't have to be historically true, and quite often, truth comes a very kind of far off second.

Shakespeare's plays, as I say, fall into a number of groups, which have been usefully labeled by critics. Now, whether Shakespeare himself would have agreed with the groupings is another question, but those groups are history plays, comedies, tragedies, Roman plays, problem plays and romances.

The year after *Richard III*, 1593, he produced a comedy which would also become a great favorite on the stage over the succeeding centuries, *The Taming of the Shrew*. It's perhaps as well known in its musical version, *Kiss Me, Kate*. The play is set in Italy, which was a favorite location for Shakespearian comedy, and with *Othello*, with tragedy as well. But why Italy? Well, because it was cultivated and fashionable. And Shakespeare seemed to have had an aversion to setting his comedies in England, although, clearly enough, the mechanicals, who are regular working guys in a play like *Midsummer Night's Dream*, are as English as plum pudding.

But in the *Taming of the Shrew*, Petruchio, a well-born Italian gentleman, marries the daughter of a prosperous Paduan merchant, Katherine. And she's a shrew. That is to say, a woman who wants what the Wife of Bath, whom we encountered in Chaucer's *Canterbury Tales*, would have called *maistrie*, that is to say, mastery. In her marriage, she wants to wear the pants, she wants to call the shots, she wants to be in charge.

Petruchio, whose motive in marrying is purely mercenary—he wants her dowry, he wants the money she brings with her—wagers his male friends that he can tame this termagant, this shrew. He can show her who really wears the pants. So after the marriage, Petruchio embarks on a systematic campaign of humiliation. He sees Katherine as a falcon which must be broken and then trained to its master's commands and wishes. Domestic tyranny is the way in which he carries this through.

He criticizes her clothes and makes her change them. Then he does the same again after she's changed them. When the food is brought to the table, he sends it away, claiming, falsely, it's burned. It's unfit to eat. And not to put too fine a point on it, he intends to starve her into submission, to beat her. You know, it's what's called mental cruelty in the divorce court today.

Let this husband speak for himself:

> Thus have I politicly begun my reign,

He thinks of himself as a king in the marriage.

> And 'tis my hope to end successfully.
> My falcon now is sharp and passing empty;

That's to say, his wife, she's hungry.

> And till she stoop she must not be full-gorged,

He won't give her a good meal until she actually bows down before him.

> For then she never looks upon her lure.
> Another way I have to man my haggard,
> To make her come and know her keeper's call,
> That is, to watch her, as we watch these kites
> That bate and beat and will not be obedient.

He's just talking about the ways in which he's going, as it were, to bring her to heel, I suppose, if she were a dog, rather than a falcon.

> She eat no meat to-day, nor none shall eat;
> Last night she slept not, nor to-night she shall not;
> As with the meat, some undeserved fault
> I'll find about the making of the bed;
> And here I'll fling the pillow, there the bolster,
> This way the coverlet, another way the sheets:
> Ay, and amid this hurly I intend
> That all is done in reverend care of her;
> And in conclusion she shall watch all night:
> And if she chance to nod I'll rail and brawl
> And with the clamour keep her still awake.

As I say, it is cruelty and it's cold-blooded cruelty as well. It is, in fact, very unpleasant, but it works, and finally Kate is broken, like the falcon. The fact that she's starved, the fact that she's, as it were, humiliated, the fact that she's sleepless means that she finally cracks and she becomes a good wife, as Petruchio thinks. And in the final scene, Petruchio wins his wager. Not only does Kate submit to her lord, she proudly philosophizes on the theme. She, as it were, speaks, as well as acts, the obedient wife.

"Thy husband," she says, and this is a general rule:

> Thy husband is thy lord, thy life, thy keeper,
> Thy head, thy sovereign; one that cares for thee,
> And for thy maintenance commits his body
> To painful labour both by sea and land,
> To watch the night in storms, the day in cold,
> Whilst thou liest warm at home, secure and safe;

He's away, killing dragons, while you're safe at home. One has to remember, of course, that at this period, and until quite recently, the marriage vows of the man and the woman were quite different. The man promised to love, honor, cherish, and the woman promised to love, honor, cherish, and obey. And so, in fact, if you want to be, as it were, defensive of Petruchio's action, you can say there is some kind of social warrant for the cruelty and rather, as I say, sort of obnoxious way in which he acts toward his wife. More so, as I say, his motives in marrying her are not idealistic, but mercenary.

It's fair to assume, I think, that most modern audiences of either sex find these two speeches—that's to say, the speech in which Petruchio lays out his intentions, and the speech in which Katherine submits—uncomfortable, very uncomfortable. There are a number of points which one should make. The Elizabethans, like all of us at all historical periods, were quite capable of what George Orwell calls doublethink.

They quite happily, for instance, indeed proudly, accepted that they themselves were ruled by a woman, even if, as she boasted, she had the heart of a man. It would have been a very brave man who tried to tame Elizabeth I or Elizabeth II, come to that. Those that tried usually ended up like Leicester, swinging at the end of a rope, or like Sir Walter Raleigh in the tower.

There are also other of Shakespeare's comedies in which shrews are not tamed, where, in fact, they're triumphant: Beatrice in *Much Ado about Nothing*, for example. There are innumerable strong women and sometimes, for that reason, bad women, it should be added, in Shakespeare's plays. Lady Macbeth, for instance, Volumnia in *Coriolanus*, Regan and Goneril in *Lear* and most magnificently, Cleopatra. Men kiss her foot, as Kate kisses Petruchio's foot in the most unpleasant moment in that play's action. Emperors, no less, have laid themselves down in homage to Cleopatra. And there are even obedient wives, like Hermione in *A Winter's Tale*, who prove themselves to be infinitely wilier than their spouses.

So there are many kinds of women in the plays. Shakespeare is anything but rigid on the subject of gender. But when all the chips are down and all the counterarguments are made, we have to accept that on many matters, the Elizabethans thought differently from us. They had soaring imaginations, huge resources of language, but they were not, in everything, socially enlightened. So we have to make that allowance when we watch Shakespeare.

The last play of the early Shakespearean cycle which I want to point to very briefly is the first of his Roman plays. Shakespeare was fascinated by Rome. Why? Because it was a kingdom without kings. It was most interesting thing, a republic. *Julius Caesar*, for example, is, in one of its many facets, a meditation on how you can have a democracy without a strong man or a strong woman at its head. And the first of the Roman plays, *Titus Andronicus*, in fact, which actually leads that way, is fascinating, but it's anything but thoughtful on such matters. That's to say, Shakespeare began his Roman plays with one which is rather different in mode.

It's a bloody revenge play in the Senecan mode. Now, revenge is very important. *Hamlet* is a revenger and one can draw a line between *Titus Andronicus* and *Hamlet*. But there's a great difference in that *Titus Andronicus* is a work of horror, a terrible horror, and terror, in fact.

The action opens with Titus, a general, returning to Rome after 10 years campaigning for the empire. The emperor has died and there is a crisis of succession. This, in fact, is the perennial situation in Shakespeare's plays. Titus has brought with him captives, the Goth queen Tamora and her lover, the Machiavellian Aaron, who is a Moor and is black.

In the succeeding scene, Tamora's sons meet the noble Roman maiden Lavinia in a wood and they rape the poor woman over the body of her slain lover. That's horrible enough, but then they cut out her tongue and cut off her arms so that she cannot identify her assailants by speech or by writing. Now, among other improbabilities in the play, Lavinia learns how to write holding a stake between the stumps which are all that survive of her arms, and she writes the names of her assailants.

Incredibly, the play gets even more violent, culminating in a "Thyestean scene," as it's called, in which Tamora is tricked into eating, with great relish, a pie containing the meaty substance of these two rapist sons. So, as this summary suggests, *Titus Andronicus* is a ne plus ultra of violence. It's over the top. It's Shakespeare's slasher play, and it's a vein of drama which the older Shakespeare did not care to pursue.

In his later tragedies, there are certainly scenes of blood and horror. One thinks of Gloucester's being blinded on the stage, for example. "Out, vile jelly!" they say as they pop out his eyeball. But it's the process by which tragedy unfolds, the quality of what Aristotle called the necessary and the probable, which creates that climactic effect which Aristotle again called catharsis, that interest Shakespeare. It's not the horror. It's the mechanical progression to the climax which interested Shakespeare and which creates, in his view, the finest kind of tragic effect.

Titus is a young dramatist's play. It's over the top and it's exploring just how far his dramatic art could go. And, one should remember of course that one could be horrified by this play, but one should remember that members of the audience would have wondered as they saw it, "Well, shall I go to the Globe and pay my sixpence entrance fee there, or shall I go across the road and watch some bear or bull baiting, or perhaps even watch a public hanging?" There was a lot of, if you like to call it, violence of a horrific kind in Shakespeare's world, and so *Titus Andronicus* perhaps draws on that appetite for blood.

But Shakespeare becomes a much more sophisticated dramatist as his career evolves, as it moves forward, as it progresses. Few writers, I think, have developed as fast and as interestingly as Shakespeare. He had huge successes, very large successes from his earliest plays onward, but he never actually stayed in the same groove. He always moved on. This, in fact, is one of the many aspects of what makes him, as I said at the beginning of this lecture, our greatest ever author: that, in fact, he moves through at least five or six kinds of mastery toward what will be, I think, regarded by posterity and by most readers of Shakespeare as his greatest achievement, the tragedies, which we'll be looking at in the next lecture.

Shakespeare—The Mature Years
Lecture 8

Every one of Shakespeare's plays is a masterpiece. Every one of them, in fact, performs very well on the stage to this day, but the very greatest of his works are those of his maturity, as we call it. And it's with those that we're occupied in this lecture.

So wonderful are Shakespeare's middle- and late-period plays that some skeptics ask how a man who left school in his early teens could possibly have written them. Some have asserted that the plays must have been written by Francis Bacon, the earl of Oxford, or even Christopher Marlowe. Such nonsensical speculation thrives because we have so little evidence of Shakespeare's existence. Most authorities believe that the plays were written by Shakespeare, but we may still ask: How did he do it? How did Shakespeare happen?

We'll never have definitive answers for those questions, but we can see how Shakespeare's work evolves and develops. The genres that he produced in his maturity—comedies, histories, tragedies, problem plays, and romances—show a gradual progression in language and plot complexity. He was obviously interested in making his plays more challenging from a literary standpoint. Shakespeare gave up comedy fairly early, and his latest comedy is the darkest he wrote in that genre, *Measure for Measure*. He would return to a version of comedy in later problem plays and romances.

In 1610, at the height of his career and while he was still in his 50s, Shakespeare decided to retire from writing and to live out the remainder of his life as a prosperous member of the gentry in Stratford. He died in 1616 of disease, possibly syphilis or typhus.

Prospero's final speech in *The Tempest*, perhaps the last great play in the Shakespearean canon, is commonly supposed to be a version of the dramatist's own farewell to the London theater. Prospero tells us that all life is drama and all drama ends. All drama is fiction and we, too, are just figments. Like Faustus, Prospero—and his creator—seem to ask: What is the worth of knowledge or power when one is faced with death? Both Prospero and Shakespeare will withdraw to contemplate their final days. Prospero, a supreme ruler with magical powers, makes this decision from strength of mind, not terror, as Faustus did. He could have retained his power and, perhaps, achieved immortality. But having freed Ariel and made a man out of Ferdinand, his daughter's future husband, Prospero breaks his staff and vows to return to the world, giving up all comforts for a hair shirt, a monk's cell, and thoughts of death: Will he die well and at peace?

It is, perhaps, pleasing for us to think that this is Shakespeare himself speaking to us, explaining why he will write no more plays. It's also frustrating to the world of literature that Shakespeare retired while still at the top of his game.

The mature comedies and problem plays contain many powerful moments. In *Measure for Measure*, the young man Claudio has been condemned to death by Angelo, the ruler of Vienna at the time. The only thing that will save him is if his sister, Isabella, will sleep with Angelo. Claudio urges his sister to prostitute herself by describing the sheer horror of mortality in an overwhelmingly powerful speech. The fact that the play is a comedy is an assurance to the audience that all will end well, but Claudio's lines hang ominously in the mind even after the curtain has fallen.

Shakespeare's Roman plays pivot on relevant dilemmas for his own time. For instance, *Julius Caesar* asks if Brutus, the noblest Roman of them all, is right to commit the supremely ignoble act of political murder to save Rome. Can assassination, even for a good cause, ever be justified? Recall that in this play, Caesar is threatening to make himself a king, to overthrow the republic, and Brutus believes that Caesar must be stopped. But how can Brutus stop Caesar, the conqueror of the world, from achieving his ambition? The only answer is to kill Caesar, but is that right? Can one do the right thing for the wrong reason or the wrong thing for the right reason?

Coriolanus presents a similar dilemma. Is Coriolanus right to invade Rome in order to save it? Where does morality stand when great affairs of state are at stake? How dishonest must a great ruler be in the interest of preserving the well-being of his country?

This issue is also explored in the mature history play *Henry V*. Henry orders the massacre of 1,500 French prisoners because he can't achieve victory at Agincourt if he is burdened with keeping them. The French have surrendered themselves with the expectation that they will be safe, but they're killed so that Henry can win his great victory and conquer France. Was Henry right to have ordered these deaths, or should he have protected the prisoners and lost the battle? Is Henry V a war criminal or a realistic battlefield commander? Shakespeare is a master at highlighting such moral issues, as well as the problems of rulership and leadership.

> The towering achievement of Shakespeare's life can be found in four tragedies, *Macbeth, Lear, Hamlet,* and *Othello,* each so different in subject that they might have been written by different authors.

The grandest of Shakespeare's Roman plays is *Antony and Cleopatra*, in which Mark Antony throws away the empire for love of Cleopatra. As she prepares for her own suicide after the death of Antony, Cleopatra launches into a magnificent eulogy for her dead lover and husband. Cleopatra's words stake a claim that Antony's "bounty" (his goodness, grandeur of spirit, nobility of mind) vindicates what history would see as his gross irresponsibility. Shakespeare himself may have had second thoughts about this message. After Cleopatra's rhapsody of praise for Antony, she turns to her servant Dolabella and asks if such a person as she has just described could ever have existed. Dolabella replies that the queen is exaggerating. This subversive exchange sums up the fascinating complexity of Shakespeare's mature drama. The audience is left in two minds—not confused but thoughtful. Do we admire Antony or not? In losing an empire for love, was he a great man or an idiot? Such questions remind us that Shakespeare is dealing with the complexity of life itself, in which decisions, dilemmas, and defining acts are rarely neat and tidy. Shakespeare stimulates as much as he gratifies our sensibilities and our minds.

The towering achievement of Shakespeare's life can be found in four tragedies, *Macbeth, Lear, Hamlet,* and *Othello,* each so different in subject that they might have been written by different authors. These works were composed in the darkest period of Shakespeare's life and are permeated by a profound sense of gloom. Consider, for example, Macbeth's response when he is informed that his wife, a woman who once meant more to him than even the throne of Scotland, has killed herself. He says, "She should have died hereafter"; that is, she would have died later anyway. Macbeth stoically goes out to meet his own death on the battlefield against the fearsome Macduff, the man who is destined, as the witches have prophesied, to kill him. But before he does so, he delivers the most eloquently pessimistic description of the human condition to be found anywhere in the 39 plays: "[life] is a tale / Told by an idiot, full of sound and fury, / Signifying nothing."

In *Lear*, another great tragedy from this high point of Shakespeare's career, an aged king with no male heir decides to divide his kingdom among his three daughters, but chaos ensues. The king, once the highest man of the land, finds himself a mad beggar, roaming the heath and ranting; he sees the institutions that he has superintended for decades as hollow, cynical shams. Lear realizes too late that there is no justice in the world. The rich are subject to a different kind of law than the poor. Is he right, or is this merely the delusion of a deranged mind? Is society really corroded to the core by moral rot?

Hamlet delivers himself of the finest testimony we have to the humanist conception of man. He is "a piece of work," "infinite in faculties," and in his actions, "like an angel," yet he is also the "quintessence of dust." Again, we're of two minds: Is man within reach of the angels, or is he closer to dirt? And is this depressing view Hamlet's or Shakespeare's?

Othello is about a man destroyed by love (or at least that's what the protagonist would like to think). The Moor has an almost magical way of speaking, marked by what has been called "Othello music." His last great soliloquy takes place when he realizes the enormity of his crime against his innocent wife, Desdemona, and faces the men who have come to arrest him for her murder. With this soliloquy, right before his suicide, Othello sloughs off the dominance of Iago and regains mastery of himself. We cannot, however, fully accept his verdict for himself: "one that loved not wisely but too well." He is both a fool, as Iago's wife has told us earlier in the play, and somehow noble and heroic. We don't quite know what to think when we finish the play, but we are mysteriously elevated by the experience of reading it.

It's said that Shakespeare contains all life. That is true, and it is equally true that life is encased in Shakespeare in a literary greatness that has never been equaled and probably never will. ∎

Suggested Reading

Dobson and Wells, eds., *The Oxford Companion to Shakespeare.*

Evans and Tobin, eds., *The Riverside Complete Shakespeare.*

Kastan, *Companion to Shakespeare.*

Questions to Consider

1. What lines of development does one see in Shakespeare's drama, over the course of the two decades of his stage career?

2. What, insofar as it is extractable from the drama, do we take to be Shakespeare's "worldview"?

Shakespeare—The Mature Years
Lecture 8—Transcript

Every one of Shakespeare's plays is a masterpiece. Every one of them, in fact, performs very well on the stage to this day, but the very greatest of his works are those of his maturity, as we call it. And it's with those that we're occupied in this lecture.

So wonderful are Shakespeare's middle and late period plays that there have always been skeptics who ask how a mere grammar schoolboy, who left school in his early teens, turned player, probably, from Stratford could have written them. I mean how on earth could he have come up with this quality of work?

These plays must, it's surmised, have perhaps been written by Francis Bacon, who had a much better education, or by the Earl of Oxford, a noble author. Oxford, in fact, is currently the favorite anti-Shakespearean candidate, or even Christopher Marlowe. People have thought that Christopher Marlowe didn't die in 1593, as we saw two lectures ago, but, in fact, survived and, like Elvis, he actually lived on and was, in fact, the person whom we know as Shakespeare.

The reason that speculation of this kind, most of which is frankly nonsensical, thrived is that we've got so little evidence of Shakespeare's actual existence. We've got no handwriting of Shakespeare's, for instance, other than signatures on documents, in which he spells his name differently every time, and some very few lines from a play on which he may have been a collaborator, but not one of his plays, *Sir Thomas More*. We're not even sure that that was Shakespeare's hand.

Anyone may, having reviewed the evidence, make up their own minds. My own view, and that of most reliable authorities, not that I'm calling myself reliable, necessarily, is that Shakespeare is Shakespeare. But still, we may wonder. We may actually sort of be curious as the Baconians, Oxfordians and Marlovians are: how did he do it? How? How did Shakespeare happen?

We'll never have a good answer to that, but what we can see is how Shakespeare's work evolves and develops. As I said at the end of the last lecture, it's one of the extraordinary things. He never repeated himself. There's no, as it were, Shakespearean pattern that we can find. He's always exploring his own art.

The large genres—comedies, histories, tragedies, problem plays, romances—which he wrote in his maturity, show a gradual, but inexorable advance or progression in language and plot complexity. That's one of the things that he's obviously interested in perfecting, making his plays more complicated machines of a literary kind, the technique, if one wants to put a word to it. Shakespeare gave up comedy fairly early. Of course, as one grows older, life seems less amusing, but I think probably he was exploring, as I say, different genres.

And he ends comedy with the darkest in that genre, *Measure for Measure*. It's an interesting play, and particularly if one thinks of it as a kind of late comedy. It's set in a wartime, pox-ridden, morally decayed Vienna. It's a very, very black comedy. Later, Shakespeare would return with his problem plays and romances, which we can see as his most daring exercises in a kind of version of comedy, but we can connect that with the sort of changes that he's making to the genre in *Measure for Measure*.

But suddenly, if one looks at the whole career, at the height of his power, Shakespeare stops writing. He's relatively young. He's still in his fifties. He's no great age, even in 1610, when he apparently seems to have retired. Shakespeare resolved to retire and to live out the remainder of his life as a prosperous member of the gentry, a leading citizen, no doubt, in Stratford, his home town. That was his ambition in life and he fulfilled it. And these final, dignified years would, alas, be very few.

Disease, as was common enough in the early 17th century, swept him off early. What that disease was, we don't know. A recent book by Germaine Greer has suggested it might have been syphilis. Another book published within three weeks of Germaine Greer's book, Rene Weis's *Shakespeare Revealed*, thinks it was typhus. The fact is we don't know, but he died young, that we do know.

As I say, he took farewell from the London stage before he returned to Stratford, where he died prematurely. And Prospero's final speech in *The Tempest*, which is, I think, the last great play in the Shakespearean canon, is commonly supposed to be a version of the dramatist's own valediction or farewell to the London theater which, for 20 years, he'd graced and dominated.

This is Prospero's speech, which, as I say, is very often seen as Shakespeare's own farewell, and could even, if we want to be fanciful about it, have been uttered by Shakespeare himself. He did take the boards, on occasion. He did act, we do know that.

This is what Prospero says. It is, as I say, a magnificent speech, but it is imbued with a spirit of leave-taking:

> Our revels are now ended. These our actors,
> As I foretold you, were all spirits and
> Are melted into air, into thin air;
> And, like the baseless fabric of this vision,
> The cloud-capp'd towers, the gorgeous palaces,
> The solemn temples, the great globe itself
> Yea all which it inherit, shall dissolve
> And, like this insubstantial pageant faded
> Leave not a rack behind. We are such stuff
> As dreams are made on, and our little life
> Is rounded with sleep.

It's a very meaningful speech. Obviously, what he's saying is all life is drama and all drama ends. All drama is fiction and we too are just figments. We're just, as it were, sort of fleeting things that pass through and are forgotten.

Remember, if you would, Faustus's last pathetic utterance, "I'll burn my books." What Faustus asks at that moment, that terminal moment of his life, "What is knowledge, magic, power when you're faced with death?" And Prospero, and behind Prospero, his creator, seems to be debating the same point, and making a similar decision. That is to say, he'll withdraw and, unlike Faustus, of course, who's doomed to go immediately to hell, he will, in fact, as it were, go into retirement, where as he later says, his every third thought shall be of death.

This decision of Prospero's is made, as I say, unlike Faustus's, from strength of mind, not terror. Prospero, if you remember, is the supreme ruler of his island. He has magical powers. He's a king with even more kingly powers than Tamburlaine could have wanted. He could have retained that power and stayed on his island and ruled there till the end of his days, and perhaps beyond. Since he's a magician, he could have perhaps been immortal, lord of all he surveyed, all he owned. The island is a domain which is as much Prospero's as, by 1616, the London theater was Shakespeare's. He was the king of the London stage. Prospero is a sovereign ruler. His soul is not at risk.

But having freed Ariel, his kind of minister, and made a man out of Ferdinand, his daughter's future husband, you'll remember he makes him pile wood until he actually becomes a real man, Prospero breaks his staff, his magic wand. He will return to the world, he says, and give up all comfort for a hair shirt and a monk's cell, and he'll turn his mind to the most important thing: death. How will he die well? How will he die at peace? How will he die, having completed his life? It's a wonderful moment and it is very pleasing to think this is Shakespeare himself talking to us and saying, "There'll be no more plays, and this is the reason why."

It's always pleasing, if frustrating to admirers, when artists, like athletes, retire while still at the top of their game. Prospero's valediction is magnificent and it's highly theatrical. And the fact is that one would never have had enough of Shakespeare. One would like another 39 plays. But in fact, he will not give them to us. He'd done enough in that sphere and then he went back to his home town and lived the rest of his life.

To return to the plays that we do have, the mature comedies and problem plays contain wonderful things. To return to *Measure for Measure*, Claudio, lying in prison, is condemned to death. What's happened is that—it's a very powerful moment—his sister, Isabella, has been persuaded to prostitute herself by sleeping with the misnamed ruler of Vienna at the time, Angelo. He's not at all angelic. And what he's done is to put Claudio, Isabella's brother, in prison, and what he says is, "If you sleep with me, you'll save his life. If you don't sleep with me, it's off with his head."

Claudio says, "Well, sleep with him. Please sleep with him. Save my life." And remember, this is a comedy. He urges his case to his sister by describing the sheer horror of mortality, death.

And this, recall, is a comedy. What does that mean? It means there's an unstated contract between playwright and audience that all will end well, that in fact, Claudio will not go to the gallows. But as the laughter and the terminal smiles fade, as we walk out of the theater, having watched *Measure for Measure*, those lines of Claudio's hang ominously in the mind. The skull is there somewhere in the background, smiling mirthlessly at us. The deaths-head, as Falstaff calls it, is always there, even in the most comic of Shakespeare's middle period plays.

Moving now to Shakespeare's Roman plays. These pivot on hugely relevant dilemmas for Shakespeare's own time. Is Brutus, for instance, the noblest Roman of them all, right to commit the supremely ignoble act of political murder to save Rome? Can assassination, even in a good cause, ever be justified? The situation, you'll remember, is that Julius Caesar is threatening to make himself a king, to overthrow the republic, and Brutus, who is a republican to the marrow of his bones, feels that this must be stopped. But how can he stop Julius Caesar, the conqueror of the world from achieving this, this ambition to become king of Rome? The only way he can do it is by killing him, but is that right? Can you do the right thing for the wrong reason, or the wrong thing for the right reason? These are questions which Brutus debates with himself.

Is Coriolanus, in a similar dilemma, right to invade Rome, which is the equivalent, in terms of the Roman plays, of maternal rape, to save Rome? Can you do this if, in fact, you're doing it for a right reason, but it's a very wrong thing you're doing? Where does morality stand when great affairs of state are at stake? How dishonest must a great ruler be in the interest of preserving the wellbeing of his country?

This is an issue explored in the mature history play, *Henry V*. Consider, for instance, Henry V, who massacres all his French prisoners. He's got 1,500 prisoners and he has them bludgeoned and killed. Why? Because, in fact, he can't go on and win Agincourt if he's got to look after all these French prisoners. It's a very bloody act. It's horrible. These are people that have given themselves up in the expectation that they'll be safe, and their throats are cut so, in fact, Henry V can win this great victory at Agincourt and conquer France. Was he right to do that? Should he, in fact, have done the honorable thing and protected the prisoners, as they expected to be protected, and lost the battle?

It's a terrible thing to be a ruler in Shakespeare's plays, and it's very embarrassing for audiences. The two great film versions of *Henry V*, that of Laurence Olivier and the Oscar-winning 1991 Kenneth Branagh version of *Henry V*, both gloss over or drop that very nasty event, but Shakespeare, to his credit, does record, that is to say, Henry V killing his French prisoners. But I mean is Henry V a war criminal, or is he simply a realistic battlefield commander? It's a very, very nice and very difficult question. Shakespeare is very, very good, it seems to me, at highlighting these issues, and highlighting the problems of what we would think of rulership and leadership.

To go back to the Roman plays, in the grandest of them, *Antony and Cleopatra*, Mark Antony, who's a very different character in *Antony and Cleopatra* from what he was in *Julius Caesar*, throws away the empire for love of the fascinating Cleopatra. *All for Love, or the World Well Lost*, as Dryden titled his anemic 18th-century rewriting of *Antony and Cleopatra*. But is the world really "well lost" or merely thrown away?

As she prepares for her own suicide, or easeful death—she's determined she's not going to suffer too much—Cleopatra launches into a magnificent eulogy for her dead lover and husband. It's one of the finest speeches in Shakespeare, it's always seemed to me. Antony is dead and she offers an obituary, in a sense, but an obituary which is in the highest vein of poetry.

> His legges bestrid the Ocean,
> his rear'd arme Crested the world:
> His voyce was propertied

As all the tuned Spheres, and that to Friends:
But when he meant to quaile, and shake the Orbe,
He was as ratling Thunder.
For his Bounty, There was no winter in't.
An Anthony it was, That grew the more by reaping:
His delights Were Dolphin-like,
they shew'd his backe aboue
The Element they liu'd in:
In his Liuery Walk'd Crownes and Crownets:
Realms & Islands were
As plates dropt from his pocket.

It's a fine speech and it stakes a claim that Antony's "bounty," which is a very difficult word to define, goodness, grandeur of spirit, nobility of mind, vindicates what history, and historians like Plutarch, who was Shakespeare's main source, would see as an outrageous and wholly romantic defense of gross irresponsibility. That's to say, Shakespeare's Antony is not one which would find favor with historians. Supreme commanders, historians think, political theorists think, like Antony, have responsibilities that go beyond the gratification of their sexual desires or romantic proclivities. The world is not "well lost" for love, any love.

And in fact, Shakespeare himself may have had second thoughts, because when she turns to her servant Dolabella after her rhapsody of praise on Antony, Cleopatra asks if such a person as she's just described could ever have been. And Dolabella, who's got nothing to lose since the queen is going to die very soon, replies honestly, "No, you know, you're exaggerating." And that subversive little exchange sums up for me the fascinating complexity of Shakespeare's mature drama.

The audience, as is usual with Shakespeare, is left in two minds, not confused, that's very different, but thoughtful. Do we admire Antony or do we not? Was Henry V right to kill those French prisoners or was he criminal? Was Brutus really that noble? Now, it is, of course, the complexity of life itself whose decisions, dilemmas and defining acts are rarely, if ever, neat and tidy that Shakespeare is dealing with. Was Antony, the man who lost an empire for love of a woman, a great man or an idiot? Well, he was both, or he was either or neither. As I say, we're left actually thinking these things through. Shakespeare stimulates, as much as he gratifies our sensibilities and our minds.

I want in the last part of this lecture to look at the towering achievement of the great tragedies. They were composed, we do know, in the darkest period of Shakespeare's life. He'd lost his son, Hamlet. They make up a majestic quartet, all so different from each other in subject that they might have been written by different authors, but equally great: *Macbeth*, *Lear*, *Hamlet*, and *Othello*.

There is, as critics and lovers of Shakespeare have observed, a profound gloom permeating these works, a worldview that seems, in many ways, embittered or profoundly saddened. Now, any number of examples of this prevailing mood may be cited, but when, for example, Macbeth is informed that his wife, the woman who once meant more to him than even the throne of Scotland, which he killed Duncan for, has killed herself—we never call her Queen Macbeth, by the way, always Lady Macbeth—what does he reply? "She should have died hereafter." That is, she would have died later anyway. No matter. He does not even bother to go and look at her body or take his last farewell.

He stoically goes out to meet his own death on the battlefield against the fearsome Macduff, the man who is destined, as the witches have prophesied, to kill him. But before going to certain death, Macbeth delivers the most eloquently pessimistic description of the human condition to be found anywhere in the 39 plays.

Let me read it:

> To-morrow, and to-morrow, and to-morrow,
> Creeps in this petty pace from day to day,
> To the last syllable of recorded time;
> And all our yesterdays have lighted fools
> The way to dusty death. Out, out, brief candle!
> Life's but a walking shadow; a poor player,
> That struts and frets his hour upon the stage,

> And then is heard no more: it is a tale
> Told by an idiot, full of sound and fury,
> Signifying nothing.

One talked about the mighty line in Marlowe, but no lines are mightier than that, and that particular line, "Out, out, brief candle!"—remember that in Shakespeare's theater, the illumination would have been candles, so he points to one. Again, there's this notion that even drama is insignificant, that life's but a drama, which, when it ends, it's just been fiction.

In *Lear*, another great tragedy in this huge, as it were, high point of Shakespeare's career, an aged king with no male heir decides, rationally enough, one might think, to divide his kingdom between his three daughters. Now, it's superficially a wisdom of Solomon thing, but chaos ensues. The king, once the highest man of the land, finds himself, like Oedipus Rex at the end of Sophocles's play, a mad beggar, roaming the heath and ranting. And in this condition, he sees the institutions which he's superintended for decades as hollow, cynical shams. There's no justice in the world.

He suddenly realizes it's too late and he has this wonderful diatribe against the law:

> Through tattered clothes small vices do appear;
> Robes and furred gowns hide all. Plate sin with gold,
> And the strong lance of justice hurtless breaks;
> Arm it in rags, a pygmy's straw does pierce it.

What he's saying is if you're rich, if you're a celebrity in our terms, you have, in fact, a different kind of law than you get if you're poor. Is Lear right, or is this merely the delusion of a deranged mind? He's a very sick man. He's mad. Is society really corroded to the core, as he says, by corruption and moral rot? As I say, I mean who, looking at celebrity trials in our own time, cannot have at least a suspicion that if you "plate sin with gold" with lots and lots of dollars, and the criminal can afford a dream team, the "strong lance of justice hurtless breaks"?

But does that mean there is no justice anywhere? Well, as I say, these are tragedies, and they're very, very pessimistic. But Shakespeare again leaves us in two minds. Hamlet, as is often observed, delivers himself of the finest testimony that we have to the humanist conception of man. You know, the kind of thing which we feel Marlowe would have actually sort of stood up and shouted, "Yes, yes."

This is what Hamlet says about humanity:

> What a piece of work is man! How noble in reason!
> how infinite in faculties! in form and moving, how
> express and admirable! in action how like an angel!
> in apprehension, how like a god! the beauty of the
> world! the paragon of animals!

But then, turning on himself, Hamlet concludes:

> And yet, to me,
> what is this quintessence of dust? Man delights not
> me.

So we have these two sort of visions of mankind, as, in fact, the paragon and as the "quintessence of dust." This subversive undercutting complicates our response. As I say, is man within touching distance of the angels, or is he, in fact, just a thing of dirt? But is the depressive view Shakespeare's or is it the melancholic Prince of Denmark's? Again, we're left in two minds.

And so too, with *Othello*, which has a very different theme. It's about a man who is destroyed by love, or at least, that's what he'd like to think. And if you look at Othello's last great soliloquy, it is wonderful. Of all the tragic heroes, the Moor, that is Othello—you can read that both ways, either that he's Arabic or that he's black—he has the most magical utterance, and his speeches are marked with what has been very aptly called the "Othello music."

When he speaks, it's almost as if time stops, but having horribly been played on and been perverted by the diabolic Iago, and killed his wife, Desdemona, wrongly, she's innocent, but he thinks that she's cuckolded him, Othello realizes finally and futilely the enormity of what he's done and he confronts the men who've come to arrest him for his crime, his murder of his wife, his uxoricide.

And this is his speech, and it is, as I say, very typical of Othello. The Othello music, I think, is never at its higher pitch than it is here:

> Soft you; a word or two before you go.
> I have done the state some service, and they know't.
> No more of that. I pray you, in your letters,
> When you shall these unlucky deeds relate,
> Speak of me as I am; nothing extenuate,
> Nor set down aught in malice: then must you speak
> Of one that loved not wisely but too well;
> Of one not easily jealous, but being wrought
> Perplex'd in the extreme; of one whose hand,
> Like the base Indian, threw a pearl away
> Richer than all his tribe; of one whose subdued eyes,
> Albeit unused to the melting mood,
> Drop tears as fast as the Arabian trees
> Their medicinal gum. Set you down this.

And then he kills himself. It's a magnificent speech. He stabs himself. He recovers at this moment his mastery. He's been dominated by Iago, he's been corrupted by Iago, and now, in fact, he's again sort of, as it were, in control. But sneakingly, we can't accept his version of what he's done. "One that is, who loved not wisely but too well." Now, has he? He is, as the down-to-earth Emilia earlier told him—Emilia is Iago's wife—a fool. He should never have been deceived by Iago, and not even a fool, he's a wife-killer. He's a brute, nothing more, nothing less. He's ignorant as dirt, she says. But at the same time, he's the heroic noble Othello, and one leaves the theater with dark clouds swirling in the mind. That's to say, we don't know what to think, but in fact, we are mysteriously elevated by the experience.

The great tragedies represent a phase in a career which has many phases. There are many Shakespeares. And the manifest depression may, it's often been surmised, have arisen from some personal disaster. I mentioned: the death of his son Hamlet. It may have been a love affair which went wrong. We'll never know. Perhaps even the glum post-Elizabethan national mood: Elizabeth was dead by this point, by the way, and James I had acceded to the throne, and with him had come a kind of national depression as well.

But when, like Prospero, Shakespeare bowed out, he seems to have been in a happier frame of mind, we'd like to say. *The Tempest*, which is, as I say, probably his last great play, is stoical, but not overly depressed. But nonetheless the wild gaiety of youth is long gone, the kind of gaiety which one associates with plays like *Midsummer Night's Dream*.

All life is there, it's said of Shakespeare, and not only is life there— multifaceted—it is encased in a literary greatness which has never been equaled, and probably never will, but we have Shakespeare. He's left us enough, I think, to actually sort of validate that judgment with which I began these two lectures on Shakespeare: that he is the greatest writer we have. And there's no dispute about that, nor is it hard for anyone who reads or sees Shakespeare to see the nature of that greatness.

Shakespeare's Rivals—Jonson and Webster
Lecture 9

One can't think of a harder act to follow in literature than William Shakespeare, and it must, one imagines, have been fiendishly difficult to write in his shadow. ... But, as usually happens, great writers happen in company. ... There's a sort of collectivity about it. ... And so it was with, and immediately after, Shakespeare's career.

In this lecture, we turn to two late contemporaries and, arguably, rivals to Shakespeare, Ben Jonson (1572–1637) and John Webster (c. 1580–c. 1634). Both of these writers were born a few years after Shakespeare, and both were major dramatists, although Jonson wrote primarily comedies and Webster, tragedies.

Both Jonson and Webster are also imbued with the darker tinge associated with Jacobean England. James I succeeded Queen Elizabeth when she died in 1603 and would reign for more than 20 years. He was a literary man himself, but some of his policies were heavy-handed, and his reign lacked the liveliness and national enthusiasm associated with Elizabeth. How do we account for this mood of Jacobean gloom? Partly, the new era was a letdown from the effervescence of the Elizabethan age. Further, the succession had been somewhat difficult. At the same time, James was politically much more contentious than Elizabeth and unable to unify the country. The Gunpowder Plot, the attempt of Guy Fawkes to blow up Parliament, took place in the early years of James's reign. England experienced social discontent at this time as new class energies were released. D. H. Lawrence attributed the gloom of the Jacobean era to the prevalence of syphilis and the fact that biblical scholars of the time had calculated the approaching end of the world. Whatever the reasons for this more somber national mood, English drama was blacker as well.

Ben Jonson was one of Shakespeare's greatest admirers, and much of what we know of Shakespeare comes from Jonson's comradely reminiscences. Jonson related for us Shakespeare's method of writing: He worked in conjunction with his actors and, it was said, "never blotted out a line."

Jonson was a university-educated man and probably believed that he was more intellectual than Shakespeare, while Shakespeare was a more natural kind of genius. Jonson was very learned, but he wore his learning lightly. His plays are not characterized by scholasticism as much as wit. Nonetheless, Jonson's comedies typically accommodate to the neo-Aristotelian unities. According to this doctrine, the events of a play must be contained in a single day (unity of time); the events must take place in one location (unity of place); and the play must not contain subplots or digressions (unity of action). Only one of Shakespeare's plays, *The Tempest*, is unified in this neo-Aristotelian sense.

Jonson knew and learned from ancient dramatists, and his so-called comedy of humors was directly derived from Classical sources. The humors were the four constituents of the human personality: phlegm, yellow bile, black bile, and blood. For Jonson, psychology was one dominant personality trait. Thus, if, as Jonson said, Shakespeare had little Latin and no Greek, he was more of the common people; Jonson, who knew those languages fluently, was an intellectual.

Even though he was a Neoclassicist, in such plays as *Bartholomew Fair*, Jonson depicted contemporary London with a documentary vividness that is not found in other dramatists. One can almost smell the wood-burning fires and sewage of early 17th-century London. Jonson brings us into a world we know from nursery rhymes, with *London Bridge* and church bells ringing throughout the city.

The early 17th century, as Karl Marx observed, was the birth of the capitalist era, and Jonson's major theme was money. Jonson did not approve of the new mercantile focus of society, and the foundation of his play *The Alchemist* is a satire on the rush for wealth. He believed that the contemporary stampede for money was akin to the promise of the alchemist's stone to transform base metals into precious metals.

The Alchemist was first performed in 1610. The play is set in fashionable residential London during one of the city's recurrent outbreaks of plague. Such epidemics occurred regularly in the summer months, spread by rat fleas, though at the time it was thought that the plague was carried in the air.

Daniel Defoe, writing a century later, tells us that perhaps 200,000 people fled the city during the summer months, mainly the wealthy, leaving their servants behind to look after their affairs and take their chances with illness. The setting of the play ties in with a kind of diseased moral climate as well. It's not just that the epidemic is a physical illness, but it's something that goes deep into the fabric of the age.

In Jonson's play, a wealthy man, Lovewit, has left his townhouse in the care of his *maestro domo*, the master of the household. This man, named Face, exhibits different faces depending on what the situation requires.

Face conspires with a conman, called Subtle, who pretends to be an alchemist. (Alchemy was sometimes called a process of subtilizing, or refining.) The third member of this conspiracy is a prostitute named Dol Common.

Ben Jonson.

This trio sets out to run a scam on the fools left in the city. They will let it be known that Subtle has found the philosopher's stone and has mastered the process of transmuting base metals into gold. The grand mystery of alchemy will, in fact, be available to anyone who pays for it. Puritans, shopkeepers, respectable citizens, and aristocrats all line up to get rich, while the tricksters compete to be the best "shark." Face, Subtle, and Dol encourage their victims' wild fantasies of wealth. One example, Sir Epicure Mammon, serves to illustrate the theme. The name Epicure indicates this character's addiction to pleasures of the flesh, and "mammon" means money. Sir Mammon wants to be rich, and he wants to indulge his appetites on a gigantic scale. Mammon imagines the wonderful universe of self-indulgence he will inhabit once he gets the fool's gold. His speech here is reminiscent of a speech by Marlowe's Faustus, when he has Mephistopheles call up Helen of Troy for his bed partner. Jonson outdoes even Marlowe in the lavishness and cloying richness of his blank verse. But most of all, this speech conveys a biting satire on human greed. Money is the root, not just of all evil, but of all human foolishness.

The Alchemist ends with a wonderfully ironic stroke of theater: Out of the blue, Lovewit, the master of the house, returns and witnesses the criminal activities that have been going on in his household. Does he punish the wicked trio and return the victims' cash? No, he laughs good-naturedly, congratulates Face, and pockets the profits. Human nature, Jonson tells us, is the same from top to bottom. Cash is God.

In contrast to Jonson, John Webster was a tragedian. His corpus of work is fairly small, with only four plays that have lasted, but all of them are powerful tragedies, carrying on the mood we find in the darkest of Shakespeare's works. Webster, as T. S. Eliot said, was much obsessed with the "skull beneath the skin." Before we look at Webster's greatest tragedy, *The Duchess of Malfi*, we should note that the Jacobeans loved reversals of conventional romantic plots. John Ford's *'Tis Pity She's a Whore* takes the *Romeo and Juliet* scenario, but the star-crossed lovers in this play are brother and sister.

The Duchess of Malfi is similarly perverse. A rich widow in Italy, the Duchess, falls in love with a respectable but lower-born man. The two marry secretly and have children. The duchess's brother finds out about the marriage, however, and brutally kills the husband. Ostensibly, the brother is protecting the name of Malfi, but his real motive is that he is incestuously in love with his sister. He wants her as his lover and he is going mad under the pressure of his lust. His is a gothic form of madness: *lycanthropia*. The brother believes that he is a wolf, and in this wolfish aspect, he tortures and kills the Duchess horribly on stage.

As this gothic tragedy unfolds, a spectator, Bosola, the brother's principal henchman, passively observes the action. He is not a bad person but will do bad things when commanded. One actor who played Bosola observed that the play reminded him of the world of the Mafia: Normal morality is suspended, and the darkest, most savage, wolfish aspects of human character are loosed. One of Bosola's speeches conveys the bleak amorality of Webster's worldview and gives some sense of the brilliance of Webster's turn of phrase. Bosola essentially tells the duchess not to resist the torments of her brother, that is, to accept her own death: "'Tis now full tide 'tween night and day; / End your groan, and come away." Using only the basic constituents of English, these lines are effective and beautifully melodic. Unfortunately, in Webster's tragedy, such lines rarely combine to create any larger dramatic effect of the kind we might expect from Shakespeare.

With Webster and his fellow Jacobean dramatists, a great moment in English literature came to an end. Increasing pressure from the Puritans eventually brought about licensing and, later, even closure of the theaters. Apart from a brief florescence during the Restoration, there would be no supremely great drama again until the 20th century. The curtain had come down on the British stage, and it would not rise again for 200 years. ∎

Suggested Reading

Jonson, *Five Plays*.

Knights, *Drama and Society in the Age of Jonson*.

Webster, *The Duchess of Malfi and Other Plays*.

Questions to Consider

1. Do the post-Shakespearian dramatists take drama forward or lose their way?

2. What are the characteristics of Jacobean gloom, and how can one account for it?

Shakespeare's Rivals—Jonson and Webster
Lecture 9—Transcript

One can't think of a harder act to follow in literature than William Shakespeare, and it must, one imagines, have been fiendishly difficult to write in his shadow, to come after him. Christopher Marlowe, who we looked at a couple of lectures ago, was lucky in that he had an open field. He came a few years before Shakespeare, and Shakespeare wasn't there. There was no competition.

But, as usually happens, great writers happen in company. You know, more of them happen at once than chance would predict. There's a sort of collectivity about it. You know, think, for example, as we shall be thinking a bit later on, about Dickens and the Victorian novel. There's an updraft of genius. And so it was with, and immediately after, Shakespeare's career.

And I want, in this lecture, to look at two late contemporaries and, arguably, rivals to Shakespeare. They weren't greater than Shakespeare, but they were up there with him. They were Ben Jonson and John Webster. They were born in 1570s, a few years after Shakespeare, and their great plays came four or five years after his great plays. So, in fact, they knew what they were up against.

One of these writers, Ben Jonson, is a comedian principally, a writer of comic plays. The other is very much a tragedian, a writer of tragedies. Both are incontrovertibly major dramatists. They matter in our map of English literature. Both are, however, imbued with that darker tinge which one associates with Jacobean England. Jacobean means the reign of James I of England, the man who succeeded Queen Elizabeth when she died in 1603. He was also a literary man. In fact, so was Queen Elizabeth. In fact, being able to write well, being able to write poetry, to write good prose was as much a valued social skill among the higher classes in England as dancing. And Queen Elizabeth wrote very creditable poetry. And James wrote some very wonderful pamphlets, including one against tobacco, which, in fact, is still sort invoked nowadays. It was a kind of very early surgeon general's report on the dangers of nicotine.

James I was called the wisest fool in Christendom. Some of his policies were rather heavy-handed. But nonetheless, his reign, and he reigned for some 20-odd years, is permeated with a darkness. There's none of that kind of effervescence, none of that kind of liveliness, that kind of sense of enthusiasm, collective national enthusiasm which one associates with Queen Elizabeth.

If one admits, and it seems to very much borne out of the literature, there is this kind of mood of Jacobean gloom, how do we account for it? Well, partly it was just a kind of hangover. The Elizabethan age had been so wonderful that there was inevitably a comedown. There was a kind of "the party's over" feeling. Particularly there was this difficult succession. James wasn't automatically the monarch you would have chosen. He was the King of Scotland, for instance, and because Queen Elizabeth had had no children, there was a certain kind of awkwardness.

But there are other factors. He was politically much more contentious than Elizabeth. He couldn't unify the country quite as well. Very famously, there was the 1605 Gunpowder Plot, when Guy Fawkes tried to blow up Parliament, and you know, that is, in fact, celebrated every November 5th in England. But there was much more, as it were, social discontent. That may well be that the country had been so successful, that new class energies had been released. People, in fact, were straining against the old system throughout James's reign.

But there were perhaps other factors. D. H. Lawrence, a writer we'll be looking at later, thought it was the prevalence of syphilis, a disease of horrifying and incurable malignancy in this period. There are lots of references in Jacobean drama to the pox, by which they mean not smallpox, but venereal disease. Others note that Biblical scholars had computed that the world would soon come to an end. That's to say, the 6,000 years in which the world was to run were nearly up—that clock was winding down. The whole universe had had, as Falstaff says to Shallow in *Henry I, Part 2*, seen the best of its time. To quote Macbeth, "the sere and yellow leaf was upon them."

These are speculations, but the fact is the mood was more somber, and with it, English drama, which is a wonderful mirror held up to the national mood, was blacker as well. It's darker hued, and sometimes, in fact, downright pessimistic.

Ben Jonson was one of Shakespeare's greatest admirers, and much of what we know of Shakespeare, which is very little, comes from Jonson's comradely reminiscences. They were fellow dramatists, and Jonson, incidentally, is the first professional writer in England, the first person to publish his works and make money out of a publication. And Jonson did feel that he and Shakespeare were fellow laborers. And it was Jonson who declared with what looks to me like a mixture of artistic generosity and jealousy that wonderful verdict on Shakespeare's artistic method. That is to say, he gives us—and one thanks him forever for that—a picture of Shakespeare at work.

This is what Jonson said of Shakespeare's method of writing. Remember that Shakespeare worked in conjunction with his actors:

> The players have often mentioned it as an honor to Shakespeare, that in his writing, whatsoever he penned, he never blotted out a line.

Remember also at this time, you'd use a quill. You'd have to dip it in ink and afterwards you would blot it, usually with sand, incidentally. But you know, it's our delete function on a computer. And what he's saying is that he was so fluent and so gifted, he never went back. But Jonson doesn't quite approve.

> My answer hath been, "Would he had blotted a thousand," which they thought malevolent …

The actors said "What are you doing, running down Shakespeare? He's our god."

> I had not told posterity this but for their ignorance, who chose that circumstance to commend their friend by wherein he most faulted;

He is saying that the actors were wrong: that a dramatist who's good for actors is not necessarily good for the printed page.

> and to justify mine own candor, for I loved the man, and do honor his memory on this side idolatry as much as any. He was, indeed, honest, and of an open and free nature; had an excellent fancy, brave notions, and gentle expressions, wherein he flowed with that facility that sometime it was necessary he should be stopped.

It's a sort of, as I say, a very generous verdict, an obituary. Jonson outlived Shakespeare by about 10 years. But what comes through, I think, and it's only too clear, is that Jonson was a university-educated man. That's to say, he felt that he was, if you like, rather more intellectual than Shakespeare, and Shakespeare was much more a kind of natural genius. Jonson was very learned. He knew the Classics very well, as Shakespeare didn't, as he thought, but Jonson wore his learning lightly. And in his plays, the hallmark quality is not scholasticism, but wit, that three-letter word which is going to be so important for the next 100 years in English literature.

Nonetheless, Jonson's comedies typically accommodate to the neo-Aristotelian unities. This is a doctrine which will become almost a tyranny for dramatists over the next 100 years. What were these unities? Well, one was unity of time: The events must be contained in a single day. The other was the unity of place: The events must take place in one location. And thirdly, the unity of action: You must not have subplots and digressions. You must have, to some extent, a concentration on a single plotline.

Only one of Shakespeare's plays is unified in this neo-Aristotelian sense, and that's his last great play, in fact, *The Tempest*. It's been speculated, and I like the speculation a lot, that he may have written it to show Jonson he could do it. "You don't think I can write an Aristotelian play? Look at this, then." Now, Jonson knew and learned from ancient dramatists. In fact, he felt himself in a kind of line going back to Greece and Rome, Aristophanes, Terence, Plautus. And his so-called comedy of humors—I'll just explain that in a second—was directly derived from classical sources.

The humors were the four constituents of the human personality: phlegm, [black] bile, [yellow bile, and] blood, and they linked in again with the four sort of elements as well. And what this meant was that for Jonson, psychology was one dominant personality trait. So if, as Jonson said, Shakespeare had little Latin and no Greek, Jonson had those languages virtually coming out of his ears. But as I say, he wears his learning very lightly. So, in fact, it doesn't, as it were, offend us when we watch a Jonson play in the theater.

Even though he was a Neoclassicist, unlike Shakespeare, in plays like *Bartholomew Fair*, Jonson depicted contemporary London with a documentary vividness which is not found in the other dramatists. Shakespeare, as I said earlier, liked to set his comedies oddly enough in Italy or in notional countries, imaginary countries, like Illyria. But when we enter the world of Jonson's plays, we can almost smell early 17th-century London, Jacobean London. You can smell the wood-burning fires, the cattle and horse droppings in the streets, wooden sidewalks, the stench of Fleet Ditch, which was the *cloaca maxima*, the main sewer, carrying down the city's waste to the hugely polluted Thames. In fact, London was probably only bearable in winter when it froze over; as it often did at this time.

England at this period is going through what's called the Little Ice Age. You'll remember when we were talking about Chaucer, medieval England was going through its warm period then. It's now very cold. As Shakespeare said, "For the rain it raineth every day." Weather is very important in English literature and the weather has rarely been worse historically than it was in the Jacobean period. Who knows? That may have actually accounted for part of their gloom.

The great river, which joined the north and south banks, was spanned— and it's a tidal river, remember, it's the main port in England—by the Old London Bridge, which had wooden houses and boat moorings on it. "London Bridge is falling down, falling down, falling down, London Bridge is falling down, my fair lady": children still sing that to this day. That, in fact, was a major monument in the city, and so too were the church towers, which told the time with their bells. People didn't have wrist watches and they were very important. And these church towers, these structures were strategically placed across the city.

Since we're in nursery rhymes, another one which is sung to this day by English children: "Oranges and lemons, went the bells of St. Clement's." Now, that's St. Clement Danes, which is on the Strand, which is just by London Bridge. Jonson, unlike Shakespeare, takes us into this world, takes us into the world of London Bridge, of the teeming streets of the capital in the early 17th century.

I want to concentrate for the next few minutes on one of those London plays, *The Alchemist*, but first, a word about Jonson's major theme. It is, in a word, money. The early 17th century, and we'll see this again and again, was, as Karl Marx observed, the birth of the capitalist era. It was mercantile. Everyone, in London at least, was on the make. It was an age of free enterprise. Alan Greenspan would have loved it.

Jonson did not approve, however. Where economics was concerned, he was a conservative, and the foundation of his play *The Alchemist* is satire on this contemporary rush for wealth, this kind of exuberance. It was a bubble, like the stampede for fool's gold, which is promised by the Alchemist's Stone, you remember, which is the very primitive kind of chemistry by which base metals, like lead and copper, are turned into precious metals, like gold and silver, by touching them with this miraculous stone.

The Alchemist was first performed in 1610, and it's set in fashionable residential London, a bit to the west of the London Bridge area I was talking about. It is a London undergoing one its recurrent outbreaks of plague. These happened regularly in the summer months. Often the epidemics of plague would close the theaters and the companies would go on tour. That may be, in fact, one of the reasons that Shakespeare became a dramatist. In fact, a touring company came through Stratford when he was a young man.

The last words of that children's nursery rhyme is "Atishoo, atishoo, we all fall down." Now, what does that mean? It's plague. That's to say, you sneezed and that was the first symptom of getting plague and then you fell down and you didn't get up again. It was the most virulent epidemic since the Black Death, and it was spread, we know, by rat fleas, though no one at the time knew that. They thought it was miasmic. They thought it was in the air. They didn't know how, in fact, these infections were communicated.

A century later, Daniel Defoe, a writer we'll be looking at later, did a work of great research on the plague and plague years, and he wrote a journal of the plague year. And he describes what happened to London during these regular summer outbreaks.

This is Daniel Defoe writing in his journal about the plague year:

> It was thought that there were not less than 10,000 houses forsaken of the inhabitants in the city and suburbs, including what was in the out-parishes and in Surrey, or the side of the water they called Southwark.

[Southwark] is where the Globe Theatre was, on the south bank.

> This was besides the numbers of lodgers, and of particular persons who were fled out of other families; so that in all it was computed that about 200,000 people were fled and gone.

This was kind of a huge number of people from a city, which was probably no more than 500,000 population in the first place. A very large city by their standards, but not a megalopolis by our standards. During the summer plagues, as Defoe says, rich men would leave their town houses and take refuge from the epidemic in the country, leaving servants behind to look after things and, if they were unfortunate, fall ill and die. "Atishoo, atishoo."

This practice of summer evacuation remains to this day in the London season, when fashionable people still leave town in summer and there's a long summer recess in Parliament. This can all be traced back to the plague years of the early 17th century. And this is the setting of Jonson's play, *The Alchemist*. Now, it also ties in, I think, to a kind of diseased moral climate as well. The time is morally sick. It's not just, as it were, an epidemic which is an illness—it's also, in fact, something which goes deep into the fiber, into the fabric of the age.

Lovewit, who's the *deus ex machina* figure, the person who's offstage, but nonetheless quite important, has left his magnificent townhouse in the care of his *maestro domo*, the master of his household, Face. He's called Face. Now,

Face, as his name implies, is a cunning fellow. He's all things to all men. He wears a mask and you never know what you're getting from him. He has many faces, depending on what the situation requires. And Face conspires with a conman, who pretends to be an alchemist called Subtle. Alchemy was sometimes called the process of subtilizing or refining, making subtle base object, base things, base materials. And there's a third member of this conspiracy, this little gang, as we'd call them, a prostitute, Dol Common. That means she's anyone's doll.

And this trio set out to run an elaborate scam on the fools left in the city. They will let it be known that Subtle has at last found the philosopher's stone. He's mastered the process, the forlorn dream of alchemists, of transmuting base metals, lead, iron, and tin, into gold. And the grand mystery of alchemy will, in fact, be available to anyone who pays for it. And they put out the word that they want investors. "Does anyone want to get rich? Come to us. Just bring your old junk to us and we'll turn it into gold."

And the suckers all line up, Puritans, small shopkeepers, respectable citizens, and aristocrats. Everyone wants to get rich. It's a kind of stampede. And the tricksters are magnificent. They love their trickery. It's an art form to them. And it's a unified play. The whole thing, near Aristotelian terms, takes place in a few hours. Before embarking on their day's work, they agree among themselves to play a game: which of them, they say, can "shark" the best. That is, which of them can skillfully and wittily rook the gulls, as they're called. That means the gullible people, their victims.

And they go to their work with a will. It's bait and sting. They encourage in their victims' wild fantasies of wealth once they get the alchemical return. One example, Sir Epicure Mammon, will serve to illustrate the theme of the play. Now, the name Epicure indicates his addiction to pleasures of the flesh, the classical philosophy which advocated "Eat, drink and be merry." And "mammon" is money. He wants to be rich, and he wants to indulge his appetites gigantically, monstrously.

And this is what Epicure Mammon fantasizes:

> I will have all my beds blown up, not stuft:

When he gets the alchemist's stone and get rich through the fool's gold, he's going to have air beds, the first mention of air beds in literature.

> Down is too hard: and then, mine oval room
> Fill'd with such pictures as Tiberius took
> From Elephantis, and dull Aretine
> But coldly imitated. …

He's going to have pictures of pornographic scenes on his walls. And then at the end, there's this wonderful moment when he fantasizes the food he'll have.

> I … will have
> The beards of barbels served, instead of sallads;
> Oil'd mushrooms; and the swelling unctuous paps
> Of a fat pregnant sow, newly cut off,
> Drest with an exquisite, and poignant sauce;
> For which, I'll say unto my cook, There's gold,
> Go forth, and be a knight.

And so it is he imagines this wonderful universe of self-indulgence that he'll have once he gets the fool's gold. And if one thinks back, I mean that speech is surely inspired by a speech of Christopher Marlowe's Faustus, when he has Mephistopheles calls up Helen of Troy for him to sleep with, when he in, fact, summons the most beautiful woman in human history as his bedmate. "Is this the face that launch'd a thousand ships?"

Jonson outdoes even Marlowe in the lavishness and cloying richness of his blank verse. The speech is both Marlovian and mock Marlovian, but most of all, it conveys a biting satire on human greed. Money is the root, not just of all evil, but of all human foolishness. And *The Alchemist* ends with a wonderful stroke of theater, and very ironic it is: Out of the blue, Lovewit, the master of the house, returns and he sees what Face has been doing in his absence, the criminal activities that have been going on in his household. So what does Lovewit do? Does he punish the wicked trio, return the victims' cash? No, he laughs good-naturedly, congratulates his servant Face, who's by now betrayed his two coconspirators, and he pockets the profits. He loves wit and he loves money. Human nature, Jonson tells us, is the same from top to bottom. Cash is God.

I want to move now to the other dramatist which I said we'd look at, John Webster. Webster, in fact, is a tragedian. He's not a comic artist like Ben Jonson, but his view of life is as black and as gloomy, though, in fact, the literary form which he chooses to communicate it with is very different.

Webster, in fact, has a fairly small corpus of work and generally speaking, there are only sort of four plays of his which have lasted, and they're all of them very powerful tragedies, and all of them, as it were, carrying on, I think, the mood which one finds in the darkest and most powerful of Shakespeare's works. I think, you know, *King Lear* must have had a very powerful impact on Webster. And his worldview is imbued with this melancholy and what's called a contempt for the world.

Webster, as T. S. Eliot put it, was much obsessed with the "skull beneath the skin." And I want to concentrate on what is generally regarded as the greatest of Webster's tragedies, *The Duchess of Malfi*. It's still very much performed and it comes over very strongly on the stage. But before looking at the play itself, one should note that the Jacobeans loved taking standby plots, conventional plots of a romantic kind, and turning them upside down. John Ford's *'Tis Pity She's a Whore*, for example, takes the *Romeo and Juliet* scenario, but the star-crossed lovers in *'Tis Pity She's a Whore* are brother and sister. It's *Romeo and Juliet* plus incest, and the plot works itself out very nastily indeed.

The Duchess of Malfi is similarly perverse. The plot again is a romantic standby. A rich lady, a widow in Italy, the Duchess, falls in love with a lower-born man, but still a respectable courtier. It wouldn't be a disgraceful match. They marry secretly and have children. And her brother finds out, and kills the husband, his brother-in-law, brutally. Ostensibly, it's for honor, to protect, as it were, the name of Malfi, but the real motive is that he himself is incestuously in love with his sister. He wants her as his lover and he's going mad under the pressure of his lust. It's a very, very gothic form of madness: *lycanthropia*. He thinks he's a wolf, and in this wolfish aspect, he tortures and kills the Duchess horribly on stage.

All the while, as this gothic tragedy unfolds, a spectator, the brother's principal henchman—his hit man, in fact—passively observes what's going on. And when commanded, he does very bad things, but he's not, we gather, a bad man. He's simply a child of the time. His name is Bosola. And when the part was played on stage by the British actor, Bob Hoskins, who's famous for his gangster performances on screen, Hoskins observed that *The Duchess of Malfi* reminded him of nothing so much as gangland. We could call it the Duchess of Mafia, if you like. Webster creates a world in which normal morality is suspended, and the darkest, most savage, wolfish, if you like, aspects of human character are loosed.

Let me give one of Bosola's speeches, first, to convey the bleak amorality of Webster's worldview, but secondly to give some sense of the brilliance of Webster's turn of phrase. He's a wonderful wordsmith. These are lines which Bosola, her servant, gentleman of her horse, delivers to the Duchess. In fact, he's working for her brother. And she's being sadistically tormented to death, and her children are killed by her mad brother, as well as her husband. And what Bosola says is, "Don't fight it. Don't resist. Simply accept it. It's life, or death, but life and death, it's the same thing."

And this is the speech:

> Hark, now everything is still,
> The screech-owl and the whistler shrill
> Call upon our dame aloud,
> And bid her quickly don her shroud!
> Much you had of land and rent;
> Your length in clay 's now competent:
> A long war disturb'd your mind;
> Here your perfect peace is sign'd.
> Of what is 't fools make such vain keeping?
> Sin their conception, their birth weeping,
> Their life a general mist of error,
> Their death a hideous storm of terror.
> Strew your hair with powders sweet,
> Don clean linen, bathe your feet,
> And (the foul fiend more to check)

A crucifix let bless your neck.
'Tis now full tide 'tween night and day;
End your groan, and come away.

What he's saying is, "Die and accept it." No dramatist, not even Shakespeare, is the author of more brilliant lines than Webster. "'Tis now full tide 'tween night and day; End your groan, and come away." Could anything be more simple? Could anything use the basic constituents of English language and yet be more effective, and of course, more poetic, more beautifully melodic?

Unfortunately, in Webster's tragedy, those wonderful lines rarely combine to create any larger dramatic effect of the kind that we are used to in Shakespeare. They lie there, like jewels in the mud of a wholly fallen world. And yet that fallen world has its, as it were, I've used the word many times, kind of gothic fascination.

So with Webster and his fellow Jacobean dramatists, a great moment in English literature comes to an end. The moment that began, I would say, with Shakespeare's first history plays. Increasing pressure from the Puritans eventually brought about a licensing, and later on, even a closing of the theaters. The theater had a very, very hard time. And apart from a brief florescence during the Restoration when Charles II came back in 1660 until he was replaced in the beginning of the 18th century, there would be no supremely great drama, I would estimate, until the 20th century. The curtain had come down on the British stage, and it would not rise again for 200 years. But still, we have the works of Shakespeare, Jonson, and Webster, and they are very great work

The King James Bible—English Most Elegant
Lecture 10

The King James Version of the Bible, published in 1611 in the same period as Shakespeare's tragedies and Ben Jonson's comedies, stands as an example of the English language at its highest pitch of eloquence, subtlety, and beauty. Nevertheless, we sometimes do not think of the King James Bible as literature. One reason for this is because it was written by committee, although there was a single-minded genius behind what we call the Authorized Version.

The publication of the Bible in English was a project motivated principally by politics. This new version of the Bible would consolidate the Reformation by supplying a central text for Protestantism in contrast to Rome's Latin Bible and liturgy. It would also widen the gulf between London and Rome.

The King James Bible is a translation of a translation and, possibly, many more translations beyond that. The New Testament was immediately translated from the Greek. The Old Testament was translated from the Masoretic Hebrew text. Latin, Greek, and Hebrew were tongues that only a handful of scholars had mastery of in the 16th century, which made the Bible very remote. Martin Luther, who published the first vernacular version in German in 1522, believed that the Bible should be the property of all men and women. English translations followed Luther's, the most significant of which was by William Tyndale in 1525. Tyndale was a devout follower of Luther and believed there should be no barriers between Christians and their scriptures. For his beliefs, he was strangled and his body was burned at the stake by English authorities. Henry VIII, in his reforming break from Rome, endorsed the Tyndale Bible, which included, essentially, the New Testament and the Pentateuch.

Between Tyndale and the King James Bible, there intervened the rule of the fanatically Catholic Bloody Mary. The five years of her reign, from 1553 to 1558, ushered in a period of religious terror as she sought to return England to Catholicism. The reign of Mary's half-sister, Elizabeth, saw a return to the Protestantism of her father, Henry VIII. Protestantism, in its Anglican version, has the secular monarch, not the pontiff, at its head. Church and state are one. Tyndale's version of the holy writings, as enlarged by refugees during Mary's reign—the so-called Geneva Bible—became current again in Elizabeth's reign.

Mary I, Queen of England.

© Corel Stock Photo Library.

James, who ruled Scotland as James VI before taking over the English throne as James I, had for some years wanted to authorize a version of the Bible in English. The increasingly powerful Puritans also called for a Bible to which they could have access in their own language. From James's point of view, an English Bible would be a safety valve, making society more stable. The Puritans would, to some extent, be defused by having their own Bible.

Thus, the project for the new Bible was outlined at the Hampton Court Conference, convened in January 1604 with the principal aim of scholarly accuracy. The new translators didn't seek to interfere with the text of the Bible, just the way in which it was articulated. Certain key terms, such as the word "priest," had not been translated precisely in the Tyndale-derived versions. Marginal notes offering interpretation of the Bible were also at issue.

From James's point of view, it was important to create an orthodox Authorized Version. This authorization was not by virtue of a sect, or the church, or the universities, but by the king who was head and patron of the established church. In England, the Bible was to be a state-owned text, as much the property of the Crown as Buckingham Palace or Regent's Park. Unlike in the United States, authorized versions of the Bible may be printed in England only under license from the Crown; that license has traditionally been awarded to Oxford and Cambridge. The Authorized Version has never been in the public domain in the United Kingdom. This fact creates a significant axis of institutional power among the throne, the church, Parliament, and the academy—the establishment in Britain.

The Authorized Version was the work of six committees using the expertise of 50 scholars, most of them men of learning from Oxford or Cambridge. Nonetheless, 80 percent of the King James New Testament is verbally unaltered from Tyndale's earlier translation. This percentage is probably comparable to estimates scholars would give of the extent of authentic Shakespeare in our possession today. Despite all the committee apparatus, the mind of William Tyndale stands behind most of the King James Bible, and Tyndale may have been a creative writer of equal stature to Shakespeare. A reading of the opening lines of Genesis translated by Tyndale and from the King James Bible shows obvious echoes in the Authorized Version from that written almost a century earlier.

> **Despite all the committee apparatus, the mind of William Tyndale stands behind most of the King James Bible, and Tyndale may have been a creative writer of equal stature to Shakespeare.**

This brings us to the question of who William Tyndale was. Little is known of his early life. He was probably born in 1494, and he died in 1536. Even his surname isn't certain; he sometimes appears in documents as Hichens. He was a student at Oxford and, after his graduation in 1512, enrolled to do advanced study in theology.

He became a tutor in a noble household but was soon in trouble for heresy. Early on, he developed two dangerous aspirations: to defy Rome and to translate the scriptures into English. His aim, he said, was that even the ploughmen of England should know the scriptures.

Tyndale went to Germany and may even have met Luther in the 1520s. He was on the continent when Luther's vernacular Bible in German was published, a text that was promptly prohibited in England. Over the years, Tyndale worked on his own translation abroad.

He fell out with the king on the issue of Henry VIII's multiple divorces and was captured, brought back to England, tried for heresy, and strangled and burned. Reportedly, his final words were: "Oh Lord, open the King of England's eyes."

We could sample the Authorized Version anywhere for its literary quality. The Book of Job gives us a complete and fascinating narrative: In the opening, note the solidity of specification, what we would call the exposition if this were a novel. We know the hero's name and place of residence; we have an exact inventory of his property; and we know his character—excessively devout and sensible, rather dull even, and very cautious. Suspecting that his sons might have sinned, he makes offerings for them. The most extraordinary feature in this exposition is the conversation between God and Satan, in which they make a wager, effectively, that Satan will visit his evil upon Job as a test. As the story develops, many tribulations fall on Job, but he survives and remains faithful.

Allegorically, the meaning is simple: Even in the extremity of hardship, one must hold the faith. God will, in the fullness of time, reward those who remain faithful. The back story here is fascinating, particularly the free hand given to Satan. God does not seem to be a particularly noble protector of mankind. He is prepared for Job to lose all that he has; it is part of his divine intention and plan to allow Job to suffer the sharpest and cruelest of pain. This is in order to win a bet with Satan, who seems, in some sense, an equal player with God. Like other great stories, the more we read the Book of Job, the more curious and perplexed we become. Above all, it is the wonderfully terse, gritty style that captivates us.

Note in the literary expression of this story the stress on monosyllables. The last line, for example, reads: "And Job died, an old man, and full of days." The line contains nothing more than the simplest constituents of English language. Note, too, that the line is in iambic pentameter, recalling the blank verse of Marlowe.

In all the literature that we'll look at in the following lectures, the Authorized Version is there. It's not always visible, and it's not always audible, but it's always present.

In addition to making the Bible accessible, the Authorized Version achieved all the goals that James had for it. It created one of the structures of the established church in England, which was one of the great foundational elements of what would become the English state. It also created a version of the English language that was heard by the population every week. In listening to weekly sermons, the people of England gained the power of understanding complexity through the ear rather than the eye (listening rather than reading), and this ability conditioned the kinds of work produced by poets, dramatists, and writers of prose. The weekly lessons read from the Authorized Version permeated the intellectual fabric of England, particularly its writers, for the next 200 years. This cultural core is attributable to the enlightened act of James I in organizing the authorized translation.

But we must not forget William Tyndale, whose words still echo throughout our literature. For 200 years, he was almost equal to Shakespeare as one of the great formers, one of the people who produced the raw material for the authors we'll look at in coming lectures, including John Donne and John Milton. ■

Suggested Reading

Daniell, *The Bible in English: Its History and Influence.*

———, *William Tyndale: A Biography.*

Prickett and Carroll, eds., *The Bible: Authorized King James Version with Apocrypha.*

Tyndal, trans., *Tyndal's New Testament.*

1. What problems do we confront in reading the Bible "as literature"?

2. What claim does the Book of Job have to be the first sophisticated prose narrative in Western Culture, the "proto-novel"?

The King James Bible—English Most Elegant
Lecture 10—Transcript

Let me begin with a trick question: Supposing one could count all the readers up who've ever read English literature for as long as we've had English literature, 15 centuries, what was been the most read book, the most read work? The answer to that trick question will be found in the drawer alongside every hotel and motel bed in the United States of America. The book I'm referring to, that most read book, is, of course, the Authorized, or, as we call it, the King James Version of the Holy Bible.

We don't normally think of this book as literature, but, of course, the Bible in this most exalted of literary forms is an example of the English language at the highest pitch of its eloquence, subtlety and beauty. And it's produced at exactly the same period, one should note, as Shakespeare's great tragedies and Ben Jonson's comedies, the works we've been talking about.

And another reason we tend not to think of the King James Bible as a work of literature is because it was team written. We can't attach to it, as we can with *King Lear* or *The Alchemist*, the name of William Shakespeare or Ben Jonson. It is not, like most of the literature of the period we revere, the early 17th century, the product of an "onlie begetter," as Shakespeare called it, an originating genius, a single mind.

We don't think of great literature as something written by committees, by groups. I want, later, to modify that conception because there was indeed, I will argue, a single-minded, individual genius behind what we call the Authorized Version. There was, as it were, one creative talent which made the book we now know as the Authorized Version. More of that later. King James, you'll remember, comes on the throne in 1603, after Elizabeth. And this project was motivated principally by politics. There's no surprise there for anyone that knows this period. It was a period of seething upheaval and politics were inevitably involved with religion, so, in fact, to do this to the Bible, to make the King James Version, was essentially a politically motivated act or project.

And what was the political motivation? Well, this new Bible in English—remember, the Bible was previously in Latin—would consolidate the Reformation, that great movement which had been started by Henry VIII, Queen Elizabeth's father. It would supply a central text for Protestantism against Rome's Latin Bible and liturgy. It would open still wider the gulf between London and Rome, so wide, in fact, that it would never be bridged again.

So the Authorized Version is there, as I say, as a political wedge, and the fact that we revere it as literature is, in fact, a happy byproduct of that. The Authorized Version is a translation. More correctly, it's a translation of a translation, and possibly even many more translations beyond that. The New Testament was immediately translated from the Greek. The Old Testament was translated from the Masoretic Hebrew text. Latin, Greek, and Hebrew were tongues that only a handful of scholars had mastery of in the 16th century, or even now. It made this work very, very remote. It was the property of what are called hierophants, people, in fact, who were almost like a secret society.

And it was the rebel cleric, Martin Luther, who published the first vernacular Bible in his native German tongue in 1522. It shouldn't be the property of a secret society. It should be the property of all men and women. Luther's was, arguably, the most revolutionary act in European history at this period. There followed English translations, the most significant of which was by William Tyndale, mark that name, in 1525.

Although not by nature obedient, in point of fact, few churchmen have been more rebellious, Tyndale was a devout follower, a disciple, one might say, of Luther. And he would have described himself, if you'd asked him, as a Lutheran. And like his German master, Tyndale believed that there should be no barriers whatsoever between Christians and their Holy Writ. Now, this wasn't a lightly maintained belief. It wasn't a dinner party opinion. Tyndale's life ended with him being strangled and having his body burned at the stake by the authorities, English authorities, for just such beliefs.

You interfered with the Bible, unless you were the king and could do it at the king's command, like King James, at your peril. Tyndale's body was consumed by the flames, but his great work, the English Bible, was not. Although, alas, and for reasons I've never been able to understand, Tyndale's name and the credit which is owing to that name, have faded from view. There's very little name recognition for this man, even though, as I say, he is one of the great figures of our literature.

Henry VIII—you'll remember, we're back in the middle of the 16th century, we've jumped back 50 years—in his reforming break from Rome endorsed the Tyndale Bible. It was useful to him, and so he said it's a good thing. It sort of actually offended the Pope. Now, the Tyndale Bible that Henry VIII endorsed was essentially the Gospels, that's to say the New Testament, and the Pentateuch, or the central five books.

Between Tyndale and the Authorized Version, there intervened the rule of the fanatically Catholic Bloody Mary, Elizabeth's half-sister. These five years of her reign, from 1553 to 1558, ushered in a period of unprecedented religious terror in England. That's why they call her Bloody Mary. She wanted to return England to Catholicism by terror. And Elizabeth's reign saw a return to her father's, Henry's, Protestantism. These half-sisters, in fact, had very different notions of what England should be, and England, in Elizabeth's view, would have to revert to that vision which Henry VIII had. That's to say, an independent country, or country independent of Rome.

Protestantism, that is, in its Anglican version, as the established church has the secular monarch, not the pontiff, at its head. Church and state are one. They're fused together. Tyndale's version of the holy writings, as enlarged by refugees during Mary's reign, the so-called Geneva Bible, became current again in Elizabeth's reign. And John Bunyan, whom we'll be looking at later, used the English or the Geneva Bible as the basis of his *Pilgrims Progress*, as indeed, many other people of his class, working class, did.

James, who ruled Scotland as James VI before taking over the English throne as James I, had for some years wanted to authorize a new, improved, English Bible, more accurately, a bible in English. There was no disagreement as to content with Rome. He didn't want to change what was in the Bible, just the linguistic form in which it could be read or heard. And the growing lobbying power of the Puritans, who'll be more and more intrusive over the next 100 years of our literary history, added to the urgency of this task. They too wanted a Bible which they could, as it were, have access to through their own language, their own tongue.

Now, from James's point of view, I return to this observation that it's principally political, an English Bible would be a safety valve. It would make society more stable. The Puritans, in fact, would, to some extent, be defused by having their own Bible. So the project for the new Bible was outlined at the Hampton Court Conference, as it's called, which James convened in January 1604, and the principal aim was scholarly accuracy.

That's to say, they didn't want to interfere with what was in the Bible, just the way in which it was, as it was, articulated. And there'd been a laxity, it was felt, particularly in key terms of translation, in the Tyndale-derived versions. They were generally all right, but there was certain kind of, as it were, features which needed correction, needed refining. For instance, Tyndale had a terrific aversion to the word "priest," which he thought was Romish, and there are all sorts of lexical problems of that kind in terminology.

Marginal notes were also an issue, that's to say, these things down the side, which told you what various crucial moments in the Bible meant. Interpretation, one has to remember, was a life and death matter on such issues as the Trinity, the divinity of Christ. Again, having the wrong doctrine could be very dangerous.

And also it was important from James's point of view to create, as it were, an orthodox Authorized Version. This authorization was not by virtue of a sect, not by the Church, not by the universities, but by the king, the monarch who, then as now, was head and patron of the established church, the appointer of the church's senior clerics, from archbishops down. Everything, it was said, was in the king's gift. You couldn't be a humble parson without, in fact, that authorization coming from the king, from the throne.

Church and state were, as I said earlier, fused, as they have never, for example, been in post-revolutionary America. In England, the Bible was to be a privileged, that is, a state-owned text, and as much crown property as Buckingham Palace or Regent's Park. To this day, unlike in the US, you may only print the authorized versions of the Bible in England under license from the Crown, and that license has traditionally been awarded to the universities of Oxford and Cambridge, but in fact, the property belongs today to Queen Elizabeth II.

The Authorized Version has never, ever been in the public domain in the UK, as it has in America. That, in fact, is a big cultural difference between the two countries. And if, in fact, the authorities have their way, it never will be in the public domain in the UK, in England. And this creates a huge axis of institutional power, consolidated power between the throne, the established church, Parliament, and the academy. These, in fact, create what in Britain is called the establishment. There's no parallel structure in America.

As I said earlier, the Authorized Version was a team effort, and a very sizable team. It comprised six committees, utilizing the expertise of 50 scholars. Most of them are Oxbridge based, most of them men of huge learning. Nonetheless, 80 percent of the King James New Testament is verbally unaltered from Tyndale's translation. Eighty percent probably seems like a fairly, as it were, ragged sort of totality, but it isn't. Shakespearean scholars, who have to rely on printed copies produced from dubious sources, well after the playwright's death, would say that probably 80 percent of what we have of Shakespeare is authentic and 20 percent is inauthentic—we have to reconstruct it. That's the same with Tyndale and the Authorized Version.

When I said earlier that there was, despite all the committee apparatus, a single, originating mind, it's probably unnecessary now to repeat the point: that mind was William Tyndale's. And Tyndale is a creative writer of equal stature, I would suggest, perhaps even to Shakespeare. Let me give an example of Tyndale's creativity, his literature, if you like.

I'll read out two versions of the opening lines of Genesis. They're among the most famous lines in our culture, the moment of creation. This is where, in fact, the world becomes the world. Without, as it were, giving you any clues; try and guess which is Tyndale's and which is the Authorized Version, that version which, thanks to the Gideon Society, you'll find in your nearest motel.

1   In the begynnynge God created heaven and erth.

2   The erth was voyde and emptie and darcknesse was vpon the depe and the spirite of god moved vpon the water

3   Than God sayd: let there be lyghte and there was lyghte.

4   And God sawe the lyghte that it was good: and devyded the lyghte from the darcknesse

5   and called the lyghte daye and the darcknesse nyghte: and so of the evenynge and mornynge was made the fyrst daye

6   And God sayd: let there be a fyrmament betwene the waters ad let it devyde the waters a sonder.

7   Than God made the fyrmament and parted the waters which were vnder the fyrmament from the waters that were above the fyrmament: And it was so.

That's one version, and here's the other version:

1:1 In the beginning God created the heaven and the earth.

1:2 And the earth was without form, and void; and darkness was upon the face of the deep. And the Spirit of God moved upon the face of the waters.

1:3 And God said, Let there be light: and there was light.

1:4 And God saw the light, that it was good: and God divided the light from the darkness.

1:5 And God called the light Day, and the darkness he called Night. And the evening and the morning were the first day.

1:6 And God said, Let there be a firmament in the midst of the waters, and let it divide the waters from the waters.

1:7 And God made the firmament, and divided the waters which were under the firmament from the waters which were above the firmament: and it was so.

As I say, one of those is Tyndale's, and it was the first passage I read out. And this, remember, was almost a century before the Authorized Version. And the echoes are so obvious. I mean it's not quite a transliteration, but so close that any kind of lawyer could actually bring a plagiarism suit against the committee who came out with the Authorized Version in 1610.

Well, who then was this man, William Tyndale? His dates, as best we can put them together, are he was born in 1494 and he died in 1536. Now, his death, which was very painful and very public, we know a lot about, but little is known of his early life. Even his surname isn't certain. He sometimes appears in documents as Hichens, but it's known Tyndale and Hichens was a student at Oxford, and on graduation in 1512, he enrolled to do what we would call research or advanced study into theology. And he was evidently a brilliant linguist.

He went on became a tutor in a noble household, which was a popular occupation for clever scholars who wished to continue their scholarship. But young Tyndale was soon in trouble for heresy. He was the most pugnacious of clerics. He loved a fight. It's a good thing he did, otherwise we wouldn't have the Bible that we have. Early on, he developed two very dangerous aspirations. One was to defy Rome and the second was to translate the scriptures into English.

His aim, as he put it, was that even the ploughmen of England should know the scriptures, and know them as well as they knew their plough handles. It was a very dangerous doctrine. And he went abroad to Germany, and he may even have met Luther in the 1520s. And this was a period when the whole continent was in a ferment about religion.

Tyndale was on the continent, in Europe, when Luther's vernacular Bible in German was published. It was a text which was promptly prohibited in England, although few ploughmen could have read German, of course. Over the years, Tyndale worked on his own great translation abroad. And he fell out with the King on the issue of Henry VIII's flagrantly multiple divorces, which was the reason, of course, that Henry VIII brought about the Reformation. He had personal, not, in fact, theological differences with Rome.

Tyndale was captured, brought back to England, where he was tried for heresy, and as I say, strangled and burned. And his final words reportedly were, "Oh Lord, open the King of England's eyes." That is, Henry VIII's eyes.

One could sample the Authorized Version anywhere for its literary quality, but I'm going to take the easiest of samples, from my point of view, the best story, if one's thinking of stories, in that wonderful compilation, the Book of Job. I've chosen it because it's a complete narrative and a fascinating one, I think.

Let me read out the opening of the Book of Job, the story of Job.

1:1 There was a man in the land of Uz, whose name was Job; and that man was perfect and upright, and one that feared God, and eschewed evil.

1:2 And there were born to him seven sons and three daughters.

1:3 His substance also was seven thousand sheep, and three thousand camels, and five hundred yoke of oxen, and five hundred she asses, and a very great household; so that this man was the greatest of all the men of the east.

1:4 And his sons went and feasted in their houses, every one his day; and sent and called for their three sisters to eat and to drink with them.

1:5 And it was so, when the days of their feasting were gone about, that Job sent and sanctified them, and rose up early in the morning, and offered burnt offerings according to the number of them all: for Job said, It may be that my sons have sinned, and cursed God in their hearts. Thus did Job continually.

1:6 Now there was a day when the sons of God came to present themselves before the LORD, and Satan came also among them.

1:7 And the LORD said unto Satan, Whence comest thou? Then Satan answered the LORD, and said, From going to and fro in the earth, and from walking up and down in it.

1:8 And the LORD said unto Satan, Hast thou considered my servant Job, that there is none like him in the earth, a perfect and an upright man, one that feareth God, and escheweth evil?

1:9 Then Satan answered the LORD, and said, Doth Job fear God for nought?

1:10 Hast not thou made an hedge about him, and about his house, and about all that he hath on every side? thou hast blessed the work of his hands, and his substance is increased in the land.

1:11 But put forth thine hand now, and touch all that he hath, and he will curse thee to thy face.

1:12 And the LORD said to Satan, Behold, all that he hath is in thy power; only upon himself put not forth thine hand. So Satan went forth from the presence of the LORD.

First, note the solidity of specification, the exposition, as we would call it, if it were a novel. We know the hero's name, we know his place of residence, we have an exact inventory, a very pedantic inventory of his property. We know his character, it's excessively devout and sensible, rather dull, even, and very cautious. Have his sons sinned? He thinks, "I must do something about that. I must pray to God."

We may suspect a certain folkloric antiquity and the business of animal sacrifice, for example, in his religious practices, but the most extraordinary feature in this exposition is the conversation between God and Satan. Effectively, they have a wager, as if they were a couple of high rollers who met in a Las Vegas casino. In the story as it develops, many tribulations fall on Job, not least, his wife, whose advice in the extremity of his suffering is "despair and die." One doesn't like her for that.

But Job holds fast, he survives and remains faithful, amidst all the tortures that the evil one can inflict on him. He declines to turn his face to the wall. In short, Satan loses, as, for example, he does in Peter Blatty's novel *The Exorcist*.

And this is the conclusion of the Book of Job:

> 42:12 So the LORD blessed the latter end of Job more than his beginning: for he had fourteen thousand sheep, and six thousand camels, and a thousand yoke of oxen, and a thousand she asses.

> 42:13 He had also seven sons and three daughters.

> 42:14 And he called the name of the first, Jemima; and the name of the second, Kezia; and the name of the third, Keren-happuch.

> 42:15 And in all the land were no women found so fair as the daughters of job: and their father gave them inheritance among their brethren.

> 42:16 After this lived Job an hundred and forty years, and saw his sons, and his sons' sons, even four generations.

> 42:17 So Job died, being old and full of days.

Allegorically, the meaning, so to call it, is simple. Even in the extremity of hardship, you must hold the faith. God will, in the fullness of time, reward you. But the back story here is fascinating, particularly the free hand given to Satan. Also, in some ways, God does not come out as a particularly noble protector of mankind. He's prepared to allow Job to lose all that he has, not just cattle, but his loved ones. He's happy to allow him, or at least it's part of his divine intention and plan to allow him to suffer the sharpest and cruelest of pain.

Why? To win a bet with Satan. And are we to consider Satan, in some sense, an equal player with God? Like other great stories, the more we read, the more curious and perplexed, but interestingly perplexed, we become. Above all, it is the wonderfully terse, gritty style which carries us forward and carries us away.

To return to the Tyndale/Authorized Version literary expression: You'll note, stylistically, the stress on monosyllables. The last line "So Job died, being old and full of days": there's not a single polysyllable there, no word which is anything more than, as it were, the simplest constituents of English language. And you'll note too that it's an iambic pentameter. Remember Marlowe, the mighty line and blank verse? "And Job died, an old man, and full of days." That, in fact, is poetry, even though, in fact, it's there, sort of set as prose in the Book of Job.

In all the literature we're going to be looking at in the following lectures, the Authorized Version is there. It's not always visible and it's not always audible, but it's always there. Now, what the Authorized Version did was obviously it made the Bible accessible. It did all the things that James wanted it to do. It created, if you like, one of the kind of structures of the established church in England, which was one of the great foundational elements of what would be the English state, and what still is the English state. The established church is still there, and the established church still depends very much on that text that King James I actually gave to succeeding generations.

So the Bible, the Authorized Version of the Bible did everything politically that its authors, and obviously its authors were not just that committee, and not even just William Tyndale, but James I as well, that its authors intended it to do. But it did something else as well. What the Authorized Version did was to create a version of English which was heard by the whole English population every week. That's to say, during the 17th century, one has, in fact, to know this fact, I think, to understand, for example, why it is that Shakespeare's plays worked so well on the stage. Every week, the whole population of England was obliged to go to church. They had to attend church and they had to listen to sermons. And so what happened was that their ears became terribly well educated.

I don't know if it's the same with you, but one of the problems I have when I go to a Shakespeare play, if I don't know that play, I have great difficulty in taking it in through the ear because, in fact, our culture, as we now have it, is very much a culture of the eye. That's to say, we read. We look at what's in front of us and then our brains actually process the visual stimuli. But for the 17th century—and this is very important because there are various other things about Metaphysical poetry that one needs to be aware of concerning this point—the whole population had, as it were, a power of understanding things through the ear, which conditioned the kinds of work which poets and dramatists and prose writers came out with.

This is a very important fact. That's to say, they understood complexity when they heard it without having to see it. Why was that? Because every Sunday, you had to go to church and you had to listen to a sermon, which would be in English, but from after 1610, you also had to listen to lessons. You had to listen to sort of the wonderful sonorous cadences of the Authorized Version as well. And this permeated, this actually soaked into the intellectual fabric of England so that every writer for the next 200 years, if they knew one text, that text was the Authorized Version of the Bible. That, in fact, if you unpeeled the onion of their culture, that was at the very, very center.

All that, of course, is attributable to the very enlightened act of this monarch, James I. I said in the last lecture that he was almost, in fact, a notable author in his own right, but his great work is understandably enough his Authorized Version.

But also there is the fact that William Tyndale, that writer who regrettably is so neglected in our history books, that his words, in fact, still roll through our literature. But for 200 years, you could argue, that he's up there with Shakespeare as one of the great formers, one of the people who's actually making, as it were, the raw material for the kinds of authors we'll be looking at in the next lecture, John Donne, John Milton. Milton, in fact, has a very, very Tyndalian sense of the Bible, which feeds through into *Paradise Lost*.

If I could actually rewrite English literary history, or at least if I could actually create a billboard, with the big names on top and the small names underneath, William Tyndale's name, for me, would be up there with the very great names. And I think it's one of the sadnesses, obviously not something that one's going to regard as a great tragedy, but it's one of the sadnesses of our literary history that he does not have the recognition which I think he duly deserves.

At the beginning of the 21ˢᵗ century, we have the best part of a millennium and a half's worth of English poetry to read and enjoy. ... Which period or school qualifies as the greatest? ... My guess is, if you took a survey among poetry lovers and scholars, and most of all, among poets, the vote would go to the so-called Metaphysicals.

The Metaphysicals were a school of poets writing in the early and the mid-17ᵗʰ century. Their work circulated in manuscript form among educated elite. Several versions of their poems exist in some cases, making it hard to assign dates to them.

Metaphysical poetry was a highly cultivated branch of literature for the highly cultivated. One had to be able to write, in a sense, to qualify as a reader. The Metaphysical poets were familiar with, and adept in, foreign styles; deeply learned; and above all, witty. Wit, meaning smartness or cleverness, was the essence of the Metaphysical project. The Metaphysical poets cultivated a particular form of wit that they called the conceit, meaning a daring idea or concept. They valued originality, uniqueness, and sometimes the farfetched. Some of the conceits were so daring they almost defy imagination, such as that used in "The Flea" by John Donne (1572–1631).

"The Flea" is a love poem addressed by the poet to his unnamed lover. The young lady to whom the poem is addressed is a virgin, and she is steadfastly resisting the poet's urgent and wittily seductive request that she remain a virgin no longer. For his part, the poet is using all the resources of his poetry as an instrument of seduction. Donne compares the size of his request—that the young lady sleep with him—to a flea. He tells her that the flea has sucked on both their bodies, and their bodily fluids have come together in this way. Christ's blood, the mark of redemption, is daringly alluded to here, as is the breaking of the virginal hymen. The sucking flea has joined the lovers as a minister might join them in the holy union of marriage. The poem is riddled with parody and jammed full of strange, heterogeneous ideas. It's so farfetched in its wittiness as to verge on the surreal. Yet clearly the poem is designed not just to impress but to seduce. The poet may have used these same arguments, even though he may not have originally formulated them in poetic language.

With the Metaphysicals, the short lyric poem became a dominant mode in English literature. Another poem in this mode is Donne's "The Sun Rising." This poem again finds the poet in bed. Here, he has woken up after a night of lovemaking alongside a woman who is not his wife. In the opening lines, the poet addresses the sun as "thou," used at the time as an informal, even contemptuous form of address, almost as if the sun is a servant who has come to empty the chamber pot. English verse has a long tradition of hailing the dawn as a beautiful moment of the day, but here, Donne turns that convention on its head. The poet continues, telling us that love doesn't have to obey the movements of the clock or the sun through the heavens. As he contemplates time, his poem becomes more metaphysical and witty. As his companion wakes up, he begins to compliment her, telling her that she is richer than all the riches of the Orient. He goes on: "She's all states, and all princes I; / Nothing else is." The poet has become solipsistic, closing out the universe beyond himself and the woman.

The poem ends with lines addressed to the Sun: "Shine here to us, and thou art everywhere; / This bed thy center is, these walls thy sphere." At first Donne addresses the Sun as an irate householder might curse his alarm clock. But then, by a kind of intellectual glide, the poem becomes the supreme lover's compliment. The poet and his paramour have become heavenly bodies, equivalent in cosmic significance to the Sun, the Moon, and Earth.

The poem moves by a series of conceits from a comic, low-life scenario, through hyperbole, through overstatement and fantastic exaggeration, to something extraordinarily stimulating intellectually. And it has carried us along with it, or has it? The poem is, in fact, extremely complicated. As mentioned in the last lecture, 17th-century audiences were much better at understanding things through listening than we are. Modern readers often have to wrestle with the words of this poetry.

The other problem with Metaphysical poetry at the time it was written was that not everyone liked its farfetched conceits or its naughty sexuality.

Censorship was very real in the 17th century, and the Puritans, in particular, hated this "libertine poetry."

Samuel Johnson said of Metaphysical poetry: "the most heterogeneous ideas are yoked by violence together." For Johnson, this tendency was indecorous; he believed that poetry should follow certain rules. The Metaphysicals were somewhat out of fashion when Johnson was writing, but he does have a point; the extravagance in this poetry offends some readers.

Despite such objections, the reputation of the Metaphysicals rose over the centuries. They were regarded as increasingly significant, not just in themselves but in the influence they had on successive poets. It was T. S. Eliot, the greatest poet of the 20th century, who most effectively celebrated and vindicated the work of his 17th-century predecessors. A poet such as Donne had what Eliot called an "undissociated sensibility." For the Metaphysicals, there were no such things as poetic subjects. A poet could write about a flea as well as he could write about the dawn, and he could write about the flea very differently from the ways in which it had been traditionally regarded. There was no such thing as a subject beneath the dignity of poetry or as poetic diction. Everything was grist to the metaphysical mill. All human experience could be put into the poetic mix. We saw in "The Sun Rising" how the poet moves from waking up in a tussled bed with a woman to imagery of the spheres that is clearly derived from the Aristotelian view of the universe. Erotic love and astronomy are not usually yoked together, but this learned poet combines them effectively. In "The Flea," theology and verminous infestation are similarly yoked together. Eliot valued Metaphysical poetry most for its willingness to transmute and refine into high poetry any area of human life.

Donne's poetry is marked by a restless intellectual energy that constantly borders on the violent. Even in later life, when he was a respectable, married dean of Saint Paul's, Donne's sacred verse is marked by a breathtaking pugnacity or violence of intellectual argument. In perhaps his most famous sonnet, "Death, Be Not Proud," Donne personifies death, then conquers it. The idea of death itself dying is a magnificent conceit, as is the catalog of abuse that precedes it.

George Herbert (1593–1633) was a Metaphysical poet of almost equal stature with Donne. Herbert, too, was a churchman, although only a humble pastor. Herbert was less pugnacious than Donne, less prone to take on the great adversaries of the Christian universe. Herbert's poetry is marked by a simplicity that works by way of economy and deceptive subtlety; it is no less clever in its conception, in its "conceitedness," than Donne's. Herbert's *The Temple* is a structured collection of verse, in which he lays out the church in architectural form. It's an early example of concrete poetry, and all the poems in the collection correlate with an architectural feature of the church.

It was T. S. Eliot, the greatest poet of the 20th century, who most effectively celebrated and vindicated the work of [the Metaphysicals], his 17th-century predecessors.

One poem from this collection, called "Vertue," addresses death but less in a spirit of aggressive confrontation than in submission to the universal facts of vegetation and decay. Everything that lives must die, but we can view that fact as both positive and negative. The first two lines of the poem read: "SWEET day, so cool, so calm, so bright, / The bridall of the earth and skie." The use of "bridall" here illustrates the Metaphysical poets' love of puns. It can mean a horse's bridle, something like a leather strap that holds the earth and sky together, or bridal in the sense of marriage. The title of the poem, "Vertue," also plays with the Latin root of that word, which means "strength." The poet is asking: What is the strength of the world? What holds the world together? The gentleness and lyricism of this poem are suddenly transformed in its powerful last stanza: "Onely a sweet and vertuous soul, / Like season'd timber, never gives; / But though the whole world turn to coal, / Then chiefly lives." These lines allegorize suffering in the human context. The poet tells us that the more we suffer and the unhappier we are, the stronger and more virtuous will we be as individuals.

"To His Coy Mistress" by Andrew Marvell (1621–1678) is another poem of seduction. The lady in this poem is not yet the poet's mistress, although he wants her to be. She is a woman of his own class who is capable of understanding complex and witty verse. Marvell tells the lady that time is their enemy; she should sleep with him now, before she dies and "worms shall try / That long preserv'd virginity." The poem is another version of the carpe diem theme but with a wittily subversive motive. It's not coyness but virtue that makes the woman hesitant, but Marvell won't celebrate that quality, as Herbert did, because calling attention to it might prevent him from getting what he wants.

The most enduring qualities of the Metaphysical school and its bequests to subsequent schools of English poetry are its go-for-broke linguistic and conceptual daring and its reckless yokings of high and low, its relish for twisting language and ideas into new shapes. The sheer cleverness of the school is a wonder. ■

Suggested Reading

Carey, *John Donne: Life, Mind and Art.*

———, ed., *Marvell: A Critical Anthology.*

Donne, *John Donne: The Major Works.*

Herbert, *George Herbert: The Complete English Poems.*

Marvell, *Andrew Marvell: The Complete Poems.*

Norbrook and Woudhuysen, eds., *The Penguin Book of Renaissance Verse, 1509–1659.*

Vendler, *The Poetry of George Herbert.*

Questions to Consider

1. What did the Metaphysicals understand by the term "wit"?

2. Why is this particular school of poetry regarded by many modern commentators as one of the very highest points achieved in the long history of English literature?

The Metaphysicals—Conceptual Daring
Lecture 11—Transcript

Situated where we are historically, at the beginning of the 21st century, we have the best part of a millennium and a half's worth of English poetry to read and enjoy and to select from. That's 1,500 years' worth of verse. We're very lucky. Shakespeare, for instance, had nowhere near as much. Reviewing and looking over that vast treasure trove of poetry, which period or school qualifies as the greatest? If one's being, as it were, evaluative about it, which, in fact, is the highest achievement in verse? Across all those centuries, where would we find the highest peak, the Everest of poetic achievement?

My guess is, if you took a survey among poetry lovers and scholars, and most of all, among poets, the vote would go to the so-called Metaphysicals. In fact, in some ways, the worst thing about them is that name. It doesn't say very much and it hangs round their necks like Coleridge's albatross.

Who were the Metaphysicals? Well, there were a school of poets, a group of poets writing in the early and the mid-17th century, from about 1620 to, say, 1650. The Metaphysicals' work circulated in manuscript form among an educated elite. It was a lot of very clever people writing for very clever people, and they didn't put their work into printed form.

In fact, this is one of the problems. It's very hard to know when some of these poems were written because they exist in any number of manuscript versions, some of which are very different from each other. But in fact, we don't have, as it were, an easy way of putting a publication date on it. There's no record written into these works as to when they were composed and, indeed, when they were made generally available.

It was, as I say, a highly cultivated branch of literature for the highly cultivated. You had to be able to write, in a sense, to qualify as a reader. That's to say, the kind of poets we're talking about as Metaphysicals would exchange their work among themselves. And they respected each other. They probably didn't respect what Dr. Samuel Johnson would have called the "common reader."

These poets were familiar with and adept in foreign styles. They were all deeply learned. Above all, they were witty. You remember, with Ben Jonson, the importance of the notion of wit. Wit, which means any number of things, but we can sort of paraphrase it as smartness or cleverness, is the essence of the Metaphysical project. This, in fact, was their fatal Cleopatra, for which they would think the world "well lost."

These poets, the Metaphysicals, cultivated a particular form of wit which they called the conceit. What that meant was a daring idea or concept. The words are linked, concept and conceit. That's to say, they liked to do things which had never been done before and never been thought before. They valued originality, uniqueness, and indeed, sometimes farfetchedness.

Some of these conceits are so daring that, you know, they almost, in fact, defy the imagination. That's to say, one would never think of them. If you locked someone in a room for a million years and said, "Come up with the basic conceit in the next poem that I'll be talking to," which is called "The Flea" by John Donne, they would never. They'd be there a million years later, without having hit on what that mind invented for this particular poem.

"The Flea" is a love poem, addressed by the poet to his unnamed lover. In fact, she hasn't yet succumbed physically to his addresses. So in a sense, he's not yet writing a poem—he's wooing her. It's a love poem in the sense that it obviously sort of records a strong emotion, but it also has an ulterior motive. That ulterior motive, not to put too fine a point on it, is he wants to get her into bed.

This young lady, this beautiful young lady, we assume, to whom the poem is addressed is a virgin, and she's sturdily resisting the poet's urgent and wittily seductive request that she remain a virgin no longer. He's, as it were, using all the resources of his poetry as an instrument of seduction. It's not clear whether or not John Donne originally sent this poem to a young lady or whether, in fact, he just wrote it to show off to his equally cultivated and clever friends, but you know, that, in fact, is a secondary consideration.

This, in fact, is the central part of the poem "The Flea":

> Mark but this flea,

And he picks off the flea. Now, usually when you do that, it's with a kind of shudder of disgust, but this is not what John Donne is going to do.

> and mark in this,

Mark in the flea.

> How little that which thou deniest me is;

You know, you won't let me sleep with you, but look at this flea and just think about what a small thing that is.

> It suck'd me first, and now sucks thee,
> And in this flea our two bloods mingled be.
> Thou know'st that this cannot be said
> A sin, nor shame, nor loss of maidenhead;
> Yet this enjoys before it woo,
> And pamper'd swells with one blood made of two;
> And this, alas! is more than we would do.

You have to imagine the poet then just squeezing the flea and the blood spurting out. And whose blood is it? It's her blood and it's his blood. The flea has, in fact, sucked on both their bodies, and their fluids are conjoined. Their bodily fluids have come together. It is a flesh of my flesh sacrament. Now, it's highly blasphemous, of course. Christ's blood, the mark of redemption, is daringly alluded to here, and in the same context, the breaking of the virginal hymen. That's to say, he's saying, "Let me sleep with you and obviously you're a virgin. They may be some blood around, but nonetheless, just think of this flea. I mean it's not a big deal for a flea, I mean, if it just takes blood and mixes blood, why should we bother so much?"

And so the sucking flea has joined the lovers, as a minister might join them in the holy union of marriage. Of course, Donne is thinking more of the joys

196

of the wedding bed, and it's fornication that he has in mind. This is not a proposal of marriage. It's, in fact, as I say, a rather kind of intense seductive move that he's making.

The poem is riddled with parody and it's full of all sorts of very, very, very heterogeneous strange ideas, which are being jammed together. And it's so farfetched in its wittiness as to verge on the surreal. And yet, one knows, of course, that the poem is designed not just to impress, but probably to seduce. These are arguments which he may have used, even though he may not have originally formulated them in poetic language. One assumes that, in fact, there was a flea, an actual flea, and it did move between the two bodies and he did actually comment on it.

And it could also be, as I say, that it's a kind of circuitous apology for the flea-ridden squalor of the environs in which the poet is carrying out his act of seduction, you know, some sort of cheap lodging house or something like that, some fleapit, as we say. But the important thing is the bed is not far away. You know, fleas like beds and so does the young lover, John Donne.

Donne's early Metaphysical poetry is saturated in sexuality. Let me quote another one. Incidentally, the Metaphysicals loved short poems and hereafter the short lyric poem becomes a dominant mode in English poetry. That's to say, you can have great poetry in short measure, but this is, in fact, I think one of the Metaphysicals great bequests to poets that come afterward.

But this next poem I want to look at is another poem which finds the poet in bed. As I say, beds are for anything but sleeping, as far as John Donne's concerned. Having had what he was denied in the previous poem about the flea, a night of love, he is satiated and he's woken up after a night's love alongside the woman that he's spent the night with. It is not, one need hardly say, Mrs. Donne.

This is the poem:

> BUSY old fool, unruly Sun,
> Why dost thou thus,
> Through windows, and through curtains, call on us?

Two things here: first of all, he uses the word "thou" instead of "you," which is informal and almost contemptuous. We've dropped that now. We just use you whether or not it's someone we know very well or someone we don't know at all. Unlike the Spanish, for instance, which has three forms of address, or French and German, which have two, we only have the one. But here, in fact, he's actually talking to the sun. And remember, the sun has divine status in most mythology. He's talking to it as if it was sort of the person who's emptying his chamber pot.

There is a long tradition of English verse which, in fact, actually hails the dawn as a beautiful moment of the day—they're called aubades—but Donne is turning that convention on its head. He says, "Dawn? I don't want dawn. I want the night to carry on." He wants more acts of love in the dark.

> Must to thy motions lovers' seasons run?
> Saucy pedantic wretch,

He's still apostrophizing, or talking to the sun

> go chide
> Late school-boys and sour prentices,
> Go tell court-huntsmen that the king will ride,
> Call country ants to harvest offices;
> Love, all alike, no season knows nor clime,
> Nor hours, days, months, which are the rags of time.

So he's saying that love doesn't have to obey the movements of the clock and the movements of the sun through the heavens, the hours of the day. But he's now thinking about time and the poem is becoming metaphysical. *Metaphysical* means thinking philosophically. And so from that original waking up, his eyes "ungum" themselves and he's angry. "Oh, is it morning already?" His brain is taking over, his intellect, and the poem is becoming both witty and, at the same time, extremely complicated in its intellectual movement.

> Thy beams,

He's still talking to the sun.

> so reverend and strong
> Why shouldst thou think?
> I could eclipse and cloud them with a wink,
> But that I would not lose her sight so long.

He says, "I could actually sort of get rid of the sun, except I really want to look at her and I want her to look at me," which, in fact, is hyperbole and in fact, clearly a conceited remark.

> If her eyes have not blinded thine,
> Look, and to-morrow late tell me,
> Whether both th' Indias of spice and mine
> Be where thou left'st them, or lie here with me.

He's suddenly starting to compliment the woman. She's woken up as well and he's sort of turning to her and giving her that kind of little compliment, which will make her presumably more accessible to what he wants from her, which, in fact, is what he's been having all night, but he wants more of it.

> Ask for those kings whom thou saw'st yesterday,
> And thou shalt hear, "All here in one bed lay."

He's saying to this woman, "You're richer than all the riches of the Orient." What woman could resist that, particularly as he says it? And then he goes on, and now his mind is taking over in a quite sort of riotous way. He's having what you might call a kind of creative brainstorm.

> She's all states, and all princes I;
> Nothing else is;

This is, of course, solipsism. If you're in love, somehow the rest of the universe sometimes gets closed out. All that matters is the person that you're with and the person you love.

Princes do but play us; compared to this,
All honour's mimic, all wealth alchemy.
Thou, Sun, art half as happy as we,
In that the world's contracted thus;
Thine age asks ease, and since thy duties be
To warm the world, that's done in warming us.
Shine here to us, and thou art everywhere;
This bed thy center is, these walls thy sphere.

Of course, on one level, it's just pure egomania. What he's saying is that we are the whole world, but the important thing is that that, in fact, expresses—for me, anyway—a truth about love. Love is a very kind of introverted, very kind of, in some ways, manic state. Donne is addressing the sun in that first stanza as an irate householder might curse an alarm clock which has woken him up too early. But then by a kind of intellectual glide, the poem has become a work of supreme lover's compliment. The poet and his paramour have become heavenly bodies, equivalent in cosmic significance to the sun, moon, and earth. And then, of course, it becomes even more a kind of reflection on, in fact, what one call might call perception.

And the poem moves by a series of conceits, from a comic, low-life scenario, through hyperbole, through overstatement and fantastic exaggeration, to something extraordinarily stimulating intellectually. And it's carried us along with it, or has it? There's one problem in that it is extremely complicated. In the last lecture, I said that the 17th century was much better at understanding things through the ear than we are, partly because, as I said, they had to sit every Sunday and listen to long, very often rhetorical, sermons. And you know, they became used to it. Their ears were much more practiced then ours are. I think, in my experience, teaching and reading Metaphysical poetry, we have to actually wrestle with the words on a page. So that's one problem.

But there's another problem: Not everyone liked the farfetched conceits of Metaphysical poetry, or, indeed, the naughty sexuality. That's to say, the impropriety offended some people. Censorship, in fact, is a very real fact in the 17th century. I mentioned several times the rise of Puritanism, and the Puritans hated this kind of poetry, which they called "libertine poetry." It was the poetry of immorality.

But there's another objection. Dr. Johnson, who we'll be visiting in more length in a later lecture, with his Neoclassical prejudices, disliked this Metaphysical poetry in which, as he pontificated in the grand Johnsonian way "the most heterogeneous ideas are yoked by violence together." Now, this was, and the term is important in Johnson's criticism, indecorous. It offended decorum. His notion was that poetry should follow rules. It should move in certain grooves, and of course, what happens in Metaphysical poetry, as we saw in that poem, is that there are no grooves. It's jumping all over the place like the flea itself.

Johnson, of course, was writing, as we'll see, a few decades later. And it is a fact of literary life that few generations value the verse of their immediate predecessors. There's a kind of rise and fall thing. And so to some extent, they were out of fashion when Johnson was writing. But nonetheless, Johnson does have a point. There is a kind of an extravagance in Metaphysical poetry which can offend.

But despite Johnsonian and quasi-Johnsonian objections, and they recur every few decades, as the centuries drew on, the reputation of the Metaphysicals rose. They were regarded as more and more significant, not just in themselves, but in the influence they had on successive poets. It was T. S. Eliot, the greatest poet of the 20th century, 300 years later, who most effectively celebrated and vindicated as supremely great the work of his 17th-century predecessors.

Now, why? Well, a poet like Donne, Eliot argued, had what he called an "undissociated sensibility," and this is very important in poetry. For the Metaphysicals, there was no such thing as a poetic subject. You could write about a flea as well as you could write about the dawn, and you could write very differently from ways in which they'd been traditionally regarded. And there's no such thing as a subject beneath the dignity of poetry. There's no such thing as poetic diction, a special way of writing, and unpoetic diction. Everything was grist to the Metaphysical mill. All experience, all human experience could be put into the poetic mix.

You note, for instance, in the poem about the sun rising, how the move is made from waking up late in a tussled bed, with a woman who is clearly not the poet's wife, and the poet then modulates into imagery of the spheres, which is derived quite clearly from the Aristotelian view of the universe. The poet, in fact, is a very learned man. Erotic love and astronomy, and these are subjects, for example, not normally brought together, but they're "yoked" as Johnson would say, "violently" but very effectively, other people would say, in that poem. As in "The Flea," the theology and verminous infestation are similarly yoked together, whether by violence or not.

There are, in this Metaphysical poetry, no fences keeping one area of human life from other areas. Everything, as I say, can come together, can be transmuted and refined into high poetry. This, in fact, is what Eliot saw as the great feature of, and, indeed, the valuable feature for him of Metaphysical poetry.

Donne's poetry is marked by a restless intellectual energy that constantly borders on the violent, as Johnson noted. Johnson hated violence, incidentally. He couldn't stand the end of *King Lear*, for instance. He just preferred endings which were happy. Later life, when he was a respectable, married dean of St. Paul's—at that point in his life—he was very embarrassed by his early love and satirical poetry, and he tried to suppress it, but he went on writing poetry, even though he was, by this point in his life, in the late 1620s, a senior churchman. He went on writing poetry, but his sacred verse, which, in fact, is holy verse, his "Holy Sonnets," particularly, are marked by a breathtaking pugnacity, violence, one could say, of intellectual argument, as for example, when, in the most famous of the "Holy Sonnets," he takes on Death mano-a-mano in his great sonnet "Death, Be Not Proud."

I'm going to read that out to you:

> DEATH, be not proud, though some have called thee
> Mighty and dreadfull, for, thou art not so,
> For, those, whom thou think'st, thou dost overthrow,

You'll notice he uses the word *thou* again, but this time contemptuously.

> Die not, poore death, nor yet canst thou kill me.
> From rest and sleepe, which but thy pictures bee,

Much pleasure, then from thee much more must flow,
And soonest our best men with thee doe goe,
Rest of their bones, and soules deliverie.
Thou art slave to Fate, Chance, kings, and desperate men,
And dost with poyson, warre, and sicknesse dwell,
And poppie, or charmes can make us sleepe as well,
And better then thy stroake; why swell'st thou then?
One short sleepe past, wee wake eternally,
And death shall be no more; Death, thou shalt die.

He personifies death and then, you know, goes 15 rounds with him and ends up with death on the canvas floor, knocked out. The idea of death dying is a magnificently clinching conceit, as is the catalogue of abuse that precedes it. You're not so big, death. Who's frightened of you? Death, that black shadow over medieval life and literature is erased in this poem.

So that is John Donne. Now, there are other masters of Metaphysical verse. George Herbert, who is, I think, a Metaphysical poet of almost equal stature. And like Donne, he was another churchman, though, in fact, he was a humble pastor, working in a parish. He wasn't, like Donne, in the great cathedral of London. Herbert is less pugnacious. He's less prone to wave his fist in the face of the great adversaries of the Christian universe.

Herbert's poetry, by contrast, is marked by a simplicity which works by economy and deceptive subtlety: It is, however, no less complex and no less clever in its conception, in its "conceitedness" than Donne's. Consider the poem which I'm going to read out from his great structured collection of verse *The Temple*. It's a wonderful collection. What he does is he lays out an architectural form the church. It's an early example of concrete poetry. And all the poems in it co-relate with an architectural feature of the church.

But the poem which I want to look at is called "Vertue," and like the "Holy Sonnet" we've just been considering, it too addresses death, but less in a spirit of aggressive confrontation, so much, as it were, a submission to the facts, the universal facts of vegetation and decay. Everything that lives must die, but that can be seen really as a positive, as well as a negative thing.

This is the poem. It's very beautiful, and it requires, I think, a much quieter recitation, much less aggressive recitation than Donne. Again, it is another apostrophe:

> SWEET day, so cool, so calm, so bright,
> The bridall of the earth and skie:
> The dew shall weep thy fall to-night;
> For thou must die.

I love that line, "The dew shall weep thy fall to-night;"

> Sweet rose, whose hue angrie and brave
> Bids the rash gazer wipe his eye,
> Thy root is ever in its grave,
> And thou must die.

> Sweet spring, full of sweet dayes and roses,
> A box where sweets compacted lie,
> My musick shows ye have your closes,
> And all must die.

And then the last affirmative stanza:

> Onely a sweet and vertuous soul,
> Like season'd timber, never gives;
> But though the whole world turn to coal,
> Then chiefly lives.

The Metaphysicals, as we're seeing, loved puns. This is part of their kind of wittiness. In the above example, for instance, from Herbert, the word "bridall" means a horse's bridle, something like a leather strap which holds the earth and sky together, and it means bridal in the sense of marriage union. Virtue, too, you remember in *The Fairy Queene*, there's a catalog of virtues. But what Herbert is doing here is playing with the Latin root of virtue, which means "strength." And he's saying, "What, in fact, is the strength of the world? What holds the world together? Even though the world is forever falling apart, the fact of mutability, that flowers die, things decay, what holds it together?" Virtue, the strength. And again, the word is being played on and many meanings are being brought into play. The Metaphysicals loved this kind of thing.

The gentleness of this Metaphysical poem of Herbert's, it's lyricism and carpe diem, "Gather ye roses while ye may" theme is suddenly overset in that powerful last stanza. "Onely a sweet and vertuous soul, Like season'd timber, never gives; But though the whole world turn to coal, Then chiefly lives." Herbert was enough of a naturalist, enough of a kind of amateur scientist—in part due to the fact that there were very great scientists in the 17th and 18th century (they didn't have a lot to do six days a week)—to know that coal is carbonized wood, purified by extreme heat. And what happens with that is that the destruction makes for something which is stronger.

That, in fact, is allegorizing suffering in the human context. What he's saying is that the more you suffer, the more unhappy you are, the richer your life will be, the stronger you'll be, the more virtuous you'll be, in the sense you'll be able, as it were, to live a good life.

No poetry has been more erotic and simultaneously intellectually adventurous than the Metaphysicals, and I want just to finish very briefly with Andrew Marvell's poem, "To His Coy Mistress." It's another love poem, another poem of seduction. The lady is coy, not in the sense of being shy, and she's not really yet his mistress. He wants to make her his mistress, but she isn't yet. What Marvell wants in this poem, quite bluntly, is the pleasure of fornication with an understandably reluctant woman of his own class, a woman who's capable of understanding complex and witty verse.

Why do we know that? Because he talks about how when she dies, she's going to be buried in a very elaborate burial place, tomb. This, in fact, is "To His Coy Mistress," one of the most famous poems of the Metaphysical Movement.

It begins:

> Had we but world enough, and time,
> This coyness, lady, were no crime. ...

Then he goes on to say we don't really have time. And then this wonderful peroration at the end:

> But at my back I always hear
> Time's winged chariot hurrying near;
> And yonder all before us lie
> Deserts of vast eternity.
> Thy beauty shall no more be found,
> Nor, in thy marble vault, shall sound
> My echoing song; then worms shall try
> That long preserv'd virginity,

Almost the most horribly erotic simile that I know of in poetry.

> And your quaint honour turn to dust,
> And into ashes all my lust.
> The grave's a fine and private place,
> But none I think do there embrace.

And so what Marvell is saying here is that as Donne would say, "Jump into bed with me." And there's that wonderful notion, nonetheless, of the metaphysical dimension: time is our enemy. Time "the winged chariot" at your back and in front of you "deserts of vast eternity." The poem teeters on the brink of vulgarity, but doesn't quite topple. And like Herbert's "Vertue," Marvell was, in fact, no rural clergyman or dean of St. Paul's, but a man of the world. He was a diplomat. "To His Coy Mistress" is another version of the carpe diem, short are the days of life theme, but it had a wittily subversive motive.

It's not coyness, but virtue, for instance, which makes the woman hesitant, that quality which Herbert was celebrating. The poet, however, wouldn't allow that thought. It might prevent him from getting what he wants, which is her body.

Metaphysical poetry, it should be noted, isn't all love poetry, nor is it short lyric poetry. There are longer works, Donne's "Satires" and his "Anniversaries," Marvell's complicatedly long poem "Upon Appleton

House," and I would say that Marvell's "Horatian Ode on Cromwell's Return from Ireland" is the best political poem in the language. But the enduring quality of the school and its bequest to subsequent schools of English poetry, right the way through to T. S. Eliot and beyond, is its go-for-broke linguistic and conceptual daring and its reckless yokings, that word again, of high and low, its relish and love of twisting language and ideas into new shapes, fantastic shapes. The sheer cleverness of the school is a sheer wonder.

Is this then a highpoint? Is this the highest point? I think probably it would get my vote, as well as T. S. Eliot's.

Paradise Lost—A New Language for Poetry
Lecture 12

It's always fun to run an imaginary Q&A session with the great writers that we've been looking at. … And what exactly, we might have asked Milton in this Q&A session of the mind … did he think that he was doing when he dictated—being, like that other epic poet Homer, blind at the time—what did he think when he dictated *Paradise Lost*?

When John Milton (1608–1674) dictated *Paradise Lost*, as mentioned in his prolegomenon, he aimed to explain the ways of God to man. Just like the English builders of cathedrals, for whom their buildings were not architecture but concrete acts of worship, Milton's motives in writing his great poem were religious, and we do him a great injustice if we don't appreciate that fact. Most of us do not read *Paradise Lost* as its author intended us to read it. For us, it is a great literary text, not Genesis poeticized or explained.

Paradise Lost is an immensely ambitious poem, bringing together the epic project of Homer and the text of the Bible. Milton faced both strategic and logistical problems in writing it. How could he achieve such a massively difficult undertaking with the tools at his disposal? What language should he write in, Latin or English? Milton could write in Latin as fluently as he could write in English, but he was also an English Puritan, and he wanted to make his poem accessible to his coreligionists.

Milton compromised brilliantly on the language question by inventing a new language for poetry that was halfway between Latin and English. In the opening lines of Book I, we hear diction, vocabulary, rhythms, and syntactic structures that are wholly alien to the language of everyday life, then and now. Note the suspension or delay of the key verb *sing*, which doesn't appear until the sixth line. This is a wholly Latinate construction. T. S. Eliot said, although he later changed his mind, that this Miltonic poetic idiom divorced poetry from the language of men. It's true that Milton went farther than most poets in re-crafting the language in the interest of his art; indeed, he invented a new dialect for poetry.

Milton's second technical problem related to genre. In *The Poetics*, Aristotle defined the two great literary genres as tragedy and epic. These two forms had intrinsic nobility, but which one should Milton adopt for his great poem? Tragedy, as Aristotle defined it, is unified. Milton's poem *Samson Agonistes* was created along strict Aristotelian lines. It rigorously obeys the unities of place, time, and action; has a classic catharsis; and avoids all scenes of blood or violence. Epic, again as defined by Aristotle, is loose, episodic, and digressive. It is narrative, not dramatic, in its organization. Whereas the material in tragedy is carefully structured, beginning strictly at the final, conclusive moment, epic typically begins *in media res*, "in the middle of things." Milton toyed with the model of the epic poets Homer and Vergil and with that of the tragedian Sophocles. He made detailed plans for the dramatic tragedy he thought of writing, tentatively called *Adam Unparadised*.

One great speech from Satan in *Adam Unparadised* was later grafted into Book IV of Paradise Lost. As the enemy of mankind, Satan debates with himself about his intent to bring sin into Eden: Will doing so damn him, or is it justifiable in his rebellion? In the end, "Disdain forbids" him from submitting to God. He is too proud. Faustus's last soliloquy is clearly echoed here, as is the line of Mephistopheles "Why, this is hell, nor am I out of it."

Even though Milton decided not to write a drama, he retained a dramatic conception of Satan in *Paradise Lost*. The best speeches in the poem are Satan's. The speech in which Satan dooms himself to fall would have occurred at a key moment in the drama, what Aristotle termed the *peripeteia* or "turning point" in the play. This is the irredeemable moment for Satan. Up to this point, he could have saved himself, but by committing himself to the destruction of Adam and Eve, he also destroys himself.

The poet William Blake observed that Milton was "of the Devil's party and did not know it." At its heart, the poem *Paradise Lost* is morally conflicted. Milton himself was a rebel and a Puritan who had taken up his pen against the king. How could he not have some sympathy for the arch-rebel Satan? Deep countercurrents in *Paradise Lost* drive against the poem's biblical orthodoxies and make the poem more complex. Milton was a firm believer in the doctrine of *felix culpa*, "happy sin," the belief that man was greater, potentially, because of the fall and redemption than he had been before. The loss and regaining of paradise, each individual's struggles in life, had the capacity for making us, given that we are possessed of free will, greater than we would have been if we were happily vegetating in Eden for all eternity.

How could a scholar like Milton think that the tree of knowledge should be forbidden to mankind? In the poem, he gets around this problem rather elegantly. The forbidden fruit, the apple, represents nothing but a test of obedience; it does not relate to sex. Adam is learned enough to debate on equal terms with the Archangel Raphael before the fall, but he hasn't gained mastery over what the Puritans called the old Adam, the propensity to rebel, sin, and break rules.

It's impossible to make sense of *Paradise Lost* unless one sets it in the context of the English Civil War.

Another countercurrent that has particularly worried modern readers is Milton's misogyny, his apparent hatred of women. The poem is very focused on the fall of man; woman is there, not as a partner, but as a subsidiary cause. Eve was created out of one of Adam's less important bones, a rib, and it's clear in the poem that while Adam is for God, Eve is for the God in Adam. When Satan gets his first look at his two future victims, he sees two magnificent specimens, but he says of Adam: "His fair large front and eye sublime declared / Absolute rule"; the implication is that he has absolute rule over Eve. When Eve succumbs to the serpent's seductive wiles, her error is really Adam's because he has not exercised his authority over her. When Eve returns, having eaten the apple, Adam's duty is clear: to spurn her. But he doesn't because his carnal desire for her is greater than his godliness. The old Adam cannot be suppressed. Adam offers the shabbiest of excuses to God: "The woman tempted me and I did eat." He goes on to ask God why women—"this fair defect / Of nature"—need to exist at all. Both Milton's life and his poetry reflect the spirit of his time, which from our point of view seems chauvinistic. Romantic myth holds that Milton, the blind poet, dictated his work to his daughters. In reality, he kept his daughters in ignorance; at least two of them probably could not even write. Milton's unhappy first marriage to the 16-year-old Mary Powell most likely led to his famous pamphlets in favor of divorce as a means of assuring liberty for men.

It's impossible to make sense of *Paradise Lost* unless one sets it in the context of the English Civil War. Milton had served the Commonwealth during its years of domination and civic power in the mid-17th century, in part by writing anti-Episcopal tracts. Bishops were an obnoxious relic of Rome and a main bone of contention during this period, as was subservience of the Church of England to the Crown of England. The rebellion made it clear that one had to oppose the king in order to oppose the church, and the goal of doing so was to create religious liberty. The Puritans maintained that God did not serve any king; individuals had a personal relationship with God, not one that was mediated through bishops or monarchs.

With the parliamentary victory in the Civil War, culminating in the beheading of Charles I, Milton used his pen in defense of republicanism and against monarchic rule. In return, he was awarded a high position in the Commonwealth, Secretary of Foreign Tongues. After the Restoration in May 1660 and Charles II's accession, Milton went into hiding, fearing for his life; a warrant was issued for his arrest, and his writings were burned. (*Paradise Lost* did not yet exist.) Despite the issuance of a general pardon, Milton was nevertheless arrested and briefly imprisoned before influential friends intervened. *Paradise Lost* was composed between 1658 and 1664 (and published in 1667 for the fee of £5 or $10). From the Puritans' point of view, the Civil War had failed, and from the larger point of view of the English nation, the war was one of the most traumatic events in modern history.

Two main problems remain for successive generations coming to *Paradise Lost*. The first problem is this: Is the poet compelled to re-create language so drastically if he or she is to write great poetry? Could one not draw, instead, on the reservoirs of natural speech? The other question is not specifically poetic, though it reverberated through literature for the next 300 years: To what extent should the poet and to what extent should the subjects that the poet deals with be subordinated or antagonistic to the order of things as they are?

In a famous essay, George Orwell said that the writer should be "outside the whale," because otherwise, the state or society could swallow the writer up, as the whale had swallowed Jonah. The writer should maintain a position on the edge of things, looking in, but not contained by what he or she is describing. Milton was on the edge of things during the time he was writing *Paradise Lost,* and that edginess gives the poem much of its power.

Paradise Lost is a work of literature that requires us to educate ourselves in order to make sense of it. It is an extraordinary achievement that has challenged readers of every generation. ∎

Suggested Reading

Milton, *John Milton: The Complete Poems.*

———, *John Milton: The Major Works.*

———, *Paradise Lost.*

Waldock, *Paradise Lost and Its Critics.*

Questions to Consider

1. Is Milton secretly, subversively, or unconsciously "of the devil's party" in *Paradise Lost?*

2. T. S. Eliot commented that, with his Latinate diction, Milton had erected a Chinese wall around English poetry, sealing it off from the language of the people. How just a criticism is this?

Paradise Lost—A New Language for Poetry
Lecture 12—Transcript

It's always fun to run an imaginary Q&A session with the great writers that we've been looking at. Take Shakespeare, for example. Did he, one might ask the author of *Hamlet*, realize that he was writing great works of literature, works which would last as long as civilization itself? "No," he would probably have replied, possibly looking slightly perplexed at the question. "No, I was just a working playwright, making enough money to provide for my family, entertain audiences, and, you know, with luck, set myself up in my years of retirement as a country gentleman." Great literature didn't come into it. He probably wanted a good reputation among his peers, but he didn't think that he was writing for posterity.

And what exactly, we might have asked Milton in this Q&A session of the mind, this literary mind game, did he think that he was doing when he dictated—being, like that other epic poet Homer, blind at the time—what did he think when he dictated *Paradise Lost*? Did he, for example, think he was writing the greatest epic in the English language, something for successive generations like us to study? "No," he would have replied, with a sharp, piercing look from those unseeing, but all-seeing eyes, under that flowing head of hair, of which we know he was so proud. He wrote the poem as, if you only took the trouble to read it, he had made crystal clear in his prolegomenon, to explain the ways of God to man.

Of course, like Homer, he'd wanted to raise English literature in the process, to give it some kind of equality with the classical works of the ancients, but that wasn't his main aim. It was a secondary aim. Divinity, not literary status, came first.

Paradise Lost has sold millions of copies since its first printing in the 1670s. Milton got just £5 or $10 for the copyright, and that too would have been a matter of utter indifference to him. He was not in it for the money. Leave that to journeyman writers, you know, like William Shakespeare. Milton's mission was higher; none higher, not even the parson's mission was higher than his, as he thought. Just like the English builders of cathedrals, for whom their buildings were not architecture but concrete acts of worship, Milton's motives were, at base, religious. And we do him a great injustice if we don't appreciate that fact. We don't have to submit ourselves to it entirely when we read the poem, but we should know it and acknowledge it.

But that is not how most of us read *Paradise Lost*, not as Milton intended us to read it. For us, it is a great literary text. It's not Genesis poeticized or explained. And few, I think, put Milton's poem down with the observation, "Well, now, at long last, I understand what God was getting at by allowing Adam and Eve to fall. Thank you for explaining it to me, John. I feel I'm a better Christian now."

Nonetheless, as I say, we have to take on board the original religious intention, if only the more effectively to put it on one side and then see the poem as a poem. *Paradise Lost* was, for the reasons I've just been talking about, an immensely—a grotesquely, even—ambitious poem. The Bible and Homer: Was there ever a more heady literary cocktail than those two? The Bible and Homer: It's literary nuclear fusion, bringing together the two hugest texts one can think of.

And the initial problems Milton faced were strategic and logistical. How could he achieve such a massively difficult undertaking with the tools at his disposal? Practically speaking, what language should he write in, Latin or English? These are the two great Biblical languages, of course, in the mid-17th century. Should he follow the King James Version or should he go back to Rome, the language of proven literary nobility?

Now, Milton was an accomplished Latinist. He could write in that language as fluently as he could write in English, and many of his poems are Latin poems, though I think very few people, for obvious reasons, read the Latin Milton nowadays. But Milton was also an English Puritan, and a very dedicated and patriotic Puritan. And he wanted to make his poem accessible to his coreligionists, the mass of who were not, like him, fluent in Latin.

So, this was the big initial question: what language should he write in, English or Latin? Now, Milton compromised brilliantly and typically. He invented a new language for poetry which was halfway between the two, halfway between Latin and halfway between English. It's in the middle and it is totally synthetic.

Let me give an example, a very famous example, from the invocation of *Paradise Lost* in Book I. That's to say, the opening, the poet coming forward and speaking to the reader or writing for the reader, the first page. You'll forgive me because, in fact, it is very, very hard, for obvious reasons, to read out Milton. He didn't write, like Shakespeare, for the human mouth. He was doing something very different with what one could call the Miltonic idiom.

But this how the poem starts:

> Of Man's first disobedience, and the fruit
> Of that forbidden tree whose mortal taste
> Brought death into the World, and all our woe,
> With loss of Eden, till one greater Man
> Restore us, and regain the blissful seat,
> Sing, Heavenly Muse, that, on the secret top
> Of Oreb, or of Sinai, didst inspire
> That shepherd who first taught the chosen seed
> In the beginning how the heavens and earth
> Rose out of Chaos: or, if Sion hill
> Delight thee more, and Siloa's brook that flowed
> Fast by the oracle of God, I thence
> Invoke thy aid to my adventurous song,
> That with no middle flight intends to soar
> Above th' Aonian mount, while it pursues
> Things unattempted yet in prose or rhyme.

Note that, "Things unattempted yet in prose or rhyme." He knows he's doing something quite unique.

> And chiefly thou, O Spirit, that dost prefer
> Before all temples th' upright heart and pure,
> Instruct me, for thou know'st; thou from the first
> Wast present, and, with mighty wings outspread,
> Dove-like sat'st brooding on the vast Abyss,

And mad'st it pregnant: what in me is dark
Illumine, what is low raise and support;
That, to the height of this great argument,
I may assert Eternal Providence,
And justify the ways of God to men.

Well, if you're like me, you get rather lost in all that. It's very, very hard. I couldn't read it without the help of annotation, without going over it several times, and it's blank verse, of course. But the only line which actually hits home and which, to some extent, the ear welcomes is that last one, "And justify the ways of God to men."

The diction, vocabulary, rhythms and syntactic structures are wholly alien to the language of everyday life, then, now, or at any conceivable stage of past history. And if the human species survives 1,000 millennia, one doubts they'll ever speak like that. I speak for myself, but the mind virtually herniates itself, ruptures itself following the syntax. Note, for instance, what's technically called suspension or delay of the key verb, which is *sing* and you don't know what the sentence means until you get at least 10 lines into that.

This is a wholly Latinate construction. If you know Latin, you'll know they quite often put the verb at the end of the sentence. This, in fact, is routine in Latin, but it's not routine in an analytic language like English. To some extent, it creates confusion.

T. S. Eliot later compared this Miltonic poetic idiom to a Chinese wall thrown around English poetry. It divorced poetry from the language of men. It's a very tricky issue, and one on which even Eliot rather changed his mind in later life. That's to say, to what degree must the poet re-craft language in the interest of his art? Milton, it's safe to say, went further than most. As I say, he invented a whole new dialect for poetry.

Would the poem have been even greater had Milton kept closer to the language of everyday intercourse, as indeed they did in the King James Bible? Well, this is a nice question, and it's one which students of literature, lovers of literature constantly debate.

Milton's second great technical problem was generic. Language was one, idiom was one, but the second one was generic. In the *Poetics*, a text which Milton knew almost as well as he knew the Book of Genesis, Aristotle defined the two great literary genres as tragedy and epic. These two forms had an intrinsic nobility. They were high, as opposed to comedy, which was low. But which of the two should Milton adopt for this great poem? Remember how ambitious this poem is, a poem which is going to fuse, which is going to conjoin Homer and the Bible, probably the most ambitious poem ever attempted by an Englishman. But which form, epic or tragedy, should he take?

And that was a genuine dilemma for Milton. Tragedy, as Aristotle defined it, and he was thinking principally of the superbly structured *Oedipus Rex* by Sophocles, was unified. It was complexly organized. It was like a Swiss watch. Milton, in another context, can claim to have created the finest tragic poem in the language on strict Aristotelian lines in *Samson Agonistes*, a work which rigorously obeys the unities of place, time and action, which has a classic catharsis, and which avoids all scenes of blood or violence. Aristotle would have given that poem an A+.

Epic, by contrast, as defined by Aristotle, was loose, episodic, and digressive. It is narrative, not dramatic in its organization. It goes all over the place. Whereas the material in tragedy was carefully organized and shaped and structured, beginning strictly at the final, conclusive moment, epic would typically begin *in media res*, "in the middle of things." It could begin anywhere and circle around aimlessly, going who knows where. But nonetheless that was intrinsic to its greatness, and this, in fact, was what Homer had done.

So what literary precedent should Milton follow in this all-important venture: the epic poets Homer and Virgil, or the tragedian Sophocles? Which was the best model for this hybrid religio-epical experiment, daring experiment?

In fact, Milton toyed with both models. There survives to us the detailed plans and dramatis personae he made for the dramatic tragedy that he was going to write, or that he was provisionally thinking of writing. And it was called tentatively *Adam Unparadised*, which, in my view, is a candidate for the unsexiest title ever come up with by an author, *Adam Unparadised*.

One great speech survives from *Adam Unparadised* as opposed to the plan: Satan's speech, which was later grafted into Book IV of *Paradise Lost*. As the enemy of mankind, Satan arrives at the edge of Eden and debates with himself whether what he is about to do is right or not right, whether, in fact, it's going to damn him or whether what he's doing is justified rebellion.

Can Satan justify bringing sin into Eden, working the downfall of this most beautiful of God's creation, mankind and womankind? And this is a speech which, as I say, we know survived from that original tragedy, as Milton projected it, *Adam Unparadised*:

> Me miserable! which way shall I fly
> Infinite wrath, and infinite despair?
> Which way I fly is Hell; myself am Hell;
> And, in the lowest deep, a lower deep
> Still threatening to devour me opens wide,
> To which the Hell I suffer seems a Heaven.
> O, then, at last relent: Is there no place
> Left for repentance, none for pardon left?
> None left but by submission; and that word
> Disdain forbids me, and my dread of shame
> Among the Spirits beneath, whom I seduced
> With other promises and other vaunts
> Than to submit, boasting I could subdue
> The Omnipotent.

"Disdain forbids me," he said. I'm too proud to do it. Pride, of course, has brought him down. It's Satan's great fault. Remember, if you would, Faustus's last soliloquy, clearly echoed here, as indeed is Mephistopheles's line "Why, this is hell, nor am I out of it." Marlowe is clearly sort of in Milton's mind and Milton clearly knew drama. He could have written a good drama, I think, but you know, it's a wonderful speech and one wishes one had more like it. It's much easier, I have to say, to recite than that earlier invocation.

But, in fact, Milton decided that that was not the route he would take, even though, he did keep a dramatic conception of Satan, one which is very interesting. And particularly that line, "Evil, be thou my good": it has a wonderfully dramatic resonance.

There are some very good speeches in *Paradise Lost* and the best speeches of all are Satan's, and I'd like to think that that's because as he began the poem, Milton was in two minds, and there was a dramatist Milton as well as an epic narrative poet Milton at work in the conception of that work. As it happens, that wonderful speech, I mean it would have been a key moment because it would have been, in Aristotelian terms, the *peripeteia*, or "turning point" in the play, the moment in which Satan entirely dooms himself to fall. And he has to fall before he can, as it were, work about the fall of man.

This is the irredeemable moment for Satan. Up to this point, Satan could have saved himself, but by committing himself to the destruction of Adam and Eve, it is not just them he is destroying, but himself as well. It would have been the key moment, the pivot of *Adam Unparadised*. And it's quite interesting that that's what Milton began with. He began by thinking of, as it were, the components of his play, and this was the key component, and he actually wrote that. And then it was so good that he couldn't leave it in the wastepaper basket. He picked it up and stuck it centrally in Book IV of his epic poem.

In the final analysis then, after carefully weighing up the options, trying them out, and test-driving them, in a sense, Milton settled on epic, not tragedy, as the best vehicle for what he had in mind. But, you know, that above speech of Satan raises another fascinating aspect of *Paradise Lost*. Milton, the poet William Blake observed later on, and we'll be coming to Blake when we get to the Romantic period, was "of the Devil's party and did not know it." That is to say, at its heart, the poem, *Paradise Lost*, is morally conflicted.

If you look at the historical biographical facts: How could a rebel and a Puritan like Milton, who'd taken arms against a king and justified cutting that king's head off, not have some sympathy for the arch-rebel, Satan? Are there not deep countercurrents in *Paradise Lost*, driving against the poem's

Biblical orthodoxies? And indeed, there are. And they make the poem not confused, but complex and intensely interesting.

For one thing, we'll see, or we can see if we read the poem, that Milton was a firm believer in the *felix culpa*, the "happy sin" doctrine, the belief that man was greater, potentially, because of the fall and redemption than he was before. The loss of paradise and the regaining of paradise, everyone's individual struggle in life, had the capacity for making us, as possessed of free will, potentially greater than we would have been, happily vegetating in Eden for all eternity.

How could an intellectual, a scholar like Milton think that the tree of knowledge, learning, that is, should be forbidden to mankind? In the poem itself, he gets around this problem very elegantly. The forbidden fruit, the apple, represents nothing but a test of obedience. Adam and Eve are fully sexual. The apple has nothing to do with sex. And Adam is learned enough to debate on equal terms with the Archangel Raphael before the Fall, but he hasn't mastered what the Puritans called the old Adam, the propensity to rebel, sin and break rules.

It is man's first disobedience—you'll recall those opening lines—which is at issue here. Blake, I think, was right, except perhaps in the "did not know it" observation. It's hard to think that, trained in spiritual introspection as Milton was, that he didn't know what was going on in his own head. But in fact, it was difficult.

There are other countercurrents in *Paradise Lost*. One countercurrent which has particularly worried modern readers is Milton's misogyny, his apparent hatred of, or scorn for womankind. It's very much the Fall of man. Woman is there, not as a partner, but as a subsidiary cause. *Paradise Lost* oozes with what later times have called male chauvinism. Eve, for example, is created out of one of Adam's less important bones, a rib (we can all spare a rib or two). And it's very clear in the poem that he is for God, and she is for the God in him.

Consider, if you would, the first visual snapshot Satan has of his two future victims, shortly after the Book IV soliloquy which I quoted earlier. The fiend sees two magnificent specimens. Both are Godlike, erect, unlike animal-kind, "with native honour clad." They walk "in naked majesty." They're not shameless, but they're wholly unconscious of what shame can be. They're the image of their divine maker. But, and this is stressed:

> Not equal, as their sex not equal seemed;
> For contemplation he and valour formed;
> For softness she and sweet attractive grace;
> He for God only, she for God in him:
> His fair large front and eye sublime declared
> Absolute rule.

Absolute rule over what? Over her. His hair is parted neatly and manly. Hers is "disheveled," pleasant to the eye "in wanton ringlets waved / As the vine curls her tendrils, which implied / subjection." That's to say, she's behind him. She's always following. Milton adds, "Nor those mysterious parts were then concealed" but exposed in sinless and spotless innocence, equally beautiful, but not equal.

So when, using the full arsenal of her feminine wiles, Eve goes off to work by herself in the garden and succumbs to the serpent's seductive wiles, it is Adam's error for not exercising his masculine authority, not making her what she is, his subject. When, having eaten the apple, Eve returns, again, Adam's duty is clear. He should cast her off, spurn her, get another rib. But he does not. Why? Because he loves her, or, more correctly, his carnal desires are greater than his godliness.

The old Adam cannot, at this critical moment, be suppressed. He fails himself and he fails his God, and it leads to that shabbiest of excuses, which he offers his maker, "The woman tempted me and I did eat." It's all her fault. Adam then goes on to ask, "Why do women need to exist at all?" And this, again, is one of the unlovelier parts of the poem, I think, for modern readers, though I think the Puritans actually sort of concurred. This, in fact, was not going against the grain of prejudice at the time in the middle to late 17th century.

Anyway, this is what Milton asked God, and effectively, it's saying, "Why on earth did you make this awful thing, womankind?"

> O! why did God,
> Creator wise, that peopled highest Heaven
> With Spirits masculine, create at last
> This novelty on earth, this fair defect
> Of nature, and not fill the world at once
> With Men, as Angels, without feminine;
> Or find some other way to generate
> Mankind?

Well, Milton, I have to say, is not at his most lovable in this frame of mind. And more so, if one goes back to the actual composition of the poem, one has to picture the blind poet, dictating to his daughters. In fact, he didn't dictate to his daughters. That is a romantic myth. What he did was to keep his daughters in ignorance. Two of them at least, we suspect, could not even write.

And so, Milton's life, as well as his poetry, has this kind of, as it were, spirit of the time, which, from our point of view, is a kind of prejudice of the time. And you know, Milton's own personal life may well be reflected in this kind of hostility to woman. His first marriage to the 16-year-old Mary Powell, a girl half his age, went very, very badly, and the same failure of that marriage led more directly to his famous pamphlets in favor of divorce.

It was liberty for the man, not for both partners, which he had in mind when he wrote those divorce pamphlets. So there may be a biographical explanation, but whether or not, it's there and it's in the poem, and it is, in fact, a kind of rough sort of surface in a poem which is otherwise an extremely polished, indeed, one could argue, overpolished, literary structure.

One won't make sense of *Paradise Lost* unless one sets it in the context of the English Civil War. Milton had served the Commonwealth during its years of domination, its Cromwellian years of domination and civic power in the mid-17th century. He wrote anti-episcopal tracts. Bishops were an obnoxious relic of Rome and a main bone of contention at the period, as indeed was subservience to the Church of England to the Crown of England. The rebellion was very, very precise on this matter, that you had to oppose the king in order to oppose the church, and by so doing, you were creating religious liberty. God did not serve any King, or so the Puritans maintained. You had a personal relationship with God, not one which was mediated through bishops and through monarchs.

And with the parliamentary victory in the Civil War, culminating in the beheading of Charles I, Milton used his pen in defense of Republicanism, against monarchic rule. And the power of his pen got him a high position in the Commonwealth. He was a Secretary of Foreign Tongues in 1649, for instance. He was what we could call a PR man for Cromwell.

After the Restoration in May 1660 and Charles II's accession, Milton went into hiding, fearing for his life, as a warrant was issued for his arrest and his writings were burned. *Paradise Lost* did not exist at this point. Despite a general pardon having been issued, he was nevertheless arrested and briefly imprisoned before influential friends, such as Andrew Marvell, he of the "Coy Mistress" poem discussed in the last lecture, intervened.

This, then, is the tangled background to *Paradise Lost*, published in 1667, for, as I say, the grand fee of $10. It was composed by the blind Milton from 1658 to 1664. This was a period when the Civil War had failed, from the Puritans' point of view. And there's a nice speculation how he might have written and how he might have conceived Satan had the work been conceived 20 years earlier, when he too was a rebel, and I think would have been much closer to Satan. It would have been a very interesting poem indeed.

What kind of poem would Milton have written had he not been writing it in this kind of turbulence, terrible turbulence? Now, England has never had a revolution like France, and it's never been broken into many pieces like Italy or Germany, but it did have this Civil War, which in fact, was historically one of the most traumatic events in modern history. And Milton, remember, is writing his poem during this.

Just to summarize some of the points of this lecture: The main sort of problem for successive generations with *Paradise Lost* was whether Milton was right, that the poet had, to some extent, to re-create language so drastically if he or she was to write great poetry. Could you not draw on the reservoirs of what we would call natural speech? Could you not, as it were, bring poetry closer to the ways in which men and women actually spoke to each other? Did you really have to, to some extent, do this kind of cookery, this kind of bizarre, in some ways, sort of linguistic sort of remodeling? That is one problem.

And the other question which, in fact, is not specifically poetic, though, in fact, it does continue to reverberate through literature for the next 300 years is, "To what extent should the poet and to what extent should the subjects which the poet deals with be subordinated or antagonistic to the order of things as they are?"

In a very famous essay in the 20th century, George Orwell said that the writer should be, as he put it, "outside the whale" because, in fact, the state, community, country, society would swallow you up, as the whale swallowed up Jonah. And what the writer had to do was to be on the edge of things, looking in, but not, as it were, contained by what he's describing.

It seems to me you can see *Paradise Lost* in exactly that situation. That's to say, Milton is not within a kind of Puritan utopia and, indeed, for a lot of the time he's writing *Paradise Lost*, he's on the run. But at the same time, he's not an outlaw, he's not a criminal, he's not being hounded by the authorities. He's on the edge of things, and that edginess, it seems to me, gives *Paradise Lost* a lot of its juice. That's a wonderful poem, but it's one of these works of literature where, to some extent, we have to educate ourselves in what it's doing in order to make sense of it. It's a very, very difficult poem.

But nonetheless it is an extraordinary achievement, and it's also, one has to say, a poem which changed English literature. It is, in fact, acknowledged and always will be acknowledged as one of the great achievements of literature, but very different from William Shakespeare's achievements. Shakespeare speaks the language which is very much, even with the passing of centuries, our language, but Milton isn't. Yet, nonetheless, in his way, on a separate peak, perhaps, one might imagine, he is doing as great things as William Shakespeare was doing. But it is, as I say, a poem which has always posed problems, both to readers, to critics and to every generation which comes to it.

Turmoil Makes for Good Literature
Lecture 13

Paradise Lost, **Milton's great poem, began … with a civil war, not in England, but in heaven. But there was civil war in England. The mid-17th century was, historically speaking, riven. … It's a strange historical fact, as historians often observe, that England's never had a proper revolution. … The nearest … England has come to a revolution is the turmoil of the last half of the 17th century, which is where we now are in our account of English literature.**

The mid-17th century in England was torn apart by civil war, a war focused on religious, intellectual, and social freedom. However, the closest England has ever come to a true revolution was the turmoil experienced in the last half of the 17th century.

The Puritans had become a strong political party, and the royalists, many of them with Catholic roots, felt the need to repress this dangerous new force. An explosion was inevitable, with Oliver Cromwell, known as the Protector, as the detonator. The king's forces were defeated, and a Commonwealth or English republic was established. Cromwell's moral illiberality and defiance of Parliament led, in a few years, to the restoration of the monarchy in the person of Charles II and the return of the court from its exile in France.

The old order was reestablished with certain modifications: More power was given to the people, specifically, to the middle classes, and to Parliament. These constitutional modifications were confirmed with the importation from Holland of William and Mary in 1689, chosen because it was believed they would follow the desires of the nation. The long era of characteristically English liberal democracy was thereby inaugurated, with a balance of forces among the Crown, Parliament, elected governments, and the people. This balance of forces exists to this day.

Literature rode out this turmoil, and in fact, as typically happens, turmoil made for some very good literature. Pamphlets, for example, played a major part in the conflict between the parliamentarians or Puritans and the royalists.

The Civil War, which had broken out in 1642, elicited Thomas Hobbes's (1588–1679) *Leviathan*, a grim and powerfully written political treatise. *Leviathan* was published in 1651, only two years after Charles I had been executed by the English people.

Leviathan was also the name used by Milton to describe Satan in Book I of *Paradise Lost*. When we're first introduced to Satan, who has been exiled from heaven, he is basking like a vast whale in a fiery lake. For both Milton and Hobbes, Leviathan is a monster.

Hobbes, in his *Leviathan*, also pictured society as a monster, made up of innumerable small units, with each small unit a human being. In Hobbes's view of human nature, these tiny components of society will constantly fight each other unless savagely restrained from doing so. The body politic—society as a whole—can only be organized and controlled by force. Without that forceful top-down control, society was, in Hobbes's best known phrase, a "war of all against all." And civil war reduces society to its simplest, irredeemably belligerent, homicidal elements. It breaks down the body politic.

For Hobbes, this is the natural condition of humanity. Not even Darwin, with his universal struggle for survival, had such a harsh view of the human condition as did Hobbes. A famous line from Hobbes's description of civil war tells us its result: "And the life of man, solitary, poore, nasty, brutish, and short."

Hobbes's view of the human condition and the social contract in *Leviathan* is jaundiced in the extreme, but it has been influential over succeeding generations. The Conservative party in England, for example, still retains a strong Hobbesian bent, particularly in the idea that society needs binding forces, what we now call law and order.

As Hobbes saw it, new structures would be needed to create the necessary stability on which civilization could found itself, but beyond forceful authority, Hobbes offered no suggestions for what those structures would be. Nonetheless, his beautifully written work infused his views into literary political discourse for generations to come.

Another image of man put forth in this period was similarly embattled but ultimately more hopeful than Hobbes's. This optimistic response to the Civil War was current among the Puritans and given literary expression by John Bunyan (1628–1688).

Bunyan was born to a working-class family in the town of Bedford, in the midlands of England. He was largely self-educated, steeped in Tyndale's Geneva Bible and Puritan polemic. Bunyan espoused a militant Protestantism and was himself a Christian soldier, serving in Cromwell's Roundhead parliamentary army. His service is recalled in his spiritual journal *Grace Abounding*. In adult life, Bunyan became convinced that he was one of God's elect. He would go to heaven, not necessarily because he was a good man, but because that's what God had decided. From 1655, he spoke to various congregations, despite the schismatism that was affecting even Puritanism at this point.

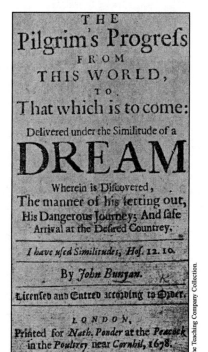

Title page of John Bunyan's *The Pilgrim's Progress*.

Bunyan's belief that he had been saved sustained him throughout his difficult life. In 1660, with the return of Charles II from France and the downfall of the Commonwealth, he was imprisoned for preaching without a license. Indeed, Restoration Puritans would have a hard time of it unless they conformed, but for Bunyan, conformity meant damnation. He spent 12 years behind bars as a prisoner of conscience and, during that time, wrote *The Pilgrim's Progress*. This book was eventually published in the late 1670s in two parts and became the most popular work in prose fiction in the English language. Along with the Bible and Foxe's *Book of Martyrs*, a catalog of people who suffered for their faith, *Pilgrim's Progress* would take its place on the mantelpiece of every respectable lower-class family for generations.

The full title of Bunyan's great work is *The Pilgrim's Progress FROM THIS WORLD TO That which is to come: Delivered under the Similitude of a DREAM Wherein is Discovered, The manner of his setting out, His Dangerous Journey; And safe Arrival at the Desired Countrey.* Puritans were inveterately suspicious of fiction, but Bunyan justified the imaginative aspect of his allegorical work with an epigraph from the book of Hosea: "I have used Similitudes." The Bible approved the use of similitudes to communicate religious truths.

The story of *The Pilgrim's Progress* is as well known: Christian leaves home and the City of Destruction, where he has lived all his life, to undertake a long journey to the Celestial City. He has been inspired by the Bible to take this journey. Christian's journey is made harder because of a burden on his back—sin, the old Adam—which he cannot slough off until he gets to the Celestial City. On his journey, Christian discovers that the majority of mankind is sinful and destined for inevitable damnation. He undergoes various trials and ordeals, encountering the Slough of Despond, the Hill of Difficulty, the Valley of Humiliation, the Valley of the Shadow of Death, and Doubting Castle. He is accompanied on his pilgrimage by his friend Faithful to the city Vanity Fair, which is London, where Faithful is put on trial and executed as a martyr. Faithful dies and, thus, takes a shortcut to the Celestial City. Christian plods on, with his new companion, Hopeful. After many trials, the two pilgrims cross the River of Death to Mount Zion and the Celestial City. It is Hope who keeps Christian going during the most dispiriting periods of their journey. Once they arrive at their destination, their burdensome packs drop away; they are free of sin. The second part of the book, dealing with Christiana, Christian's wife, is a parallel story of trial, ordeal, and salvation. There are no passengers on her journey. Everyone must save themselves, even wives, husbands, and children.

Bunyan's allegory is mechanical and, compared to Spenser's, for example, primitive, but the texture of the prose, nourished by vernacular English and the Geneva Bible, is as pure as crystal. The opening of the book describes Bunyan's vision of Christian in a dream at the moment in Christian's life when he decides that he must save himself. Bunyan sees a man clothed in rags reading from a book. As he reads, he weeps and trembles, finally crying out, "What shall I do to be saved?" Evangelist appears and points to the book Christian is reading, telling him that he must "fly from the wrath to come." The message is that everyone must find individual salvation; seekers cannot even take their loved ones with them, but they have a book as a guide. It's by reading that one will be saved.

In complete contrast to Bunyan, we turn to John Wilmot (1647–1680), Earl of Rochester and the most depraved poet in all of English literature. Rochester was active and writing while Bunyan was in prison, but he was a member of the royal court, as well as a libertine. While the Puritans believed in repressing the flesh, the libertines believed in expressing it. Rochester's poem "To His Mistress" uses religious imagery for starkly irreligious ends. His salvation is not found in the Celestial City but in the fornicator's bed.

Looking at the Puritan and the libertine literature produced simultaneously during this period, it's safe to say that never has English society been as split as it was in the Restoration period. After the brief experiment with republicanism and the Commonwealth, the court returned from France, willfully intending to annoy and affront the Puritans, who had killed the king. This effrontery reached its highest pitch in Restoration comedy. Such dramatists as William Congreve, William Wycherley, and George Etherege deliberately offended Puritanism and middle-class sensibility with witty depictions of cuckoldry, seduction, and indifference to common morality.

These excesses eventually led to the virtual extinction of drama. The Puritans and the middle classes would win, and the English theater would be a casualty of their victory for at least 200 years. William and Anne, who came to the English throne in 1702, were monarchs who embodied middle-class virtue, Protestantism, and parliamentary democracy; their reign inaugurated a stable England.

John Dryden, reviewing the tumultuous years from 1640 to 1700, wrote: "Thy wars brought nothing about; / Thy lovers were all untrue. / 'Tis well an old age is out, / And time to begin a new." We will look at that new age in the next lecture. ■

Suggested Reading

Bunyan, *The Pilgrim's Progress.*

Hill, *Intellectual Origins of the English Revolution.*

———, *Puritanism and Revolution.*

———, *Society and Puritanism in Pre-Revolutionary England.*

———, *A Tinker and a Poor Man: John Bunyan and His Church, 1628–1688.*

Hobbes, *Leviathan.*

Johnson, *A Profane Wit: The Life of John Wilmot, Earl of Rochester.*

Rochester, *Rochester: Complete Poems and Plays.*

Sharrock, *John Bunyan.*

Zwicker, ed., *The Cambridge Companion to English Literature, 1650–1740.*

Questions to Consider

1. Is literature itself at war in this period? If so, what weapons can literature effectively use?

2. How far can the "virtue" or "vice" of a writer influence the reader's response to literature, and how does such a response vary over time?

Turmoil Makes for Good Literature
Lecture 13—Transcript

Paradise Lost, Milton's great poem, began, as you'll recall, with a civil war, not in England, but in heaven. But there was civil war in England. The mid-17th century was, historically speaking, riven, it was torn apart by that most detested of conflicts: internecine war, Englishman against Englishman. The English Civil War of the 1640s was, unlike the American Civil War, less about authority, independence, taxation or the pursuit of life and happiness, but about ideas, ideas principally about religious freedom, intellectual freedom and social freedom, liberty.

It's a strange historical fact, as historians often observe, that England's never had a proper revolution, nothing equivalent to the storming of the Bastille, the invasion of the Winter Palace in Moscow, or tea chests bobbing around in Boston Harbor. The nearest the country England has come to a revolution is the turmoil of the last half of the 17th century, which is where we now are in our account of English literature.

In brief, Protestantism, as it always tends to do, went political. Puritans became a major force in the land. They became effectively a strong political party. And the royalists, who are traditionalists, and many of them with old Catholic roots like their Jacobite king, Charles I, they repressed these new forces, this Puritanism, which was to dangerous to them. Now, that was a big mistake. There was the inevitable explosion, with Cromwell as the detonator. The king's forces were defeated, and a Commonweal or English republic was set up.

It didn't last long, but it was very important while it did last. Now, the Protector's—that's what Cromwell called himself—moral illiberality and defiance of Parliament led, in a few short years, to the restoration of the king, or at least the king's son, Charles II, and the court, which had been in exile in France. So England's briefest of experiments with republicanism was over. The English decided that, for any number of reasons, they didn't like it. They tried it and it didn't work for them.

The old order was established, or reestablished, but with certain modifications: notably, more power to the people—and, specifically, to the middle classes, who were also becoming a dominant force—and to Parliament. And these constitutional modifications—I'm sorry, this little history lesson is really necessary—were confirmed with the importation from Holland of William and Mary. The monarchs which Britain eventually chose came from overseas, and they were chosen because, in fact, they would do what the country wanted.

And the long era of characteristically English liberal democracy was thereby inaugurated, with a balance of forces between the Crown, which increasingly was symbolic, between Parliament, which made decisions, between elected governments, with regular elections, regular polls, and the people. Now, that balance of forces lasts to this day. It's worked very well for the best part of 300 years.

Now, literature, like a cork in a storm, rode out this turmoil, but, as it typically happens, turmoil made for some very good literature. That's to say, authors very often thrive on turbulence. Literature, for example, played a major part in the Roundhead versus Cavalier conflict, that's to say, the parliamentarians or Puritans against the royalists.

There was a pamphlet war. Words, in fact, were weapons, and sometimes the pen was indeed mightier than the sword. It was certainly mighty, but generally speaking, the sword was, if not mightier, more horrible, more terrible.

The actual war, the Civil War in [1642], was, for thinking people, dreadful. It elicited that grimmest and most powerfully written of political treatises, Thomas Hobbes's *Leviathan*, and that's what I want to talk about over the next few minutes, *Leviathan*.

Leviathan was published in 1651. Dates are very important at this moment because, in fact, the mood of the country's changing almost day by day. And it was published with the smell of Cromwell's cannon still reeking in the nation's nostrils. It was virtually a kind of traumatized wartime reaction, as well as being a great book. Civil War had broken out in 1642. Charles I was executed in 1649, the only king to be so treated by the English people.

Leviathan, which is Hobbes's title, you may recall, is the name and image used by Milton—who's also mixed up in all this, by the way, as a kind of political player and as, in fact, a parliamentarian—to describe Satan in Book I of *Paradise Lost*, back to that great poem. Perhaps you don't remember, but I'll describe it to you: when we're first introduced to Satan, he's seen as basking like a vast whale, Leviathan, which is the biblical term, in the fiery lake. He's been exiled from heaven, and he's the great rebel.

This, in fact, is Miltonic quotation. Like all Milton, it's rather hard to take in, but this, I think, is probably more vivid and more comprehensible than a lot of the early section of *Paradise Lost*:

> Thus Satan, talking to his nearest mate,
> With head uplift above the wave, and eyes
> That sparkling blazed; his other parts besides
> Prone on the flood, extended long and large,
> Lay floating many a rood, in bulk as huge
> As whom the fables name of monstrous size,
> Titanian or Earth-born, that warred on Jove,
> Briareos or Typhon, whom the den
> By ancient Tarsus held, or that sea-beast
> Leviathan, which God of all his works
> Created hugest that swim th' ocean-stream.
> Him, haply slumbering on the Norway foam,
> The pilot of some small night-foundered skiff,
> Deeming some island, oft, as seamen tell,
> With fixed anchor in his scaly rind,
> Moors by his side under the lee, while night
> Invests the sea, and wished morn delays.
> So stretched out huge in length the Arch-fiend lay,
> Chained on the burning lake.

The image there is that, of course, it's wholly kind of legendary, that some mariners see, as they think, an island and they get on it at night and it turns out to be the back of a whale, as they discover the next morning, quite disastrously. The important thing for Hobbes, as for Milton, Leviathan is a monster. Now, Hobbes in his *Leviathan* pictured society, or the body politic, as he saw it, as just such a monster, made up of innumerable small units, each small unit a human being.

It's a kind of very atomistic view of society, but the atoms are all, as it were, at each other. And these units, these tiny little components of society, were by nature not cooperating, but fighting with every other unit. That, for Hobbes, is human nature. It turns on itself unless savagely restrained from doing so. Lock two people in a room forever and one will sooner or later kill the other.

And the body politic—that's to say, all these little units put together, making up one huge body, one huge corpus—can only be organized and controlled by force. This is what Hobbes thought. By tyranny, to give it another name, by dictatorship, by Cromwell.

Without that forceful top-down control, society was, in Hobbes's best known phrase, a "war of all against all," not, in fact, conflict, but war. And civil war reduces society to its simplest, irredeemably belligerent, murderous, homicidal elements. That's what civil war does. It breaks down the body politic into all these little atoms, who then actually sort of go against each other, hammer and tongs.

This, for Hobbes, is the natural condition of humanity. Now, not even Darwin, with his universal struggle for survival, had such a harsh view of the human condition as did Thomas Hobbes. This, for instance, is Hobbes's word picture of civil war. And reading it, as I'll do in a second, one can almost feel the concussion of the muskets, the shrieks of the wounded. In fact, one can feel the "war of all against all."

This is what Hobbes writes:

In civil war, every man is Enemy to every man. ...

There's a kind of punch that line has, and it's not speculative, it's not hypothesis. This, in fact, is the rule of the universe.

In such condition, there is no place for Industry; because the fruit thereof is uncertain;

You never know whether you're going to be able to bring your goods to market because of the war.

and consequently no Culture of the Earth; no Navigation, nor use of the commodities that may be imported by Sea; no commodious Building; no Instruments of moving, and removing such things as require much force; no Knowledge of the face of the Earth; no account of Time; no Arts; no Letters; no Society;

This is a huge catalog of negatives.

and which is worst of all, continuall feare, and danger of violent death;

And then this terrible last line:

And the life of man, solitary, poore, nasty, brutish, and short.

It's beautifully written and horrible to read, or horrible to hear. And that last word, "short," hits the reader, I think, like a pistol shot.

Hobbes's view of the human condition and the social contract in *Leviathan*, a work which was actually written during the Civil War, are jaundiced in the extreme. They're unbalanced, but who would not be unbalanced with the world actually going crazy around you? And Hobbes's views, even though, in fact, they're a response to the immediate circumstances, have been hugely influential over succeeding generations, and they still are influential.

If you look at the doctrines, for instance, of one of the two main political parties in England, the Conservative party, there's still a very strong Hobbesian vein going through it: the notion that society needs binding forces, and sometimes those binding forces have to be what we now call law and order. The whole kind of law and order debate, in fact, is very often

Hobbesian in its origin. And of course, that debate rages on in the UK, as it, at every election time, rages on in the United States.

As Hobbes saw it, new structures would be needed to create the necessary stability on which civilization could found itself. And what those were, other than forceful authority verging on dictatorship, Hobbes could not see. But in fact, nonetheless, he puts a kind of, as it were, an impulse into political discourse and literary political discourse for generations to come.

And what's important, of course, is he writes like an angel. In fact, when one hears that passage as it's read out about life being "solitary, poore, nasty, brutish, and short": I mean once you hear that, it's almost like it's engraved on your brain. You never forget it, and very few people can write that way, and certainly, very few political thinkers can write that way. And when they do, they tend, in fact, to rise head and shoulders above their contemporaries.

There was another image of man current in this period, and it was similarly embattled, but ultimately more hopeful than Hobbes. I mean Hobbes is pessimistic, but there is an optimistic version of the response to the Civil War. And that view was current among the Puritans and was given literary expression by the greatest Puritan writer in English, John Bunyan.

Bunyan's dates are 1628 to 1688. Bunyan was born in Bedford, in the working class of that small town, which is located in the midlands of England. He was largely self-educated. Specifically, he was steeped in the Bible and Puritan polemic. There are those that think there's only one book that he ever read, which was the Geneva Bible, which, in fact, is Tyndale, who we talked about before. In fact, there is a direct link, I think, between Tyndale and Bunyan, which one could investigate, had one time.

Like many of his class, the pulpit was Bunyan's university, and preachers were his teachers. And as I say, Tyndale's influence through the Geneva Bible was immensely strong on him. Now, Bunyan espoused a militant Protestantism. It was Protestantism which believed in the Christian soldier, not, in fact, passive suffering. Religion, in Bunyan's view of life, involved battle. He was, as I say, a Christian soldier, forever marching as to war, and literally he served in Cromwell's Roundhead parliamentary army. He carried a musket.

And he recalls his service in the spiritual journal, *Grace Abounding*. The Puritans believed in the exercise of looking into themselves and writing journals so that they could understand the state of their own soul, the state of their own salvation.

In adult life, Bunyan became convinced that he was saved, that he, in fact, John Bunyan, was one of God's elect. And this, in fact, was the strongest conviction of his life, that he would go to heaven because God wanted him to go to heaven. Not necessarily because he was a good man, but because, in fact, that's what God had decided.

From 1655, Bunyan spoke to congregations, one can hardly say that he preached, but he spoke to congregations as a kind of Baptist. And there's a lot of schismatism, breaking up of even Puritanism in this period, and, for instance, Bunyan loathed Quakers. He loathed them almost as much as he loathed royalists, but it's very, very hard, I mean there was more and more, as it were, sort of internal fighting in the Puritan movement, one of the things which brought it down at the end of the century.

As has been said, Bunyan believed in election. That is, he believed he'd been pre-selected by God, and it wasn't works which would be his royal road to salvation. God, in Bunyan's view of the universe, had already decided in his grand plan who would join him in the eternity of celestial reward. So this, in fact, conviction that he had been saved was what sustained him because there were, as it happened, very few rewards for Bunyan on earth. His life was an extremely hard one.

In 1660, with the return of the new King Charles, Charles II, from France and the downfall of the Commonweal, Bunyan was imprisoned for preaching without a license. There was a general amnesty, but he was too much of a fighter to submit to the king, and so he continued preaching, and preaching against authority.

Restoration Puritans like Bunyan, those, in fact, who would not wear the yoke, would have a very hard time of it for years to come unless they conformed. Not a huge degree of conformity was required. They wouldn't be burned at the stake, but they had, to some extent, not to cause too many waves. But Bunyan, as I say, was not of that mind. For men of conviction like him, conformity meant damnation, or more importantly, it meant going against God's ordinance. He wouldn't do it.

And Bunyan spent 12 years in prison, as what we would call a prisoner of conscience. He hadn't done anything wrong. He was in prison because of what he believed, and his conviction, his belief that he had to pass on to others the nature of his belief. And it was in Bedford prison, suffering for his faith, that he wrote *The Pilgrim's Progress*.

The Pilgrim's Progress was eventually published in two parts, and it came out in the late 1670s. And it went on to become the most perennially popular work in prose fiction in the English language. With the Bible and Foxe's *Book of Martyrs*, which, in fact, is a catalog of people who've suffered for their faith, it would take its place on the mantelpiece of every respectable lower class family for generations, for centuries.

It still sells. It's still a best-seller. Children learned to read from *The Pilgrim's Progress*. Their elders consoled themselves with the message of Christian hope that *The Pilgrim's Progress* contained. Forget *The Da Vinci Code. The Pilgrim's Progress*, as I say, has been a bestseller for over 200 years, and still going strong. You'll find it in your local bookstore.

Bunyan, on his release after 12 years, was lucky not to be imprisoned again. The man just couldn't be stopped from preaching. Of course, we can be very grateful for that because, in fact, had he not had that kind of obstinacy, we wouldn't have *The Pilgrim's Progress*. But that, in fact, if you like, is a byproduct of the misery of his life.

Now, the full title of Bunyan's great work is: *The Pilgrim's Progress FROM THIS WORLD TO That which is to come: Delivered under the Similitude of a DREAM Wherein is Discovered, The manner of his setting out, His Dangerous Journey; And safe Arrival at the Desired Countrey.*

Bunyan justified the imaginative aspect of his allegorical work—Puritans, incidentally, were inveterately suspicious of fiction—with the epigraphic quotation from the Book of Hosea, "I have used Similitudes." Similitudes, allegory, was okay. The Bible had said so, so in fact, he could do this. He could actually create his dream world, which, in fact, is a wonderful fictional universe. He was liberated by finding this one sentence in the Bible, which said "If you want, you can write effectively what is a poetic structure, if, in fact, by so doing, you're trying to communicate religious truths."

The story of *The Pilgrim's Progress* is as well known as that of *Cinderella*. Christian leaves home and the City of Destruction, where he's lived all his life, to undertake a long journey to the Celestial City. And he's been inspired to take this journey by a book, the book of books, in fact, the Bible, which he can now read himself. It's now in English. If it had been still in Latin, of course, he would have had a hard time of it.

Christian's journey is the harder because of a burden on his back, which is sin, the old Adam, which Christian can never slough off until he gets to the Celestial City. He undergoes various trials. He's, at best, one of a tiny minority. There aren't many people of his kind around, he discovers, as he journeys through the world. The majority of sinful mankind, as the Puritans unkindly believed, was destined for inevitable damnation. Christian is one of a very few brands who will be saved from the burning.

He undergoes trials and ordeals. He has to pass through the Slough of Despond, what we would call depression:

> This miry [place] is such a place as cannot be mended: it is the descent whither the scum and filth that attends conviction for sin doth continually run, and therefore it is called the Slough of Despond.

It's one of the finest descriptions I know of the condition of melancholy or depression.

There's the Hill of Difficulty, the Valley of Humiliation, and the Valley of the Shadow of Death, Doubting Castle. Now, Christian is accompanied on his pilgrimage by his friend Faithful to the city, Vanity Fair, which is London, where Faithful is put on trial and executed as a martyr. Faithful dies, faithfully, and thus takes a short cut to the Celestial City. It's very hard, but he gets there. He takes the high road, or the low road, and gets there before Christian.

Christian plods on, with his new companion, Hopeful. And after many trials, the two pilgrims cross the River of Death to Mount Zion and the Celestial City. It is Hope who keeps Christian going during the most dispiriting periods of their journey. And once they arrive at the heavenly destination, their burdensome packs drop away. In fact, they are free of sin.

The second part, dealing with Christiana, Christian's wife, is a parallel story of trial, ordeal and salvation. There are no passengers on this journey. Everyone must save themselves, even wives, husbands and children.

Bunyan's allegory, as even my brief summary will have revealed, is mechanical and, compared to Spenser, for example, primitive, but the texture of the prose, nourished by vernacular English and the Geneva Bible, is pure as crystal.

Let me give a taste of what I'm talking about. It's the very opening, Christian's flight from the City of Destruction: "As I walk'd through the wilderness of this world," says the narrator,

> I lighted on a certain place, where was a Denn; And I laid me down in that place to sleep: And as I slept I dreamed a Dream. I dreamed, and behold I saw a Man cloathed with Raggs, standing in a certain place, with his face from his own House, a Book in his hand, and a great burden upon his Back. I looked and saw him open the Book, and Read therein; and as he read, he wept and trembled: and not being able longer to contain, he brake out with a lamentable cry; saying, what shall I do?

And what Christian decides to do is that he must, at this primal moment in his life, save himself. He duly goes home and tells his wife, their city, and they with it, are doomed. You know, they're all going to die. It's a dark day, we assume, in the Christian household. And the dreamer sees him again, walking in the fields:

> reading in his Book, and greatly distressed in his mind; and as he read, he burst out, as he had done before, crying, What shall I do to be saved?

And enter Evangelist, who tells him by pointing to the book's contents what he must do, namely he must "fly from the wrath to come." And then the narrator goes on, how he saw in his dream the pilgrim ran:

> from his own door [and] his Wife and Children perceiving it, began to cry after him … but the Man put his fingers in his Ears, and ran on crying, Life, life, Eternal Life: so he looked not behind him, but fled towards the middle of the Plain.

As I said before, everyone has to find their own salvation. There are no passengers. They can't even take their loved ones with them. They had to abandon them. And what will guide them to salvation? A book will guide them. It's by reading that one will be saved, and this concept furnishes one of the very greatest books in the English language: of course, *The Pilgrim's Progress*. And it is, in fact, a work of great language. It's extraordinary what you can do with just the Bible and your own sort of native tongue.

As they used to say on *Monty Python*, now for something completely different. John Wilmot, Earl of Rochester, dates 1647 to 1680, the most depraved poet in all of English literature, and he was active and writing while Bunyan was in prison, but he was one of the royal court. He, in fact, had friends in high places and was himself a very top person. And he was legendarily debauched, and his writings reflect that.

Among the more repeatable of Rochester's libertine poems is that which is entitled "To His Mistress." So on one side, you've got the Puritans and on the other side, you've got the libertines. And the Puritans believe in repressing the flesh, and the libertines believe in expressing it. This, in fact, is Rochester's poem. As I say, a lot of his poetry is wholly unrepeatable in decent company.

WHY dost thou shade thy lovely face? O why
Does that eclipsing hand of thine deny
The sunshine of the Sun's enlivening eye?

Without thy light what light remains in me?
Thou art my life; my way, my light 's in thee;
I live, I move, and by thy beams I see.

Thou art my life—if thou but turn away
My life 's a thousand deaths. Thou art my way—
Without thee, Love, I travel not but stray.

It is, needless to say, religious imagery which is used for starkly irreligious ends. Rochester's salvation is not the Celestial City, but the fornicator's bed. And he goes on:

Thou art the pilgrim's path, the blind man's eye,
The dead man's life. On thee my hopes rely:
If I but them remove, I surely die.

It's a very different kind of pilgrimage which is indicated here from Bunyan's. Rochester, a libertine poet, wrote very obscene works. Even by the standards of a free-speaking time, they're outrageous. One of his more infamous works is called *Sodom*, and it gets worse after that.

Looking at the Puritan and the libertine literature produced simultaneously at this period, thinking of it in bipolar terms with Bunyan on one side and the Earl of Rochester on the other, it's safe to say that never has English society been as bifurcated, as split as it was in the Restoration period. After the historically brief experiment with republicanism and the Commonweal, the court returned from France, willfully intending to annoy and affront the Puritans who had killed their king's father. And this effrontery reached its highest pitch in Restoration comedy. We'll talk more about that when we come to Aphra Behn, a couple of lectures on. But just for the moment, think of the merry monarch, Charles II, going into the theater, seeing a play, perhaps Wycherley's *The Country Wife*, or that new play by Congreve, *The*

Way of the World. And the saucy orange girl, Nell Gwynn, and her sly jest "Oranges, sir, are not the only fruit." Of course, she becomes his mistress.

As I say, we've got dramatists like Congreve, Wycherley, Etherege, who deliberately affront Puritanism and middle class sensibility with witty depictions of cuckoldry, sort of husbands whose wives are unfaithful to them, aggressively and self-righteously, seduction, lordly indifference to common morality. They're above that kind of thing.

The excesses led to a virtual extinction of the drama. The Puritans and the middle classes would win. They eventually sort of combined and they had the numbers and the tide of history on their side. And the English theater would be a casualty of the Puritan victory for at least 200 years. All that changes with what I mentioned earlier, the bloodless revolution which brought William and Anne to the throne. This was a crucial event for literature and for drama. Writers like Rochester, like Wycherley, like Congreve henceforth would actually be reined in, or at least they wouldn't really have an arena in which to perform. Monarchs who embodied middle class virtue, Protestantism and parliamentary democracy: these were what William and Anne represented. They brought with them a new ethos, a new, as it were, sense of what England should be, and it was a very stable England that they inaugurated, that they put in motion.

Dryden, who was the poet laureate, wrote in 1700, and he looks back at those tumultuous years which I've been talking about in this lecture, and he reviews what had gone on from 1640 to 1700. He's writing at the dawn of a new century, and he says:

> Thy wars brought nothing about;
> Thy lovers were all untrue.

And then this wonderful couplet:

> 'Tis well an old age is out,
> And time to begin a new.

And we'll be looking at that new age in the next lecture.

The Augustans—Order, Decorum, and Wit
Lecture 14

> There is a distinctive mood which settles over English literature and the
> cultivated elite which creates literature in the 18th century. Critics have
> called that mood the "peace of the Augustans." ... The country was now
> prosperous and it could see itself, interestingly, as the leader of Europe
> in commerce, in science, and in international diplomacy.

Under Marlborough, the brilliant general who took the British army into mainland Europe, Britain would establish itself as a major military power. Of course, the navy was more important than the army. As James Thomson's 18th-century anthem put it, Britannia ruled the waves. The Hanoverian dynasty, the German monarchs who were now on the throne of England, created a strong Protestant leadership at the top of society.

Literature in this period was moving inexorably toward cultivation and civilization. The aspiration was to match the great cultural achievements of Rome under Augustus, which is why writers called themselves Augustans. Literature, it was believed, should be polished and should reflect the values of the great emerging British civilization.

Old English masters, such as Chaucer and Shakespeare, were polished into 18th-century styles of correctness. John Dryden's *All for Love*, for example, attempted to improve upon Shakespeare's *Antony and Cleopatra*. Shakespeare gives to Enobarbus, a minor character, a speech describing the beauty of Cleopatra as she sails down the Nile. The poetry is rich but still conversational and sinewy. Dryden's version of the same speech is cool, correct, and in comparison to Shakespeare's, anemic.

The English Augustans loved rules, order, and decorum. It's no accident that Samuel Johnson's great dictionary was produced in this century, when organization was paramount. In architecture, Sir Christopher Wren built huge Neoclassical structures after the Great Fire of London. Chastity of design, purity of form, and reverence for style were the orders of the day.

The theater still enjoyed royal patronage, but it was strictly licensed. Words on the page dominated the world of literature, and one literary genre dominated all others: satire.

In poetry, one small component dominated: the heroic couplet. Unlike blank verse, invented earlier by Marlowe, the heroic couplet rhymes. This form had been brought back by the court literati from France after the Restoration, modified with 10 feet (syllables), not 12. The strong, or masculine, final rhyme syllable in a couplet creates closure, as we hear in the first two lines of Samuel Johnson's poem "The Vanity of Human Wishes": "Let observation with extensive view / Survey mankind from China to Peru." Another recurrent feature in the heroic couplet is the *caesura*, or cut, which creates a half-line silent pause. The heroic couplet lends itself to epigram and closed statements. It's not as successful with long narrative because it breaks ideas down into linear units.

In terms of diction, 18th-century poetry was addicted to *periphrasis*, which means high-sounding circumlocution. A school of fish, for example, might be a "finny tribe." At the same time, poetry and satire of this period were equally addicted to generalized abstraction. Again, think of Johnson's line "Let observation with extensive view," rather than "Let observers with extensive view."

Another quality valued by the Augustans was wit. In this period, "wit" implies knowledge or learning in its most elegant form. The poet Alexander Pope (1688–1744) gave a classic definition of wit in his treatise poem *An Essay on Criticism*: "True wit is nature to advantage drest; / Which oft was thought, but ne'er so well exprest." The poet takes what we think and makes it more polished, striking, and epigrammatic. Conversely, the Augustans detested dullness. Pope wrote a Miltonic-length mock epic against dullness that he called *The Dunciad*, the great epic of duncery, in which he attacked his personal enemies for their lack of wit.

A smaller, equally effective squib on dullness was penned by John Dryden (1631–1700). Dryden was, for entirely personal reasons, antagonistic toward one of his fellow poets laureate, Thomas Shadwell. Dryden tended to be flexible about such issues as Catholicism, shifting with the winds of change and producing poems for whatever party seemed to be in power. Shadwell had satirized Dryden for his much-turned coat.

Such satire was dangerous, however, because Dryden was an infinitely greater poet. He turned the tables on Shadwell with a poem that pictures a mock coronation in which Shadwell succeeds as king of dullness Richard Flecknoe, an obscure poet of significant dullness himself. Dryden's poem embodies an appeal to Classical Augustan standards, a genuflection to wit, and a satirical ad hominem venom in its wonderful final couplet: "The rest to some faint meaning make pretence, / But Shadwell never deviates into sense."

The English Augustans loved rules, order, and decorum. It's no accident that Samuel Johnson's great dictionary was produced in this century, when organization was paramount.

Even more masterful than Dryden with the couplet and in personal satire was Alexander Pope. Pope was afflicted by bodily disfigurement, and his life, as he put it in one of his verse epistles, was "one long disease." Enemies loved to portray him as a hunchback, dwarfish ape. He was born and brought up Catholic, which exacerbated his sense of being on the edge of his world, never able to join elegant society. He was educated at home because he was too frail to go to school or university. He was, however, precocious, and wrote exquisitely accomplished verse in his early teens.

Although his life was short, Pope's works were long and many. His corpus includes bestselling translations in couplets of Homer and Vergil; an edition of Shakespeare; and philosophical treatises, some written in verse, such as the *Essay on Man* and *Essay on Criticism*, all of them in couplets. His works were extremely popular with an increasingly literate public, but it is his satires that have preserved his name as, arguably, the greatest poet of the 18th century.

Lighter in touch and more representative of Pope's genius than the two versions of *The Dunciad* is his mock epic *The Rape of the Lock* (1714). The poem revolves around a petty quarrel in English upper-class life. In a country house, Ingatestone Hall in Essex, a beau had cut a lock of hair from the head of a belle without her permission, creating a huge fuss between the two families, both, incidentally, Catholic. Pope satirized the pettiness of the quarrel by casting the event in a mock heroic mold, but he did it so diplomatically that the satire served to heal the rift between these two warring families. Pope describes for us Belinda (known in life as Arabella Fermor), whose locks will be ravished. She is a somewhat featherbrained beauty, but she is described in Pope's poem as if she were a Homeric goddess. Underlying the apparent tribute to this paragon of beauty is a subversive note of criticism, an element of bathos. The reference to "patches" among Belinda's cosmetics, for example, implies that she might use these faux beauty marks to cover syphilitic sores. It leads us to wonder if her love letters are of equal importance to her scriptures.

The kind of satire and heroic couplet that Pope specialized in was called Horatian after the Augustan-era poet Horace. Horatian satire is conversational and relaxed in tone; it flows effortlessly off the page.

Another variety of satire popular in the period was called Juvenalian after the post-Augustan poet Juvenal. This satire, although still decorous, is harsher, more moralistic, and angrier than Horatian satire. The master of the Juvenalian genre was Samuel Johnson (1709–1784), and his masterpiece was *The Vanity of Human Wishes*, an imitation of Juvenal's 10th *Satire*.

Following his Classical model, in *The Vanity of Human Wishes* Johnson surveys human greatness in all its multiple examples, illustrating the fact that, inevitably, any triumph always ends in decay and disappointment. Interestingly, Johnson turns the satire in this poem on himself, the scholar who spent decades laboring on the first dictionary in English. Johnson had worked his way through university, toiled for years to produce his monumental work, and finally, it was dust in his mouth. Johnson gives us a long list of obstacles that opposes scholarship, and if one manages to surmount these, the scholar's life is summed up as "Toil, Envy, Want, the

Patron, and the Jail." Johnson had a bad time with patrons, particularly during his 20 years of hard labor on the dictionary. Lord Chesterfield refused the obscure dictionary-maker's help at the beginning of his project but later, after Johnson was already famous, offered assistance in return for a flattering dedication. Johnson retorted with a magnificently contemptuous refusal.

Surprisingly, *The Vanity of Human Wishes* is not, ultimately, a depressing poem. Johnson's Christian stoicism—the idea of putting up with one's lot in life—comes through in the poem, and indeed, echoes of this doctrine can be found in Juvenal's original. But in the climax of his poem, Johnson turns away from Juvenal's pagan nihilism to Christian acceptance. It is the divine plan, he suggests, that our great achievements in life should end in failure. We would do well to take Johnson's message to heart. However much we love to read literature, we should not forget also to live.

In reading Johnson, we admire his facility with words, but we also feel that enshrined in his poetry is a truth. We read literature to be entertained and, perhaps, because we hope that we will be better people for having read it. ∎

Essential Reading

Dryden, *John Dryden: The Major Works*.

Ferguson, Salter, and Stallworthy, eds., *The Norton Anthology of Poetry*.

Mack, *Alexander Pope*.

Nokes, *Raillery and Rage*.

Pope, *The Poems of Alexander Pope: A Reduced Version of the Twickenham Text*.

Richetti, ed., *The Cambridge History of English Literature, 1660–1780*.

Rogers, *The Alexander Pope Encyclopedia*.

———, ed., *The Cambridge Companion to Alexander Pope*.

Zwicker, ed., *The Cambridge Companion to John Dryden*.

1. The English Augustans aimed at "polish" and "refinement" in their verse. Did they go too far?

2. Which of the Classical styles suited English genius best—Horatian or Juvenalian?

The Augustans—Order, Decorum, and Wit
Lecture 14—Transcript

There is a distinctive mood which settles over English literature and the cultivated elite which creates literature in the 18th century. Critics have called that mood the "peace of the Augustans." England, but not Europe, alas, was, if not quite at peace, no longer in a condition of civil war, that Hobbesian condition, "war of all against all," in which life is "nasty, brutish, and short."

The country was now prosperous and it could see itself, interestingly, as the leader of Europe in commerce, in science, and in international diplomacy. Under Marlborough, the brilliant general who took Britain into mainland Europe and won battles, Britain would establish itself as a major military power. Blenheim Castle, a jewel of Neoclassical architecture, would be the nation's reward to its great commander, in fact, a great ancestor of Winston Churchill, as it happens.

The navy was, if anything, more important than the army. And Britannia, as James Thomson's 18th-century anthem put it, ruled the waves. And the second verse of this ultra-chauvinistic tribute to England's greatness in 1740 is still sung out on ceremonial occasions, and it still, to some extent, expresses a lot of what the British like to think about themselves.

This is how Thomson's *Rule, Britannia* goes, the second stanza:

> The nations, not so blest as thee,

Not so blessed as you, England.

> Must, in their turns, to tyrants fall;
> While thou shalt flourish great and free,
> The dread and envy of them all.

Who would not be English if they had the choice? Well, that's what they thought. And of course, there's a famous refrain to Thomson's poem, as it's put to music.

This is how it goes as poetry:

> Rule, Britannia! rule the waves:
> Britons never will be slaves.

But as it's sung out, it's:

> Rule Britannia, Britannia rule the waves
> Britons never, never, never shall be slaves.

I know that song very well. It was the regimental march of the regiment I was in in the army. But in fact, it's still sung out, as I say. It's known to every schoolchild in Britain.

The Hanoverian dynasty—in fact, these were the German monarchs who were now on the throne of England—created a strong Protestant leadership at the top of society. And in literature over this period, the grand project, what, in fact, they were moving toward inexorably, was cultivation and civilization. And the aspiration was to match the great cultural achievements of Rome under Augustus. That's why they called themselves Augustans. And that was a golden age. And Britain wanted itself to be moving toward a golden age as well, the golden age of England, if you like.

And literature, it was felt, should be polished. It should be civilized. It should reflect the values of this great civilization which was happening around them. Old English masters, such as Chaucer and even Shakespeare, were burnished, were polished into 18th-century styles of correctness. It's not to our taste at all, I think.

Let's take one example. Who now reads John Dryden's *All for Love*? What he did was to improve, to polish, Shakespeare's *Antony and Cleopatra*. Now, let me give an example of what Dryden understood by polishing, by improving, by correcting, by bringing into a new sort of mode of much more acceptable verse the rough and barbarous, but still work of genius, of Shakespeare.

I'll just take one example, which is Enobarbus's description of Cleopatra sailing down the Nile, or flowing down the Nile, coming down the Nile and how beautiful she looked at the time. It's very typical of Shakespeare, incidentally, something that Dryden wouldn't do, to give this speech to a minor character. It's one of the finest speeches in all the plays:

> The barge she sat in, like a burnished throne,
> Burned on the water: the poop was beaten gold;
> Purple the sails, and so perfumèd, that
> The winds were lovesick with them; the oars were silver,
> Which to the tune of flutes kept stroke, and made
> The water which they beat to follow faster,
> As amorous of their strokes. For her own person,
> It beggared all description: she did lie
> In her pavilion, cloth-of-gold of tissue,
> O'erpicturing that Venus where we see
> The fancy outwork nature. On each side her
> Stood pretty dimpled boys, like smiling Cupids,
> With divers-coloured fans, whose wind did seem
> To glow the delicate cheeks which they did cool,
> And what they undid did.

It's poetry so rich that one almost salivates on hearing it, but it's also conversational and sinewy. One hears the accents of everyday speech in it, the way in which people were talking when they left the theater.

And this is how Dryden corrects that passage in his *All for Love*, which is his rewriting of *Antony and Cleopatra*:

> Her galley down the silver Cydnus rowed,
> The tackling silk, the streamers waved with gold;
> The gentle winds were lodged in purple sails:
> Her nymphs, like Nereids, round her couch were placed;
> Where she, another sea-born Venus, lay.
> She lay, and leant her cheek upon her hand,
> And cast a look so languishingly sweet,
> As if, secure of all beholders' hearts,
> Neglecting, she could take them: boys, like Cupids,

> Stood fanning, with their painted wings, the winds
> That played about her face.

I've been very unfair to Dryden, but you'll get the point. It's cool, correct and, with the Shakespeare still ringing in our ears, anemic. It gets rid of that mind-bending paradox at the end of the Shakespeare speech about the boys' fans simultaneously heating and cooling "what they undid did" which Dryden clearly thought didn't make sense. But somehow, Dryden has missed the point of what Shakespeare was doing.

Nonetheless, I mean there were failures, but there were also huge achievements. The English Augustans loved rules. They loved order, they loved what they called decorum, and order was the greatest of the values which they aimed at. And it's no accident that the greatest dictionary, Dr. Johnson's, that we have in the English language was produced in this century. Theirs was a time when they wanted to organize everything, put everything in its place.

And architecture: after the Great Fire of London, Sir Christopher Wren was charged with rebuilding London, and he built huge structures like St. Paul's Cathedral, but it was orderly. It was a Neoclassical rebuilding that he undertook, and a Neoclassical revision was really what the Augustans were aiming at. Neoclassicism ruled. And this went with a chastity of design, a purity of form and a reverence for style.

The theater still enjoyed royal patronage, but it was, as I said in the last lecture, strictly licensed, and it declined, really. It was words on the page which dominated. And one literary genre on those pages dominated all others: satire. And, in poetry, one form, one small component above all others rides high: the heroic couplet.

Unlike blank verse, that mighty instrument which we saw Marlowe virtually invent all those years ago, the heroic couplet rhymes. And it's not intrinsically English. It had been picked up and brought back by the court literati from France after the Restoration in 1660. But unlike the French alexandrine, the heroic couplet has 10, not 12, feet or syllables.

Let me illustrate what I'm talking about because I think the ear understands the couplet better than the eye. I'm going to take the first two lines of Samuel Johnson's poem, a great satire, *The Vanity of Human Wishes*.

This is how it goes:

> Let observation with extensive view
> Survey mankind from China to Peru.

You'll note or hear the strong or masculine final rhyme syllable, which creates closure: view, Peru. It clangs the couplet shut.

There's another recurrent feature in the heroic couplet, namely the *caesura* or cut, division. This creates a half line silent pause. Half lines, of course, take us right the way back to *Beowulf*, though we won't go there just at the moment.

> Let observation with extensive view
> Survey mankind from China to Peru.

The heroic couplet lends itself to epigram and closed statements. It's not as successful with long narrative because it breaks everything down into these small line briquets. The couplet, in fact, tends to disintegrate along narrative, unlike blank verse. I don't think you could have written *Paradise Lost* in couplets. It wouldn't work.

In terms of diction, that's the choice of words, poetry of the 18th century is addicted to *periphrasis*. What that means is high-sounding circumlocution. You want to talk about fish and you don't say fish. That's a common word. They use that in the marketplace. You talk about the "finny tribe." And at the same time, poetry, satire of this period, is equally addicted to generalized abstraction. You'll notice, to go back to those lines of Johnson which I quoted, the use of observation rather than observers in "Let observation with extensive view." It would scan as well if you said "Let observers with extensive view" but Johnson wanted to abstract and generalize.

The heroic couplet was, as Lytton Strachey later put it, the Augustans' "criticism of life." It incarnated on the page in words their ideal of order. A quality which the Augustans most valued in writing their work, getting it out, was wit. "Wit" is a three-letter word of infinite complexity. It implies knowledge or learning in its most elegant form, or at least it does at this period. And Alexander Pope, the poet, gave a classic definition, among many others, in his treatise poem, *An Essay on Criticism*.

And what he said was:

> True wit is nature to advantage drest,

The next line will strike you as very familiar because you've heard it:

> Which oft was thought, but ne'er so well exprest.

"Yes," we think, "yeah, those are my thoughts exactly, but I could never have put it quite as succinctly or as brilliantly as the poet does." That's wit. He takes what we think, or she takes what we think, and makes it more polished, makes it more striking, makes it more epigrammatic.

Conversely, what the Augustans most detested was dullness, which is kind of wit on its day off, the other side of wit. Alexander Pope, arguably the wittiest of them all, wrote a Miltonic-length mock epic against dullness, which he called *The Dunciad*, the great epic of duncery—attacking personal enemies, and always labeling them for their incorrigible dullness, their lack of wit, the kind of wit which his work manifested so brilliantly.

A smaller, equally effective squib on dullness was penned by John Dryden, at one period the poet laureate, and who comes immediately before Pope in the great tradition of English Augustan poets. Dryden was, for entirely personal and less than admirable reasons, very antagonistic to one of his fellow rivals, Thomas Shadwell, who was another poet laureate, as it happened, like Dryden. There was an awful lot of what was called caballing and literary feuding in this period. It's very interesting to us and it enlivened their lives as well.

And the issue between Shadwell and Dryden was essentially political. Dryden was very flexible about such things as Catholicism, and he shifted with every wind of change, producing poems for whatever party it was prudent to ally himself with. Shadwell had satirized him for his much turned coat. He thought that Dryden, in fact, was just a fair-weather friend to whoever was in power. And that was a dangerous thing to do because Dryden was infinitely the greater poet, and he hit back. And the context is an obscure poet of huge dullness, Richard Flecknoe, who had just died. No one read his word.

Dryden, in his satire on Shadwell, pictures a mock coronation—coronations, of course, were a big deal at the time of the Restoration—in which Shadwell is, in succession to Richard Flecknoe, created the new king of dullness or son of Flecknoe. Mac in Scots, as you probably know, means son of, so MacFlecknoe means the son of Flecknoe. It's very unfair, but deliciously funny.

This is part of it:

> All human things are subject to decay,
> And, when Fate summons, Monarchs must obey:
> This Fleckno found, who, like Augustus, young
> Was call'd to Empire, and had govern'd long:
> In Prose and Verse, was own'd, without dispute
> Through all the Realms of Non-sense, absolute.
> This aged Prince now flourishing in Peace,
> And blest with issue of a large increase,
> Worn out with business, did at length debate
> To settle the succession of the State.
> And pond'ring which of all his Sons was fit
> To Reign, and wage immortal War with Wit;
> Cry'd, 'tis resolv'd; for Nature pleads that He
> Should onely rule, who most resembles me:
> *Shadwell* alone my perfect image bears,
> Mature in dullness from his tender years.
> Shadwell alone, of all my Sons, is he
> Who stands confirm'd in full stupidity.

The rest to some faint meaning make pretence,
But *Shadwell* never deviates into sense.

It's all there: the appeal to classical Augustan standards, the genuflection to wit, the satirical ad hominem in that wonderful final couplet, "The rest to some faint meaning make pretence, / But *Shadwell* never deviates into sense."

Shadwell, as his supporters insist to this day, was by no means a bad poet and he was a goodish playwright. He did his literary work as best he could, competently and honorably, but he will never now rise from the literary grave with Dryden's satire staked through his heart.

Even more masterful than Dryden with the couplet and in personal satire was Alexander Pope, who was born in 1688 and came on the scene about 20 years after Dryden. Pope's background was very unusual. He was afflicted by bodily disfigurement. Enemies loved to portray him as a hunchback or a round-shouldered, dwarfish ape. And his life was, as he put it in one of his verse epistles, "one long disease." He suffered.

He was born and brought up Catholic, which exacerbated his sense of being on the edge of his world, able to see it and comment on it, but never quite to join it, and never, of course, to be an elegant member of society, handicapped as he was. He was educated at home. He was too frail to go to school or university. And he was very precocious and was writing exquisitely accomplished verse in his early teens. He "lisped," as he said, in his cradle.

His life was short, but his works were long and many. And Pope's work makes up a huge corpus, including bestselling translations in couplets of Homer and Vergil, an edition of Shakespeare, and also philosophical treatises, such as the essays, which includes philosophical treatises in verse, such as the *Essay on Man* and *Essay on Criticism*, all of them in couplets. He is the master of the couplet.

His works were hugely popular with an increasingly literate reading public, and Pope is often regarded, with Johnson, as the first purely professional writer in England, one, that is, who could live off sales, not patronage. He didn't require great rich people to help him on his way. His readers were enough. It's Pope's satires which have preserved his name as, arguably, the greatest poet of his century, the 18th century.

I mentioned the two *Dunciads*, but lighter in touch and more representative, I think, of his genius, is the mock epic *The Rape of the Lock*. It was published in 1714 and it revolves around a tiny episode in English upper-class life. Mainland Europe at the time, incidentally, was in flames, but as I say, the Augustans had their peace.

It's hard to think of a more petty quarrel than *The Rape of the Lock* deals with. In a country house, Ingatestone Hall in Essex, a beau had cut a lock of hair from the head of a belle without her permission. It created a huge fuss between the respective families. Both, incidentally, were old Catholic families. Pope satirized the pettiness of the quarrel by casting the event in a mock heroic mould with great Homeric epic machinery, but he did it so diplomatically that the satire did not wound. And, in fact, *The Rape of the Lock* served to heal the rift between these two warring families.

The following is the famous description of Belinda, she whose locks will be ravished. She was called Arabella Fermor in real life, and she's preparing her morning toilette, putting on her makeup, as we would say. Now, she's a somewhat featherbrained beauty, a kind of leading figure, a leading beauty in the contemporary *monde*, but she's described in Pope's poem as if she were a Homeric goddess, girding herself, assisted not by maidservants, but nymphs and priestesses.

> And now, unveil'd, the Toilet stands display'd,
> Each silver Vase in mystic order laid.
> First, rob'd in white, the Nymph intent adores,
> With head uncover'd, the Cosmetic pow'rs.
> A heav'nly image in the glass appears,
> To that she bends, to that her eyes she rears;
> Th' inferior Priestess, at her altar's side,
> Trembling begins the sacred rites of Pride.

And so it goes on, describing the objects on Belinda's dressing table.

> Here files of pins extend their shining rows,
> Puffs, Powders, Patches, Bibles, Billets-doux.

The maids do their duty with Belinda's coiffure, the last cosmetic act before she enters the world, the morn, before showing herself off for her admirers.

> The busy Sylphs surround their darling care,
> These set the head, and those divide the hair,

Notice how cleverly Pope uses the *caesura* here, dividing the two functions with the division of the line.

> Some fold the sleeve, whilst others plait the gown:
> And Betty's prais'd for labours not her own.

Underlying the apparent tribute to this paragon of beauty, there's a subversive note of criticism. It's what they called at that time bathos or clash, that's to say, something which doesn't sound quite right. Consider that line "Puffs, Powders, Patches, Bibles, Billet-doux." Are such cosmetic trifles as "patches"—those are black beauty spots, black stickers on the face. Some say they were there to mask syphilitic sores. That's why they became fashionable—and *billet-doux* which are love letters: are they of equal importance with Bibles? It's not entirely flattering, but so charmingly done, so light-handedly that who, even Belinda, Arabella, could resent it?

The kind of satire and heroic couplet which Pope specialized in was called Horatian after the Latin poet Horace, the great Augustan. Horatian Satire, as I hope has been evident, is conversational and relaxed in tone. It flows effortlessly off the page. And Pope was, of course, famously fluent. I mean he seems just to have been able to actually turn out this elegant verse as easily as other people could actually converse.

There was another kind of satire, another variety of satire popular in the period, which is called Juvenalian after the post-Augustan poet, Juvenal. It's harsher, more moralistic and angrier, though it's still very decorous. It's still within the rules which the Augustans laid down for themselves.

In Juvenalian satire, we hear not civilized conversation, but the voice of the preacher talking down to the congregation. And the master of the Juvenalian genre is Samuel Johnson, and his masterpiece is called *The Vanity of Human Wishes*. It's an imitation, very key word at this period, of Juvenal's 10th *Satire*. That's to say, he's doing a Juvenal.

Effectively, what Johnson does, following his great classical model, is to survey human greatness in all its multiple examples, and show how, inevitably, any triumph always ends in decay and disappointment. "Vanity of vanities, all is vanity saith the preacher." And so saith Dr. Johnson as well. "All careers," said the English politician Enoch Powell, "end badly." And so too it is with Johnson. His examples, which are multiple in the poem, display the fact or demonstrate the fact that no human achievement can, as it were, survive the corrosive blast of time.

What is fascinating in this poem is how Johnson turns the satire on himself, the scholar who spent decades laboring on the first great dictionary in English. What for? Samuel Johnson had worked his way through university, toiled for years and produced his monumental work, and finally, it was dust in his mouth.

Let Johnson himself speak of the hardship of being a scholar. And I think anyone who's educated, and all of us are, in a sense, nowadays, will feel the truth of what he's saying:

> When first the College Rolls receive his Name,

That's the aspirant scholar.

> The young Enthusiast quits his Ease for Fame;
> Resistless burns the Fever of Renown,
> Caught from the strong Contagion of the Gown;

He wants, in fact, to graduate from Oxford.

> O'er Bodley's Dome his future Labours spread,
> And Bacon's Mansion trembles o'er his Head;

He walked round Oxford and sees the buildings in which these previous
great scholars have worked.

> Are these thy Views? proceed, illustrious Youth,
> And Virtue guard thee to the Throne of Truth,
> Yet should thy Soul indulge the gen'rous Heat,
> Till captive Science yields her last Retreat;

If, in fact, you make it there.

> Should Reason guide thee with her brightest Ray,

This is the list of things which, sort of, oppose scholarship.

> And pour on misty Doubts resistless Day;
> Should no false Kindness lure to loose Delight,
> Nor praise relax, nor Difficulty fright;
> Should tempting Novelty thy cell refrain,
> And Sloth's bland Opiates shed their Fumes in vain;

I love that, "Sloth's bland Opiates shed their Fumes in vain;"

> Should Beauty blunt on Fops her fatal Dart,
> Nor claim the Triumph of a letter'd Heart;

You won't have any time for sex, believe me.

> Should no Disease thy torpid Veins invade,
> Nor Melancholy's Phantoms haunt thy Shade;
> Yet hope not Life from Grief or Danger free,
> Nor think the Doom of Man revers'd for thee:
> Deign on the passing World to turne thine Eyes,

And pause awhile from Letters to be wise;
There mark what Ills the Scholar's Life assail,
Toil, Envy, Want, the Patron, and the Jail.

Originally, that last line read "Toil, Envy, Want, the Garret, and the Jail." But Johnson had a very bad time with patrons, particularly so during his 20 years' hard labor on the dictionary, and in the dictionary, Johnson exacts some small revenge by defining a patron as "Commonly a wretch who supports with indolence, and is paid with flattery."

Lord Chesterfield, whose letters on manners to his son are a minor classic of the Augustan period, haughtily refused the obscure dictionary-maker help at the beginning of his project:

> But My Lord [Chesterfield] intimated, as it [the dictionary] reached its glorious conclusion [and Johnson was now a famous man], that he [Chesterfield] might, after all, indeed be minded to help with a few hundred pounds: in return, of course, for a flattering dedication in the Dictionary.

Johnson retorted with a magnificently contemptuous refusal:

> Is not a Patron, my Lord, one who looks with unconcern on a man struggling for life in the water, and, when he has reached ground, encumbers him with help? The notice which you have been pleased to take of my labours, had it been early, had it been kind; but it has been delayed till I am indifferent, and cannot enjoy it: till I am solitary, and cannot impart it; till I am known, and do not want it.

And he ends "Your Lordship's most humble, Most obedient servant, Sam. Johnson." And that he certainly wasn't. Now, the letter has a larger significance. The writer need truckle no more. He no longer needed patrons, those damned "wretches" who had oppressed literary genius for centuries. The public would henceforth support the man of letters' literary endeavors.

So is *The Vanity of Human Wishes* finally a depressing poem? Surprisingly, it isn't. Consider the passage above and the line "pause awhile from Letters to be wise": now, letters here, of course, means literature. What does being wise mean, as Johnson understands it? It means Christian stoicism, putting up with our lot, a doctrine, in fact, which one can find echoed in Juvenal, the original of *The Vanity of Human Wishes*.

Life, as Johnson saw it, was a condition in which, as he said, much was to be endured and little enjoyed. But in the climax of his poem, he turns away from Juvenal's pagan nihilism to Christian acceptance. It is the divine plan, he suggests, that our great achievements in life should end in failure. And Johnson's, I think, is a message which we ourselves would do well to take to heart. However much we love literature, we should pause awhile and ask ourselves: reading is good, but let us not forget also to live. Is that not good as well? And is not living well better than reading well?

Johnson, I would suggest, does that most difficult of things in literature. We admire what he's doing with words, we admire what he's doing with poetry, but at the same time, we feel that enshrined in what he's doing is a truth. That is to say, why do we read literature? Well, we read literature to be entertained. We read literature, in fact, to learn things.

But I think if we're really honest with ourselves, if we do a kind of spiritual introspection of the kind the Puritans loved, we say that we read literature because we do hope that we will be better people for having read it. We do hope not just to learn tricks, not just to learn how to actually sort of impress people and perhaps even to get degrees, think of the scholar's life, "the Fever of Renown," "the strong Contagion of the Gown;"—we don't do it necessarily for that, though that, in fact, is one of the kind of incidental rewards. We do it because, in fact, we want to be good. We want to be better. We want, in fact, to fulfill ourselves.

Whether or not you agree with Johnson, and not everyone will,—I think probably there is a slight temperamental melancholy or depression in his view of life;—nonetheless, it seems to me that this great poet does, if taken on board in the spirit in which he intends us to take it on board, in fact, makes us, or at least I speak for myself, hope that we are a better person. It's great poetry.

Swift—Anger and Satire
Lecture 15

> In the last lecture, we looked at how English poetry refined itself in the 18th century. ... But English prose, as much as English verse, cultivates itself ... during this Augustan period. ... One great satirist became the wielder of the sharpest and most savage satire in the English language, and he [Jonathan Swift] dominates all others.

In this lecture, we'll see that English prose, as much as verse, also cultivated itself during the Augustan period. We find, in this period, a new generation of essayists, who are writing what we would now call higher journalism for magazines. These essays were also composed in a language more cultivated than ever before. They were often addressed to the woman reader, and the presence of women raised the tone of literature. Addison and Steele, in *The Spectator* magazine, introduced a new civilized voice into the already many-voiced English literature.

In the 18th century, we also find one great and excoriating satirist—Jonathan Swift (1667–1745). When we read Swift, we forget good manners and cultivation. Anger seethes underneath his pure and sublimely simple prose. Swift held up a model of plain writing that has been followed by innumerable disciplines, notably, the great 20th-century writer George Orwell.

Swift can claim to be, among his many other achievements, the first great Irish writer in English literature. As we know, England has oppressed Ireland, and in return, Ireland has given England some of its greatest literature: Richard Sheridan, the dramatist; Oscar Wilde, the greatest wit in English literature; Bernard Shaw, arguably the greatest 20th-century dramatist; Samuel Beckett, who challenges Shaw for that title; and the Nobel laureate, Seamus Heaney.

Swift was born in Dublin seven months after the death of his father. He was a Protestant in a predominantly Catholic country and a member of the Ascendancy, that is, one of the privileged class who were supported by the English to run their colonial property, Ireland. The oppression of Ireland was at its most intense during the period when Swift was there.

Swift received his higher education at Trinity College in Dublin. He excelled at university and might well have become a university teacher, but the Revolution of 1688 and the importation of William and Mary to the throne of England forced him to come to the mother country if he wanted to get ahead in the world.

In England, Swift became a secretary to a nobleman and a diplomat, Sir William Temple. Through Temple, Swift was introduced to the court and given access to the king. During his three years of service with Temple, Swift became politicized.

During this same period, Swift was closely involved with one of the two women in his life, to whom he would give the pseudonyms Stella and Vanessa. He also, at this time, began to show signs of the mental illness that would, in late middle life, spiral into full-blown madness.

In the meantime, Swift earned a doctorate from Trinity College and became an ordained priest in the Church of Ireland. He was given a series of parishes and enjoyed a comfortable income. Swift was bitterly disappointed, however, that he didn't receive more patronage from the court, and this disappointment stoked his anger. Around the turn of the century, his serious writing career began, nurtured by that anger.

On various trips to England, Swift formed a friendship with Alexander Pope, and together, they founded, in 1713, the Scriblerus Club. The members vied with one another to see who could write the wittiest satires. It was in the context of the Scriblerus Club that *Gulliver's Travels* found its genesis.

Swift was always, unlike Pope, the most political of the 18th-century satirists. As the battles between the Whigs and the Tories (liberals and conservatives) evolved, he fired off pamphlets from a radical Tory position. Swift's services to the Tory party did not bring him the rewards he craved. Queen Anne didn't like him, and the best position his friends at court could secure for him was the deanery of Saint Patrick's in Dublin. As the Whigs came into ascendancy, Swift returned to Ireland, to live, as he said, "like a rat in a hole." From Dublin, he fired off the most powerful of his pamphlets demanding justice for Ireland. The most famous of these pamphlets is *A Modest Proposal* (1729).

The pamphlet is written in the persona of an English economist, who is imbued with the rational principles of Adam Smith and free enterprise. This social scientist has turned his mind to the perennial problems of Ireland—hunger and overpopulation—and come up with an ingenious solution: state-sponsored cannibalism. Swift's anger bleeds through in his detailed plan for breeding Irish children and selling one-year-olds as meat "at an entertainment for friends; and when the family dines alone. ..." We are horrified by the proposal, but we also find it funny. Satire was never more powerfully relevant to man's inhumanity to man.

> **Where, then, is the satire in the fourth book of *Gulliver's Travels* going? ... The satire is unstable in the fourth book. Although the book is very powerful, we can't seem to organize our response to it.**

Around the 1720s, Swift began putting into shape the work for which he is most well known, *Gulliver's Travels*. After the death of Stella, one of the pseudonymized women in his life, Swift became increasingly melancholy and began to show clear signs of madness. In 1742, he appears to have suffered a stroke, losing the ability to speak and realizing his fears of becoming mentally disabled. At his death, his fortune was left to found a hospital for the mentally ill. In the 1720s, however, working on *Gulliver's Travels*, Swift gave the book a great pseudo-authenticity. In fact, the original readers were fooled, at least for the first few pages, into thinking that they were reading an actual account of exotic travels.

Gulliver's Travels encompasses four books, or voyages, the first of which is to Lilliput, where the people are tiny. Here, Swift satirizes the court around Queen Anne. Despite their size, the characters fondly imagine themselves to be people of consequence. The second book takes Lemuel Gulliver to Brobdingnag. Here, the inhabitants are rural giants, and the hero himself is doll-sized. Brobdingnag is the most pleasant of the imaginary countries created by Swift, who hated progress, because it is the most traditional. In the third book, Gulliver travels to Laputa (Spanish for "whore"), a scientific utopia. We should note that Swift also loathed science, which he thought contrary to religion and unnecessary. Here, he pictures the advanced scientific thinkers of his age as geeks, laboring, for example, to extract sunbeams from cucumbers. The third book also contains the Struldbrugs, who live forever and decay forever, suffering an eternity of pain and mental infirmity as they fall to pieces but cannot die.

The fourth book takes Gulliver to Houyhnhnm Land, the pronunciation of which represents the neighing of a horse. Here, the rulers are horses, and *Homo sapiens* are horrific apes. In this final book, Lemuel Gulliver seems to go mad; his madness takes the form of believing that the horse people are wholly admirable and his own species, the Yahoos, as they're called, are nauseatingly disgusting. The narrative of Book IV begins with Gulliver, the captain of his vessel, cast adrift by his men. This is an important detail because it indicates the cruelty of man to man. Gulliver sets out to find the "savages" in this strange land but will encounter, instead, a civilized species. As he walks, he notices several animals in a field, partially covered with hair and standing on their hind legs. They are able to climb trees and leap with tremendous agility, but their appearance is disagreeable, and Gulliver feels contempt toward them. The reader begins to realize, before Gulliver does, that these creatures are human beings, *Homo sapiens*, in a sense, but more along the lines of *homo excrementus*. The scene in which these animals rain feces down on Gulliver from the trees is an excremental vision of humanity.

The horses, given that they eat grain and grass, have less offensive bodily wastes, and they live lives of utter rationality. Gulliver turns away from the distorted version of humanity to this species. Of course, horses have no technology, no institutions, no culture, and no literature.

Where, then, is the satire in the fourth book of *Gulliver's Travels* going? It is sometimes suggested that the Houyhnhnms are themselves being satirized; they're deists, super-rational thinkers similar to the economist from *A Modest Proposal*. We can't be sure of this conclusion because the satire is unstable in the fourth book. Although the book is very powerful, we can't seem to organize our response to it, except to feel the same nausea and disgust that Swift himself feels for his own kind.

When Gulliver returns to England, he becomes a strange sort of satirized figure himself. He can't bear his wife and family and goes to live in a stable.

Five years after his return, he is able to have his wife and children in his presence but much prefers the company of his two horses. Has Gulliver gone mad, or should any rational human being, as Swift suggests, hate the human race? When one reads the fourth book of *Gulliver's Travels*, one feels that one's own sanity is teetering.

Gulliver's Travels, like everything in Swift's life and writing, is both terrifying and wonderful. The book makes us wonder with genuine anxiety what we are, what we have done, and whether our accomplishments as a species are as worthwhile as we'd like to think. Much of the literature of the Augustan period entertains and even instructs us, but Swift frightens us. ■

Suggested Reading

Fox, ed., *The Cambridge Companion to Jonathan Swift*.

Swift, *Gulliver's Travels*.

———, *The Writings of Jonathan Swift*.

Questions to Consider

1. Is Swift's satire too savage?

2. How different is the fourth, and last, book of *Gulliver's Travels* from the previous three books?

Swift—Anger and Satire
Lecture 15—Transcript

In the last lecture, we looked at how English poetry refined itself in the 18th century, became decorous, became civilized, became, as the poets would like to think, golden. But English prose, as much as English verse, cultivates itself during this century, during this Augustan period.

On the one side, we discover a new generation of essayists, who are, in fact, writing what we would now call higher journalism in magazines, and in a language more cultivated than ever before, cultivated and well-mannered and often addressed to the woman reader. The presence of women, in fact, raises the tone of literature. Addison and Steele, for example, in *The Spectator* magazine, which was designed to be enjoyed over teacups, introduced a new voice into the already many-voiced English literature.

But one great satirist became the wielder of the sharpest and most savage satire in the English language, and he dominates all others. If you think of this period, you think of one great writer in prose. Forget good manners when you read Jonathan Swift. Anger seethes underneath the purest prose that ever flowed from an English pen. Pure and sublimely simple: that's the quality of Swiftian prose. "The rogue never hazards a metaphor," observed Johnson, and he meant it as praise, as much as criticism.

Swift held up a model of plain writing, which has really been followed through the ages by innumerable disciplines, notably by his great 20th-century disciple, Orwell, in fact, the direct descendant of Swift and also a great satirist in his own period. Now, Swift can claim to be, among his many other achievements, the first great Irish writer in English literature, if that isn't too Irish a formulation, an Irish English writer.

That western island's population has contributed disproportionately to its colonizing neighbor's literature. England has oppressed Ireland and in return, Ireland has given England some of its greatest literature: Sheridan, the dramatist, Oscar Wilde, the greatest wit in English literature, Bernard Shaw, arguably the greatest of 20th-century dramatists, Samuel Beckett, who challenges Shaw for that title, Seamus Heaney, all these are names which we'll encounter in these lectures. And I could extend the list, practically to the end of this particular lecture.

But let's revert to Jonathan Swift. Swift was born in Dublin. His father at the time was seven months dead when he was born, so he was born fatherless. He was a Protestant in a predominantly Catholic country, and a member of what is called the Ascendancy. That's to say, he was one of the privileged class who were supported by the English to run their colonial property, Ireland.

That huge running sore, the oppression of Ireland, still suppurates today, two centuries later, though we may hope that over the last few years, we're at last seeing the removal of what Gladstone called "the thorn from England's thigh": the Irish problem. But it was at its most intensely sick and oppressive, and really, in some ways, insoluble, at the period when Swift was there. It was a very bad period in Irish history and probably as bad as almost anything until the Great Famine in the mid-1840s.

Young Jonathan received his higher education at Trinity College in Dublin, and he received his BA in 1686. He was a scholar. In fact, he excelled at university and he might well have become himself a university teacher, a don, as they're called. But the great Revolution of 1688 and the importation of William and Mary to the throne of England, which we were talking about in previous lectures, forced him to come to the mother country if he wanted to get ahead in the world.

And here he became a secretary to a nobleman and a diplomat, Sir William Temple. And Temple would go in his turn to become a friend and patron to the young Jonathan Swift. And through Temple, Swift was introduced to the court and given access to the king, William III himself. He was on his way.

Swift was, during these three years of his service with Temple, politicized. And during this period also, he became closely involved with one of the two women in his life, women whom he gave the pseudonyms Stella and Vanessa to. Now, Swift's sexuality was famously tortured and he also ominously, even at this early age, began to show signs of the mental symptoms which would, in late middle life, spiral into full-blown madness. But in the meanwhile, Swift scooped up more degrees, culminating in a doctorate from Trinity College. And he became an ordained priest in the Church of Ireland. This, in fact, was a very useful qualification for scholars at the time. The two institutions, university and church, were very closely connected.

He was given a series of livings, that's to say parishes, in which he was nominally a pastor, and enjoyed a comfortable income. And he had very few parish duties. These were all delegated to curates. And he was still very much in Ireland, by the way. The Church of Ireland was the Church of England in its, as it were, exported form.

But Swift was bitterly disappointed that he didn't get more preferment, more patronage, more success from the king and the court, and later from Queen Anne, who took over from William. This disappointment stoked up his anger, which was always there. It was burning away. And around the turn of the century, his serious writing career began. And it was nurtured by that anger that I've just been talking about.

In various trips to England—and he was moving between the two countries, it wasn't hard to do: there were only a few miles of water between Ireland and England—he formed friendships with, among others, Alexander Pope, who we were talking about in the last lecture. And Pope and Swift were founder members of the Scriblerus Club, which they founded in 1713, in which they were both very witty, probably the wittiest men of their time. And they would vie with each other and with other friends to see who could come up with the wittiest satires. It was a kind of contest between two great satirical geniuses. And they got on well together as well. They were, if you like, congenial.

And here it was in the Scriblerus Club that *Gulliver's Travels* found its genesis. But Swift was always, rather unlike Pope in this respect, the most political of the great 18th-century satirists. As the battles between the Whigs and the Tories, liberals and conservatives, evolved, he, in fact, was a main player and he would fire off pamphlets and squibs from a very radical Tory position. George Orwell, the disciple I talked about earlier, called Swift a "Tory anarchist." He was very old-fashioned and yet, at the same time, he had this terrific destructive urge to tear it all down. Tear it all down for what? To re-create the old world, the world of the past.

It's a particularly sort of, as it were, aggressive form of conservatism. And that's very much Swift's allegiance. Now, Swift's services to the Tory party did not bring him the rewards he craved. He didn't actually come out as well as he always hoped to. Queen Anne didn't like him, and that was very bad. The clouds covered your sun if the queen took a dislike to you. And the best position his friends at court and in high places could secure for him was the deanery of St. Patrick's in Dublin.

And as the Whigs came into the ascendant, Swift returned to Ireland, to live, as he said—it's a very Swiftian phrase—"like a rat in a hole." And from Dublin, in anger, he fired off the most powerful of his pamphlets demanding justice for Ireland, a country suffering the extremity of persecution, as he saw it. He didn't want independence for Ireland. He wanted justice for Ireland. The most famous of these pamphlets is *A Modest Proposal*.

It came out in 1729, or, to give it its full title: *A Modest Proposal For Preventing the Children of Poor People in Ireland from Being a Burden to their Parents or Country, and for Making them Beneficial to the Public.*

The pamphlet is written in the persona or assumed character of an English economist, an economist imbued with the rational principles of Adam Smith and free enterprise. This social scientist, the kind of character that Swift's invented, has turned his mind to the perennial problem of Ireland and come up with an ingenious solution.

And this is what he writes, the modest proposal:

> It is a melancholy object to those who walk through this great town or travel in the country, when they see the streets, the roads, and cabin doors, crowded with beggars of the female sex, followed by three, four, or six children, all in rags and importuning every passenger for an alms. These mothers, instead of being able to work for their honest livelihood, are forced to employ all their time in strolling to beg sustenance for their helpless infants: who as they

grow up either turn thieves for want of work, or leave their dear native country to fight for the Pretender in Spain, or sell themselves to the Barbadoes.

So, in fact, it's a mess. "I shall now," the modest proposer goes on to say, "humbly propose my own thoughts, which I hope will not be liable to the least objection."

And his thought is state-sponsored cannibalism. Way back, talking about Spenser, I quoted *A Modest Proposal* as an example of irony, and I want to quote it again, but this time to highlight the anger, not the irony. It is a furious onslaught but all done with the instrumentality of high satire.

This, again, is *A Modest Proposal*:

> I have been assured by a very knowing American of my acquaintance in London, that a young healthy child well nursed is at a year old a most delicious, nourishing, and wholesome food, whether stewed, roasted, baked, or boiled; and I make no doubt that it will equally serve in a fricassee or a ragout.

He gets carried away with the delights of the menu.

> I do therefore humbly offer it to public consideration that of the hundred and twenty thousand children already computed, twenty thousand may be reserved for breed, whereof only one-fourth part to be males; which is more than we allow to sheep, black cattle or swine; and my reason is, that these children are seldom the fruits of marriage, a circumstance not much regarded by our savages, therefore one male will be sufficient to serve four females.

He's going to breed them, as one might breed beasts of the field.

> That the remaining hundred thousand may, at a year old, be offered in the sale to the persons of quality and fortune through the kingdom; always advising the mother to let them suck plentifully in the last month, so as to render them plump and fat for a good

table. A child will make two dishes at an entertainment for friends; and when the family dines alone, the fore or hind quarter will make a reasonable dish, and seasoned with a little pepper or salt will be very good boiled on the fourth day, especially in winter.

I mean was ever satire angrier? Was ever satire funnier? It's very odd. One's horrified and yet at the same time, one giggles. Was ever satire more powerfully relevant to man's inhumanity to man?

It was at the same period, around the 1720s, that Swift began putting into shape the work with which his name will forever be associated, *Gulliver's Travels*, or, to give it its mock serious title, *Travels into Several Remote Nations of the World, in Four Parts, by Lemuel Gulliver, first a surgeon, and then a captain of several ships*.

After the death of Stella, one of the pseudonymized women in his life, Swift became increasingly melancholy, and, as I said earlier, in his middle and later years, he began to show tragically clear signs of madness. And in 1742, he appears to have suffered a stroke, losing the ability to speak and realizing his worst fears of becoming mentally disabled. Once, when walking through the countryside, he said, "I shall be like that tree, I shall die at the top." He had seen a tree which was dying down and what he meant was his head would go first.

Swift, as Johnson wrote in *The Vanity of Human Wishes*, "expires a driveller and a show." People would come and laugh at his madness, to be amused. Swift died and he was buried by Esther Johnson's side, one of the two women in his life, in accordance with his wishes. And the bulk of his fortune was left to found a hospital for the mentally ill, originally known as St. Patrick's Hospital for Imbeciles, which opened in 1757, and which still exists as a psychiatric hospital. It's a very tragic life, though a life, in fact, which was very productive in literary terms.

Let's turn now to *Gulliver's Travels*. Now, the book itself has great pseudo-authenticity. In fact, the original readers were fooled, at least at the moment of purchase, that they were buying, and perhaps on the first few pages, reading an actual account of exotic travels, until, of course, they got into the story.

There are four books or voyages in *Gulliver's Travels*, and the first of them is to Lilliput, where the people are tiny. And what Swift is satirizing in the Lilliputian book is the court around Queen Anne. These, in fact, are midgets who fondly imagine themselves to be people of consequence. It's delightfully funny. I don't think it was all that funny in the court of Queen Anne, but he, by that point, had lost all chance of royal favor.

The second book takes Lemuel Gulliver to Brobdingnag, and here the inhabitants are rural giants, and the hero himself is now a doll-sized midget. Brobdingnag, as it happens, is the most pleasant, the most livable in of the imaginary countries because it's the most traditional and the least modern. Swift hated progress. He hated the modern world and Brobdingnag is an agricultural community, and he thought that was just about bearable.

In the third book, Gulliver travels to Laputa. *La puta* is Spanish for "the whore," and it's a scientific utopia. Swift loathed science. He thought it was contrary to religion and unnecessary. And he pictures the advanced thinkers of his age, those members of the newly formed Royal Society, which was, in fact, taking science forward at a huge rate, and it's one of the things that we most admire in the 18th century, but Swift did not admire it.

He pictures the members of the Royal Society as geeks, laboring, for example, to extract sunbeams from cucumbers. You know, obviously the cucumber absorbed sunbeams. How do we get the sunbeams out? Of course, for us, he's quite rational because we extract energy from garbage and think we may even save the world by recycling. Swift saw it very differently and very satirically.

Book III also contains the most horrible of the Dean's conceptions. These are the Struldbrugs, who live forever, but who also decay forever, suffering an eternity of pain and mental infirmity as they fall to pieces, but cannot die. Who would want 1,000 years of progressive Alzheimer's? That's the kind of question which Swift is asking in the Struldbrug part of Book III.

The fourth book takes Gulliver to Houyhnhnm land, one of the most difficult words to pronounce in English literature. And it's supposed to be like the neighing of a horse. And here, the rulers are horses, and homo sapiens, people like us, are horrific apes. And Lemuel Gulliver seems, in this final book, to go mad, and his madness takes the form of believing that the horse people, the equine people, are wholly admirable and his own species, the Yahoos, as they're called, are nauseatingly disgusting.

And the narrative of Book IV begins with Gulliver, the captain of his vessel, cast adrift by his men. This is an important detail because it indicates the misanthropy of man to man, that men treat each other very badly. Human beings treat each other very badly, without humanity.

Anyway, Lemuel finds himself washed ashore in a very strange land. And it begins:

> When I was a little refreshed, I went up into the country, resolving to deliver myself to the first savages I should meet, and purchase my life from them by some bracelets, glass rings, and other toys, which sailors usually provide themselves with in those voyages, and whereof I had some about me.

You'll notice, incidentally, how beautifully simply Swift writes. And you'd think it'd be very easy to write like that until you try. You'll find it's very, very difficult. In fact, it's impossible unless you're a genius like him.

Now, he notes:

> The land is divided by long rows of trees, not regularly planted, but naturally growing;

It was a very orderly place.

> there was great plenty of grass, and several fields of oats. I walked very circumspectly, for fear of being surprised, or suddenly shot with an arrow from behind, or on either side.

In fact, this is really quite exciting stuff, because we, at this stage, do not know what kind of adventures, what kind of "savages" as he says, he will find. In fact, he finds not savages, but a very civilized species.

> I fell into a beaten road, where I saw many tracts of human feet, and some of cows, but most of horses. At last I beheld several animals in a field, and one or two of the same kind sitting in trees. Their shape was very singular and deformed, which a little discomposed me, so that I lay down behind a thicket to observe them better. Some of them coming forward near the place where I lay, gave me an opportunity of distinctly marking their form.

In fact, he doesn't recognize them at first, but in fact, he soon will.

> Their heads and breasts were covered with a thick hair, some frizzled, and others lank; they had beards like goats, and a long ridge of hair down their backs, and the fore parts of their legs and feet; but the rest of their bodies was bare, so that I might see their skins, which were of a brown buff colour.

These wonderful sort of details.

> They had no tails, nor any hair at all on their buttocks, except about the anus, which, I presume, nature had placed there to defend them as they sat on the ground, for this posture they used, as well as lying down, and often stood on their hind feet.

He doesn't recognize what they are, of course, but he will soon, and it will be a terrible recognition.

> They climbed high trees as nimbly as a squirrel, for they had strong extended claws before and behind, terminating in sharp points, and hooked. They would often spring, and bound, and leap, with prodigious agility. The females were not so large as the males; they had long lank hair on their heads, but none on their faces, nor any thing more than a sort of down on the rest of their bodies, except about the anus and pudenda.

The reader, of course, is beginning to understand rather more than the ingenuous Lemuel Gulliver does.

> The dugs hung between their fore feet, and often reached almost to the ground as they walked. The hair of both sexes was of several colours, brown, red, black, and yellow. Upon the whole, I never beheld, in all my travels, so disagreeable an animal, or one against which I naturally conceived so strong an antipathy. So that, thinking I had seen enough, full of contempt and aversion, I got up, and pursued the beaten road, hoping it might direct me to the cabin of some Indian. I had not got far, when I met one of these creatures full in my way, and coming up directly to me. The ugly monster, when he saw me, distorted several ways, every feature of his visage, and stared, as at an object he had never seen before; then approaching nearer, lifted up his fore-paw, whether out of curiosity or mischief I could not tell; but I drew my hanger, and gave him a good blow with the flat side of it, for I durst not strike with the edge, fearing the inhabitants might be provoked against me, if they should come to know that I had killed or maimed any of their cattle. When the beast felt the smart, he drew back, and roared so loud, that a herd of at least forty came flocking about me from the next field, howling and making odious faces; but I ran to the body of a tree, and leaning my back against it, kept them off by waving my hanger. Several of this cursed brood, getting hold of the branches behind, leaped up into the tree, whence they began to discharge their excrements on my head; however, I escaped pretty well by sticking close to the stem of the tree, but was almost stifled with the filth, which fell about me on every side.

These animals, of course, are human beings, homo sapiens, but in no sense sapiens. They are *homo excrementus*. It's what's called an excremental vision of humanity. Now, the thing about horses, given their graminivorous habits, the fact they eat grain and grass, they have the least offensive of bodily wastes. The vegetarian horses, Houyhnhnms, live a life of utter, not to say sterile, rationality.

What Gulliver has seen is a kind of distorted version of humanity, and he turns away in disgust to another species, the horse. Now, horses have no technology, no institutions, no culture, no literature. And one of the questions in the fourth book of *Gulliver's Travels* is where is the satire going? Now, it could well be, and this is sometimes suggested, particularly by Swiftian apologists, that the Houyhnhnms are themselves being satirized. They're the deists, they're super-rational thinkers. They're rather like that economist whom we encountered in *A Modest Proposal*.

But we can't be sure because all the satire is so unstable in the fourth book. We do feel there's a sort of rhythm, a kind of energy of madness in it. It's very powerful, but we can't, as it were, organize our response terribly easily, except, of course, we feel this nausea and disgust that Swift himself feels. And what does Swift feel it for? His own kind.

We have to remember, as I say, that Gulliver—he's so called because he's very gullible—is anything but a reliable narrator, and when he comes back to England, he, in fact, becomes himself a kind of very strange satirized figure. The last sight we have of him is that he goes to live in a stable. He can't bear his wife and family, even though they receive him back with great joy because they thought he was dead. He was washed overboard and they never heard from him again.

And this is what he says of his wife and children:

> I must freely confess the sight of them filled me only with hatred, disgust, and contempt; and the more, by reflecting on the near alliance I had to them. For although, since my unfortunate exile from the Houyhnhnm country, I had compelled myself to tolerate the sight of Yahoos.

He had actually, as it were, accepted there were such horrible things. Nonetheless he could not accept that he himself was one such. And then there comes this terrible line:

And when I began to consider that, by copulating with one of the Yahoo species I had become a parent of more, it struck me with the utmost shame, confusion, and horror.

As soon as I entered the house, my wife took me in her arms, and kissed me; at which, having not been used to the touch of that odious animal for so many years, I fell into a swoon for almost an hour. At the time I am writing, it is five years since my last return to England. During the first year, I could not endure my wife or children in my presence; the very smell of them was intolerable; much less could I suffer them to eat in the same room. To this hour they dare not presume to touch my bread, or drink out of the same cup, neither was I ever able to let one of them take me by the hand. The first money I laid out was to buy two young stone-horses, which I keep in a good stable; and next to them, the groom is my greatest favourite, for I feel my spirits revived by the smell he contracts in the stable. My horses understand me tolerably well; I converse with them at least four hours every day. They are strangers to bridle or saddle; they live in great amity with me and friendship to each other.

Gulliver has, we assume, gone stark staring mad, or has he? Does not any rational human being, Swift suggests, hate the human race? When one reads the fourth book of *Gulliver's Travels*, one feels that one's own sanity is teetering.

Gulliver's Travels, like everything in Swift's life and writing, is terrifying and at the same time, wonderful. *Gulliver's Travels* is a work which makes us wonder with genuine anxiety what we are, what we have done, and whether what we are and what we as a species have done is as worthwhile as we'd like to think.

Much of the literature of the Augustan period, this golden age, interests us, entertains us. It astonishes us with its virtuosity, and it may even instruct us, if you read, for instance, Alexander Pope's *Essay on Man*. But Swift, I think, and this is the word which is inescapable, Swift frightens us. And that, after all, perhaps is one of the many functions of literature. And no one has done it more effectively than Jonathan Swift in *Gulliver's Travels*.

Johnson—Bringing Order to the Language
Lecture 16

Few authors can claim as legitimately as ... Johnson can claim ... to be one of the great founders of a literature that came after him. In terms of style and preferred ways of writing, Johnson ranks as the most authoritative Neoclassicist in our long survey.

S amuel Johnson (1709–1784) is always referred to as Dr. Johnson, his title bringing with it a sense of discipline and literary authority. His achievement was to bring order to the English language and English literature. Few people have had more direct authority over their subject matter than Johnson. His contemporaries and successors might rebel against his constraints—and many did, including Wordsworth and Coleridge— but Johnson established a bedrock for English literature that still exists to this day.

In terms of style and preferred ways of writing, Johnson ranks as the most authoritative Neoclassicist in our survey. He believed that in order to be a proper literature, not just an effusion, English literature needed three elements: principles, cataloging, and tradition. Those were the foundations on which a great national literature could be erected and on which native English genius could flourish.

Classicism, as Johnson conceived it, did not imply elitism. What Johnson's classicism demanded was an architecture, a shaping principle to the literary project. He believed that one could no more create literature without critical principles than one could improvise the building of a cathedral.

We've already looked at Johnson's Juvenalian theory and practice of satire in our examination of his greatest poem, *The Vanity of Human Wishes*. In this lecture, we will turn to his achievements in lexicography.

Few authors and critics have been as farsighted as Johnson was. Other critics have judged literature in terms of touchstones or golden lines, fragments, but for Johnson, the essence of literature was not in fragments. The famous 11ᵗʰ chapter of Johnson's novel *Rasselas* is relevant here. The novel is a kind of prose version of *The Vanity of Human Wishes*. In the book, Prince Rasselas goes out into the world only to discover that all human aspiration is doomed to disappointment; he then returns to where he started, the Happy Valley. In the process of being in the outside world, Rasselas learns that stoical acceptance is the only rational response to the inevitable disillusionment of living. Life, said Johnson, is a condition "in which much is to be endured, and little to be enjoyed." One has to live one's life, but art and literature can soothe or "sweeten" one's existence.

> **The *Dictionary of the English Language* preoccupied Johnson from 1745 to the late 1750s. [When published], it contained more than 40,000 words with definitions and, as the most innovative feature, a historical set of usages.**

Also according to Johnson, however, art and literature must also always adhere to certain iron principles if they are to aspire to greatness or even to worth. These principles are explained early on in the narrative of Rasselas. The character Imlac, Rasselas's teacher, who is based on Johnson himself, explains that the poet "must write as the interpreter of nature and the legislator of mankind, and consider himself as presiding over the thoughts and manners of future generations, as a being superior to time and place."

Such authority was also needed to embark on Johnson's project of organizing the English language. He would create the laws of literature.

Johnson's commanding influence comes through on nearly every page of the magisterial *Life of Johnson*, written by James Boswell (1740–1795). In Boswell's description of his first encounter with the great man, we note Johnson's schoolmasterly tone, followed by the detail that the two men drank "a couple of bottles of port." Boswell's portrait of Johnson's personality is sublime.

The other quality that comes through in the *Life of Johnson* is the doctor's vast commonsense. In one conversation, Boswell records that he asked Johnson, a former teacher, what he thought were the best subjects for children to learn first. Johnson's reply was that it didn't matter: "Sir, while you are considering which of two things you should teach your child first, another boy has learnt them both." On another occasion, the two men were discussing the idea that matter does not exist and everything in the universe is "merely ideal." Boswell observed that this theory couldn't be refuted, but Johnson responded by kicking a large stone and saying, "I refute it thus."

Why was Johnson so fond of this romantic young Scot, Boswell? Johnson tells us that he prefers the company of young people for pragmatic reasons: First, he doesn't like to think of himself as growing old; second, young people won't outlive him and leave him friendless in his old age; and finally, young people have "more generous sentiments in every respect" than old men.

Johnson's life was undramatic but interesting, as everything about him was interesting. And thanks to Boswell, we know that life in great depth. Johnson was the son of a poor bookseller in Lichfield, a small town in central England. He would be surrounded by books and poverty all his life. He was educated at grammar school and proved to be a student of unusual ability. He went on to earn a place by merit at Oxford University but couldn't afford to stay for more than a year.

Like many great writers, life for Johnson was financial hardship and struggle, but he wrote in spite of these circumstances. For a while after leaving Oxford, he eked out a living as a schoolteacher and even started his own school. One of his pupils would later become famous as the greatest actor of the age, David Garrick.

As a young man, Johnson married a 54-year-old woman; the union was likely based on affection at best and Johnson's need for money. His married life was probably less than blissful. Once widowed, Johnson enjoyed the company and friendship of women but nothing more.

At age 28, Johnson set off for London with the hope of making his way in literature. He found work as an essayist, editor, hack writer, poet, and journalist, all the while developing his distinctively authoritarian literary style and manner. An essay in *The Idler* from this period stands as an example of Johnsonian sentiment (humans would be happier if unencumbered by memory) and style.

In 1745, Johnson embarked on his magnum opus, the *Dictionary of the English Language*. This project would take him 10 years to complete and would ruin his eyesight. It was undertaken without any financial assistance, although Johnson applied in vain to Lord Chesterfield for patronage at the outset of his task.

Late in life, the dictionary and Johnson's growing body of work finally brought him fame and a modicum of prosperity. He was awarded a government pension of £300 per annum for his work, appropriately enough because the dictionary was for the English nation as much as it was for the English language or literature. It was a national monument.

Fame in his later years brought Johnson the adulation of "young dogs," such as Boswell, and those years were much more comfortable than his early ones. By the 1760s, Johnson was probably the most famous man of letters in literary London. People traveled from abroad to take tea with him, and he became an institution in coffee houses. Joshua Reynolds painted his portrait. In 1773, Boswell took Johnson on a "jaunt" to the far western Hebridean Isles, what Boswell thought of as a glorious wilderness. Johnson, always the Neoclassicist, saw it merely as a wasteland.

Johnson is buried with his literary peers in Westminster Abbey. His career was a landscape marked with mountainous infrastructural projects. In addition to the dictionary, he compiled a complete edition of Shakespeare and wrote *Lives of the Poets*, the first account of the literary tradition of England.

The *Dictionary of the English Language* preoccupied Johnson from 1745 to the late 1750s. When it was published, the dictionary was the size of a small coffee table. It contained more than 40,000 words with definitions and, as the most innovative feature, a historical set of usages. Johnson cited such writers as Shakespeare and Milton to show how words evolved. In this way, the dictionary was as much a work of linguistic archeology as it was of current correct usage. This practice has since become accepted as standard for all dictionaries.

The principles on which Johnson worked are clearly laid out on the title page. The dictionary was to be descriptive rather than prescriptive. In other words, the meanings of words would be rooted in how people actually used the words rather than how they ought to use the words. As mentioned earlier, Johnson was always on the side of the public.

Johnson's definitions are infused with his inextinguishably egotistic spirit. He is the most personal of lexicographers. The definition of lexicographer, for example, reads as follows: "a writer of dictionaries; a harmless drudge that busies himself in tracing the original and detailing the signification of words." His definition of oats is: "a grain which in England is generally given to horses, but in Scotland supports the people." Obviously, Johnson believed that dictionaries need not be dull.

Another achievement of Johnson's was the professionalizing of the trade of writing. Along with Pope, he freed literature from the tyrannies of aristocratic patronage. As you will recall, Lord Chesterfield had refused Johnson assistance at the beginning of the dictionary project, then offered money when the dictionary was complete in the hope of receiving a complimentary dedication. Johnson's letter in response to Chesterfield was a declaration of independence for English literature. Writers are rarely rich, even in the present day. But Johnson's letter to Chesterfield asserts the dignity of the profession and frees the writer to answer only to the public.

From the 18th century onward, booksellers and book buyers would support the writer, including those whom we will discuss in lectures to come. Aristocratic patronage, which is also a kind of aristocratic ownership, would become a thing of the past. Johnson was by no means a revolutionary; he believed in the English class system, in stability, and in order. Nonetheless, one of his greatest achievements was in giving writers a new sense of liberty. ■

Suggested Reading

Bate, *Samuel Johnson*.

Boswell, *The Life of Samuel Johnson*.

Johnson, *A Dictionary of the English Language: An Anthology*.

———, *Samuel Johnson: The Major Works*.

Questions to Consider

1. What claim does Samuel Johnson have to be considered a great writer, as opposed to a great critic, lexicographer, and conversationalist?

2. What view of life does the reader come away with from a reading of *The Vanity of Human Wishes*?

Johnson—Bringing Order to the Language
Lecture 16—Transcript

How we refer to great writers, how, when we discuss them, we address them, so to speak, is a curious aspect of what one might call literary etiquette. Why does one say William Shakespeare, but Ben Jonson? I mean if you say Geoff Chaucer, it would sound wrong. The fact is, there's no question about how we are compelled to refer to the subject of this particular lecture. He is Dr. Johnson, if you please, not Samuel Johnson and never, never Sam Johnson, although he sometimes signed his letters that way.

Johnson's title, his doctorate, is an honorary doctorate of divinity, which was awarded by Dublin University, but, nonetheless, it brings with it a sense of order, of discipline, of literary authority. That Johnsonian order, discipline, and authority is the theme of this lecture.

In this lecture, we'll be looking less at what Johnson did as an author on his account, though that's quite considerable, than what he did for English literature, for English culture, his larger achievement, so to call it, and in the largest sense of all, it's what he's done for us.

To simplify, Johnson brought order into the language, and for a time, he brought order into English literature. Few people have had more direct authority over their subject matter than Johnson.

His contemporaries and successors might rebel, and many of them did, against Johnsonian constraints, as Romantics like Wordsworth and Coleridge did in the *Lyrical Ballads* with their protest against his "gaudy and inane phraseology" and the straitjackets of Neoclassicism. We'll be looking at that in one of the future lectures, but Wordsworth, for example, as we shall see, specifically targets Johnson's poetry as a prime example of what was wrong, corrupt, stylistically wrong, if one wants to put it that way, with Augustanism, which the author of *The Vanity of Human Wishes* espoused and wanted others to follow.

But nonetheless it's there, and one can query it and one can build on it according to whatever line one wants to take, but, as I say, whatever one's sentiments, the literary bedrock is there, and it's a Johnsonian bedrock. And it'll be there for as long as there's an English literature.

Few authors can claim as legitimately as Samuel Johnson can claim, Dr. Johnson, to be one of the great founders of a literature that came after him. In terms of style and preferred ways of writing, Johnson ranks as the most authoritative Neoclassicist in our long survey. The most influential, if you want to put it that way. He's one of those, nonetheless, who went outside English literature to make English literature.

If English literature was to be a literature proper, Johnson thought, and not just an effusion, it needed three things: it needed principles, it needed cataloging, and it needed tradition. And those were the foundations, Johnson believed, on which a great national literature could be erected and on which native genius, English genius, could flourish.

Now, classicism, as Johnson conceived it, did not imply elitism. One should be very clear on that point. Johnson rejoiced, as he said, to "concur with the common reader." He was, throughout his life, on the side of the public. What Johnson's classicism implied and demanded was an architecture, a shaping, grand principle to the literary project. He believed you could no more create literature without critical principles than you could improvise the building of a cathedral. And, like the great cathedrals of England, literature was for all, not for the few.

We've already looked at Johnson's Juvenalian theory and practice of satire in our examination of his greatest poem, *The Vanity of Human Wishes*. And in this lecture, what we'll be looking at principally are his achievements in lexicography, in the elements, that is, of language, the *primum materium* of literature, its DNA. "Words, words, words" as Hamlet says. Without them, you cannot have a literature, and Johnson did more for verbiage, for the words of literature than anyone before or since.

Johnson saw things very large. Few authors and critics have been as longsighted, as farsighted as he was. Other critics have actually judged literature in terms of touchstones or golden lines, fragments. But for Johnson, the essence of literature was not in fragments. Someone, he thought, who tried to capture the essence of English literature with quotations, for instance, was like the fool who tried to explain the glories of Palladian architecture by carrying a brick round in his pocket. "This, in fact, is Palladian architecture." Of course, it isn't. It's the way in which all those bricks are put together.

The famous 11th chapter of Johnson's novel *Rasselas* is relevant here. It's a kind of prose *Vanity of Human Wishes*. The enthusiast of the title, Prince Rasselas, goes into the world only to discover that all human aspiration is doomed to disappointment, and he returns to where he started, the Happy Valley. It's very like the garden to which Candide finally returns in Voltaire's great satire And in the process of being in the outside world, one of the things that Rasselas has learned the hard way is that stoical acceptance is the only rational response to the inevitable disillusionment that living brings with it.

It's the same conclusion which we found at the end of *The Vanity of Human Wishes*. It's a doctrine of life which is both tough and pessimistic, these two things together. Pessimism, of course, in Johnson's case, has a personal explanation. He wrote this work *Rasselas*, which is the only work of fiction which was designed to sell, in a fortnight to defray the cost of his mother's funeral. And we're not talking Henry James here. We're talking a very practical man of letters.

Life, said Johnson, is a condition "in which much is to be endured, and little to be enjoyed." But, nonetheless, one had to live one's life. And, nonetheless, there was art and literature to soothe or "sweeten"—one of his favorite words—one's existence. But, as Johnson saw it, that art and literature must adhere always to certain iron principles if it was to aspire to greatness or even to worth.

What those principles are, what literary principles are, is explained very early on in the narrative of *Rasselas* to the hero prince, Prince Rasselas. They're explained by his teacher Imlac. We should perhaps call him Dr. Imlac because he's so clearly based on Dr. Johnson. What is poetry? What, more properly, should poetry be? Now, Imlac lays down the law on that subject.

And this is what is written:

> "This business of a poet," said Imlac, "is to examine, not the *individual*, but the *species*; to remark general properties and large appearances. *He does not number the streaks of the tulip*, or describe the different shades of the verdure of the forest. He is to exhibit in his portraits of nature such prominent and striking features as recall the original to every mind, and must neglect the minuter discriminations, which one may have remarked and another have neglected, for those characteristics which are alike obvious to vigilance and carelessness … He must write as the interpreter of nature and the legislator of mankind, and consider himself as presiding over the thoughts and manners of future generations, as a being superior to time and place."

Kind of a huge assumption of authorial authority. And Imlac goes on. "To be a poet," I think he says rather unnecessarily, "is indeed very difficult." Well, amen to that. But, difficult as it is, that is what the artist must do, in Johnson's view of things.

Just by the way, later poets, such as Wordsworth, would see attention to the streaks of the tulip or, more famously, the golden daffodil, as very much the prime duty of the poet, and we'll say more of which later when we come to the Romantics. They're very much anti-Johnsonians.

But huge authority was needed to embark on what Johnson embarked on. And what was it? Nothing less than, he uses that word in Imlac's discourse, "legislation" for literature, laying down the literary law, creating the literary laws, devising the literary laws. Personally, as every page of Boswell's magisterial *Life of Johnson* indicates, the doctor, the great Cham, as he was nicknamed—that's not sham in the sense of phony, but in the sense of emperor—had the necessary authority, and more, to lay down the law with the authority of a literary Solomon.

This is how the young Scot, Boswell, describes his first encounter with the great man, Dr. Johnson. Now, it was, we should remember, the most important meeting of James Boswell's life. It was overwhelmingly important to him.

> I complained to him that I had not yet acquired much knowledge, and asked his advice as to my studies. He said, "Don't talk of study now. I will give you a plan; but it will require some time to consider of it." "It is very good in you (I replied,) to allow me to be with you thus. Had it been foretold to me some years ago that I should pass an evening with the authour of The Rambler, how should I have exulted!" What I then expressed, was sincerely from the heart. He was satisfied that it was, and cordially answered, "Sir, I am glad we have met. I hope we shall pass many evenings and mornings too, together." We finished a couple of bottles of port, and sat till between one and two in the morning.

One of the great blessings of literature is that we have the greatest biography in English literature, Boswell's *Life of Johnson*. It gives us a wonderful sense of the man himself. If only one had other Boswells around at every point in English literature.

And it is the personality of the man, of Dr. Johnson, which makes Boswell's portrait so sublime: the schoolmasterly tone with the implication of stern discipline, followed by those "couple of bottles of port." They got right royally drunk. Johnson, in fact, was an alcoholic and he gave up drink in later life and turned to tea, which, as contemporaries record, he drank by the oceanful. He did everything greater than life, bigger than life.

The other quality which comes through on virtually every page of Boswell's *Life of Johnson* is the doctor's vast commonsense. To take an example at random, Boswell, who is by now an intimate confidant and friend, they've been together for some time, for years, indeed, records that on one occasion:

> We talked of the education of children; and I asked him what he thought was best to teach them first. JOHNSON. "Sir, it is no matter what you teach them first, any more than what leg you shall put into

your breeches first. Sir, you may stand disputing which is best to put in first, but in the mean time your breech is bare. Sir, while you are considering which of two things you should teach your child first, another boy has learnt them both."

It's the bare buttock theory of education, and Johnson, we remember, had once been a schoolteacher. And we cannot but think that what Johnson says is surely right. You know, for all its Neoclassical doctrine, Johnson's thought is distinguished by an invincible pragmatism.

Let me cite another famous example, again from Boswell. The two men have just attended divine service, they've been to church, and they're conversing afterward on metaphysical matters.

And this is what Boswell writes:

> After we came out of the church, we stood talking for some time together of Bishop Berkeley's ingenious sophistry to prove the non-existence of matter, and that every thing in the universe is merely ideal. I observed, that though we are satisfied his doctrine is not true, it is impossible to refute it. I never shall forget the alacrity with which Johnson answered, striking his foot with mighty force against a large stone, till he rebounded from it, "I refute it thus."

Wonderful moment, "I refute it thus." Now, one can see him doing it. And one never hears the theory that the universe is imaginary, *esse est percipi*, again without seeing that "mighty" refuting Johnsonian boot.

Why did Johnson take to this romantic young Scot, Boswell? Why did he like him so much? Why was he so fond of Boswell? Boswell was a young fellow, possessed of high talents, but also of undisguised moral weaknesses where drink, women, and money were concerned. Johnson himself gives the reasons for consorting with ostensibly worthless young fellows like Boswell, rather than greybeards of his own generation.

Incidentally, this is a hint: you can make any quotation sound "Johnsonian" by prefacing it with the word "Sir!" as in "Sir, you are sitting in my seat" or "Sir, I believe you are in error on that matter."

Anyway, this is what Johnson said in defense of his liking to have young people like Boswell around him:

> Sir, I love the acquaintance of young people; because, in the first place, I don't like to think myself growing old. In the next place, young acquaintances must last longest, if they do last; and then, Sir, young men have more virtue than old men: they have more generous sentiments in every respect. I love the young dogs.

"Young dogs" is wonderful. Boswell was a young dog. Few have been more doggishly mischievous, and Johnson loved him for it. And it's hard not to love Johnson for loving Boswell. You'll note too the pragmatism of that comment that if you have young friends, the chances are you won't outlive them, you won't have to grieve for them and die friendless. Johnson actually thinks very practically about these things.

Johnson's life itself is undramatic, but interesting, as everything about him is interesting. And thanks to Boswell, we know that life in great depth and minute detail. Johnson was born in 1709, the son of a poor bookseller in Lichfield, a small town in central England. He would be surrounded by books and poverty all his life. Lichfield, as I say, is a midlands rural town of no great historical distinction or interest. Like Shakespeare in his undistinguished rural town Stratford, young Samuel Johnson was educated at grammar school and he was a pupil of unusual ability. That was clear to everyone. He went on earn a place by merit at Oxford University.

Alas, he couldn't earn also the wherewithal to stay at Oxford University. Having no money, he was obliged to leave without a degree after only a year. It was a great consolation to him that very late in life, Oxford awarded him an honorary doctorate. It's nice to think that young Samuel Johnson got more out of that one year than most undergraduates get out of four.

Like many great writers, life for Johnson was financial hardship and struggle. He wrote in spite of circumstances. He wrote against all sorts of obstacles. For a while, after leaving Oxford, he eked out a living as a schoolteacher. Now, he retained many schoolteacher's mannerisms throughout life. He even started his own school, which attracted only three pupils, but one of those pupils, oddly enough, was the boy who was to become famous later as the greatest actor of the age, David Garrick.

Johnson married a woman who, at 54 years old, was some 30 years older than himself. It was clearly a union which was based, not on physical passion, but on affection, at best. And she brought him some needed money. That may also have been a motive. Now, his married life was probably less than blissful, although, as in everything, Johnson did his best to be a good husband while Mrs. Johnson lived. Once widowed, he enjoyed women's company very greatly and he enjoyed their friendship, but nothing more.

At age 28, Johnson, with young Garrick in attendance, one of his three pupils, took off on the road to London, with the hope of making his way in literature. Now, this has never been a road paved with gold. He found work in London as an essayist, as an editor, as a hack writer, as a poet, and as a journalist, as a kind of writer of all trades, developing all the while his distinctively authoritarian literary style and manner.

Here's a typical example from one of his essays in a magazine which he edited called *The Idler*:

> It would add much to human happiness, if an art could be taught of forgetting all of which the remembrance is at once useless and afflictive, if that pain which never can end in pleasure could be driven totally away, that the mind might perform its functions without incumbrance, and the past might no longer encroach upon the present.

That, in fact, is a very Johnsonian sentiment, but could you, having heard that, repeat it word for word? You need a very good memory to do so. But it's the style which we instantly recognize as Johnsonian, and it's the power, the authority which comes through, that use of language, which I think, you know, really does make an impression, even if one can't remember exactly what he's saying.

In 1745, Johnson embarked on his magnum opus, the *Dictionary of the English Language*. It was a work whose completion would take him 10 years, which is 7 years longer than he originally scheduled. The task would also ruin his eyesight, which had been weakened since childhood from an attack of scrofula. He was a famously ugly man. And this undertaking, the dictionary, was done without any financial assistance from patrons like Lord Chesterfield, to whom he applied, vainly, at the beginning of the task. It was the publishers and the book trade and, of course, beyond them, the readers, the great English public which supported his project.

The dictionary and his growing body of work at last, quite late in life, brought him fame and a modicum of prosperity, and the last two decades of his life were passed reasonably comfortably. And he also got a government pension of £300 per annum in 1762, which was awarded by the king, George IV, for his work on the dictionary: He received some 1,500 guineas from the publishers who commissioned it, which was a really good payment at the time. The award of the pension was very appropriate. Johnson's dictionary was for the English nation, as much as it was for the English language or English literature. It was a national monument that he was erecting.

And, of course, fame in his later years brought the adulation of "young dogs" such as James Boswell. So in fact, as I say, his last years were much more comfortable than his early years. By the 1760s, Johnson was probably the most famous man of letters in literary London. People traveled from abroad to take tea with him He was an institution in the coffee houses. Taverns he no longer frequented in these abstemious last years. He'd given up drink.

His portrait was painted by Reynolds, a magnificent portrait, which is a "warts and all" portrait. Dr. Johnson was, after his fashion, a celebrity. And in 1773, James Boswell, by dint of heroic persuasion, took him on a "jaunt" as he called it, to the far western Hebridean Isles, a glorious wilderness, Boswell the Scottish nationalist thought. And Johnson, of course, saw it merely as a wasteland. He's a Neoclassicist. He could see nothing there, except rocks and scrub, and the occasional pheasant. It was the one trip of

Johnson's life. I mean he is the archetypal Londoner. He very rarely put his foot outside the capital.

He died, famous, in 1784 and is buried with his literary peers in Westminster Abbey. Johnson's literary career is a landscape marked with mountainously huge infrastructural projects. He did a complete edition of Shakespeare, which is still one of the best editions that we have. He did *Lives of the Poets*, which is the first sociology of English literature which we have, the first, as it were, sort of account of what the literary tradition of the country was, and what, in fact, the job and work of writers is. He took the 100 greatest writers and wrote up little biographical and bibliographical capsules on them.

I want, very briefly, though, to look at the very greatest of those great projects, the *Dictionary of the English Language*, which preoccupied him in his prime from 1745 to the late 1750s. The published dictionary was physically large. It was the size of a small coffee table. It contained over 40,000 words with definitions and, as the most innovative feature, a historical set of usages. For instance, Shakespeare and Milton are the most cited examples. What he was doing was looking at the ways words evolved. The dictionary was as much a work of linguistic archeology, of digging into the language, as it was of current correct usage. This, in fact, was a novel thing to do, and it's become accepted as standard practice for every dictionary-maker since.

The principles on which Johnson worked are clearly laid out on the descriptive title page. Title pages were very descriptive in those days because they didn't have blurbs. It described itself as:

> *A Dictionary of the English Language*: in which the words are deduced from their originals, and illustrated in their different significations by examples from the best writers.

There is a whole theory of linguistics in that title. It wasn't a cheap purchase. It cost £4.10s, which probably translates into something like $300 or $400 in modern currency. Now, the rooting of meanings of words in usage, how people actually used those words, rather than in prescription, how they ought to use words, was revolutionary. Again, I said some time ago that Johnson was always on the side of the public. They were always right, and if they chose to use a word in a certain way, that was what it meant. You didn't tell them what it meant and then make them change the way they used words. That was wrong. He was authoritarian, but not tyrannical on these matters.

As I said, all great dictionaries have been compiled on the same principle as Johnson's ever since notably the greatest dictionary of all, the *Oxford English Dictionary*. And famously also, Johnson's definitions—and this is perhaps one of the many Johnsonian aspects of the dictionary—are infused with the inextinguishably egotistic spirit of the dictionary-maker. He's the most personal of lexicographers.

For instance, how did he describe the word lexicographer? What he says is "a writer of dictionaries; a harmless drudge that busies himself in tracing the original and detailing the signification of words." Lexicographers, oh, forget it. Of course, he's making fun of himself, and one loves Johnson for that.

What happens when he describes oats? For us it's a kind of breakfast cereal. He says oats are "a grain which in England is generally given to horses, but in Scotland supports the people." Of course, the Scots eat porridge, and Johnson was a Scotophobe, even though Boswell was his closest friend. I don't think Boswell must have liked that definition of oats very much. The point is that Johnson believed that dictionaries need not be dull. There was enough dullness in life without that. He was on Pope's side where dullness was concerned.

Another huge achievement of Johnson, the great literary builder, as I've called him, founder, putter into order, was that he may take much of the historical credit for professionalizing the trade of writing. Along with Pope, with whom he had great sympathies, he freed literature from the tyrannies of aristocratic patronage.

The famous letter to Lord Chesterfield: I've alluded to it once in this lecture and quoted from it earlier, but I want to quote from it again because Chesterfield was the man who refused to help when Johnson supplicated assistance at the beginning of the dictionary, but sent an unwanted check with the hope of some complimentary dedication when the dictionary was complete, when this Herculean labor was complete. That, in fact, is a very all-important moment in English literature. It's a declaration of independence.

When Johnson returned Chesterfield's check, his money order, with contempt, he wrote, and I repeat myself, but it's worth repeating, I say: "Is not a Patron, my Lord, one who looks with unconcern on a man struggling for life in the water, and, when he has reached ground, encumbers him with help?"

And then he goes on to say that he's done the work. In fact, it's been a very sad and melancholy task. He's done the work, but he doesn't need patrons any more. And he's speaking not for himself alone. He's speaking for the writer. The writer has been freed, in a sense. It's not easy; writers, in fact, are rarely rich. Even in the present day, a successful novelist does not make as much as a hedge fund manager. It's not, in fact, a way of getting rich, and most writers do their work in poverty.

The author's purse is usually empty, but what Johnson did was to say that it may not be an enriching profession in terms of cash reward, but, nonetheless, it is dignified. What Johnson did was to say the writer can be free. The writer can, to some extent, throw himself onto the public, and the public can return his efforts with whatever reward they see appropriate. And the writer can therefore, to some extent, sort of go his own way or her own way.

This, I think, is a very important moment. It happens in the 18th century, when writers, to some extent, create their own domain within which they can do their stuff. Booksellers and book buyers hereafter support the writer, and they support not just writers like Johnson, but almost every writer whom we shall look at in the next lectures. Aristocratic patronage, which is also a kind of aristocratic ownership, will be a thing of the past.

Johnson, one should insist, was by no means a revolutionary. He respected rank. And Boswell confirms this point. Johnson believed in the English class system. He believed in meritocracy. He believed in stability and in order. He was an Augustan. He did not want revolution. He did not want upheaval, but nonetheless he was a man who gave the writer a new sense of liberty. That, in fact, is one of his great achievements.

It is a wonderful life and in reading that life, it seems to me that one has this kind of aching sense if only Shakespeare had had a Boswell. Well, we may wish that.

Defoe—*Crusoe* and the Rise of Capitalism
Lecture 17

Our long journey through English literature has brought us almost 1,000 years now, from the ale hall and that distant epic *Beowulf*, to the Neoclassical grandeur and coffeehouse elegance of Dr. Johnson, the great literary lawgiver. But during that long voyage, one important word has been largely missing from our discussions. … And that word, of course, is the novel.

The novel is the one major literary form whose emergence we can date almost precisely. We can see the modern form developing from traditional forms of narrative at the beginning of the 17th century. Narrative storytelling is as old as literature is itself; indeed, it's probably as old as humanity itself. Together with song, narrative is what the ancients called the *primum materium*, the basic substance of one of the most important traditions in literature. However, we should note that a novel is not the same thing as a story. *Beowulf*, for instance, tells a story. *The Canterbury Tales* tell many stories, as does the work of Shakespeare. But none of the storytellers who wrote those works was writing a novel. In this lecture, we'll look at the first great novelist in English literature, Daniel Defoe (1660–1731), and the archetypal work of fiction that came from his pen, *Robinson Crusoe*.

Why did the novel "happen" at this particular time (1719, to be precise) and in this particular place (London)? To help answer those questions, we can point to another occurrence in that time and place: the birth of capitalism. Robinson Crusoe is *homo economicus*, a new kind of man for a new kind of economic system. One of the features that make this novel so fascinating is that it describes a world with which we are familiar, even though, in fact, that world is now 300 years old.

The critic Ian Watt, in his classic study *The Rise of the Novel*, ties together the rise of the novel and the rise of capitalism. Watt sees the novel as inextricably connected with what was going on financially in the city of London—in the counting houses, banks, shops, warehouses, and markets on the Thames. Everyone was a moneychanger, and the moneychangers had, in biblical terms, taken over the temple. This was an age of capitalism and entrepreneurship. Entrepreneurship depends on an idea of society as made up of individuals, each with his or her own store of property and each eager to acquire more property. Through acquisition, these individuals rise in the world. The class system becomes fluid because the more money one has the better chances one has of promotion. Social mobility is part of this complicated system. Worth, at this point in history, is not something that is inherited but something that can be made or earned.

One way of looking at this kind of society, as Adam Smith did, is as an aggregate of individuals coming together. The principal and most dynamic factor in capitalism is the accumulation of individual, not communal or collective, wealth.

The story of *Robinson Crusoe* is familiar, even to those who have never read the novel. A merchant seaman, Robinson, goes to sea to trade; among the goods that he will deal in are slaves. Robinson's vessel is wrecked, all the crew is lost, and he is marooned on an island for 28 years.

We can learn a good deal from the title page of *Robinson Crusoe*; for example, it lists the name of the publisher but not the author. Why was Defoe's name omitted? The answer is that this book purported to be an authentic tale of travel and adventure. Many first readers assumed there was a real Robinson Crusoe who spent 28 years in total isolation on an island off the mouth of the Oroonoko River in South America. With the novel, we encounter for the first time a convention of literary representation known as realism. Is this a true story, or is it a factual fiction? This creative confusion is compounded by the fact that we're not told what kind of book this is. Four years before *Robinson Crusoe*, a similar account of a sailor marooned on an island had become a bestseller. The gullible reader in 1719, looking at Defoe's title page, would have no way to know that *Robinson Crusoe* wasn't the same kind of book.

Literature changes and so do reading practices. Today, we are more sophisticated readers, but the novel was only just emerging in the early 18th century, and not all readers would understand the "doublethink game" (the balance between a real story and a fiction of knowing) that is the essence of literary realism.

The prosaic opening paragraph of the novel doesn't offer any clues that we are not reading an authentic autobiography. Thus, the novel, we may say, is a genre that looks like something else, a chameleon genre. Recall that *Paradise Lost* proclaims Milton's intention to "sing" from the very beginning. The reader knows exactly what literary form to expect. Defoe, by contrast, is deceptive. This story may be fact, he insinuates, or it may not, but the reader must actually be in that state of confusion to get the maximum benefit from the novel.

Daniel Defoe.

The opening paragraph of *Robinson Crusoe* reads like journalism. This makes sense in light of the fact that Defoe worked as a journalist for 30 years.

The novel is sometimes called the "bourgeois epic," meaning that it takes as its subjects characters from classes in society that have generally been beneath the interest of literature, except for comedy. Unlike Shakespeare's Henry V or Marlowe's Dr. Faustus, Robinson Crusoe and Moll Flanders, the heroine of Defoe's next novel, are ordinary people with whom we can identify. At the beginning of the book, Robinson describes himself to the reader, pulling us in. We have a sense of his life in a way that we do not with Dr. Faustus. Further, the fact that Robinson is not a hero but an ordinary fellow impresses us.

Why should the bourgeoisie, the ordinary middle class, require an epic? In the dynamic mercantile world that was emerging in England at this time, the middle classes were the driving force. The middle classes were, as Marx says in *The Communist Manifesto*, the "revolutionary class" in this period, transforming the world around them as the proletariat would do in 1917 in Russia. As the dominant class in society, the middle class wanted its own literature to express itself and to enshrine its ideals in literary form. The middle class was riding high, and the novel was its form.

Robinson leaves from home, not because he wants adventure, but because he wants to make his fortune. He must make his own way in the world as an individual, starting from nothing. Life as a merchant seaman presents the prospect of getting rich.

As the story progresses, Robinson has a series of adventures: He is almost drowned, he's captured by pirates, he's enslaved by Arabs, and he becomes a wealthy plantation owner in South America. In the process of making even more money, he finds himself alone on an island, having lost everything. On the simplest of narrative levels, Robinson's story is exciting. How will he survive against the elements, wild animals, and cannibals without supplies or other people?

Below the narrative surface, however, Robinson is *homo economicus*. He is an economic man, making it himself in the world, without any assistance other than what he has, what he is, and what he does. Money remains the main purpose of his existence, along with the acquisition of more money. Shortly after the wreck, Robinson makes several trips back to the ship before it breaks up to bring back whatever materials he can find, and he gives us an exact inventory of what he has scavenged. At one point, he finds about £36 and, while noting that it is useless to him on the island, takes it anyway. The incident is amusing yet also offers insight into what the novel is about: Money is important.

Over the next 28 years, Robinson uses what he scavenges from the ship to sustain himself, and gradually, he cultivates the island. Everything on the island, all that he grows and can plunder from it, is his property. Thus, we see this novel also as an allegory of empire and of England, which at this time was taking great chunks of the world as its property.

After many years, Robinson acquires a companion, a native from a neighboring island, who has escaped from cannibals. Robinson names his companion Man Friday, teaches him English, and makes him a servant. More importantly, Friday becomes his chattel. Here, the allegory is of slavery. In the sequel to *Robinson Crusoe*, Robinson sells Friday. This, too, is an allegory of English colonialism in the 18th and 19th centuries.

As Britain acquired more and more of the globe, it was transformed into the largest empire the world had ever known. Its vast territories, however benignly or malignly they were ruled, were, in the geopolitical sense, property of the English Crown. Robinson refers to himself as the sovereign of his island and all that it contains, including Friday. Robinson converts his companion to Christianity but retains Friday as his property, and of course, Friday exists principally in Robinson's terms to turn a profit.

Below the narrative surface, however, Robinson is *homo economicus*. ... Money remains the main purpose of his existence, along with the acquisition of more money.

It's interesting to note that many thinkers, such as Marx, Max Weber, and R. H. Tawney, have argued that the rise of capitalism is intimately connected with Protestantism and Puritanism. Just as capitalism stresses the individual acquisition of wealth, so do Protestantism and Puritanism stress the individual's private, personal relationship with, and responsibilities to, God. The individual has credit with his maker and must earn his salvation.

On his island, Robinson, who began his adventures as a version of the prodigal son, gradually becomes a devout and God-fearing Christian. Fear is the key word here. When Robinson finds a single footprint on the shore—not Friday's—he is terrified. This is a key moment in his moral and religious growth because his terror turns him toward God

Robinson was swept up on the island a godless fellow and destitute. He leaves the island, by a series of adventures, rich and a good Christian. As readers, we are to understand that this was God's plan for Robinson. God clearly loves him, and he is finally saved by the rescue vessel and in his soul.

Defoe's life was long, eventful, and full of literary achievement. He was a pamphleteer, a government spy, and the father of English journalism. Born around 1660, he lived in turbulent and dangerous times, more so because he was a dissenter. He found himself in the stocks at one time for having offended the authorities in his writing. Defoe was never well off and downright impoverished in his last years, but it was in those last years that he invented the English novel. Over the next three centuries, the English novel will become a major form, one of the principal arenas in which literary talent will express itself.

Robinson Crusoe is, in its own right, a great novel, but more importantly, it creates a genre. It's rare in literary history that we can see things happening with this clarity, and it's a great privilege because we understand the novel better as a result of our understanding of its origins. ■

Suggested Reading

Defoe, *Robinson Crusoe*.

Earle, *The World of Defoe*.

Richetti, *Defoe's Narratives*.

Questions to Consider

1. How can one explain a work as influential on the subsequent course of English literature happening in 1719?

2. *Robinson Crusoe* is commonly seen to mark "the rise of the novel" in England. Why?

Defoe—*Crusoe* and the Rise of Capitalism
Lecture 17—Transcript

Our long journey through English literature has brought us almost 1,000 years now, from the ale hall and that distant epic *Beowulf*, to the Neoclassical grandeur and coffee house elegance of Dr. Johnson, the great literary lawgiver. But during that long voyage, one important word has been largely missing from our discussions. It's been out of the frame. And that word, of course, is the novel.

The word novel literally means new thing, and that, in literary historical terms, is exactly what the novel is or what it was when it first happened. We've now arrived at the moment at which that new thing, that literary novelty, the novel, came into being.

The novel is the one major literary form whose emergence we can date more precisely, which we can see emerging in its modern form out of the traditional forms of narrative at the beginning of the 17th century. I think that literary evolution is as fascinating as the evolution of any other species. It's interesting. It's more than interesting. It's, in fact, a privilege to see something of this importance coming into being.

It's not difficult to see where, in the most primal sense, the novel comes from. It's primal soup, so to speak. Narrative storytelling is as old as literature itself. It's probably as old as humanity itself. And along with the song, narrative is what the ancients called the *primum materium*, the basic substance, the DNA, we might say, of one of the big aspects, one of the big trends or traditions in literature.

But one has to be precise about this. The novel is not, is not, the same thing as a story. *Beowulf*, for instance, tells a story. *The Canterbury Tales* tell many stories. Shakespeare tells stories. A best-seller of the 19th century was Charles Lamb's *Tales from Shakespeare*, taking Shakespeare and turning them into stories. But none of these storytellers are novelists writing novels.

In this lecture, we'll look at the first great novelist in English literature, the maker, if you want to call him that, the creator of the literary form, if that's not too grand. I think he would have given us a wry smile had we put that label round his neck. And I'm talking about Daniel Defoe, not a very English name, but he was a very English writer. And we're also talking about the archetypal work of fiction which came from his pen, *Robinson Crusoe*. Again, not a terribly English name, which is quite important. I think Defoe is on the edge of society. That's important, given the views which he has of England.

But first the question why did the novel "happen" at this particular point in historical time? And why did it arise in this particular place? That place is England, London, specifically, at the beginning of the 18th century, 1719, if we want to be pinpoint precise about it. To help answer those questions, why then and why there, we may note that something else simultaneously was happening, and that very simply was the birth of modern capitalism.

Robinson Crusoe is, as I'll try to show, *homo economicus*. He's a new kind of man for a new kind of economic system. It's not new to us, but it was new to the 18th century. One of the things that make *Robinson Crusoe* so fascinating is that it talks to us very directly because he's, to some extent, describing our world, even though, in fact, of course, we're looking at something which is 300 years old.

The critic Ian Watt in his classic study *The Rise of the Novel* ties these two phenomena very stimulatingly together: namely, the rise of the novel and the rise of capitalism. Watt, to simplify, sees the literary form, the novel, as inextricably connected with what was going on financially, not in the publishing houses of the city of London, but the city of London, in the counting houses, the banks, the shops, the great Thameside warehouses and the great markets, Covent Garden for vegetables, Smithfield for meat, Billingsgate for fish. Everyone was a moneychanger. The moneychangers, in biblical terms, had come back into the temple. They'd taken it over. This was capitalism. Very simply, this was capitalism, entrepreneurship.

Entrepreneurship depends on a notion of society which is made up of individuals, each with their own store of property, and each keen to acquire more property, each with their own wallet, which they're trying to fill. And by doing this, they're going to rise in the world. The class system becomes very fluid because, in fact, the more money you have, the better chances you have of promotion.

Social mobility is part of this very complicated system. Worth, at this point in history, is not something that's inherited, like a title, blood, good breeding or an estate. Worth is something that can be made or earned. You can die a very different person from what you were born, in a very different station of life.

Worth at this period of history has a pound sterling sign at the front and lots of zeroes at the end: money. Society at this point, one way of looking at it—and thinkers like Adam Smith did see it in this way—is just an aggregate of such individuals coming together. And the greatest conservative leader in the United Kingdom in the postwar period, Mrs. Thatcher, famously said, "there is no such thing as society," only individuals cooperating.

But, to repeat, the principal and most dynamic factor in capitalism is the accumulation of individual, not communal or collective, wealth and property. Everyone knows the story of *Robinson Crusoe*, homo economicus, as I called him. It's one of those works of literature that's familiar, even to those who've never read it and never will read it. It starts in 1651, a very interesting year because the Civil War's going on, though Robinson never mentions it.

A merchant seaman, merchant, here, is the operative word, Robinson, goes to sea to trade, indirectly, the novel hints, and in some points makes very clear, slaves are among the goods that he's going to deal in. The vessel he's on is wrecked and all the crew are lost, and he is marooned on a desert island for 28 years, a lifetime, practically. Why don't I just read the title page, as *Robinson Crusoe* was published in 1719, and spend a couple of minutes just digging around in it for what first readers and first purchasers saw? This, one must a remember, is a commodity, this is a world where nothing is for nothing, people bought and sold this novel, and listen to this title page and work out exactly what it's telling us, with all the hindsight that 300 years gives us, looking backward.

This is the title page:

THE

LIFE

AND

STRANGE SURPRIZING

ADVENTURES

OF

ROBINSON CRUSOE,

Of YORK, MARINER:

Who lived Eight and Twenty Years,

all alone in an un-inhabited Island on the

Coast of AMERICA, near the Mouth of

the Great River of OROONOQUE;

Having been cast on Shore by Shipwreck, where-

in all the Men perished but himself.

WITH

An Account how he was at last as strangely deli-

ver'd by PYRATES.

Written by Himself.

LONDON:

Printed for W. TAYLOR at the Ship in Pater-Noster-

Row. MDCCXIX.

One can learn a lot from this pedantic signage which is hanging over the novel, not least, of course, there's no author's name. It's a hugely, bulgingly expansive subtitle and it gives us the name of the publisher. We know who he is, Mr. Taylor, but one name is missing: that of Daniel Defoe. Why? Because this purports to be an authentic book of travel and adventure. And many first readers, and this is a well-authenticated fact, assumed that there was a real Robinson Crusoe, who spent 28 years in total isolation on an island off the mouth of the Oroonoko River in South America.

With the novel, in short, we encounter for the first time a convention of literary representation which we know as realism. Is this a true story or is it a factual fiction? Now, this confusion, and it's a very creative confusion, is compounded by the fact that we're not told what kind or what variety of book this is.

There had, as it happened, been a recent best-seller four years before *Robinson Crusoe* on exactly the same lines, an authentic account of a sailor who'd been marooned on a desert island, Alexander Selkirk. And Defoe's story was most likely influenced by it. It was a knock-off, if one wants to be blunt about it. It was a homage or a kind of imitation or plagiarism of the real life experiences of Alexander Selkirk, a Scottish castaway who lived more than four years on the Pacific island that was called Más a Tierra. It's now, by a nice turn of fate, called Robinson Crusoe Island.

How would the gullible reader in 1719, looking at this title page, know that *Robinson Crusoe* wasn't exactly the same kind of book as Selkirk's book? As I say, many early readers were fooled. We are not fooled because we have become, and this is very important, sophisticated readers. That's to say, literature changes and so do reading practices. And generally speaking, they've become more skilled. And without the kind of sophistication that we have, the novel *Robinson Crusoe* simply wouldn't work, and neither would any novel, to be honest.

And, of course, we're also helped by the fact that *Robinson Crusoe* in our bookstores and libraries is not placed in the travel section, but in the fiction section. That's to say, we have a sense of genre, which is, at that point, only emerging, only becoming worked out.

We could play the "doublethink game"—this is a real story, this is a fiction—simultaneously, and we can actually do that and it is necessary if we're to get a kind of maximum benefit from the novel. This, in fact, is the essence of literary realism and it's a trick which the reading public has learned in the 18th century. And it's necessary to the writer of the novel.

And not every reader, one suspects, when the novel was still a new arrival on the literary scene, was able to do this, this kind of, what I call the doublethink which realism requires—it is, as I say, not in our DNA. One has to learn it as a kind of skill, a trick or as a technique.

With that in mind—realism—let's look at the wonderfully prosaic opening paragraph. And as you listen to it, try and work out "Is this true or is it false? What markers, what kind of clues are there in this?" And of course, the fact is it teases us.

This is how it goes. This is the opening paragraph, wonderfully so direct. Defoe has this capacity of writing so simply and yet so powerfully.

> I was born in the year 1632, in the city of York, of a good family, though not of that country, my father being a foreigner of Bremen, who settled first at Hull. He got a good estate by merchandise, and leaving off his trade, lived afterwards at York, from whence he had married my mother, whose relations were named Robinson, a very good family in that country, and from whom I was called Robinson Kreutznaer; but, by the usual corruption of words in England, we are now called—nay we call ourselves and write our name—Crusoe; and so my companions always called me.

If you read that blind, so to speak, without knowing where it's coming from, how would you know that it's not autobiography written *in propria persona*, that is to say, by a real person in the real world who's really called Robinson Crusoe?

So the novel, we may say, is a genre which, characteristically, looks like something else. It's a chameleon genre. Indeed, some theorists of literary aesthetics argue that it's not a genre at all, but an anti-genre. We have, as it were, to change the whole framework if we're to understand how the novel works.

Recall, if you would, how Milton, a mere 40 years before, begins *Paradise Lost*: "Of Man's first disobedience ... etc., etc., I sing" In that epic poem, the poet proclaims what he's doing. You know from the beginning. He says "I'm singing. This is a song. This is a poem." We know exactly what literary form it is. Adjust your sets. You know, we know exactly where we're going to and where he's coming from. There's no deception.

Defoe, by contrast, is deceptive: that whole business of leaving his name off the title page, for instance. This may be fact, he insinuates, or maybe not, but you have to be actually be in that state of confusion to get a maximum benefit from the novel.

That opening paragraph reads like journalism. And, in point of fact, Defoe was a journalist. He'd been one for 30 years. And he's the first and, arguably, one of the greatest journalists England ever produced. He wasn't by background a creative writer. Indeed, he would have rather despised that description. For him, it was facts, facts, facts. He was a reporter.

How it was he came to evolve or transmute his journalistic style, his reportage, into this new thing, prose fiction, is not known. It seems to have been intuitive, a happy leap into the literary unknown. What we do know, however, is that Defoe began writing fiction very late in life, at a time when he was hard up, when he was short of money. The novel has always been a commercial form of literature. Novelists, unlike Milton with his measly £5, $10, to continue the analogy, write for money. On the whole, they, like everybody else, are in the big capitalist game.

The other feature of the novel is that it's what's sometimes called the "bourgeois epic." Now, what that means is that it interests itself, the novel interests itself, takes its heroes and heroines from classes in society that have generally been beneath the interest of literature, unless it's comedy. Ordinary people, that is, people, in fact, with whom the readers of fiction can, and this is an important word, identify. It's much easier, for instance, to identify with Robinson Crusoe than it is with Shakespeare's Henry V or Milton's Adam or Marlowe's Dr. Faustus. We can actually almost do it, but there are big differences. I mean these are people, in fact, who are above us, beyond us, different from us in many ways.

But Robinson Crusoe, as I say, or Moll Flanders, the heroine of Defoe's next novel, these are ordinary people. They may not be exactly like us, but we can, so to speak, get inside them. We have more access to them and their lives than we do to the traditional heroes and heroines of literature.

Consider, for instance, Robinson, as he goes on to describe himself to the reader, and note how, in fact, he pulls us in. We can actually feel his life in a way which, I think, is very difficult if you compare it to the first soliloquy in what I just mentioned earlier, Marlowe's Dr. Faustus.

This is how Robinson describes himself and his background:

> Being the third son of the family and not bred to any trade, my head began to be filled very early with rambling thoughts. My father, who was very ancient, had given me a competent share of learning, as far as house-education and a country free school generally go, and designed me for the law; but I would be satisfied with nothing but going to sea; and my inclination to this led me so strongly against the will, nay, the commands of my father, and against all the entreaties and persuasions of my mother and other friends, that there seemed to be something fatal in that propensity of nature, tending directly to the life of misery which was to befall me.

And somehow, it's a very mysterious thing, this, one feels that one is Robinson Crusoe. It's a terrific trick that literature is performing at this stage of its evolution.

Anyway, to go back to the story, Robinson runs away to sea. As I said earlier, it's 1651, some 50, 60 years before the novel was published. And he never sees his family again. But, as I say, it is the unexceptional nature of Robinson which impresses us. "I'm not a hero," he seems to say, "just an ordinary kind of guy, just an ordinary fellow."

Why should the bourgeoisie, the ordinary middle class, require an epic? Because in the new mercantile, dynamic world which was happening in England at this time, the middle classes were the driving force. They were, as Marx says in *The Communist Manifesto*, the "revolutionary class" at this period of history. It's very hard for us to think of the middle class as a big revolutionary, but they were transforming the world around them as much as the proletariat would do in 1917 in Russia.

They were dominant. They were the dominant class in society, and the dominant class always wants its own literature, always wants to articulate, express itself, to, as it were, enshrine its ideals and its notions and its doubts and its confusions in literary form. And the middle class was riding high, and the novel was their form.

Robinson runs away from home, not because he wants adventure, but because he wants to make his fortune. He wants to get rich. He won't inherit his fortune because he's a third son, and primogeniture means all the money gets left to the first son. So, in fact, he's going to be left out. And he doesn't want to be a lawyer, which is a drudging kind of work, so he has to make his own way in the world as an individual, starting from zero. And, of course, by becoming a mariner, a merchant, he does have the prospect of getting rich, getting very rich, but of course, he has to do so and take a lot of risks in doing so. And he doesn't know how it's going to work out, but he's going to take his chances in life.

Robinson, as the story progresses, does, in fact, have a series of very exciting adventures in his quest to make his fortune. This novel is, as 300 years of its being a best-seller testifies, a page-turner. I mean the bits I was reading out, you probably felt, even though I was reading them out, that you'd like to read on. Anyway, Robinson, to summarize, is almost drowned. He's captured by pirates, he's enslaved by the Arabs, he escapes, he finds his way to an exotic South America where, as a plantation owner, he makes a lot of money. And it is in the process of making even more money that he finds himself alone on his island, having lost everything.

On the simplest of narrative levels, it's exciting stuff, page-turning, as I say. How will Robinson survive against the elements, against wild animals, against cannibal raiders—these appear rather late in the narrative, but they're promised in the title page—without supplies, without people around him, without an army, without all the things that we need to defend ourselves in life?

But below the narrative surface, Robinson is, as I said earlier, homo economicus. He's an economic man, making himself, without other assistance than what he himself has, what he is and what he does. He's an individual, and a very successful individual. And money remains the main purpose of his existence, money and the acquisition of yet more money.

Let me cite an example. It's one of my favorite moments in the novel, and not least for a quality which may be unexpected, but which we'll encounter time and time again in fiction: humor, a very sly, ironic humor. This is the situation: the wreck of the ship on which Crusoe was voyaging has been washed up onshore. It will only be a few days before it breaks up, and our hero laboriously makes his way aboard, and even more laboriously brings back what utensils and what materials he can by an improvised raft. He salvages, he scavenges. And what he scavenges will make the difference between life and death to him. And the inventory of what he scavenges is given with a shopkeeper's exactitude.

This is the quotation I'm talking about: "I had been now thirteen days on shore,"—and you'll notice the emphasis on numbers—

> and had been eleven times on board the ship, in which time I had brought away all that one pair of hands could well be supposed capable to bring; though I believe verily, had the calm weather held, I should have brought away the whole ship, piece by piece. But preparing the twelfth time to go on board, I found the wind began to rise: however, at low water I went on board, and though I thought I had rummaged the cabin so effectually that nothing more could be found, yet I discovered a locker with drawers in it, in one of which I found two or three razors, and one pair of large scissors, with some ten or a dozen of good knives and forks:

Why, one wonders, does it matter whether there are a dozen or 100 knives and forks? Because they represent property, and property is important, and you have to, as I say, inventory it. And he does this all the way through. We don't know the name of the ship which is wrecked, but we do know how many knives and forks there are.

The passage goes on:

in another I found about thirty-six pounds value in money—some European coin, some Brazil, some pieces of eight, some gold, and some silver. I smiled to myself at the sight of this money: "O drug!" said I, aloud, "what art thou good for? Thou art not worth to me—no, not the taking off the ground; one of those knives is worth all this heap; I have no manner of use for thee—e'en remain where thou art, and go to the bottom as a creature whose life is not worth saving."

This is very pious, we think. It's the stuff of a good sort of sermon. Well done, Robinson. But remember, this is money. And then our hero adds, rather shamefacedly, we may think, "However, upon second thoughts I took it away." It might come in useful. Now, of course, it'd be much more useful to go and get a lump of rope from the deck, but in fact, he takes the money. It's both deliciously funny and amusing, and it's an insight into what this novel is all about: money is important.

Over the next 28 years, Robinson uses what he scavenges from the ship to keep body and soul together, and gradually, he cultivates the island. He colonizes it. Everything in the island, all that he grows and can plunder from it, is his and his property. And among other things, we can see this novel *Robinson Crusoe* as an allegory of empire. This is what England was doing at the time, taking over great chunks of the world as its personal property.

Famously, after many years, Robinson acquires a companion, a native from a neighboring island, who has escaped from cannibals who would eat him. Now, Robinson teaches Man Friday—he's named after the day on which Robinson found him—English, and he makes him his servant. More importantly, Friday becomes his chattel. He becomes human property. It's an allegory, if you like, of slavery.

In the sequel to *Robinson Crusoe*, which was called for by the huge success, the best-selling success of the first volume, Robinson sells his companion of his solitude. He sells Friday because he is property. Now, this too is an allegory of English colonialism over the 18th and 19th centuries. Britain acquired more and more of the globe, transforming itself, principally by sea power, into the largest empire the world had ever known. These vast territories were owned by the mother country. However benignly or malignly they were ruled, they were, in the geopolitical sense, property of the English Crown.

And Robinson refers to himself as the sovereign or monarch of his island and all that it contains. He owns it. It's his. He might just as well have put a little flag on there, saying "Robinson Crusoe." That includes the luckless Man Friday, who is taught English, civilized and converted to Christianity. He's lucky in that respect because he'll go to heaven, but, nonetheless, he remains as much Robinson's property as the scissors and the money which he took from the ship all those years ago. And of course, Man Friday exists principally in Robinson's terms to turn a profit.

A word, incidentally, on Christianity: the rise of capitalism, as thinkers like Marx, Max Weber and R. H. Tawney have argued, is intimately connected with Protestantism and Puritanism. As capitalism stresses the individual acquisition of wealth, so Protestantism and Puritanism stress the individual's private, personal relationship and responsibilities to his maker. The individual has credit with his maker. He earns his salvation, as the individual has credit with his bank, and has his little store of wealth.

On his island, Robinson, who began life all those years ago in 1651 as a version of the prodigal son, becomes gradually a devout and God-fearing Christian. Fear, as it happens, plays a major part in this, and that famous moment, as folklorically famous as anything in the story, when he finds a single footprint on the shore—it's not Man Friday's, by the way—Robinson is terrified. Now, we never discover whose foot left the print, but it is a key moment in Robinson's moral and religious growth because this terror turns him toward God.

He was swept up on the island a Godless fellow and destitute. He leaves the island by a series of adventures rich and a good Christian. And this was, we are to apprehend, God's plan for him all the time. It was providential. God clearly loves him and he's finally saved in more than one sense: not merely saved by the rescue vessel which, after almost 30 years, takes him back to civilization, but his soul is saved. The ways of providence are strange, but those whom God smiles on can expect, in addition to the eternal salvation of their souls, a healthy bank balance as well. This is a point which, as I say, those thinkers Marx, Max Weber and R. H. Tawney demonstrate, I think authoritatively.

Defoe's life was extraordinary. It was full of event and literary achievement. He was a great pamphleteer, a government spy—about which we'd like to know more, but never will—and, as was said earlier, the father of English journalism. He was born around 1660, and he lived in turbulent and dangerous times, more so as he was a dissenter. He didn't actually conform to the state religion and he had a very foreign name, which is never a good thing in England.

He found himself in the stocks at one time for having written things which offended the authorities. He lived a long life, dying in his early 70s in 1731. He was never well off, and downright impoverished in his last years. And it was in those last years, at the age of 60, a fact which, incidentally, I find very cheerful, that he invented the English novel. What if he'd died 10 years earlier? Well, we can only be grateful that, like his hero, he was spared to give us this wonderful literary bequest.

And what was that bequest? Well, the English novel over the next three centuries will become a major form. To some extent, it will be one of the principal arenas in which literary talent will express itself and will also find ways of carrying the novel a long way forward, from the starting point that Defoe gave it.

Robinson Crusoe is, in its own right, a very great novel, but more importantly, it creates a genre. I said earlier that this is a very rare event in literary history that we can see things happening with this clarity, and it's a great privilege because we understand the novel better because we understand its origins, its genesis. And we have to thank Daniel Defoe for that fact and, if you'll forgive the pun, for that fiction.

Behn—Emancipation in the Restoration
Lecture 18

Aphra Behn, I would argue, is the first woman author who can, in every respect, hold her own with any male writer of her time. ... Virginia Woolf, arguably one of the two or three greatest writers of the 20th century, irrespective of gender, sees Aphra Behn as the first important woman writer in literary history.

Much of 18th-century England that we see in literature is familiar to us; many of the country's modern institutions were, at this time, in place. The 18th century in England saw the emergence in modern form of the Crown, Parliament, the political parties of the Whigs and Tories (known now as the Labour Party and the Tory Party), the Church of England, the Bank of England, the fourth estate, the educational institutions of Oxford and Cambridge, and the ever-growing empire of Britain itself, kept in line by the Royal Navy.

Among these new institutions and entities also emerged the profession of authorship called "Grub Street," because writers had to grub for money like maggots. Professional authors in the 18th century were working a commercial trade in which literature was manufactured as a popular commodity—the book—sold at retail or borrowed from libraries. Literature was no longer circulated in manuscript among an elite group. There was now a reading public and, with it, new forms of literature to satisfy its gargantuan appetites.

The one element missing from this general account of the modern state in the 18th century is women. Although women were a passive presence in the 18th century, they were an important component of the reading public. Many writers were aware that their readership included females; in fact, the novel would not exist in the form that we have it if it were not for women readers, because the novel is a domestic form. Women are also present in literature as subjects, from Chaucer's Wife of Bath to Shakespeare's Cleopatra, to Defoe's heroine Moll Flanders. Literature pays its dues to the other sex, but where are women actively in the making of literature?

English society can be read, from the woman's point of view, as a long history of oppression, subjugation, and exclusion. It was not until the late 19th century, for example, that women in England had full property rights, which effectively liberated them from being men's property themselves. Women could not even sign a literary contract until the early 19th century. Jane Austen needed her brothers to handle this kind of business for her.

In this lecture, we'll look at the first wholly independent woman's voice in literature, that of Aphra Behn (1640–1689), a female author who can hold her own with any male writer of her time. To understand Aphra Behn, we must first understand her time: the Restoration. We discussed this period earlier, but let's return to it briefly, keeping in mind Behn's position within that upheaval in English society.

After the Civil War and the execution of the king, Cromwell went on to overrule Parliament and set up a republic known as the Commonwealth. He also imposed on the country an iron Puritan dictatorship, backed by the formidable army of the Protectorate. While Cromwell held the country down for 11 years (1649–1660), King Charles's son, who would later come to the throne as Charles II, took refuge with his court in France, enjoying that country's sophisticated pleasures. Meanwhile, in England, Cromwell and his regime were ferociously moralistic. Many taverns were closed, along with the racecourses, cockfight pits, houses of prostitution, and theaters. The printed word was rigorously censored, and any hint of light morality or blasphemy was sternly punished.

Eventually, pressure from below for more liberty brought about the restoration of the monarchy. Charles II returned from France, a compromise was reached on the issue of religious toleration, and Cromwell's corpse was exhumed from Westminster Abbey and torn into fragments.

England, in 1660, breathed freely. The theaters, brothels, and taverns reopened under royal and noble patronage. Charles loved the theater, and the court brought with it from France styles of drama that included new definitions of wit, cleverness, politesse, and gallantry. Women, for the first time, became theatrical players in a number of senses.

In Shakespeare's theater, female characters were played on stage by young boys whose voices had not yet broken. But during the Restoration, women played women and became stars on the stage for the first time. Women on stage were portrayed as fiercely independent and powerful. Restoration comedy clearly makes the point that women aren't playthings of men; they are agents in their own right. For example, Millament, in William Congreve's great comedy *The Way of the World*, dominates high society.

She [Behn] is buried in Westminster Abbey, the first woman writer to be so honored.

The principal subject matter of Restoration comedy is, in French style, cuckoldry or adultery. For the women in Restoration comedy, adultery is frequently a way of evening up the score with the tyrant sex, man. William Wycherley's most notorious Restoration comedy, *The Country Wife*, involves such a situation among a merchant called Pinchwife; his young, virtuous wife; and a rake named Horner. The Puritans, although they were no longer politically dominant, were infuriated by this kind of drama, which in turn, was designed to affront them.

Aphra Behn took full advantage of this new emancipation in the world of the theater, writing a number of plays in the Restoration period. The titles of Behn's plays give us some idea of their content and of the female twist they typically contain: *The Forced Marriage*, *The Amourous Prince*, *The Dutch Lover*, *The Revenge: Or a Match in Newgate*, and *The Woman Turned Bully*, all of which were comedies. In 1676, Behn tried her hand at a tragedy, *Abdelazer*, which flopped. Wisely, she returned to comedy with *The Town Fop* and, a year later, her most famous and much revived work, *The Rover*. *The Rover* has a rather conventional plot about a woman who has two suitors of different kinds—one old and rich, one young and poor—neither of whom she wants. The play is about marriage dilemmas, but on a deeper level, it's also about female independence and choices.

If we look at Behn's life, it's not hard to see why she was such an accomplished dramatist. She was born Aphra Johnson near Canterbury. We know little about her upbringing, but while she was still in her teens, her father was appointed lieutenant general of Surinam, a British colony off the

South American coast. Behn's father seems to have met the fate that often accompanied such unfashionable postings, dying of fever. Surinam would be the setting of Behn's later work *Oroonoko*. Behn scholars argue about whether she spent time in the colony in her early 20s, but it seems, from the accuracy of her descriptions and the vividness of her depiction of life in a slave colony, that she must have been there.

Around the age of 24, Aphra Johnson seems to have married a Dutch or German merchant named Hans Behn. We know nothing about him, and indeed, Aphra may have invented him so that she would be seen as a respectable married woman. If he existed, Hans Behn died within a couple of years, leaving Aphra a young widow and a free agent.

In her later 20s, Aphra served as a spy for the newly returned Charles II in Antwerp during the war between England and Holland. Although she did good work in this endeavor, she seems not to have been paid and, in 1668, found herself in debtors' prison. Behn managed to be released from debtors' prison and wrote her way out of hardship. Occasionally, Behn's plays got her into hot water, but she also wrote poetry and, late in what would be a short life, turned to fiction, of which *Oroonoko* (1688) is judged her masterpiece.

Behn died almost simultaneously with the end of the Restoration, and it's not clear that she would have thrived in the post-Restoration period. She is buried in Westminster Abbey, the first woman writer to be so honored.

The full title of Behn's masterpiece is *Oroonoko: Or The Royal Slave. A True History*. We can learn much from the book's title page, not least that Behn was well enough known to have her name listed as an enticement to purchase. Kings, of course, were of great interest during this period, and the paradox of a "royal slave" would have stimulated curiosity. Calling the work "a true history" gives it the veneer of authenticity.

Oroonoko is the story of an African prince, who is brought to Surinam as a slave, along with his wife, Imoinda. The story is narrated by a young English woman, the daughter of the new deputy governor, who has just died. We can easily assume the narrator to be Aphra, and her detailed description of the island lends credence to the supposition that the young author had indeed been there. The narrator befriends Oroonoko and Imoinda and learns their story. Like Charles II, the African prince can speak both French and English. The narrator is struck with their native beauty, their nobility, and their moral innocence.

Oroonoko is definitively not an abolitionist work. Behn seems, indeed, to be much more interested in the divinity that resides in kings—the qualities of moral, spiritual, and human superiority—than she is in the oppression of Africans.

Early in the story, we get a flashback to western Africa and the first meeting of Oroonoko, a prince, and Imoinda, the daughter of a general who has just died saving Oroonoko's life. The king, Oroonoko's grandfather, is also taken by Imoinda's charms and orders her to join his harem. Imoinda is locked away for the king's private enjoyment. Oroonoko breaks into the harem but is discovered by the king. He is forced to flee, and Imoinda is sold into slavery. Oroonoko is told that she has been executed.

The British colonists now arrive, looking for slaves. Oroonoko is tricked, captured, and taken to Surinam to work on a plantation. As a prince, he feels the humiliation keenly. He discovers, however, that Imoinda is also a slave in Surinam, and the two marry. Imoinda becomes pregnant, but Oroonoko does not want his son to be born into slavery. He organizes a revolt, and the narrator herself flees at this point. Oroonoko is foiled in his attempt to escape and cheated into surrendering. When he realizes the end is near, he kills Imoinda; Oroonoko is executed sadistically by a white slave-owner, who is infinitely below him in moral worth.

Thus ends the novella *Oroonoko*. Although it lacks complex narrative machinery, it is nonetheless a good tale, a powerful and readable work. ∎

Suggested Reading

Behn, *Oroonoko, The Rover, and Other Works*.

Hughes and Todd, eds., *The Cambridge Companion to Aphra Behn*.

1. *Robinson Crusoe* or *Oroonoko*? Which claims first place, and why, in the history of English fiction?

2. According to Virginia Woolf, Behn gave women for the first time in literary history the right to speak their minds. What specifically womanly aspects do we find in Behn's work?

Behn—Emancipation in the Restoration
Lecture 18—Transcript

In our long trawl through English literature, we've arrived, chronologically speaking, at the 18th century, the 1700s. We're well into the 1700s, in fact, with the Augustan giants we've been talking about, Alexander Pope, Dr. Johnson and the father of the English novel, Daniel Defoe. As we look round 18th-century England, as it is illumined by the literature, much of it's very familiar to us. Many of the country's institutions which still preside over it are now, at this point in history, in place.

For example, the Crown of England, with its carefully limited prerogatives, as laid down in the reign of William and Mary at the beginning of the century, and consolidated by the accession of the Hanoverian dynasty, a sovereign rule which, of course, England still has. Queen Elizabeth II is a Hanoverian, unlike Queen Elizabeth I. Parliament, with its political party system; we see that too emerging in its modern form in the 18th century. The Whigs and the Tories are, in fact, the two large political interest groups which we still know as the Labour Party and the Tory Party.

We can see the Church of England, which is now unthreatened by nonconformity. The Civil War has, to some extent, placed it on a rock, from which it will never be shaken. Nonconformity is there and it's still very active in the literary fringe, but it doesn't, as it were, threaten the establishment.

There's the Bank of England, the great commercial headquarters of the empire. There's the fourth estate: newspapers begin to come out in the 18th century, very much in their modern form. *The Times*, for instance, the "Great Thunderer," the newspaper of record, begins to emerge or comes out, and is, in fact, launched in the 18th century.

We have the great educational institutions of Oxford and Cambridge. They're imposing themselves. They've been around for a while, but in their modern form, we recognize them in the 18th century. And of course, there's the ever-growing empire, kept in line by Britain's Royal Navy. And, of course, there is, among all these new institutions and entities which we see happening in the 18th century, the profession of authorship: "Grub Street," as it was called.

Why was it called Grub Street? Because writers like Defoe write, they grub for money like little maggots. A lordly writer, such as Edmund Spenser, a virtuoso amateur, such as Donne: they were above any such grubbing. These professional authors of the time—think Defoe—write in a commercial book trade, where literature is now manufactured in the form of the popular commodity, the book, which is sold as retail or borrowed from circulating libraries. It is, as I say, a commodity, as well as a medium, a modem of literary expression.

Literature is no longer circulated in manuscript among a tight coterie or in-group, as it had been, say, in Chaucer's or Spenser's or even John Donne's time. There is now a reading public. And comes the reading public, comes new forms of literature to satisfy its gargantuan appetites. The reading public is very large. It can, at times, be very tyrannical. And of course, the novel is there right in the center. The novel, in fact, is what the reading public is most hungry for.

Now, one could go on in this anatomy of the modern state of the 18th century, but one thing is missing, has been missing from the general account which I'm giving. There is a large, gaping vacancy, and you've probably already guessed what it is. Where, oh where, are the women?

Of course, women are there en masse as a passive presence, as an important component within the reading public I was just alluding to. Writers like Pope were well aware that many of their readers, their most discriminating, genteel readers, were probably female. And without women readers, the novel, for example, could never have happened, at least, not in the form that we have it because, in fact, novels are very much a domestic form. You read them in the home, in the household, and part of that household is the woman listener or the woman reader.

Women are universally there in literature as subjects, from Chaucer's feisty Wife of Bath, through Shakespeare's saucy wench, Queen Cleopatra, to Defoe's plucky whore heroine Moll Flanders. Literature pays its dues to the other sex, but where, to repeat the question, are women actively in the making of literature? Why is not the woman's hand holding the pen? More bluntly, where is the woman author?

Society, English society, that is, from the woman's point of view, can be read, and indeed, has been read by feminists, as a long history of oppression, subjugation, and exclusion. Sometimes it's mild, sometimes, it's tyrannical, but oppression, whether strong or weak, is always there and always effective. It's not until the late 19th century, for example, that women in England have full property rights which, effectively, liberate them from being men's property themselves. What I mean by men's property is the property of fathers, husbands or brothers, chattels.

Women could not even sign a literary contract until well into the late 18th, early 19th century. Even Jane Austen needed her brothers to do this kind of business for her. Jane Austen, one of the greatest writers we have, could not, as it were, negotiate her own career interests.

In this lecture, we'll be looking at the first loud and clear, wholly independent woman's voice in literature. It's, I would argue, an extremely important moment. Now that voice is the voice of the magnificently named Aphra Behn, an author in skirts, something new. Now, of course, there's a background chorus of quieter voices writing in the corners of literature, women who wrote verse, and we'll reserve them for a later lecture.

Aphra Behn, I would argue, is the first woman author who can, in every respect, hold her own with any male writer of her time. This, of course, is a value judgment, but it's one which I think one can confidently make. She's front of stage. Virginia Woolf, arguably one of the two or three greatest writers of the 20th century, irrespective of gender, sees Aphra Behn as the first important woman writer in literary history. And by the end of this lecture, I trust that you'll agree with Woolf's assessment—I certainly do. Cometh the time, cometh the author.

We shall not understand how Aphra Behn happened unless we understand when she happened: the Restoration. I've talked about it before, but let's return to it briefly, keeping in mind Aphra Behn's position within that upheaval in English society. It was, as I've said earlier, an unprecedentedly tumultuous period of English history. After the Civil War, which tore England apart on class and religious lines, Roundheads against Cavaliers, Cromwell the great republican against the king, and the king, of course, lost and was executed. Cromwell went on to overrule parliament and set up the Commonweal, as he called it, which was, in fact, a republic. And to impose on the country an iron puritan dictatorship, backed by the formidable army which the Protectorate, he Cromwell, commanded.

So, Cromwell, the Protector, held the country down for 11 years, the 11 years from 1649 to 1660. King Charles's son, another Charles, later to be Charles II, after an abortive attempt to restore the monarchy in 1650, narrowly escaped with his life, famously by hiding in a tree after a battle and then taking refuge with his court in France. When in France, Charles and the people around him became half French and very sophisticated. They enjoyed life. He was called the merry monarch.

England, meanwhile, during the period of the Protectorate, across the Channel, did not enjoy life. The Protector and his regime were ferociously moralistic. "No more cakes and ale," as Falstaff puts it. Literally, many taverns were closed, along with the racecourses, cockfight pits and houses of easy virtue, and, of course, the playhouses, the theaters. They were worse, even, than the brothels or the Papist churches in the eyes of the Puritans.

The printed word was rigorously censored. Any hint of light morality or blasphemy was sternly punished. It was a dictatorship of moral virtue. The English people decided that such virtue was all very well for the life hereafter, but in the present life they wanted more liberty, more pleasure, more freedom, more sex. And eventually, the pressure of public demand from below in 1660 brought about the Restoration of the Monarchy.

Charles II came back in state from France. Parliament, having thrown off the Cromwellian yoke, exacted certain concessions from the monarch, an amnesty, religious toleration. His own Catholic beliefs would not be enforced. So what we had was that beloved English thing, a compromise. Charles, as I say, returned to London on a wave of popular support to be crowned Charles II in 1660.

Cromwell's corpse was exhumed from Westminster Abbey, where it had lain in state, and he decreed it should lie forever, and it was torn into fragments. No one's quite sure what happened to his head, but the rest of it was actually fragmented and desecrated. Charles II would go on to rule for 25 relatively stable years, but remember, he'd come back from France and he brought with him a lot of foreign things.

There was lots of cake and ale again. England, in 1660, breathed freely. It was as if the whole country relaxed. And as part of this relaxation, the theaters opened again, the theaters which had been closed by the Puritans, as did the brothels and the taverns. More importantly, they, all three of them, opened under royal and noble patronage. Charles loved the theater. He also loved women and his most notorious mistress, Nell Gwynn, was, in fact, an orange seller within the theaters, and then went on to become a distinguished actress.

Members of the court, the king himself, would sit on the stage, at the side. This has now been put a bit further back, as the royal box, as they're called in theaters, but they would sit with their legs stretched out, very close to the actors. In fact, almost close enough to exchange badinage with them. And they would choose which of the handsome women they might entertain or have some conversation with that evening. Conversation could graduate into other things, of course.

From France, the court brought back with it new styles of drama. These are the important patrons. These are the people which the proprietors of the theaters, which the actors, are trying to please. And the court brought back with it new codes, new definitions of what wit was, what it was to be clever, and politesse, and what it was to be gallant. And women, for the first time, were theatrical players in a number of senses.

In Shakespeare's theater, as you'll recall, women characters, Lady Macbeth, for example, were played on stage by young boys whose voices had not yet broken. Cleopatra alludes to this practice when she talks of being "boy-ed forth" if she's foolish enough to be taken back in captivity to Rome. But in the Restoration theater, women played women and there were women stars on the London stage for the first time: Anne Bracegirdle, a wonderful name, Elizabeth Barry, Nell Gwynn herself, who graduated, as I say, from selling oranges to lead parts in Restoration comedy and tragedy.

Women on stage are portrayed as fiercely independent and powerful entities. Restoration comedy makes this point very clearly, that women aren't just playthings of men. They are agents in their own right. They can do things. Congreve's Millament, in his great comedy, *The Way of the World*, for instance, dominates that play. In fact, it is her world, and, of course, *world* here has the overtone of the French *monde*, which means high society. Millament dominates high society like a queen.

the principal subject matter of Restoration comedy centers, in French style, around cuckoldry, adultery. But for the women in Restoration comedy, adultery is frequently an act of revenge. It's a way of evening up the score with the tyrant sex, man.

In William Wycherley's most notorious Restoration comedy, *The Country Wife*, there's a merchant called Pinchwife, who decides he wants a very virtuous woman to be his mate, to be his spouse, to be his wife. And so he gets a little girl from the country and he puts her, effectively, in a prison in town. And there's a rake, that word is very important in Restoration comedy, called Horner—you can guess why he's called that—who's put it about that because of syphilis, he's impotent, so any woman is safe with him. And foolishly, Pinchwife lets Horner into his little *purdah*, or harem, where he's kept his wife. And the inevitable happens.

There's a notorious scene on stage, in which behind a screen on stage, Horner cuckolds, in fact, a nobleman, who, thinking that Horner is impotent, doesn't realize what he's doing to his wife. It's called the China scene because Horner says, "I'll just go into this corner of the room and show your wife some fine china." When they're behind there, of course, the inevitable happens. And on the front of stage, the husband's saying, "I hope you're enjoying that china." And you know, this is a very typical scene.

It was very extreme, and in fact, the Puritans, who were still around—the amnesty had left them more or less intact as a kind of church, but they were no longer politically dominant—were infuriated by this kind of drama. It was a slap in the face to them. It was designed to be a slap in the face. It was designed to affront common low morality.

So, to go back, my original point, in the London theater world, from 1660 to 1700, it was a socio-literary arena where a woman could be a woman and hold her own with the men. That is, if she had what was called spirit, esprit, as they say in French, and wit, which brings us, at last, to Aphra Behn.

Aphra Behn took full advantage of this new emancipation. She wrote a large number of plays in the Restoration period. The titles give you some idea of their content, and also, I think, of the female twist which typically they contain. Her first comedy, produced when she was 30, was called *The Forced Marriage*. It came out in 1670. It was a huge success. It ran for six nights, and all that money which was taken on the third night from the box office went to the dramatist. And so she was, as it were, sort of commercially viable and very successful. Her plays are good.

It was followed by such hits as *The Amourous Prince*, *The Dutch Lover*, *The Revenge: Or a Match in Newgate* (Newgate is the prison), *The Woman Turned Bully*. And they were all Restoration comedies. In 1676, she tried her hand at a tragedy, *Abdelazer*, and it flopped. We, in fact, in our sort of evaluation of the Restoration period, ourselves don't reckon much of Restoration tragedy. Comedy, in fact, is where their strength was.

Wisely, Aphra Behn returned to comedy with *The Town Fop*—fop's another important word in this period—and a year later, her most famous and much revived work, *The Rover*. Nell Gwynn played the lead part of the whore, Angellica Bianca. That must have got some laughs on stage. *The Rover*, in fact, is a rather conventional plot about a woman who has two suitors of different kinds, one's old, one's young, one's rich, one's poor. She doesn't want either of them. She wants something else.

It's about marriage dilemmas, but the important thing is it's also, at a deeper level, about female independence, the woman making choices, the woman as captain of her own destiny, and forced marriage, which is a recurring situation in Restoration comedy, and particularly nagged away at by Aphra Behn, is at the center of this play. Women should not be forced into marriage, is, if you like, the subtext.

It's not hard to see why Behn was such an accomplished dramatist if one looks at her life, which let's now just do that. She was born in 1640 as Aphra Johnson. She was born near Canterbury, though we know very little about her upbringing. In fact, we know very little about any aspect of her life. The whole thing is shrouded in uncertainty.

Her father was appointed, while she was still in her teens, Lieutenant General of Surinam, a British colony. Now, this wasn't as grand as it sounds. He was a barber by profession in England, lower middle class, and Surinam was not a fashionable posting. It was what was called a white man's grave. You went there, you got fever, and you died, which seems what's happened to her father. He died out there. But Surinam would later be the setting for her later work, *Oroonoko*, about which I'll be talking.

Behn scholars argue furiously about whether she spent time in the colony in her early 20s. And it seems, from the accuracy of her descriptions of the place, Surinam, and the vividness of her depiction of what a slave colony was like, that she did spend time there. It seems, again, the details are uncertain, that around the age of 24, Aphra Johnson married a merchant called Hans Behn, and he, apparently, was Dutch or German. We know nothing at all about him.

She may indeed have invented him to make herself a respectable married woman, and then a free agent, a widow. Widows, in fact, were freer than unmarried women because they had seen the world. They had a certain status in society. He may have been a fiction, but if he existed—if Hans Behn existed—it seems he died within a couple of years, leaving her, as I say, a youthful widow, still in her 20s, but a woman with interesting connections in Europe, and, indeed, perhaps the larger world.

Again, in her later 20s, Aphra served as a spy for the newly returned Charles II in Antwerp, the area which is now Belgium and was then sort of vaguely Holland. And there was a war going on between England and Holland. Aphra Behn did good work as this 18th-century James Bond, this female 007, but she did not, evidently, make much money. In fact, the king seems to have actually welched on the money he owed her as a spy, and in 1668, as a 28-year-old, Aphra Behn found herself in debtors' prison.

Once you were in there, it was very hard to get out, but she seems somehow to have done it, and she wrote her way thereafter out of the hardship in which she found herself as she approached her 30s, with her first play, mentioned earlier, *The Forced Marriage*, 1670, when she's exactly 30. Thereafter, Aphra Behn's career, and it was a highly successful career, was in authorship.

She wrote plays, which, as I say, did very well, and they occasionally got her into hot water. She could be very reckless in the things that she said, particularly in the prologues. That's to say, when the character comes forward and talks directly to the audience. She took lovers. She wrote goodish poetry. And late in what would be a short life, in her 40s, Aphra Behn turned to fiction, of which, *Oroonoko*, published in 1688, is judged her masterpiece.

And she died almost simultaneously with the end of the Restoration period, in which she had, as an author, triumphed, partly, as I said, because the Restoration was the Restoration period. She died around 1770, in the period in which James II—during the Glorious Revolution—was forced to abdicate and a new regime came in. It's not clear that she would have thrived terribly well in the successive years of the post-Restoration period. She's buried in Westminster Abbey, the first woman writer to be so honored. And all women, declared Virginia Woolf, should drop flowers on her tomb in Westminster Abbey.

Let's now turn to the work which I've been talking about and pointing to. The full title of that work is: *Oroonoko: Or The Royal Slave. A True History* by Mrs. A. Behn, London, 1688.

One can learn much from that title page, not least that Mrs. A. Behn, Aphra Behn, was well enough known to be an attraction. In the bookseller's mind, she was a name. And kings, of course, were of great interest at this period. And the paradox of a *"Royal Slave"* was piquant. It stimulated the curiosity. Royal exiles, such as Charles, were very familiar, but a "royal slave," what could that mean? *"A True History"*: now, it is, of course, a fiction, but the word novel had not yet been invented. Mrs. Behn could have called it a romance, but that would have stripped the veneer of authenticity off, and she wanted to keep that veneer. She wanted to seem authentic.

In the first paragraph of the introduction, that authenticity is played with. What she says, and this is an address to the reader, is:

> I was myself an eye-witness to a great part of what you will find here set down; and what I could not be witness of, I received from the mouth of the chief actor in this history, the hero himself.

So she vouches for its truth. Briefly, *Oroonoko* is the story of an African prince, who, along with his wife, Imoinda, is brought to Surinam, not in any kingly way, but as slaves, to make money for plantation owners back in England. This story, the story of Oroonoko, is narrated by a young English woman, who's the daughter of the new deputy governor, who has just died. And we can easily assume that to be Aphra, if you recall her own personal history. But how true is this history?

There's a very close and detailed description which lends credence to the supposition that the young author had indeed been there.

Let me read a section of it. She's describing the flora and fauna of Surinam:

> as marmosets, a sort of monkey, as big as a rat or weasel, but of marvelous and delicate shape, having face and hands like a human creature; and cousheries, a little beast in the form and fashion of a lion, as big as a kitten, but so exactly made in all parts like that noble beast that it is it in miniature.

And so she describes the peculiar sort of vegetation and animal life on Surinam. That, as I say, persuades us that she'd actually been there. The narrator makes friends with Oroonoko and Imoinda, and learns their story. He can speak both French and English like Charles II. She's struck with their native beauty, their nobility, and their moral innocence.

How much protest against slavery is contained in the story is a moot point. It is not, repeat not, an abolitionist work. Behn seems, indeed, to be much more interested in royalty, a quality of moral, spiritual and human superiority, the divinity that there is in kings than she is in the oppression of

Africans. Oroonoko, for instance, has Roman not Negroid features. He has straight hair.

there is, as the story starts, a flashback to Western Africa and the first meeting of Oroonoko, a prince, and Imoinda, a daughter of a general who's just died saving Oroonoko's life. The love between the two, between the prince and Imoinda, becomes very fraught. The king, who's "100 and odd" years old, the grandfather of Oroonoko, in fact, has also been taken by Imoinda's physical charms and he orders her to join his harem. She may not refuse.

She is locked away for the king's private enjoyment, among all these other wives. Oroonoko breaks into the harem. The king discovers him. Oroonoko is forced to flee, and the luckless Imoinda is sold into slavery. Oroonoko is told that she's been executed. Enter the British colonists, looking for slaves.

Oroonoko, who is now, a slave himself, though he's previously been a slave-trader, is tricked, captured and taken to Surinam to work on a plantation. As a prince of the blood royal, he feels the humiliation keenly. He's no ordinary slave. He's described as killing two tigers and also has a very closely described battle with an electric eel. But to his amazement, he discovers that Imoinda is also a slave in Surinam. They marry. She becomes pregnant. Oroonoko is desperate that his son should not be born into slavery.

He organizes a revolt, an uprising, and the narrator herself flees at this point. Her life's in danger. Oroonoko is foiled in his attempt to escape and cheated into surrendering. Amnesty is promised and denied. He's whipped, pepper is poured into his wounds. And he realizes it's the end. He kills Imoinda, cutting off her face after he's cut her throat, so no one will ever see her beauty again. He is executed sadistically by a white, slave-owning rabble, infinitely below him in moral worth, but he refuses to be tied down.

This is how the execution is described:

> He had learned to take tobacco; and when he was assured he should die, he desired they would give him a pipe in his mouth, ready lighted; which they did. And the executioner came, and first cut off his members, and threw them into the fire; after that, with an ill-

favored knife, they cut off his ears and his nose and burned them; he still smoked on, as if nothing had touched him; then they hacked off one of his arms, and still he bore up, and held his pipe; but at the cutting off the other arm, his head sunk, and his pipe dropped, and he gave up the ghost, without a groan or a reproach. My mother and sister were by him all the while, but not suffered to save him ...

That's the end of the novel. *Oroonoko* is a very short work. It's a novella, in fact, not a novel, though it almost qualifies, but it has none of the complex narrative machinery which Defoe invests *Robinson Crusoe* with. It's a tale, a very good one. But that Defoe knew Behn's work and learned from it is suggested by his shipwrecking Robinson, as the title page of *Robinson Crusoe* records, at the mouth of the Oroonoque River.

So it may not be a novel, *Oroonoko*, at least, not quite a novel, but it is very, very readable and very, very powerful, as that last description of the hero's mutilation and death suggests.

The Golden Age of Fiction
Lecture 19

It's fascinating to see the high points and low points of literary genres and ... styles. As we saw, the late 16th and early 17th centuries can fairly be called a golden age of drama. Similarly, we can label the early 18th century a golden age of satire. ... The middle and late period of that same century, the 18th, is a golden age of fiction.

Several material and cultural factors combined to make the middle and late 18th century fiction's golden age. One of these factors was the growth of new mass literacy. The fact that large numbers of people could read, especially women, was an essential precondition for the emergence of the novel. Other factors included urbanization and technological advances in printing. With these came an infrastructure in the book trade that facilitated manufacture, distribution, and purchasing. Contingent entities, such as reviewers and reviews, which subject books to critical judgment, also played a part in the rise of fiction.

The novel is, physically, the longest literary form we have encountered and the most expensive to produce and purchase. A work such as Henry Fielding's *Tom Jones*, for example, ran to about 1,000 printed pages. Even in its first printing, hundreds of copies were simultaneously produced and made available. The size, scale, and speed of that operation dwarfs anything that had come before, and it presupposes a large audience that can read a work of that length.

London and, to a lesser extent, Edinburgh and Dublin were the only cities capable of sustaining a fiction industry. This industry was, in the mid-18th century, a huge, empty, inviting field for literary talent and innovation.

Let's review some of the works and some of the movements that emerged in the field of fiction, bearing in mind that every great novelist of the 18th century was a pioneer. The originality quotient of literature has never been higher than it was in fiction in this period, especially in the work of Laurence Sterne (1713–1768). Sterne was perhaps the most mischievous, eccentric writer of fiction, not merely in the 18th century but in the whole of English literature. He was a North Country parson and was renowned as one of the most stylish and rhetorically brilliant Anglican preachers of his time.

The son of an army officer, Sterne was university educated; he spent most of his life as a vicar in Yorkshire. He contracted tuberculosis as a young man and would die at the age of 54. He married and, at the same time, pursued what he called "spiritual adulteries" with ladies outside his marriage by exquisitely written correspondence.

Sterne began writing his great novel, *The Life and Opinions of Tristram Shandy, Gentleman*, to supplement his income as a churchman. *Tristram Shandy* began to appear in 1759, then continued in serial publication over successive years. The novel was hugely successful, not least for its naughtiness.

Sterne's favorite work of fiction was *Don Quixote* by Cervantes, and he called his style of writing "Cervantick." The impossible quest, like the don's impossible quest, is the basic joke in *Tristram Shandy*. One can never do the things in life that one sets out to do. Life is always too complex and seems always to defeat the individual.

Sterne, in the person of his narrator-hero, Tristram, sets out to tell the whole story of his life. He begins with the comical moment of his own conception, in which his father is interrupted by his mother's question: "[H]ave you not forgot to wind up the clock?" Squire Shandy curses her for her silly question and, at the same moment, fathers Tristram; our hero's unlucky life has begun.

After this daring introduction, the novel rambles on for nine volumes, published over 10 years. The great joke is that the novel is supposed to be the story of the whole of Tristram's life, but it's logistically impossible for Tristram to write it. No matter how many volumes he produces, the novel can never contain everything that happens to him.

As Tristram observes, narrative has two axes, one of which he calls the progressive and the other, digressive. To write that a man enters and walks across a room is progressive. To note the wallpaper in the room or the color of the man's tie is digressive. For Tristram, the digressive—what he calls the "sunshine" of the narrative—keeps getting in the way of the progressive. At one point, he calculates that it takes him a year to fully narrate the events of a single day. He will never catch up with himself. This self-reflexive work of literature obviously brings us into postmodernist territory, 150 years before the term "modernism" even came into existence.

A quarrel between two major practitioners of fiction in the mid-18th century laid down the main tracks that the form would follow over the ensuing centuries. These two practitioners were Samuel Richardson (1689–1761) and Henry Fielding (1707–1754).

Richardson began writing fiction late in life, but he was involved in the book trade as a printer and publisher. He knew what the public wanted, particularly that silent component in the public, the woman reader. Richardson's three great works of fiction are *Pamela: Or, Virtue Rewarded* (1740), *Clarissa: Or, The History of a Young Lady* (1748), and *Sir Charles Grandison* (1753), written to prove that Richardson could produce a novel with a male at its center. All of these were epistolary novels, novels written in the form of letters. This form solves the problem of creating suspense in the novel by giving the appearance of "writing to the moment," rather than relating events in the past tense. The two narratives of Pamela and Clarissa concern young women protecting their virtue. Pamela is successful in this endeavor; Clarissa, not so, although both ultimately reach a kind of marital happiness.

The epistolary form gives both novels their immediacy and impact. Clarissa, for instance, is drugged and raped in a brothel. Of course, in her letter written before these events, she doesn't know what will happen, so the rape comes as a surprise to the reader, too. Its impact is shocking because it is unexpected. In a letter written after the rape, Clarissa describes the drinks that were given to her that led to her loss of purity.

The letter form solves the immediacy problem but introduces other problems related to the narrator. Is it likely, for instance, that a recently raped woman would sit down to write composed and intricate letters? Further, wouldn't an 18-year-old girl lack sophistication and narrative skill? In some sense, Pamela and Clarissa become puppets for Richardson's own voice. Nonetheless, *Pamela* was vastly popular. Armies of female fans, who called themselves "Pamela-ites," formed reading groups to share their enthusiasm for the novel.

Henry Fielding was no Pamela-ite. His career in fiction began as a contradiction to everything that Richardson set out to do in his novels. Fielding believed that the moral of Richardson's story—be good and you'll be rewarded—was nothing more than a sermon coated in fictional sugar. It lacked realism, which Fielding thought was the primary purpose of fiction.

This self-reflexive work of literature [Sterne's *Tristram Shandy*] obviously brings us into postmodernist territory, 150 years before the term "modernism" even came into existence.

Fielding's background was very different from that of Richardson. His family was country gentry and had aristocratic connections. Fielding received a classical education at Eton and wrote a few plays in a gentlemanly amateurish spirit. Professionally, Fielding was a lawyer and a magistrate. One of the advantages of this career was that he came to know life and people, particularly rogues.

Fielding's career in fiction began with *Shamela*, a spoof or burlesque of Richardson's *Pamela*. This work was developed into a more thoughtful satire on Richardson, *The History of Joseph Andrews* (1742); the hero in this book is the brother of Richardson's Pamela Andrews, an invention of Fielding's. Like Pamela, Joseph Andrews is a servant, and his virtue, too, is under assault from a lecherous mistress, Lady Booby. Shortly after her husband dies, Lady Booby summons Joseph to her bedroom, where she tries her best to tempt him, but like his sister's, Joseph's virtue is invincible. Joseph loses his position in Lady Booby's house and makes his way back home. The narrative then begins to remind us of *Don Quixote*, a work that Fielding admired as much as Sterne did. The novel spoofs Richardson hilariously, mocking and contradicting his notion of virtue.

Fielding's career in fiction would, after this anti-Richardsonian launch, develop significantly. In the preface to *Joseph Andrews*, Fielding ruminates on Aristotle and asserts that comedy can achieve the same greatness as epic and tragedy. He seems to suggest that the novel can be a respectable literary venture.

In his masterwork, *Tom Jones*, the story of a foundling, Fielding gives us a novel that is confident in itself and confident in the power of fiction. It continues, but in a much less polemical way, the quarrel with Richardson.

Tom Jones begins life as an illegitimate child; adopted by Squire Allworthy, he grows up to become a scoundrel. He has a good heart, but can't stop himself from getting drunk, brawling, and wenching. He is no Pamela or Joseph Andrews but a human being. By the end of the novel, Tom wins his love, Sophia, and discovers the identity of his parents. He settles down as a good English squire and magistrate. He will administer justice and look after his estate.

Library of Congress, Prints and Photographs Division.

Henry Fielding, engraved by J. C. Buttre.

Fielding's point, made with great artistry and irresistible humor, is that virtue is not something to be hoarded. Pamela preserves her virtue, but she does so by not doing anything. Virtue, Fielding demonstrates, is something that one must earn by living, by experiencing life. It must be achieved, not preserved.

Both Richardson's and Fielding's doctrines founded great fictional traditions. Richardson helped to establish the tradition of romance, and Fielding, realism.

We could explore numerous other works in 18th-century fiction, from the delicate pornography of John Cleland's *Fanny Hill*, to Oliver Goldsmith's wonderfully sentimental *Vicar of Wakefield*, to Tobias Smollet's Quixotic picaresques and the work of a host of women writers. Suffice it to say that the novel took off during this period and would continue to soar for the next 200 years. ■

Suggested Reading

Fielding, *The History of Tom Jones.*

————, *Joseph Andrews and Shamela.*

Kinkead-Weekes, *Samuel Richardson.*

Rawson, ed., *The Cambridge Companion to Henry Fielding.*

Richardson, *Pamela:Or Virtue Rewarded.*

Rivero, ed., *New Essays on Samuel Richardson.*

Sterne, *The Life and Opinions of Tristram Shandy, Gentleman.*

Questions to Consider

1. In which different directions do Richardson, Fielding, and Sterne take English fiction?

2. How justified is the term "bourgeois epic" for fiction of this 18th-century period?

The Golden Age of Fiction
Lecture 19—Transcript

Taking the long view as we're doing in these lectures, it's fascinating to see the high points and low points of literary genres and literary styles. As we saw, the late 16th and early 17th centuries can fairly be called a golden age of drama. Similarly, we can label the early 18th century a golden age of satire. Think Pope, think Johnson, think Dryden.

So, as I trust we'll see in this lecture, the middle and late period of that same century, the 18th, is a golden age of fiction, that form which was introduced, as we saw, by Daniel Defoe, the novel. I want, in this lecture, to give some sense of the multiplicity, the richness, and the finest fruits of the century's fictional crop. Material factors and cultural factors combined to help make it a golden age of fiction.

Let's review those factors. They've been gradually, invisibly almost, happening behind the texts we've been looking at in earlier lectures. First, there was the growth of the reading public and with it a new mass literacy. People could read. That, in fact, is an essential precondition for the novel. Women, who learned to read at home from their mothers often, were a major force. And the novel, in the hands of early masters of romance like Samuel Richardson, is very much a woman's thing. Men had adventure, male action fiction as well, but women were, in fact, a large element in this new mix, which as I say, was necessary for the emergence of fiction as a dominant literary form.

Another factor is urbanization. A third factor, technological advance, in printing, for instance. And with it, was an infrastructure, a social, technological book-trade infrastructure, which facilitated the manufacture, distribution, cultivation, and buying. So, one's got the reading public and you have a delivery system via bookshops, libraries, and the coterie. That's to say, people, in fact, who talk about books among themselves, word of mouth, as we call it.

There were contingent entities, such as the reviews, which subject the superfluity of fiction on offer to critical judgment. All these things are happening at the same time, and they're all coming together to create an ensemble, which buoys up, which actually brings to the top the novel as a dominant form. It's all very complex.

The novel is, physically, the longest literary form we have hitherto encountered and the most expensive to produce and to purchase. It's not an easy thing, to make a novel. And you have to dig quite deep into your pocket sometimes to buy novels. A work like Fielding's Tom Jones, for example, is around half a million words, 1,000 normally printed pages in length. And even in its first edition or printing, hundreds of copies were simultaneously produced and made available. That's a huge operation, commercially.

The cost was substantial. The size, scale, and speed of operation dwarfs anything that had come before. And to go back to that issue of the reading public, a novel like Tom Jones presupposes and necessitates readers who can perform the athletic task of reading half a million, often complicated, words. It's not an easy thing.

London, and to a lesser extent, the other capitals of the United Kingdom, Edinburgh and Dublin, were the only metropolises capable of sustaining a fiction industry, and London particularly. And it helps, I think, to picture the world of fiction, the world of the novel in the mid-18th century as a huge, empty, inviting field: Inviting, that is, to literary talent to come and fill it, to invent new, exciting subforms of this new, exciting dominant form, the novel, the literary genre which has happened in this time, and which everyone was talking about, everyone wanted to read.

Let's review some of the works and some of the movements that happened within that big field, that big field of fiction. Every great novelist of the 18th century is, and I stress this fact, a pioneer. The originality quotient of literature has never been higher than it was in fiction in this period. Every novelist, to some extent, was breaking new ground.

With this in mind, let's look at the most mischievously, eccentrically original writer of fiction, not merely in the 18th century but, arguably, in the whole of English literature as we now have it. I'm referring to Laurence Sterne, more properly, the Reverend Laurence Sterne. He was a north-country parson, and was renowned, in addition to his work in fiction, as one of the great—that means one of the most stylish and rhetorically brilliant—Anglican preachers of his time. Theology didn't really come into it. It was all style.

Sterne was born in 1713, the son of an army officer, who very quickly dropped out of Laurence's life. He was university educated. He was over-educated, as he would wryly have admitted. He was ordained into the Anglican church and spent his life, very comfortably, as a vicar in Yorkshire. He had a modestly successful career, church career, that is, around the great diocesan cathedral in York, York Minster.

It was, however, an invalid's life. He had tuberculosis, which was epidemic and incurable at the time. There are poignant references in his comic fiction to the amount of blood he'd spat out that morning. Sterne would die young, at 54, and he knew he would. The skull was always on his desk. There were lots of "Alas, poor Yorick" jokes in his fiction—Hamlet, you'll remember—picking up the skull in Shakespeare's play.

The Church of England at this period was famously lax. Latitudinarian was the word which was applied to it. Parsons, for example, hunted the fox. Unlike their Catholic counterparts, they could marry. Think about Jane Austen's family. If parsons couldn't marry in England, we wouldn't have Pride and Prejudice.

Sterne married, and at the same time, he pursued what he called "spiritual adulteries" with congenial ladies outside his marriage by exquisitely written correspondence. It's probable that he was faithful, at least physically, but emotionally, he was a libertine. They lived well, these parsons. They were gentlemen. They were respected. And they could write novels and they could write poetry, if that's how their fancy took them. They could become amateur scientists. Many were.

Sterne actually began writing his great novel, The Life and Opinions of Tristram Shandy, Gentleman, to supplement his income, to live, that is, in an even more gentlemanly fashion than his stipend as a churchman allowed. Tristram Shandy, the novel, it's not saying it is a novel, but we'll call it that, began to appear in 1759 and then continued to come out serially, volume by volume, over successive years. It bore Sterne's name on the title page. He's a clergyman, but there was no objection to that.

And it was hugely successful. And it patented, it, as it were, sort of put its brand mark on a variety of humor, which we give the name Shandean to. And the novel was successful, not least for its naughtiness, of which I'll be saying something in a moment or two. He subtitled it *A Cock and Bull Story*, and the bawdy pun is deliberate. Sterne's favorite work of fiction was *Don Quixote* by Cervantes, and he called his style of writing "Cervantick." And the impossible quest, like the don's impossible quest, is the basic joke in *Tristram Shandy*. You can never get the things done in life that you've set out to do. Life is always too complex and always defeats you.

Tristram Shandy is written very much in the spirit of the magician who comes on stage and says, "My next trick is impossible." What Sterne sets out to do in the person of his narrator hero, Tristram, is to tell the whole story of his life. After all, that's what novels do. They recount, they narrate lives. But where should he begin? Well, at the moment of conception, of course. And we move to the first paragraph of the novel now, which is the moment of conception for Tristram, and very comical it is.

His father, who's a squire in Yorkshire, master of Shandy Hall—shandy, by the way, I should say, is English means small beer. It's a mixture of beer and lemonade. It's very tame, small beer, which in fact, is another joke that nothing very big is going to happen in this novel. Anyway, Tristram's father, Squire Shandy, likes to get all his household business out of the way at the same time. On Sunday evenings, he winds the great grandfather clock and then he puts on his nightdress, his night hat, and he performs his similarly once-weekly husbandly duties with his wife.

At the moment of climax, however, a thought comes to his wife, by the association of ideas, John Locke's notion of the association of ideas going on infinitely, one idea suggests another, suggests another, suggests another, and so do sense impressions. That, in fact, is very much a dynamic principle in Tristram Shandy. But his wife, by the association of ideas, thinks, "He's wound the clock, what will he do next? Oh, I remember." She remembers there's something else he does at this time, and prepares herself.

But then she thinks, and I'll quote now from the first paragraph This, remember, is the first paragraph of Tristram Shandy, of a novel:

> Pray my Dear, quoth my mother, have you not forgot to wind up the clock?—
>
> Good G..! cried my father, making an exclamation, but taking care to moderate his voice at the same time,—Did ever woman, since the creation of the world, interrupt a man with such a silly question?

He's creating something very different, of course. He's creating Tristram. At this unpropitious moment, the moment of ejaculation, our hero little Tristram, as he'll be called, sparks into life. That life, alas, thereafter, will be unlucky. How could it be anything else? I mean the homunculus, the little fellow, is being cursed in conception. But the life won't be entirely miserable. This is not a tragedy.

I don't know about you, but even today, that first paragraph strikes one as daring. I mean it really does actually slightly take your breath away. It's comic and it's nonetheless rip-roaringly funny. It's a terrific way to get a novel going. One reads on, as they say.

Well, we read on, and the novel rambles on, volume by volume, year by year, nine volumes, 10 years, a very sort of long time coming out. But the great joke in this novel is that it's supposed to be a story of the whole of Tristram's life and of his opinions, but Tristram can never write it. It's logistically impossible. That's to say, he can never contain everything that happens to him, however many volumes he turned out. If he turned out a million volumes, he couldn't do it.

We get at this moment to one of the interesting critical principles, which is at the heart of Tristram Shandy, and indeed at the heart of all fiction, because this is very much a theoretic as well as a comic work. There are, as Tristram the narrator observes, two axes or cross-spars in narrative, one of which Tristram calls the *progressive*, A, B, C, D, and the *digressive*, what happens on the way. That's to say, a man comes into a room, he walks across the room. That's progressive. In the room, there's interesting wallpaper. He's wearing a certain color tie. That's digressive.

One of these spars keeps on getting in the way of the other. You can't do them both at the same time. And at one crucial point in the narrative, Tristram calculates that it takes him a year to fully narrate the events of a single day: It's the hare and the tortoise. He'll never catch up with himself. He can't give up the digressions, which he calls the "sunshine" of his narrative, to speed up the progression. So his trick is, like the magician's, literally impossible. You cannot write a novel, or you can't write the life of someone in a novel. It has to be imperfect.

Well, not to labor the point, we're in experimental fiction, postmodernist territory here, the self-reflexive work of literature. And this, recall, is the birth of the novel, the kind of wind-up-the-clock moment. It's the moment of the genre's conception. A hundred and fifty years before the term comes into existence, Laurence Sterne is the father of modernism, which, in fact, I suspect, is his greatest joke.

Sterne then marks out the parameters of the new literary form, but I'm going to progress now. I mustn't digress too much by talking about Laurence Sterne, whom, as a novelist, I have to say I love. Let's look at another part of the field: that big, empty field that I was talking about. Sterne is fascinating and obviously is demarcating all sorts of interesting new areas, but it is a quarrel, a ferocious quarrel between two major practitioners of fiction in the mid-18th century which lays down the main tracks that the form, prose fiction, will follow over the following centuries.

In the one corner, we have Samuel Richardson, and in the other corner, we have Henry Fielding. First, let's talk about Richardson. He's a contemporary of Sterne's. His dates are 1689 to 1761. Richardson, like Daniel Defoe and Aphra Behn, began writing fiction late in life, at 51. And as I said with reference to Behn and Defoe, there are good reasons for novelists delaying the start of their fictional enterprises. Unlike, say, Pope, who was writing great poetry at the age of 14, you need, as I said, to have lived, to have seen the world to create whole lives and whole worlds, which is what the novel sets out to do. You have to have experienced it before you can write about it.

Richardson, significantly again, worked in the book trade as a printer and a publisher. He knew what sold. He knew what the public wanted, particularly that silent component in the public, the woman reader. Richardson, in fact, began his writing career with manuals on how to compose letters, which, in fact, was one of the forms of writing which was open to women at the time. They could write letters to each other.

Richardson's three great works of fiction are *Pamela: Or, Virtue Rewarded*, which came out in 1740, *Clarissa: Or, The History of a Young Lady*, which came out in 1748, these are the two most influential works, and *Sir Charles Grandison*, which came out in 1753, which he wrote really to prove that he could write a novel with a male, as opposed to a female, at the center.

All of them are what's called epistolary novels, novels written in letter or correspondence form. As Sterne noted, one of the epistemological or theoretic problems of the novel is that it is written in the past tense. It is, as Aphra Behn put it, a history. It's already happened. Now, what that means is that the end, the happy ever after, if you want to call it that, must logically be known at the beginning. And an honest author should surely give the story away, but of course, they don't. They hold the story back. We call it suspense, and without it, we wouldn't even bother to turn the page.

How, then, do you create suspense, reader interest? Writing a novel is very difficult. This, in fact, is a kind of an initial and really rather intractable problem. Writing a novel in the form of letters, in the form of correspondence, solved the problem brilliantly. It was, as they said, "writing to the moment." Richardson's two greatest narratives, that of Pamela and Clarissa, concern young women protecting their virtue, that is, their virginity. One does so successfully, the other, Clarissa, unsuccessfully. Both win through, ultimately, to a kind of marital happiness, but the immediacy of the story, its impact, its vividness is due to this form, this writing in the epistolary or letter form.

Clarissa, for instance, is drugged and raped in a brothel by the man, Lovelace, to whom she has refused to surrender her virtue. She does not know—the letter before—that it will happen. So it's a surprise. Hence, when it does happen, it, in fact, hits you. It hits the reader with shocking impact because, in fact, it's unexpected.

Take, for example, the letter describing the drugged drink, which will render her incapable so that she is susceptible to the assault, the loss of her virtue, which, in fact, is the worst thing, Richardson intimates, that can happen to a young woman.

> I was made to drink two dishes, with milk, complaisantly urged by the pretended ladies

She's in a brothel but she doesn't know that.

> helping me each to one. I was stupid in their hands; and when I took the tea almost choked with vapours; and could hardly swallow.

> I thought, transiently, that the tea, the last dish particularly, had an odd taste.

"Dish" because she pours it from the cup into the saucer.

> They, on my palating it, observed that the milk was London milk; far short in goodness of what they were accustomed to from their dairies.

They keep a cow in the back.

> I have no doubt that my two dishes, and perhaps my hartshorn,

That's her medicine.

> were prepared for me; in which case it was more proper for their purpose that they should help me than that I should help myself. Ill before, I found myself still more and more disordered in my head; a heavy torpid pain increasing fast upon me. But I imputed it to my terror.

She doesn't know what's going on. Well, she's writing this the day after, still groggy with the effects of the drugs which are still coursing through her veins, and which have led to her losing that most valuable thing in her life, her purity. The letter form got you round one problem, what we call the immediacy problem, got you out of that thing, everything is historical, everything happened in the past by putting it into the present.

But it runs you right into another problem. Is it likely, for instance, that a recently raped woman would write letters, and letters as composed and intricate in their prose as what I've just read? And surely one wants a more sophisticated tone and narrative skill—not to say a range over the whole kind of narrative field—than an 18-year-old virtuous girl, who knows nothing of the world, can bring to narrative? As I said earlier, to write a novel, you have, to some extent, to have experienced life, but Richardson's heroines are inexperienced. And to some extent, that confines the ways in which they can write, the ways in which they can reflect on their world.

And of course, the only way round that is for Pamela and Clarissa to just be glove puppets for Samuel Richardson, so the male voice comes through the female pen. As I say, you solve one problem in a novel, and you run into another. Sterne loved these problems, but for other novelists, they were trouble.

Pamela, particularly, Richardson's first novel, was vastly, hugely popular. It was a best-seller. An army of fans, calling themselves "Pamela-ites," mobilized to share their enthusiasm for the novel, reading groups, as we would call them. They were overwhelmingly female.

Henry Fielding—you'll remember, he's the great opponent in the other corner—was no Pamela-ite. His career in fiction began as a wholehearted contradiction or objection to everything that Richardson had set out to do in his novels. Think again of that title, *Pamela: Or, Virtue Rewarded*. The novel tells the story of a young servant girl, respectably born, but whose family has come down in the world, Pamela Andrews, who, over the course of many months and 1,000 pages, holds off a young man, the master of the household, who wants to rob her of her virtue. And by retaining her purity, she is rewarded. With what? The frustrated young man as her husband.

Be good, Richardson says, and you'll be rewarded. Now, this, Fielding felt, was a sermon coated with fictional sugar. It lacked that quality, realism, truth to life which he thought was the primary purpose of fiction. Now, Fielding's background was very different from that of Richardson. Remember, Richardson is a tradesman. Fielding was, by birth, upbringing and career not a tradesman, and trade is always suspect at this period, but a gentleman. Fielding's family were country gentry. They had aristocratic connections, and writers, too, were in the kind of outlying parts of that extended kinship group. Pope's friend, Lady Wortley Montague, for instance, was a friend of the Fielding family.

Fielding went to Eton, which is the best school in England. It's where our Prince Harry and Prince William went a few years ago. And he got there a solid classical education. He wrote a few plays in a gentlemanly amateurish spirit, but the theaters were going through a very bad period at this time. There was no great literary opportunity for the dramatist, as there had been, for example, during the Restoration.

Professionally, Fielding was a lawyer and he was a magistrate. He sat on the bench and passed out sentences. He was a very good magistrate, as it happened, but one of the advantages of this was that he got to know life. He got to know people. He got to know rogues. Fielding's fictional career began with *Shamela*, which is a spoof, or burlesque—and Fielding loved burlesques—on Richardson's *Pamela*, obviously enough.

This was developed into a more thoughtful satire on Richardson, *The History of Joseph Andrews*, which came out in 1742, just a couple of years after *Pamela*. The hero of *Joseph Andrews* is the brother of Richardson's Pamela Andrews, and, of course, he doesn't figure in Richardson's novel. It's an invention of Fielding's.

Joseph Andrews too is a servant, and his virtue, too, is under assault from a lecherous mistress, Lady Booby. Lady Booby's husband dies, and on the seventh day after—it hasn't been a terribly passionate marriage, his having been much older than her—she summons the handsome young servant Joseph to her bedroom, where she's been mourning. He's to bring her tea kettle. Tea, in fact, is one of the big things that women have. You'll remember it in the *Clarissa* quotation.

Anyway, he finds Lady Booby naked under the sheets, and this is the description:

> The lady being in bed, called Joseph to her, bade him sit down, and, having accidentally laid her hand on his, she asked him if he had ever been in love. Joseph answered, with some confusion, it was time enough for one so young as himself to think on such things. "As young as you are," replied the lady, "I am convinced you are no stranger to that passion. Come, Joey," says she, "tell me truly, who is the happy girl whose eyes have made a conquest of you?" Joseph returned, that all the women he had ever seen were equally indifferent to him.

He's virginal and virtuous, just like Pamela. But nothing discouraged, Lady Booby, the term then, as now, was slang for the female breast:

> [Lady Booby] raised herself a little in her bed, and discovered one of the whitest necks that ever was seen; at which Joseph blushed. "La!" says she, in an affected surprize, "what am I doing? I have trusted myself with a man alone, naked in bed; suppose you should have any wicked intentions upon my honour, how should I defend myself?" Joseph protested that he never had the least evil design against her.

He protests and she continues to urge him and tempt him, until, furious, she realizes she can't overcome his invincible virtue, just like Pamela. He loses his position. And after a rueful letter to his sister Pamela, he makes his way back home. And the narrative becomes like *Don Quixote*, who Fielding admired as much as Sterne admired, picaresque. It goes everywhere.

The novel spoofs Richardson hilariously. His notion of virtue is mocked, and, more importantly, contradicted. But Fielding's career in fiction would, after this anti-Richardsonian launch, develop significantly, carrying the genre forward to interesting places and in a different fork of the road from Richardson.

In the preface to *Joseph Andrews*, Fielding ruminates on Aristotle. Fielding was, remember, a trained classicist. And he thinks about that part of the poetics which has not survived for us, Aristotle's treatise on comedy. And the novel, Fielding proposes, can be a comic epic form, as great, that is, as anything that Homer achieved. What he's doing here is, I think, suggesting that the novel can be respectable. It can be a respectable literary venture. It can be a great form. He's actually raising the novel to the level of those other distinguished forms of literature, epic and tragedy.

And in his masterwork, *Tom Jones*, the story of a foundling, he demonstrates this greatness. He makes this greatness. It is a very confident novel, a very great novel, and it's a novel which is also confident in the power of fiction to do things. It continues in a way, but in a much less polemical way, his controversy, his quarrel with Richardson

Tom Jones, the hero, is a bastard. He's called Jones because no one's quite sure of his surname. He grows up, adopted by Squire Allworthy, and he grows up a scapegrace. But he has a good heart, does Tom, even though he can't help, on occasion, getting drunk, brawling, and wenching. He is, that's to say, no paragon, he's no Pamela, no Joseph Andrews, but a human being.

By the end of the novel, which is huge, sprawling and picaresque, he wins his love Sophia, and discovers who his parents really were. Allworthy's sister is his mother, it turns out. And he settles down, himself a good English squire and magistrate. He's going to administer justice, as well as to look after his estate.

The point which is being made by Fielding with great artistry and irresistible humor is that virtue is not something that you hoard, which you keep under your mattress, like your life's savings. Pamela preserves her virtue and she does it by not doing anything, except saying, "La, sir, unhand me." Virtue, Fielding suggests or argues, demonstrates, is something that you have to earn, by living, by experiencing. It comes only if you work at it. It's something that must be achieved, must be done, not preserved.

Whichever side one takes, Richardson's or Fielding's, both doctrines founded great fictional traditions. Richardson's went into romance: Harlequin, Troubadour, Danielle Steel, you can trace all those back to Samuel Richardson; Fielding's into the realistic mode: Jane Austen, Thackeray.

There's much more in 18th-century fiction. I began by saying it's a golden age. Well, we don't have time to look at it, but just to run through some names. We have the delicate pornography of John Cleland's *Fanny Hill*. It's a story of a resourceful lady of easy virtue, very improper, but very readable. We have Oliver Goldsmith's wonderfully sentimental *Vicar of Wakefield*. We have Tobias Smollet's Quixotic picaresques, and a host of women writers.

But suffice it to say, the novel took off at this period. It soared, and it would continue to soar for the next 200 years, dominating that great game of English literature.

Just to pause, what justification can there be for a course like this, a course on English literature, trespassing, one might think, on the preserves of another discipline, [history]? One justification is that term which has been used frequently in this course's discussion of 18th-century literature, namely, Augustanism. That term relates, of course, to the rule of the first Roman emperor, Augustus, from 27 B.C. to A.D. 14, and the golden age which Augustus presided over.

Edward Gibbon's great *The Decline and Fall of the Roman Empire* begins with the rule of Augustus. Thereafter, for reasons that Gibbon describes at great length, the empire deteriorated. In this lecture, we'll examine some of the causes that Gibbon perceived for Rome's decline, principally, Christianity.

Gibbon's initial description of the high point of the empire in the time of Augustus forecasts everything that follows and chimes exactly with the idealism of English literature in the middle of the 18th century. Gibbon notes that the first seven centuries of Rome's rise do not interest him. He is interested in the high point and why that high point did not last.

He discusses the decline as a rapid series of "triumphs," but notes, "it was reserved for Augustus to relinquish the ambitious design of subduing the whole earth, and to introduce a spirit of moderation into the public councils." The Augustan period achieved greatness because Augustus didn't overextend Rome. The early centuries of Rome were those of expansion, but under Augustus, Rome turned away from the project of global conquest. Instead, Augustus turned toward the project of Rome civilizing itself, creating its great institutional and cultural monuments. Did this, in some sense, doom the empire? This is the enigma that accompanies our reading of the history.

A second justification for our foray into history is that, at the time that Gibbon's great work was conceived, composed, and published, the fences between disciplines were lower than they are today. One of the most striking features of public discourse in the 18th century was that everything—sermons, writing on science, political speeches—was literary. Edmund Burke's speech to Parliament on conciliation with America a year before the American Revolution stands as an example of such high literature. Dictionary definitions, such as those devised by Dr. Johnson, were also literary in the heyday of the 18th century. If we credit Boswell, even coffeehouse conversation was literary in a way that our interchanges today aren't. This trend was nowhere more in evidence than in the field of history. Gibbon himself was a literary artist, as well as a great historian.

> **The Decline and Fall is hailed as a key text of the Enlightenment and Gibbon himself as "a giant of the Enlightenment." Gibbon took history beyond mere chronicle into a much more philosophical realm.**

Let's begin with a look at the life of Edward Gibbon (1737–1794). Like Fielding, Gibbon was born into the landed gentry. From childhood on, his health was poor; thus, he devoted himself to study and books. He was educated at Oxford, but the main source of his intellectual growth was the European and, to a lesser extent, the Scottish Enlightenment, both based on the notion that the universe was comprehensible by human reason.

In 1753, Gibbon converted to Roman Catholicism; a year later, after travel in Europe, he reconverted to Protestantism. Thereafter, he seems largely to have been a skeptic about religion. During the same period, he fell in love with a Swiss girl, but the relationship did not last, and Gibbon would never marry.

While taking the Grand Tour of Europe, Gibbon first visited Rome and experienced a sense of history among its ruins. In Gibbon's lifetime, England was elevating itself to a Roman level of imperial power. His *History* would stand as a reminder that even the greatest empires fall. Gibbon claimed that on October 15, 1764, he resolved to write a history of the decline and fall of Rome while watching a group of friars sing vespers in the temple of Jupiter. The injection of Christianity here marks one of the sub-narratives in the *History*.

In his late 20s, Gibbon's father died, and the young man set himself up as a rich scholar in London. There, he came to know Dr. Johnson and others who would become his first readers.

Gibbon's standing as a landowner allowed him to slip easily into Parliament as an MP in the Whig party, mildly progressive but unenergetic. This position involved no duties, responsibilities, or vexatious calls on Gibbon's time.

The first volume of the *History* was published in 1776, while America was falling away. The next two volumes appeared in 1781, and the final volume was completed for publication in 1788. The effort of this vast enterprise exhausted a frame that had never been strong. Gibbon moved between Switzerland and England as his health failed in his last years. He died in 1794.

The Decline and Fall is hailed as a key text of the Enlightenment and Gibbon himself as "a giant of the Enlightenment." Gibbon took history beyond mere chronicle into a much more philosophical realm. What conclusions, he asked, can we draw from our contemplation of history? What is the "big picture" that only the reflective mind can see?

Research, for Gibbon, did not involve digging into hitherto unvisited archives and primary materials. For Gibbon, the practice of history was to apply the powers of his mind to the facts, then to express his conclusions in clear prose of the highest eloquence.

Gibbon's subject was large and so was his conclusion. The most explosive reflection in Gibbon's great history of Rome from A.D. 1 to the 15th century concerned the other Rome, the Catholic Church, which erected itself on the ruins of the first Rome. Gibbon decided that the first Roman Empire fell as a result of moral corruption, self-indulgence, and the loss of civic virtue. It lost what had once made it great, the raw energy of its early conquests and the civilized moderation of Augustus. Christianity rose, not because it was God's plan that it should rise, but because it had just those qualities that, over time, the first Roman Empire had lost. What Gibbon called "the pure and austere morals of the Christians" gave them eventual victory. Christian

Rome retained its spiritual hardness, forged in persecution and martyrdom, while Imperial Rome went soft.

Christianity also, after it gained a foothold under Constantine, corroded the militancy of Rome. "The Jewish religion was admirably fitted for defence," writes Gibbon, "but it was never designed for conquest." It could survive the decay of the Roman Empire and thrive on what was decaying underneath it.

This conclusion was not flattering to orthodox sensibilities in England in the late 18th century. Christianity, as Gibbon saw it, could never create an empire; it could only inherit one. The Christian virtue of passive suffering was, as Gibbon saw it, disastrous to ancient Rome.

This analysis and skeptical appraisal of Christianity are contained in the 15th and 16th chapters of the first 1777 volume, leading Gibbon to be branded a heretic and his work banned. Chapter 15 opens with a reference to "rational inquiry."

Augustus of Primaporta.

Gibbon tells us that we must exclude faith, hope, and authority and shine the light of reason on the facts. What follows in chapters 15 and 16 is incendiary. Even to a modern audience, it reads, at some points, like Swiftian satire.

Gibbon, civilized cosmopolitan that he was, had little affection for the ruggedness of the Jewish people, and anti-Semitism is one criticism that is frequently leveled at his work. Why, he asks, would a rational deity not choose the English or even the French instead of the Jews? On the subject of miracles, Gibbon is at his most deadly satirical. Why did God reserve proof of his existence—miracles—"for the convenience" of the Israelites alone? Further, why is it that none of the historians or philosophers of the early empire observes any of the extraordinary social and cosmic events recorded in the New Testament? Gibbon assumes a mask of mock amazement in his "rational inquiry" into this conundrum.

Gibbon uses a range of high literary effects to make a historian's point, which is: Where is the evidence? The gospel asserts, but it gives no evidence, and if we look for collateral evidence, we cannot find it. Even the account of the crucifixion, Gibbon implies, may not stand up to reason.

Whether we agree with Gibbon or not, we cannot but admire the sinewy strength, the sheer rhetorical elegance, and the forensic force and rhythm of his prose. We have later, more thorough and more reliable scholarly accounts of what happened in Rome, but the literary quality of Gibbon endures. His work also tells us much about the world of the 18th century and its literature, a literature of great confidence.

The English truly believed that they were creating something equivalent to what Augustus had wrought in the early years of the Roman Empire. At the same time, a sense of unease accompanied their great imperial achievements—the knowledge that their empire was also fragile and could fall. Thus, Gibbon's text provided a needed *memento mori* to the Augustans of the 18th century. ∎

Suggested Reading

Gibbon, *The History of the Decline and Fall of the Roman Empire.*

McKitterick and Quinault, *Edward Gibbon and Empire.*

Questions to Consider

1. What are the specifically literary characteristics of Gibbon's historical work?

2. Why, in Gibbon's analysis, did Rome fall? And what lessons might subsequent empires learn from that fall?

Gibbon—Window into 18th-Century England
Lecture 20—Transcript

The subject in this lecture is Edward Gibbon's great historical work on the decline and fall of the Roman Empire. Just to pause, what justification can there be for a course like this, a course on English literature, trespassing, one might think, on the preserves of another discipline? One justification is that term which has been used frequently in this course's discussion of 18th-century literature, namely, Augustanism.

That term relates, of course, to the rule of the first Roman emperor, Augustus, from 27 B.C. to A.D. 14, and the golden age which Augustus presided over. Augustus, incidentally, appears in Shakespeare's Antony and Cleopatra as Octavian, not a terribly nice person, but that's by the way.

This, the rule of Augustus, is where Gibbon's great history begins. Thereafter, for reasons which Gibbon describes at great length and with massive scholarly apparatus, it was decline all the way. We'll examine some of the principal causes that Gibbon perceives for Rome's decline, principally Christianity, interestingly enough, more about that later. But consider Gibbon's initial description of the Augustan highpoint in the opening paragraphs of the work. They forecast everything that follows, and they chime exactly with the idealism which writers of English literature had in the middle of the 18th century.

This is how the great work begins, the beginning of the first chapter:

> In the second century of the Christian era, the empire of Rome comprehended the fairest part of the earth, and the most civilized portion of mankind. The frontiers of that extensive monarchy were guarded by ancient renown and disciplined valor. The gentle but powerful influence of laws and manners had gradually cemented the union of the provinces. Their peaceful inhabitants enjoyed and abused the advantages of wealth and luxury. The image of a free constitution was preserved with decent reverence: the Roman senate appeared to possess the sovereign authority, and devolved on the emperors all the executive powers of government. During a happy

period of more than fourscore years, the public administration was conducted by the virtue and abilities of Nerva, Trajan, Hadrian, and the two Antonines.

I love the way that Gibbon weighs every word, and the precision, and the conversational way in which he writes: more of that later. The seven first centuries of Rome's rise, Gibbon notes parenthetically, don't interest him. The actual rise of the empire is something which he almost doesn't have time for. He's interested at the high point and why that high point did not last, and he talks about the decline as a rapid series of "triumphs": "but it was reserved for Augustus to relinquish the ambitious design of subduing the whole earth, and to introduce a spirit of moderation into the public councils."

This is why the Augustan period was so great, because Augustus didn't really overextend Rome. The early years, the early centuries of Rome were those of expansion, as he says, of vanquishing and of valor, of actually spreading the boundaries limitlessly in an Alexander the Great way, "more worlds to conquer." But what Augustus realized was something quite different. Augustus, Gibbon suggests, allowed Rome to turn away from that project of global conquest.

But if that's what Augustus was turning away from, from global conquest, what was he turning toward? Well, he was turning toward Rome civilizing itself, creating its great institutional and cultural monuments, among which, of course, was literature. But did that turning away, that introversion back to this civilizing mission, did that in some sense doom the empire? That is the great enigma which accompanies our reading of the history that follows.

A second justification for this raid that we're conducting on another discipline's territory, on history, is that, at the time that Gibbon's great work was conceived, composed, and published, the fences between disciplines were lower than they are today. One of the most striking features of writing, of public discourse in the 18th century is that everything, whatever the genre or discipline, is literary.

Sermons, such as Laurence Sterne's, for instance, are literary. Science is literary. The Royal Society, in its opening manifesto, enjoined a "close, naked, natural way of speaking," a literary style on scientists. Isaac Newton can be read for his style. Hymns are high literature. Political speeches, those of Edmund Burke, for example, are as literary as anything Alexander Pope did.

Let me just quote from Burke's speech to Parliament on conciliation with America. This is a year before the American Revolution and two years before Gibbon published the first volume of his Decline and Fall of the Roman Empire.

This is Burke speaking to his fellow parliamentarians:

> Let the colonies always keep the idea of their civil rights associated with your government—they will cling and grapple to you, and no force under heaven will be of power to tear them from their allegiance. But let it be once understood that your government may be one thing and their privileges another, that these two things may exist without any mutual relation—the cement is gone, the cohesion is loosened, and everything hastens to decay and dissolution.

Can one imagine any modern politician addressing Parliament, the House of Lords, Congress or the Senate using this elevated oratory? Does it sound to the ear like political science or, rather, what it surely is, high literature?

Even, God help us, dictionary definitions, as devised by Dr. Johnson, are literary in the heyday of the 18th century. And, if we credit Boswell, so was coffee house conversation literary in a way which our interchanges aren't. It was, to summarize, a high literary age and its tone was literary. And it articulated itself everywhere, in the finest prose and poetry, and nowhere more so than in the field of scholarship we're looking at in this lecture: history.

Historians today write well, they write functionally, they write accurately, but they do not, in general, see themselves as great stylists, on a par with, say, Philip Roth or Salman Rushdie. Some of them, indeed, might think that would get in the way of doing history. For most, it would seem irrelevant whether they, as the phrase goes, "write like angels." Just so long as they get it right, that's what matters.

But Edward Gibbon most definitely is a literary artist, as well as, arguably, one of the very greatest historians England has produced. But he's also, and this is my assertion in this lecture, one of the country's very greatest prose writers, up there with Jane Austen or William Tyndale.

First, something about the man himself, Edward Gibbon: he was born in 1737 into the landed gentry, like Fielding, for example. Like Sterne, Gibbon's health was, from childhood on, poor. Had he been more robust— who knows?—he might have been a great politician, a judge, or a prince of the church. But his hold on the world was always weak, which perhaps made that world particularly interesting to him.

So, a retired life, one of study and books, was dictated by his fragile health. We can be grateful, perhaps, for that illness that made him what he was, a great writer. As a child, nursed by a devoted aunt, Gibbon developed "the taste for books which is still the pleasure and glory of my life." He read voraciously. He was educated in a more or less desultory way at Oxford, but that place, rigid in its ways, had little to teach him. He learned a lot there, but it didn't teach him very much.

The main source of his intellectual growth was overseas. He was imbibing the spirit of the European, and, to a lesser extent, the Scottish Enlightenment. What was that? Well, the Enlightenment was based on the notion that the universe was amenable, it was comprehensible by human reason. You could, by looking and thinking, know everything that's worth knowing in life. Mind was king. It could spread light.

How does Samuel Johnson's great poem begin?

> Let observation with extensive view
> Survey mankind from China to Peru

And that's exactly what Edward Gibbon would do, but survey it from Rome to England and back again. Gibbon's great history is, apart from being a great history, a major monument of the English Enlightenment.

There was a strange interlude in Gibbon's youth in 1753, when he converted to Roman Catholicism. A year later, after travel in Europe, he reconverted to Protestantism. Thereafter, it seems, he was largely a skeptic about religion, like that other great philosopher historian, David Hume.

At the same period—he's still a young man—Gibbon fell in love with a Swiss girl. It fell through, and Gibbon would have no distractions, as his great predecessor, Francis Bacon, said:

> He that hath wife and children hath given hostages to fortune; for they are impediments to great enterprises, either of virtue or mischief. Certainly the best works, and of greatest merit for the public, have proceeded from the unmarried or childless men.

Well, Gibbon would have no such impediments. There would be no Mrs. Gibbon and little Gibbons. His work, as he noted in the preface to the fourth book, required health, perseverance, and, leisure, and no domestic distractions, so vast was its scheme. If Laurence Sterne wittily exhibited the impossibility of compressing a single life into a printed book, how could the largest empire history had ever known be so recorded and so compressed? Nonetheless, Gibbon would do it, at the expense of his life, as it turned out, he would do it.

Gibbon's steeping in Europe, the Europe of the High Enlightenment, continued with the grand tour. This, in fact, was the finishing element in a gentleman's education of his class. And, momentously, on that grand tour, his first experience of the Eternal City, Rome.

As he recalled later in a famous passage in his *Memoirs*, this is what he wrote:

> I can neither forget nor express the strong emotions which agitated my mind as I first approached and entered the eternal city. After a

365

sleepless night, I trod, with a lofty step, the ruins of the Forum; each memorable spot where Romulus stood, or Tully spoke, or Caesar fell, was at once present to my eye; and several days of intoxication were lost or enjoyed before I could descend to a cool and minute investigation.

You'll note, even in that short wonderful passage, the move from high, hot emotion to "cool and minute" ratiocination, as it was called. But was it? Was Rome, in point of fact, eternal? It was surely ruined. It is said, Gibbon himself would record the fact that Roman emperors and generals riding back in triumph to Rome would have a slave behind them in the chariot, reminding the hero of the day that he too must die.

As he wrote and lived, Gibbon's England, the England celebrated in James Thompson's anthem, *Rule, Britannia*—do you remember that?—was elevating itself to a Roman level of imperial power. Gibbon's *History*, like the skull on the desk or the slave in the chariot, is a reminder that the greatest empires, even though they touch Augustan heights, will fall, but why? How could something as solid as Rome dissolve into ruins?

Perhaps this is to advance things. Suffice it at this point to say that it was precisely on 15th October, 1764, that the 27-year-old Edward Gibbon resolved, as he said:

as I sat musing amidst the ruins of the Capitol, while the bare-footed fryars were singing vespers in the temple of Jupiter, that the idea of writing the decline and fall of the city first started to my mind.

That may be apocryphal, but it's important that Christianity is there somewhere as well. How was it that Christianity took over the ruins? Well, that, in fact, is one of the great narratives, one of the great subnarratives in the history which follows.

Back to Gibbon's life: his father died a couple of years later, when Edward was in his late 20s, and this meant the young man could now set himself up as a rich scholar in London. It was very fortunate when a rich father dies because otherwise you might find yourself in a kind of position of just being a pensioned person until that happy event occurred. But it occurred early for him, which liberated him again.

He moved to London, where his research materials were, in the newly established archive that would, eventually, become the British Library. In London, he came to know figures like Dr. Johnson and all the other literary worthies and grandees of the time. They, in fact, were his first readership. They were, in a sense, his coterie. And the power of the coterie or the club, as they called it, was immensely potent at this period.

Gibbon's standing as a large landowner allowed him to slip easily into Parliament as an MP, a Whig, mildly progressive, but very unenergetic. It involved no duties, responsibilities, or vexatious calls on Gibbon's time whatsoever. The first volume of the history was published in 1776, while America was falling away. Was this the fall of the English Empire? Who knows, or who knew? At the same period, as I say, while Edmund Burke was orating nobly on the subject in Parliament.

That first volume was commercially successful. The next two volumes appeared in 1781, and the final, sixth, volume was completed for publication in 1788. Gibbon recorded the moment that his pen completed the great work. He's very good at annotating his own creativity: "it was on the ... night of the 27th of June, 1787, between the hours of eleven and twelve, that I wrote the last lines of the last page in a summer-house in my garden."

The effort of writing this heroic and vast enterprise exhausted a frame that had never been strong. He moved between Switzerland, which was then a center of the European Enlightenment, and England as his health failed in his last years. A whole range and battery of organic ailments assailed him and he died in 1794, relatively prematurely.

When one hails the *History* as a key text of the Enlightenment and Gibbon himself as "a giant of the Enlightenment," what does one mean? Where, precisely, is one putting him for that judgment? Principally it means that he takes history beyond mere chronicle, calendar, and record, what happened, when, how and with what consequences, and so on. He takes it into the more philosophical realm of "What conclusions should we draw from our contemplation of history? What is the 'big picture' that only the reflective mind can see?"

Research, for Gibbon, was not digging like a mole in hitherto unvisited archives and primary materials, what, in fact, historical research means to the typical doctoral student or practicing historian today. What history meant for Gibbon was applying the powers of a formidable mind like his to the facts, as they were arranged in orderly style in front of him.

As it happens, he had higher scholarly standards than historians such as David Hume and Tobias Smollet, two historians of England, one primarily a philosopher, the other a novelist. But nonetheless, Gibbon remains a thinker, not, in fact, as it were, a digger, an archeologist. And thinking and then expressing the conclusions of that thought in limpid, crystal clear prose of the highest eloquence, that was Gibbon's intention, and that was his achievement as well.

So, reflection, in a word, is what one understands by enlightenment or his enlightenment, his peculiar program of enlightenment. Now, Gibbon's subject was big, but so was his conclusion. And the most explosive reflection in Gibbon's great history of the rise and fall and Rome from the 1st century AD to the 15th century was on the other Rome, which erected itself on the ruins of the first Rome: Christianity, that is. The Catholic Church, that entity with which, since Henry VIII broke away, had been a constant obsession in England.

Very simply, Gibbon conceived that the first Roman Empire fell because of moral corruption, self-indulgence, and the loss of civic virtue. It lost what had once made it great, the raw energy of its early conquests and the civilized moderation of Augustus. Christianity rose, not because it was God's plan that it should rise, but because it had just those qualities which, over time, the first Roman Empire had let slide.

What Gibbon calls "the pure and austere morals of the Christians" gave them eventual victory. Christian Rome retained its spiritual hardness, forged in terrible persecution and martyrdom, while Imperial Rome went soft. Christianity also, after it gained a foothold under Constantine, corroded the militancy of Rome. "The Jewish religion was admirably fitted for defence," writes Gibbon, "but it was never designed for conquest." It could survive triumphantly. It could survive the decay of the Roman Empire, and, parasite-like, thrive on what was decaying underneath it, drawing sustenance from what it was insidiously destroying.

This conclusion, this reflection was certainly not flattering to orthodox sensibilities in England in the late 18th century. Christianity, as Gibbon saw it, could never create an empire, it could only inherit one, or it could inherit the corpse of one. The Christian virtue of passive suffering, turning the other cheek, was, as Gibbon saw it, disastrous to Ancient Rome, suckled as it was—you know, Romulus and Remus, remember—on wolf's milk, it could never survive on the milk of human kindness.

This analysis and the offensively skeptical appraisal of Christianity are contained notably in the 15th and 16th books of the first 1776 volume. These chapters led to Gibbon being branded heretic, and from time to time and in various places, his magnum opus being banned as a corrupter of Christian faith. And this criticism provoked Gibbon to write a passionate and eloquent *Vindication*.

But let's look at the 15th chapter. It opens:

> A candid but rational inquiry into the progress and establishment of Christianity may be considered as a very essential part of the history of the Roman empire. While that great body was invaded by open violence, or undermined by slow decay, a pure and humble religion gently insinuated itself into the minds of men, grew up in silence and obscurity, derived new vigor from opposition, and finally erected the triumphant banner of the Cross on the ruins of the Capitol.

You'll notice that key phrase at the very opening, "rational inquiry." This is the keynote, the starting line for what will follow. Exclude faith, hope, and authority, Gibbon instructs, shine the bright light of reason on the facts as they lie in front of us. What follows in those two chapters, chapters 15 and

16, is incendiary in the highest degree. Even today to the modern reader, at points, it reads like Swiftian satire.

The first point to make is that Gibbon, civilized cosmopolitan that he was, had little affection for the ruggedness of the Jewish people. Now, anti-Semitism is one criticism which is frequently leveled at Gibbon. He does not like God's chosen people. Why, he suggests, would a rational deity not choose the English, or, if he had to, the French, for heaven's sake? What was God thinking of by choosing the Jews?

It's in the matter of miracles that Gibbon waxes most deadly satirical, most Swiftian. Why, he asks, with the most cultivated of sneers, did the Almighty reserve these proofs of his existence, miracles that is, "for the convenience," that's Gibbon's word, of the Israelites alone? A couple of striking miracles in Imperial Rome, or present-day England, come to that, would speed up conversion no end. It would make us all Christians.

Why, Gibbon asks, raising his eyes quizzically from the documentary evidence, do none of the historians of the early empire observe any of the extraordinary social and cosmic events recorded in the New Testament? Gibbon assumes a mask of mock amazement, as he continues his "rational inquiry" into this conundrum, with the most wonderfully winning of proseLet me read some to you:

> How shall we excuse the supine inattention of the Pagan and philosophic world, to those evidences which were represented by the hand of Omnipotence, not to their reason, but to their senses? During the age of Christ, of his apostles, and of their first disciples, the doctrine which they preached was confirmed by innumerable prodigies. The lame walked, the blind saw, the sick were healed, the dead were raised, daemons were expelled, and the laws of Nature were frequently suspended for the benefit of the church. But the sages of Greece and Rome turned aside from the awful spectacle, and, pursuing the ordinary occupations of life and study, appeared unconscious of any alterations in the moral or physical government of the world. Under the reign of Tiberius, the whole earth, or at least a celebrated province of the Roman empire, was involved in

a preternatural darkness of three hours. Even this miraculous event, which ought to have excited the wonder, the curiosity, and the devotion of mankind, passed without notice in an age of science and history. It happened during the lifetime of Seneca and the elder Pliny, who must have experienced the immediate effects, or received the earliest intelligence, of the prodigy.

He avoids the word "miracle," by the way.

Each of these philosophers, in a laborious work, has recorded all the great phenomena of Nature, earthquakes, meteors comets, and eclipses, which his indefatigable curiosity could collect. Both the one and the other have omitted to mention the greatest phenomenon to which the mortal eye has been witness since the creation of the globe.

It's done with a whole range of effects, which one must call high literary effects. What he's doing here, of course, is he's making a historian's point, "Where is your evidence?" The Gospel asserts, the Gospel records, but they give no evidence, and if we look for collateral evidence, we cannot find it. And even the Gospel account of the Crucifixion, Gibbon infers, could be superstitious nonsense, or, as he would say, it does not stand up to "rational inquiry."

Innumerable Christian apologists have confuted, perhaps even they've refuted Gibbon over the ages. And our business in these lectures is not with matters of theological faith or biblical authority. Just as we need not be Puritans to love *Paradise Lost* as literature, not as Christian doctrine, which is what Milton intended, so whether we agree with Gibbon or not, one cannot but be astonished, as I admit I'm astonished, or won over, perhaps, more than astonished, by the sinewy strength, the sheer rhetorical elegance, the forensic force and rhythm of his prose.

It's great history, yes, although I think few modern students would return to Gibbon's great work for the historical information it contains. At least, it wouldn't be their first port of call, but undeniably it's great writing. One will always, I think, return to it for that.

We have later, more thorough, more reliably scholarly accounts of what happened in the many centuries of Rome's greatness and Rome's fall, but the literary quality of Gibbon endures, and gives it, I think, a prominence, which would mean, where do we shelve it? Well, obviously we shelve it in history, but it also belongs, I think, in whatever Dewey Decimal Classification one can find for it in the great library of English literature.

Also, I think, this work tells us an awful lot about the 18th century. The 18th-century literature is a literature of great confidence. They really did believe that they were re-creating something which was equivalent, which was parallel, which was, if you like, even greater than what Augustus had done in those early years of the high point of the Roman Empire.

But at the same time, there was that uneasiness, which I think is always there in great imperial achievement. "We are the masters," but then there is always that slave behind you, saying, "Well, remember, you too must die. Remember, your empire as well is fragile. It will fall."

And so, whatever else one says by way of praise for Gibbon's text, it seems to me that it was necessary, that in the 18th century, the Augustans needed the afterthought, the after-reflection, let's put it that way, which Gibbon brings to the greatness of that time, the greatness which, as I say, we've seen articulated principally in literature.

Equiano—The Inhumanity of Slavery
Lecture 21

Equiano's works, but principally his autobiography, are now regarded as classics, pioneering classics. They are up there with the most important works produced in the 18ᵗʰ century. And they're as important in English literary history as, for example, Frederick Douglass's and other slave narratives are in American literary history.

In our earlier lecture on Aphra Behn, we noted the paucity of women in the history of English literature, but that vacancy would gradually begin to fill in during the 18ᵗʰ and 19ᵗʰ centuries. Of course, there is another vacancy in the literary chronicle of English that would be even slower to fill in: that of writers of color.

We have seen some glimpses of black figures in literature, including Othello, Man Friday in *Robinson Crusoe*, and the prince in *Oroonoko*. The first major black author we encounter whose background is that of the enslaved masses and who writes about them on an equal standing with any other writer of the period was Olaudah Equiano (c. 1745–1797).

Equiano merits our attention primarily by virtue of his talents as a writer, principally an autobiographer. His story is both gripping in its narrative outline and wonderfully told. Equiano's account of his life and experiences was widely circulated in the abolitionist movement, which successfully ended the slave trade. We should note, however, that the use of slaves, principally in the West Indian colonies, was not abolished at this time.

Equiano's major publications were not generally known to later generations, even in Britain, until a group of academics publicized them in the 1960s. These works, principally the autobiography, are now regarded as classics.

Equiano, who was also known as Gustavus Vassa (although this was not his birth name), was born around 1745 in what is now the Ibo region of Nigeria. In his autobiography, he calls the area Essaka; it was then a part of the Abyssinian Empire. Equiano's father was a village elder and a slave-owner, but after the fashion of the country, he was a kind master. By his own account, Equiano was brought up in a condition of rural simplicity and happiness with his siblings. His home was removed from the upheavals that were shaking Europe, the Indian subcontinent, and North America during the second half of the 18th century, when the "civilized world" was reorganizing itself dramatically.

In the early description of his childhood, Equiano notes that his village society had little use for money and stresses the high standards of virtue, cleanliness, abstemiousness, and decency they obtained there. In this, he opposes the conventional images of savagery, such as we find in *Robinson Crusoe*, where the natives are bloodthirsty cannibals.

When he was about 11 years old, Equiano was kidnapped while playing with his sister and carried off to be a slave. The description of his capture gives a good idea of the overlays of high Augustanism in his literary style and, at the same time, the extraordinarily powerful and moving tale he has to tell.

This woodcut image appears on the 1837 publication of John Greenleaf Whittier's poem, "Our Countrymen in Chains."

Initially, Equiano was an African slave among his own people, but he was ultimately taken to the coast and put aboard a slave ship. His first encounter with white people inspires one of the most vivid sections in the narrative: He assumes the white monsters are cannibals and fears they will eat him. It is they who are the inhuman savages, not Equiano. He faints from shock, fear, and despair. The description of the middle passage is the most affecting and horrifying in the book. The stench and noise are overwhelming, and Equiano becomes sick; as he writes, "I now wished for the last friend, death, to relieve me."

For white traders in black human cargo, slavery was a profitable—and necessary in economic terms—line of international commerce. At the time of the American Revolution, British forces were moved to the West Indies to protect the plantations there, which were worked by black slaves, from the French. The calculation was made in London that the plantations of these islands were worth more to the Crown than what would eventually become the United States of America. What made the West Indian colonial properties so valuable was slave labor, which produced the sugar and other commodities for which there was a huge demand in Europe. Thus, the financial base of the British Empire was built on human exploitation.

Equiano was sold a number of times, eventually purchased by white slavers, and transported to Barbados. He ultimately found himself in the colony of Virginia, where he was bought by a Royal Navy officer, Michael Pascal. Pascal renamed his slave Gustavus Vassa in honor of Gustavus I, the king of Sweden, who had been, to some extent, a liberator of that country. The irony here seems to have escaped Pascal.

Equiano was the personal slave of Pascal and, thus, traveled extensively. He became a trained, able-bodied seaman under the royal flag of England and fought the French, manning the ship's guns.

Equiano endeared himself by loyal service to his master. When they made port in England, Pascal sent him to school to learn how to read and write in English. Clever as well as good-natured, Equiano learned English better than most of the English population at the time. Pascal's actions were highly unusual and generally considered, by slave-owners, to be dangerous. Literacy was, like a sword or a knife, an edge tool. It rendered slaves restless, discontent with their lot, and potentially rebellious. In Aphra Behn's *Oroonoko*, it is the prince's superior mind and intellect that inspires him to start an uprising. Ignorance was seen as one approach to keeping the slave population under control.

During this period, Equiano also became a devout Christian and persuaded his master to allow him be baptized so that he might go to heaven. Church registers record that Equiano was duly baptized in a church near Westminster in February 1759. Heaven might be possible for Equiano when he died, but freedom in life wasn't, nor was he given his share of the money from captured ships, which was usually divided among the crew.

Equiano was inevitably sold yet again, this time into the Caribbean, the jewel in England's imperial crown. He possessed remarkable skills: He could read and write English and, if necessary, navigate a ship. Given his abilities, he was too valuable to work under the overseer's whip in the sugar fields.

Equiano gives us a graphic firsthand account of the extraordinary mixture, not merely of brutality and callousness, but of calculation and commercial ruthlessness with which the slave trade was conducted, particularly in the British West Indies. This was the most profitable and extreme of the slave-driving colonies; its inhuman practices were actually written into law as the West India code. Under this code, no plantation owner could be held guilty for whatever he chose to do to his slaves, and as Equiano tells us, these slaves might easily be his own children.

Equiano also gives us a beautifully written and poignant description of the parting of slave husbands and wives, children and parents, as they were sold off to other islands. Reading his autobiography, we get the sense that Equiano is much more human than his owners. Slavery, he intimates, brutalizes the slavers more than it brutalizes the slaves.

In 1765, when he was around 20 years old, Equiano was bought by a Quaker merchant, Robert King of Philadelphia, who had many uses for Equiano's unusual abilities, principally in matters of inventory. The Quakers were an enlightened sect, and King promised that if Equiano could repay his £40 purchase price, he would receive his freedom. A good master by the standards of the time, King further educated Equiano, instructed him in the Christian faith, and enabled him, by trading, to earn the necessary sum for his freedom.

Equiano resolved that it would be unwise to remain in the American colonies as a freed black man. Such men were at risk and generally resented. Equiano was almost caught himself and carried off again to be a slave in the southern region of the colonies.

Equiano was an accomplished merchant or trader in his own right; he traded for a number of years—possibly even in slaves—before he allied himself with the emergent abolitionist movement in England. This movement was sponsored by evangelicals, nonconformists, and Quakers, whose idiom Equiano knew well. Women were also a major force in the abolitionist movement in Britain, as well as in America.

Now in England, Equiano gave speeches and preached; he also married, in 1792, an English woman, Susannah Cullen. He became a leading figure in the abolitionist movement, not by virtue of having suffered, but by virtue of being able to articulate the suffering of slaves with great eloquence and literary skill. It was Equiano who publicized the case of the slave ship called Zong, in which 133 slaves were thrown overboard to drown in their chains for the insurance money.

In 1789, with the help of patrons, Equiano published his great work, *The Interesting Narrative of the Life of Olaudah Equiano*. The book enjoyed lively sales and set Equiano up for life. It was the first important slave narrative in English literature, with a style evocative of Dr. Johnson and the Augustans. Recent scholarship has rendered parts of Equiano's autobiography dubious. It has been suggested, although this is a matter of great dispute, that he might have been born in the American colonies, in what is now South Carolina. This debate may be worth conducting in the context of Equiano's insistence that his story is genuine. From the point at which he becomes Pascal's slave, however, Equiano's experiences can be authenticated by documentary record. Even if the early descriptions of his childhood are secondhand, those descriptions were true for thousands of others taken by force from Africa to work in the British colonies.

Equiano gives us a graphic firsthand account of the extraordinary mixture, not merely of brutality and callousness, but of calculation and commercial ruthlessness with which the slave trade was conducted, particularly in the British West Indies.

Equiano's married life was evidently happy, and he became a celebrity in England. His success in middle age may have served as some compensation for the suffering that had been inflicted on him earlier. His marriage resulted in two daughters, but his wife, Susannah, died in 1796, at just age 34, and Equiano followed her a year later, probably at about age 52. It is not known where he is buried, although he did leave a sizable fortune to his surviving daughter.

Britain has appropriated Olaudah Equiano for English literature, although many anthologies include him as an American writer by virtue of his long periods of enslavement in that country. Of course, by origin and as the early sections of his history make clear, he is a Nigerian writer. The fact that we have this awkwardness about who "owns" Equiano is testament to one of the cruelest, most indelible, and most objectionable aspects of slavery, which is that it robs humans of the basic fabric of their identity.

Equiano's book is, as its title tells us, "interesting." He writes in the highest manner of literature current in the 18th century, unquestionably handling his prose instrument, the English language, like a master. In literary expression, no writer of the period is less the slave. ∎

Suggested Reading

Equiano, *The Interesting Narrative of the Life of Olaudah Equiano*.

Gates, *The Classic Slave Narratives*.

Questions to Consider

1. In what sense is Equiano's *Interesting Narrative* interesting literature?

2. A number of national traditions can claim Equiano's remarkable text as their own: It has variously been identified as an "African" work and a work of "American" literature. Can it authentically be classified as a work of 18th-century English literature?

Equiano—The Inhumanity of Slavery
Lecture 21—Transcript

If I can begin on a personal note, I've devoted my professional life to the study of English literature, and from time to time, I've asked myself why did I do it, but more importantly, was it worth doing? Is it worth spending years and years and years looking at, effectively, this kind of entertainment? And it seems to me there is a justification in that literature expresses or embodies the noblest aspirations, the finest articulations of idealism, which a culture, a society has. That, for me, justifies it.

But in an earlier lecture on Aphra Behn, I noted a large, in fact, one could go further than that and say a shameful vacancy in English literature, as we've been looking at it over the centuries, and as it's canonized in our curricula in our educational programs. That vacancy was the place where women authors should be. As we moved through the 18th century into the 19th century, that hole is gradually filling in. Women writers, thank heavens, are beginning to make their presence felt. One feels a certain kind of emancipation, long before political emancipation, long before social emancipation, long before professional emancipation, but, nonetheless, women's voices are being heard. There's another vacancy or vacuum in the literary chronicle of English, and, alas, it will be centuries slower filling in, and some would say it hasn't filled in even yet. What I'm referring to, it's obvious to you, I imagine, is where writers of color should be, those multitudes who, even at this early stage of imperial growth, are laboring, slaving, why mince our words, for the English Crown and the English state and the English people, white people.

There have been glimpses of dark pigmentation in literature. We've actually seen them on the edges and sometimes near the front of stage: *Othello*, for example, Man Friday in *Robinson Crusoe*, and *Oroonoko*. But the first major author whose skin is black and whose background is that of the enslaved masses and who writes about them on an equal standing with any other writer of the period is the subject of this lecture, and his name is Olaudah Equiano.

Equiano is, and I stress this point, an author who merits our attention primarily by virtue of his merits as a writer, principally an autobiographer.

Equiano's story, his narrative, is himself, and that story is both gripping in its narrative outline, in its plot, and it's wonderfully well told.

Equiano's account of his life and his experiences and his opinions, I'm echoing *Tristram Shandy*, of course, was widely circulated in the abolitionist movement, which, under William Wilberforce, successfully abolished the slave trade. And there's a slight kind of dishonesty there because it abolished the trade, the movement of human cargo from Africa to the colonies, but not the use of slaves, principally in the West Indian colonies, which were very profitable at this period. I'll say a bit more about that later. So in fact, there were still slaves, but you couldn't move them across the ocean.

Wilberforce's reform was carried through in 1807, and in 2007, there have been celebrations of that. Wilberforce was coming, of course, from the evangelical wing of English society, which, in fact, brought about numerous reforms throughout the 19th century, belatedly as I say, the abolition of the slave trade.

Equiano's major publications were not generally known to later generations, even in Britain, until a company of pioneering academics in the 1960s publicized them, made them in fact, sort of necessary reading for anyone who considered themselves well read. I'm very proud of the fact that that was done primarily by colleagues of mine at the University of Edinburgh in the 1960s. And sometimes you have to move authors from one place, from the hinterland to the front of sort of state, and that was done, I think, very successfully, but very belatedly, in my professional lifetime.

It was done initially under the aegis of what in Britain was called commonwealth studies. Commonwealth was the word that they used after empire was no longer fashionable, and is now termed post-colonial scholarship. We'll be saying a lot about that when we come to the modern period.

Equiano's works, but principally his autobiography, are now regarded as classics, pioneering classics. They are up there with the most important works produced in the 18th century. And they're as important in English literary history as, for example, Frederick Douglass's and other slave narratives are in American literary history.

Olaudah Equiano, who was also known, though it was not his birth name, as Gustavus Vassa, was born around 1745 in what is now the Ibo region of Nigeria. In his autobiography, in his narrative, he calls it Essaka. It was then a part of the Abyssinian Empire. Africa has been owned by external states ever since recorded history.

Equiano's father was a village elder, a governor, a local dignitary, a chief. He was also a slave-owner, but after the fashion of the country, a kind master, as it were, not an oppressive or cruel slave-owner, and certainly not a slave trader. By his own account, and it does have a ring of authenticity, it seems very trustworthy, Equiano was brought up in a condition of rural simplicity and happiness, with numerous siblings.

As he described it, it wasn't quite Edenic, it wasn't Adam and Eve, but it was innocent and it was certainly innocent of the upheavals which were shaking Europe at this period, and shaking the Indian subcontinent and North America during the second half the 18th century when, what was called the "civilized world"—one can question that term—was reorganizing itself more drastically than ever before.

This is part of Equiano's description of his early life before, in fact, he was ripped out of it and plunged into horror and the hellish conditions of slavery:

> As we live in a country where nature is prodigal of her favours, our wants are few and easily supplied; of course we have few manufactures. They consist for the most part of calicoes, earthern ware, ornaments, and instruments of war and husbandry. But these make no part of our commerce, the principal articles of which, as I have observed, are provisions. In such a state money is of little use.

It's quite interesting. He's obviously studied the work of the great economists and thinkers, philosophers of the 18th century. And in the early description of his childhood, Equiano stresses the high standards of virtue, cleanliness, abstemiousness, and general decency, which obtained throughout that village society where he was born and in which he grew up, at least until he was 11 years old.

What he's doing in this, rhetorically, is opposing conventional imagery of savagery, such as one finds, for example, in *Robinson Crusoe*, where the natives are the most bloodthirsty of cannibals and just waiting for the white man to come and civilize them. That's the best hope they have. There was an abolitionist medal, a very famous one, which was put out, which was circulated at the period, which had underneath the inscription the motto "Am I not a man and a brother" and a depiction of a slave in chains. Equiano's early account makes the Ibo seem nobler brothers, even, than those who cast that medal and circulated it among the abolitionist movement.

Well, to return to the narrative: still a child, around 11 years old, Equiano was kidnapped while playing with his sister, and carried off to be a slave. The description of how he was captured gives a good idea, I think, of the overlays of high Augustanism in his literary style and, at the same time, the extraordinarily powerful and moving tale he's telling us.

This is the description of his culture:

> I was trained up from my earliest years in the art of war; my daily exercise was shooting and throwing javelins; and my mother adorned me with emblems, after the manner of our greatest warriors. In this way I grew up till I was turned the age of eleven, when an end was put to my happiness in the following manner:— Generally when the grown people in the neighbourhood were gone far in the fields to labour, the children assembled together in some of the neighbours' premises to play; and commonly some of us used to get up a tree to look out for any assailant, or kidnapper, that might come upon us; for they sometimes took those opportunities of our parents' absence to attack and carry off as many as they could seize. One day, as I was watching at the top of a tree in our yard, I saw one of those people come into the yard of our next neighbour but one, to kidnap, there being many stout young people in it. Immediately on this I gave the alarm of the rogue, and he was surrounded by the stoutest of them, who entangled him with cords, so that he could

not escape till some of the grown people came and secured him. But alas! ere long it was my fate to be thus attacked, and to be carried off, when none of the grown people were nigh.

Initially, he's an African slave for Africans, among his own people, like those his father owned. But it was as a slave at the coast that he first encountered white people, and it inspires one of the most vivid sections in the narrative because these white people, these first white faces he's seen, strike him as monsters, demons, inhuman.

This is how he describes it:

> The first object which saluted my eyes when I arrived on the coast was the sea, and a slave ship, which was then riding at anchor, and waiting for its cargo.

The cargo of human beings.

> These filled me with astonishment, which was soon converted into terror when I was carried on board. I was immediately handled and tossed up to see if I were sound by some of the crew;

They were treated like cattle, in other words.

> and I was now persuaded that I had gotten into a world of bad spirits, and that they were going to kill me. Their complexions too differing so much from ours, their long hair, and the language they spoke, (which was very different from any I had ever heard) united to confirm me in this belief. Indeed such were the horrors of my views and fears at the moment, that, if ten thousand worlds had been my own, I would have freely parted with them all to have exchanged my condition with that of the meanest slave in my own country.

He's going to a worse condition of slavery. These white devils, with their "red faces, and loose hair" must be cannibals, he assumes. They're going to eat him. It is they who are the inhuman savages. He is human, not they. He faints with shock, horror, fear, and despair.

The description of the middle passage is the most affecting and horrifying, and, it has to be said, the most interesting section in the book. This is how he describes it:

> I was soon put down under the decks, and there I received such a salutation in my nostrils as I had never experienced in my life: so that, with the loathsomeness of the stench, and crying together, I became so sick and low that I was not able to eat, nor had I the least desire to taste any thing. I now wished for the last friend, death, to relieve me.

For white traders in black human cargo, slavery was a profitable, and very necessary in economic terms, line of international commerce. To give some idea of how profitable it was, at the time of the American Revolution in the mid-1770s, British troops and forces, largely mercenaries, were moved to the West Indies to protect the rich plantations there, which were worked by black slaves, away from the rebellious American colony. The French were threatening these West Indian possessions. The calculation was made in London that the plantations of these islands were more important, were worth more to the Crown than what would eventually become the independent United States of America.

And what made the West Indian colonial properties so valuable, of course, was slave labor, which produced the sugar and other commodities for which there was a huge demand in Europe, and which was unbelievably profitable, building, if you like, the financial base of the British Empire on, it has to be said, human exploitation.

Well, initially taken captive and enslaved by fellow Africans, Equiano was sold on a number of times. He's just like a piece of money. He passed from hand to hand. Eventually he was purchased by white slavers and transported to Barbados. Work in the sugar plantations required muscle. It required a certain kind of physical development, and Equiano, and portraits confirm this, was physically slight. He was very, very clever, but he wasn't a big man. And work in the fields would probably have killed him very quickly, and that would have meant a write-off of his value to his owner.

He eventually found himself in the colony of Virginia. The slaves were among the most traveled people in the world at this time, passing around all over the globe, though, in fact, it was anything but tourism. And in the colony in Virginia, principally, he was bought by a Royal Navy officer, Michael Pascal. Pascal renamed him Gustavus Vassa. You remember how Crusoe, in order to establish his ownership of Man Friday, gives him a name, Man Friday. It doesn't matter what the name is. The importance is that it is Robinson Crusoe who christens him.

And Equiano's new master, Pascal, calls him Gustavus Vassa in honor, surreally enough, of Gustavus I, the much admired King of Sweden, who'd been, to some extent, a liberator of that country. The irony seems to have escaped this naval officer.

Equiano was the personal slave of this man, Michael Pascal. He was part of his entourage, and since Pascal was in the navy, Equiano also traveled extensively, and he became himself a trained able-bodied seaman. He was very quick at picking things up, not least, of course, picking up eventually the skills of authorship. But initially, he's now a mariner, he's now a sailor under the royal flag of England.

One of the intermittent wars with France was going on at the time, and Equiano fought the French loyally for the king of England, manning his master's ship's guns. He was a powder monkey. If you can imagine, someone had to stick the powder down the barrels and then the cannonball, and then you'd light the fuse, and you were away.

Equiano endeared himself by loyal service to his master. He seems to have been a particularly lovable and nice man, incidentally. That's by the way. And when they made port in England, Pascal sent him to school to learn how to read and write, in English, of course. It'd be interesting to know what language he was thinking of. You know, what language did he dream in at this period of his life? We'll never know. But he learned English very well, better than most, as it happens, of the English population at the time.

What Pascal was doing was highly unusual and was generally reckoned, by slave-owners, to be somewhat dangerous. Literacy was what was called at the time an edge tool. Like a sword or a knife, it had a sharp edge. It rendered slaves restless, discontent with their lot and potentially rebellious. It was a bad thing. In Aphra Behn's *Oroonoko*, it is the prince's superior mind and intellect which inspires him to start an uprising. If, in fact, he'd been ignorant, he wouldn't have done it, so you keep them in ignorance. That's a way, to some extent, of keeping the population under control.

Equiano at this period also became a devout Christian, and he persuaded his master to let him be baptized so he might go to heaven. And church registers record that Equiano was duly baptized in a church near Westminster. Westminster, of course, was the mother of Parliament and the epicenter of the English Empire and where this poisonous slavery was authorized, if you like: another historical irony. He was baptized in February 1759.

Heaven might be possible for Equiano when he died, but freedom in life wasn't, nor was he given his share of the prize money. Captain Pascal had been promoted at this stage, and his ship had won in the war. Normally, what happened was that if you took another ship, you got a portion of the value of that ship, and it was divided throughout the crew. But Equiano, being a slave, didn't get his share.

As was the fate of slaves, inevitably he was sold on yet again, this time into the Caribbean. As I said earlier, this was the jewel in England's imperial crown. But Equiano was that remarkable thing: he was an African slave who could read and write English, and if necessary, he could navigate a ship. He had all sorts of skills which he'd picked up in a very adept fashion in what had been already a very remarkable life. And given his kind of abilities, he was too valuable to work under the overseer's whip in the sugar fields.

Equiano gives a graphic and certainly firsthand account of the extraordinary mixture, not merely of brutality and callousness, but of calculation and commercial ruthlessness with which the slave trade was conducted, particularly in the British West Indies. As I say, that was the most profitable and the most extreme of the slave-driving colonies. And it embodied an extremity of inhumanity which, amazingly, was actually written into law as the *West India code*. And effectively, what this meant was no plantation owner could be held guilty for whatever he chose to do to his slaves. He could do whatever he liked, and he was above the law. It was inevitably a he, I have to say.

This is what Equiano writes:

> Shocking as this and many more acts of the bloody West India code at first view appear, how is the iniquity of it heightened when we consider to whom it may be extended! Mr. James Tobin, a zealous labourer in the vineyard of slavery, gives an account of a French planter of his acquaintance, in the island of Martinico, who showed him many mulattoes working in the fields like beasts of burden; and he told Mr. Tobin these were all the produce of his own loins! And I myself have known similar instances. Pray, reader, are these sons and daughters of the French planter less his children by being begotten on a black woman? ... I have often seen slaves, particularly those who were meagre, in different islands, put into scales and weighed; and then sold from three pence to six pence or nine pence a pound. My master, however, whose humanity was shocked at this mode, used to sell such by the lump. And at or after a sale it was not uncommon to see negroes taken from their wives, wives taken from their husbands, and children from their parents, and sent off to other islands, and wherever else their merciless lords chose; and probably never more during life to see each other! Oftentimes my heart has bled at these partings; when the friends of the departed have been at the water side, and, with sighs and tears, have kept their eyes fixed on the vessel till it went out of sight.

Beautifully written, very poignant. And again, one feels that Equiano's so much more human than his owners, than the society which had been brutalized by slavery. Slavery, he intimates, brutalizes the slavers more than it brutalizes the slaves. I think he's right about that.

Equiano was luckier, if one can use that word in this context, than those he's describing here. He was eventually bought by a Quaker merchant, Robert King of Philadelphia. King had many uses for Equiano's extremely unusual abilities, principally in matters of inventory. He was very good at counting, very good at keeping catalogues of property. And the Quakers were an enlightened sect. In England, they were leaders in the abolitionist movement, but in the colonies, you know, neither Philadelphia and brotherly love nor the Quaker doctrine forbade the ownership and exploitation, as property, of fellow human beings.

But King—who, as I say, was a rather better owner than any, with the possible exception of Pascal that Equiano had previous experience—promised that if and when Equiano could repay his £40 purchase price—just think of the impertinence of that, £40 for a human being—anyway, if Equiano could repay that money, which King had paid out, of course, he could receive his manumission or freedom.

We've now reached 1765 and Equiano is around 20 years old. A good master by the standards of the time, King further educated Equiano, instructed him yet further into the Christian faith with his Quaker inflections, and enabled him, by trading, to earn the necessary sum for his freedom, £40.

And at this point, Equiano resolved it would be unwise to remain in the American colonies as a freed black man. They were at risk and generally resented. He was almost caught himself and carried off again to be a slave in the southern regions of the colony. And there he could expect no owner as mild or as enlightened as Mr. King.

He was an accomplished merchant or trader in his own right, and Equiano traded for a number of years—he may even have traded in slaves, we don't know about that—before he allied himself wholeheartedly with the emergent abolitionist movement. This movement was sponsored by English evangelicals, nonconformists, and Quakers, to a large part, whose idiom Equiano knew well. Women were also a major force in the abolitionist movement in Britain, as well as in America.

Equiano, now in England—he must have been among the most traveled men, incidentally, of his century—gave speeches, he preached, and he married, in 1792, an English woman, Susannah Cullen, and he became a leading figure in the abolitionist movement, not by virtue of having suffered, but by virtue of being able to articulate and express, and describe those sufferings with an eloquence and a literary skill which was greater, I think, probably than almost anyone else at the time.

It was Equiano who publicized the case of the slave ship called *Zong*, in which 133 slaves were thrown overboard to drown in their chains for the insurance money. That was the kind of thing that went on, and the kind of thing that he protested against. And he did, in fact, help change history. Very few writers can be said to have done that, but Equiano was one of them.

In 1789, with the help of noble patrons, including two senior members of the royal household and rich philanthropists, Equiano published his great work, *The Interesting Narrative of the Life of Olaudah Equiano, or Gustavus Vassa, the African*. I think that last word was a proud affirmation of what he was. The book enjoyed a lively sale and set him up for life. It can claim to be, I think, the first important slave narrative in English literature.

But the style, as the first paragraph makes clear, is Dr. Johnsonian to the core. Let me quote it:

> I believe it is difficult for those who publish their own memoirs to escape the imputation of vanity; nor is this the only disadvantage under which they labour: it is also their misfortune, that what is uncommon is rarely, if ever, believed, and what is obvious we are apt to turn from with disgust, and to charge the writer with impertinence.

The diction there is Latinate. There's a wonderful use of antithesis. He inserts the word *vanity* into that first sentence. As I say, this, in fact, is Augustan.

Recent scholarship has rendered parts of Equiano's autobiography dubious. It's been suggested, and this is a matter of great dispute, that he might conceivably have been born in the American colonies, in what's now South Carolina. As I say, there's debate about this.

In the context that, in his first sentence, he insists that his story is genuine, it's a debate which is worth conducting, but what is clear is that the principal section, from his becoming Pascal's slave onward, can be authenticated by documentary record. In fact, he's telling the truth. It is a truth-telling memoir. And even if the early descriptions of his childhood are secondhand, those descriptions are true for thousands of others taken by force from Africa to work in the British colonies.

Moving to the last phase, Equiano's married life was evidently happy, and he was at last a free man and a celebrated free man. He was a celebrity in England, and one's glad of that. It must have been some restitution, some compensation for the horrible experiences and sufferings which had been inflicted on him.

But that last phase of his life was unhappily short. There were two daughters to his marriage, but Susannah died in 1796, at just 34, and Equiano followed his wife just one year later, probably at about 52. It's not known where he's buried, although he did leave a sizable fortune to his surviving daughter.

In conclusion: I'm conscious of a certain embarrassment in appropriating Olaudah Equiano for English literature. You know, many anthologies include him as an American writer, by virtue of his long periods of enslavement in that country. And, of course, by origin and as the early sections of his history make clear, he's a Nigerian writer. He belongs to his own continent, which is not Europe. And the fact that we have this awkwardness about who "owns" him, this uncertainty, witnesses to one of the cruelest and most indelible and objectionable facts of slavery, which I stress and which he makes clear is one of the most horrible things man can do to man. It uproots you, it robs you of the basic fabrics of your identity.

Equiano's book is, as he says in his title, "interesting." It was his intention, of course, to make us read his work by virtue of the quality of what he writes, and he does write, I would suggest, in the highest manner of literature current in the 18th century. He writes like the best of the Augustans. It creates a rather odd effect, but there's no question in my mind that Equiano handles his prose instrument, the English language and the devices of English prose narrative, like a master. In language, in literary expression, no writer of the period is less the slave.

And it has to be said, in the light cast by his true history on the fictions of Defoe and Behn, those works, *Robinson Crusoe* and *Oroonoko*, which we've looked at, fine as they are, do look momentarily a little shabby. When one looks again at Man Friday, one thinks, not quite "Shame on you, Daniel Defoe" but "Daniel Defoe, if only you'd lived to read Equiano's narrative, you would have changed that section of your novel." At least, we hope he would have done.

Women Poets—The Minor Voice
Lecture 22

In the last few lectures, we've been looking at figures, writers, who've been, if not entirely excluded, relegated to the edge of English literature. … In this lecture, we'll be looking at poetry, which is self-consciously minor and typically private, written by women, and one suspects, written for women as well.

Women have always found it difficult to write for the stage because it's so public. The theater requires women to display themselves, and the conventions of society, almost through to the 20th century, forbid that. At the same time, epics are too big for women. They require some large presence in the outside world, a public grandeur that has historically been denied to women.

Some forms of literature do lend themselves to the private domestic arena, where women can feel comfortable and express themselves. In the 19th century Elizabeth Gaskell (known as Mrs. Gaskell), wrote her novels at night, after she'd put the children to bed and the house had been tidied up. Jane Austen often wrote in the drawing room amid company, who might assume that she was merely writing a letter. If someone came close enough to read her work, she might push the paper out of sight because she wasn't ready to share it.

The short lyric poem also lends itself to domestic composition, and we can follow the line of female writers in this form from the 17th century through to the 20th. Some of the poems of Sylvia Plath can be connected to the writing of women 300 or 400 years earlier.

We'll begin with a surprising example from Queen Elizabeth (1533–1603). Elizabeth was a remarkable orator. Her most famous speech is the one she gave at Tilbury on the eve of the invasion of England by the Spanish Armada. Her words are as rousing as those of Winston Churchill when he addressed the nation at a similarly perilous moment. The Tilbury speech represents the public Elizabeth, but in private, Elizabeth, like her father, Henry VIII, also wrote poetry. Skill in writing poetry would have been akin to talent in dancing or proficiency in horsemanship for a woman of Elizabeth's station.

The poem "On Monsieur's Departure" records a moment when its author was left by a lover. (Despite furious speculation, the existence or identity of a lover for Elizabeth is unknown.) In Elizabeth's case, she feels the loss, but she cannot, out of pride of position and rank, display her emotion. It must be bottled up, to be released cathartically in a private poem. The poem is wholly unexpected if compared to the rousing speech at Tilbury. There, Elizabeth had the heart and stomach of a man; here, she is "soft and made of melting snow."

In the United States, Anne Bradstreet (1612–1672) is generally regarded as the first great American poet. In Britain, she is seen as standing in a line of British Metaphysical poets. She was born Anne Dudley in Northampton, the daughter of a steward or land agent, who served an aristocratic estate owner. As a result, young Anne had access to books and a superior library. She was fascinated by the then-fashionable style of Metaphysical poetry. As you recall, in the early 1700s, such poets as Donne, Herbert, and Marvell were writing intricate, clever poems based on elaborate conceits. At age 16, Anne married Simon Bradstreet. Both her father and her husband would later serve as governors of the Massachusetts Bay Colony. Anne went to the colony with them in 1630 and stayed there for the rest of her life. Nonetheless, her literary pedigree remained English.

Life was hard in 17th-century New England. Mortality rates were high, and the amenities of life were lacking. To some extent, Anne had to adapt to a new lifestyle, and in this, she was helped by religion.

Anne contracted smallpox and later tuberculosis, both of which were chronic and debilitating medical conditions. Both her hardship and her joys were increased by giving birth to eight children.

In 1666, her house burned down and, with it, her large, treasured personal library. Anne wrote a poem on that occasion, "Verses upon the Burning of Our House, July 18th, 1666," in which she grits her teeth and gives thanks to God, in simple Anglo-Saxon diction.

Of course, losing children is much harder than losing books, and Anne also experienced this tragedy, but she consoled herself that they were in a better place. Her poem titled "In Memory of My Dear Grandchild Anne Bradstreet, Who Deceased June 20, 1669, Being Three Years and Seven Months Old" is almost unbearably poignant.

We can follow the line of female writers in this form [the short lyric poem] from the 17th century through to the 20th.

The poem is written, Anne says, with a "trembling hand" and a "troubled heart." The poet likens her granddaughter to "a bubble, or the brittle glass, / Or like a shadow turning as it was." She seems to be thinking of an hourglass with the sand running through it. As with the poem of Queen Elizabeth, there is an element of privacy here. This is a woman talking to herself about intensely personal subjects. The poem is a classic meditation, which was a standard Puritan exercise, as well as one of the bases of Metaphysical poetry. Such a poem purifies the spirit through introspection and articulating the results of that introspection with a subtle use of language. The simplicity of Anne's expression, when combined with her complex similes, creates an amazingly understated effect.

The next poet we'll turn to is Margaret Cavendish (1623–1673). Cavendish was high born and, in adult life, would bear the title duchess of Newcastle-upon-Tyne. In early life, she was a courtier attached to the queen of England, and members of her family, the Lucases, were prominent royalists during the English Civil War. Cavendish went into exile in France with the king and his court. She also wrote prolifically and, like Aphra Behn, published under her own name. Her works include prose fantasias, such as *The Blazing World*; a memoir called *A True Relation of my Birth, Breeding, and Life*; philosophical treatises; and a good deal of poetry. Unlike many other women writers, Cavendish was a known figure in the literary world, although that world was not always kind or polite to her. She was resented by male writers, many of whom regarded her as aggressive and self-advertising. She had no children, which gave her greater opportunity, with her prosperous lifestyle and access to the booksellers of London, to pursue a literary career than almost any other woman of the time, with the possible exception of Aphra Behn.

One poem from early in her career, "A World made by Atomes," is clearly Metaphysical in style. It's one of a cluster of atomic poems written by Cavendish, this one dealing with what we would today call particle physics. Cavendish uses the atom as a conceit, and she does well with it, although John Donne probably would have done better. The poem is also interesting in that it inaugurates Cavendish as the first *bluestocking* (female intellectual) in English literature. She launches a line that we can follow from such figures as George Eliot to Iris Murdoch.

Another private poet of the period was Katherine Philips (1631–1664), known also by her pen name, the Matchless Orinda. Katherine was born in London, the daughter of a nonconformist merchant. The household was excessively pious. Katherine is recorded as having read the Bible from cover to cover before she was five years old and to have learned several languages in childhood. In her teens, Katherine turned royalist, probably in a spirit of rebellion, and at age 16, married a Welsh MP, James Philips, almost 40 years her senior. The two moved to Wales, where Katherine set up a salon of likeminded people, particularly women writers.

Philips earned a reputation for herself as a writer from her Welsh base. There is some speculation that some of her poems addressed to fellow females may be, under their veneer of literary affectation, Sapphic or lesbian. We see in an example in "A Retir'd Friendship." Philips beckons her friend to a bower, where lovers traditionally enjoy their bliss. But the poet here insists on innocence, or is that merely a convenient mask or disguise? What's interesting about such poems is the sly use of male love conventions. The writer intrigues us by forcing us to question the poem's innocence.

High in this female poetic company is another aristocrat, Anne Finch, the countess of Winchilsea (1661–1720). She was one of the first female poets to make it into print under her own name. Finch's father, Sir William Kingsmill, had the unusual belief that women should be educated. Thus, her poetry, like Cavendish's, is clever, witty, and well controlled.

Finch's enigmatic poem "Glass" is based on an interesting conceit. Glass is, paradoxically, something one looks into to see one's reflection and looks through to see the world outside. In the poem, Finch both addresses the window in her living room and alludes to the looking glass in her bedroom. The poem lists the range of things one can do with glass, focusing mainly on household objects, the things a woman would see about her every day: a mirror, a window, or a vase.

We could look at other female poets, such as Anna Laetitia Barbauld, Joanna Baillie, or Hannah More, but the point is, however repressed women may have been, literature, specifically a characteristic kind of poetry, forced its way through the barriers. If we listen to this poetry, we always hear voices that are interesting, different, and womanly.

Suggested Reading

Greer, *Kissing the Rod.*

Lonsdale, ed., *Eighteenth Century Women Poets: An Oxford Anthology.*

Todd, ed., *Be Good, Sweet Maid: An Anthology of Women and Literature.*

Questions to Consider

1. Is it relevant to think of these writers as women poets? Are they not merely poets?

2. How did early women writers make a space for themselves to create literature in? Was there any available space in the normal life of women in these times?

Women Poets—The Minor Voice
Lecture 22—Transcript

In the last few lectures, we've been looking at figures, writers, who've been, if not entirely excluded, relegated to the edge of English literature. They are, as the technical phrase is, extracurricular.

In this lecture, we'll continue that excursion, that *Shandean* digression, if one wants to use that phrase, off the main highway into some of the less beaten byways of literature. It's going on all the time. There's more literature than we can ever read, and infinitely more than we shall ever study or that makes Great Books 101.

In this lecture, we'll be looking at poetry, which is self-consciously minor and typically private, written by women, and one suspects, written for women as well. That's to say, women who see a kind of invisible readership out there, with which they, nonetheless, have a connection.

Women have always traditionally found it difficult to write for the stage because it's so public. They have to display themselves, and the conventions of society, almost through to the 20th century, forbid that. Epics are too big for women. They require some large presence in the outside world, a grandeur, a public grandeur which has historically been denied the other sex, women.

But some forms of literature do lend themselves to this private domestic arena where women can feel comfortable and express themselves. In the 19th century, for example, to look forward, the admirable Mrs. Gaskell, whose work we'll encounter a bit later on, would often write her novels chapter by chapter on the mantle piece, at night, after she'd put the children to bed and the house had been tidied up and she'd done all the duties of a good wife and mother.

Jane Austen, we're told, who, again, will figure very largely in later lectures, would write in company in the drawing room at her escritoire, those elegant little writing desks that they had in the 18th and 19th century. So there'd be people around her. And people would think she was inscribing or writing an everyday letter. Women could write letters, of course. But if someone came close to read what she was actually doing, she might well push the paper out of sight, because it was fiction. She didn't want to share that. At least, she didn't want to share it until she was ready to share it. I always find it very nice to picture that protective gesture of Jane Austen's, "This is my work and I'm keeping it to myself."

Short poems, lyric poems, lent themselves to domestic composition, and it is with that form of literature, the short lyric poem, that we'll be principally concerned in this lecture. It's a line one can follow from the 17th century, through the 18th, to the 19th century—Elizabeth Barrett Browning, for instance—to the 20th century—Sylvia Plath, for instance. Some of the poems she wrote when she was living in Devon among her beehives and her kitchen, they, in fact, can be connected right the way back to what women were doing 300 or 400 years earlier, when they sat down to write this poetry for themselves.

I'd like to begin with a rather surprising example. Everyone knows that Queen Elizabeth was a great queen, that she was a great orator. She could actually speak, and remember, if you would, her speaking at Tilbury, her most famous speech. The Spanish Armada is just over the horizon. It's approaching. It was a mighty Spanish fleet, sent by Philip. It would surely, as the Spanish enemy thought, crush puny England, as the low countries had been crushed by imperial Spain.

And Queen Elizabeth stood there, physically defying the foe, and delivered herself of this magnificent speech:

> My loving people, we have been persuaded by some that are careful of our safety to take heed how we commit ourself to armed multitudes for fear of treachery;

She's using the royal *we*, of course. It's her she's talking about, not any kind of collective entity.

> but I assure you, I do not desire to live to distrust my faithful and loving people.

You'll notice how she actually changes from *we* to *I*, very, very powerful rhetorical movement, that.

> Let tyrants fear. I have always so behaved myself that, under God, I have placed my chiefest strength and safe guard in the loyal hearts and good will of my subjects, and therefore I am come amongst you, as you see, at this time, not for my recreation and disport, but being resolved, in the midst and heat of the battle, to live or die amongst you all, to lay down my life for my God and for my kingdom and for my people, my honour, and my blood, even in the dust.

The emphasis is on my, my, my.

> I know I have the body of a weak and feeble woman, but I have the heart and stomach of a king, and a king of England too, and think foul scorn that Parma or Spain, or any prince of Europe should dare to invade the borders of my realm; the which, rather than any dishonour shall grow by me, I myself will take up arms, I myself will be your general, judge, and rewarder of every one of your virtues in the field.

She's talking to her troops, really getting them fired up:

> I know, already for your forwardness, you have deserved rewards and crowns; and we do assure you,

She changes again to *we* because she's now going to be bountiful. She's going to be the queen and give out honors:

> in the word of a prince, they shall be duly paid you.

> In the meantime my lieutenant-general shall be in my stead, than whom never prince commanded a more noble or worthy subject, not doubting but by your obedience to my general, by your concord in the camp, and your valour in the field, we shall shortly have a

famous victory over those enemies of my God, of my kingdom, and of my people.

The woman who wrote that could surely hold her own with the flattering Sir Edmund Spenser and his *Faerie Queene*, a picture of which is behind me at the moment. One feels, hearing in the mind's ear those rousing words at Tilbury, as with the speeches of Winston Churchill, addressing the nation in a similarly parlous moment in World War II, which I can just as a child remember, that one wants oneself to pick up one's pike or musket and go down to the beach and do battle with the foe.

In this, of course, she's expecting that the Spaniards will land and there'll be a land battle. The troops are massed, but as it happened, "God blew" as the commemorative medal put it, and the Spanish fleet was destroyed by a terrible storm, and they never reached the British shore. God, in fact, protected England, as the English like to think. But, nonetheless, at that moment, Elizabeth didn't know that was going to happen. She thought there'd be bloody battles and that, in fact, her kingdom, their kingdom was in dire peril.

That, if you like, is the public Elizabeth. Like her father, however, there's a private Elizabeth. Her father, Henry VIII, allegedly, I'd like to think it's true, but allegedly wrote that famous lyric "Greensleeves": "Alas, my love, you do me wrong, / To cast me off discourteously." You know it well. Everyone knows it. But she too was a versifier. She wrote good poetry.

People sometimes find that surprising, but I think we should find it no more surprising than the fact that Queen Elizabeth II is a good horsewoman, or that Charles, who's to be the next king of England, one expects, the heir apparent, is a good shot, you know, he goes out shooting. Because, in fact, being able to write poetry was a skill like dancing or like horsemanship in Queen Elizabeth's growing-up period, and Queen Elizabeth I was a very good poet. In fact, she could, in other sort of situations, have been an author in her own right.

The poem of Queen Elizabeth I which I'd like to read out is called "On Monsieur's Departure," and it commemorates a moment or records a moment when a lover, and despite furious speculation, no one can work out who, if, indeed, there ever was a lover, that lover was. A lover has left her. It's a typical situation for a woman. She's been left in the lurch, jilted. But in Queen Elizabeth's case, she's embarrassed. She feels the loss, but she cannot, out of pride of position and rank, display the loss she feels. It must be bottled up, to be released cathartically in a private poem.

And this is the poem. It's very beautiful, I think, and as I say, wholly unexpected if you contrast it with that rousing speech which I read out.

> I grieve and dare not show my discontent,
> I love and yet am forced to seem to hate,
> I do, yet dare not say I ever meant,
> I seem stark mute but inwardly do prate.
> I am and not, I freeze and yet am burned,
> Since from myself another self I turned.
>
> My care is like my shadow in the sun,
> Follows me flying, flies when I pursue it,
> Stands and lies by me, doth what I have done.
> His too familiar care doth make me rue it.
> No means I find to rid him from my breast,
> Till by the end of things it be supprest.

That second stanza deals with her melancholy, her sense of being abandoned.

> Some gentler passion slide into my mind,
> For I am soft and made of melting snow;

This is the woman who has the heart and the stomach of a man? But she's also in another department of her life, "soft and made of melting snow;"

> Or be more cruel, love, and so be kind.
> Let me or float or sink, be high or low.
> Or let me live with some more sweet content,
> Or die and so forget what love ere meant.

This, surely, as I say, reveals to us the heart and stomach of a woman, and a woman who has a full range of womanly feelings and responses to the intimate relations of life.

I want to move on now to another woman poet, Anne Bradstreet. Britain and America are at good-natured war over the literary ownership of Anne Bradstreet. That's to say, her dates are 1612 to 1672, well before the American War of Independence, and yet she is generally regarded as the first great American poet. And on the other side of the Atlantic, she's regarded as being in the line, a very interesting line, of British Metaphysical poets. So, in fact, she's got, if you like, a kind of dual literary personality. She carries two passports, in literary terms.

Anne Bradstreet was born Anne Dudley in Northampton, which is in the Midlands of England. She was the daughter of a steward or land agent, who served an aristocratic estate owner. This was important because it meant that young Anne had access to books and a superior library. She was, as it were, a member of the household with privileges. She could actually read what her father's employer had in his house.

And she was a young Englishwoman at this time, without question. She clearly took full advantage of this privilege, of being able to read books. She was also very clearly attracted, fascinated even, by the currently fashionable style of poetry in the early 1700s, the Metaphysicals, Donne, Herbert, Marvell, if you can cast your mind back. These poets, as you'll recall, wrote clever, knotty, highly conceited stuff. You'll remember that word, conceit. That's to say, a poem which was constructed around an elaborate conception or an intricate conception.

At the age of 16, which, in fact, was a normal age of marriage, life being that much shorter in those days, she married Simon Bradstreet. Both Anne's father and her husband Simon would later go on to serve as governors of the Massachusetts Bay Colony. And she went to the colony with them in 1630. And she was henceforward an American woman. She resided there and never left the colony.

But, as the English proverb has it, as the twig is shaped, so the tree is bent. Anne's literary pedigree remained English, whatever her later residence, and even though her poems continued to be published in England, and they were about America, of course, they, nonetheless, have this kind of, I think, binocularity. They're English and American.

Life was very hard in 17th-century New England. Mortality rates were high, particularly among the young and the old. The amenities of life, the kind of thing routinely enjoyed in a rich household in England that Anne had been brought up with, these were singularly lacking. She had, to some extent, to change her lifestyle, adapt to a new lifestyle. She was helped by religion in doing this. It was God's wish that she should be in America, but the religious atmosphere in Massachusetts was harsh, necessarily, because in fact, the environment was so harsh.

There was a lot of illness. Anne contracted small pox, and later TB, both of which were chronic and debilitating medical conditions. Her hardship, and, as she would protest, nonetheless, her joys, were increased by giving birth to eight children. Her house burned down, and with it her large, treasured personal library, in 1666. It was a tragedy which was scarcely less terrible to her than the great 1660 London Fire was to that city's inhabitants. And at least in London, they had Sir Christopher Wren there to rebuild London, but she couldn't get her books back.

Anne wrote a poem on that occasion, gritting her teeth and, nonetheless, thanking God. This is what she wrote, and remember, she's standing there, we have to imagine, in the ruins of what little she had by way of household property and house:

> I blest his grace that gave and took,
> That laid my goods now in the dust.
> Yea, so it was, and so 'twas just.
> It was his own; it was not mine.
> Far be it that I should repine.

He and his there refers, of course, to God. It's wonderful, isn't it, the way in which she uses those very simple words? Almost every one of those words is an Anglo-Saxon monosyllable, except the last one, *repine*. It comes in with a kind of an extra force because, in fact, in terms of diction, it is different from what's gone before.

Losing books is one thing—it was even harder when God took children from her—but they too, she had to console herself, were in a better place. The Almighty must be submitted to. Consider the poignant poem, the almost unbearably poignant poem, which is entitled "In Memory of My Dear Grandchild Anne Bradstreet, Who Deceased June 20, 1669, Being Three Years and Seven Months Old." It's a poem written, as she says, with a "trembling hand" and a "troubled heart."

This is the poem:

> I knew she was but as a withering flour,
> That's here to day perhaps gone in an hour;

This kind of carpe diem thing about flowers are beautiful, but they last not long.

> Like as a bubble, or the brittle glass,
> Or like a shadow turning as it was.

It's a very complex image, that, "a bubble, or the brittle glass, / Or like a shadow turning as it was." She's thinking, I think, of an hourglass, you know, like the egg timer, and the sand running through it. It's faintly visualized there, and, of course, it ties in with the perennial theme of vegetation and decay. Everything that lives must die. Of course, this child has died very prematurely.

> More fool then I to look on that was lent,
> As if mine own, when thus impermanent.

She should never regard her children as her own property.

> Farewel dear child, thou ne're shall come to me,
> But yet a while and I shall go to thee.

Mean time my throbbing heart's chear'd up with this
Thou with thy Saviour art in endless bliss.

Children often died at this period. Life was so hard and, of course, their infant mortality was so widespread. And Anne had to write more than one poem of this funerary kind, elegies for the prematurely departed. Bitter experience can often result in sweet poetry. One knows that, but what I would point to here, as with Queen Elizabeth, is the privacy. It is a woman, taking a few minutes, as one suspects, to talk to herself, to talk about very womanly things, what a woman feels when she loses what she's labored so hard to produce, children and grandchildren.

It is, of course, in one sense, a classic meditation, which was a standard Puritan exercise, which was also one of the bases of Metaphysical poetry. It's a way of purifying the spirit by introspection and articulating the results of that introspection, very often in poetry because, in fact, that exercise requires a very subtle use of language, a very subtle use of consciousness, expressing itself through language.

But the simplicity of Anne Bradstreet's expression—it's as simple as the colonial kitchenware around her—when it's tied in with those complex similes, the one I was referring to about the hourglass, it creates an amazingly subtle effect.

It renders it, to my mind, at least, a woman's poem, and I must say, in my mind's ear, I hear it in an English accent, but that, again, as I say, is a matter of dispute, who owns Anne Bradstreet. Whatever ownership she submits to, she is, I would submit, a very great poet indeed.

The next poet I want to look at is Margaret Cavendish. She's high born, unlike the woman we've been talking about previously, Anne Bradstreet. Obviously, no one's higher born than Queen Elizabeth. Cavendish is high born and she'd bear the title in adult life of Duchess of Newcastle-upon-Tyne, a title which came to her by marriage. In early life, she was a courtier attached to the queen of England, and her own family, the Lucases, were prominent royalists during the Civil War.

She went into exile, into France, with the king. She wrote prolifically and, like Aphra Behn, under her own name, and published. Her works include prose fantasias like *The Blazing World* in 1666, a memoir called *A True Relation of my Birth, Breeding, and Life*, philosophical treatises, and much, much poetry.

Her poetry is unusual because unlike many other women writers, Cavendish was in the literary world and she was known as a literary figure, although that world was not always kind to her or polite about her. They rather resented the fact that this woman had barged in. She was often regarded as aggressive, self-advertising and fantastical. Self-possessed women were typically thus stigmatized.

She had no children, which, with her prosperous and leisured lifestyle and access to the booksellers of London, supplied more opportunity to pursue a literary career as such, than almost any other woman of the time, with the possible exception of Aphra Behn, who we were talking about earlier, and whose talent, incidentally, is by far the greater. One has to make this point.

Cavendish's epistles are, however, landmarks in literature, and I want to look at just one of her poems. It's very early in her literary career, 1653. It's called "A World made by Atomes," and it's extraordinary. It would have been extraordinary from any poet's pen, but it's a poem about particle physics and it's clearly Metaphysical in style. And it's one of a cluster of what are called *atomic poems* which she wrote.

I'll read just a bit of it, and you'll get the sense of it:

> Small Atomes of themselves a World may make,
> As being subtle, and of every shape:
> And as they dance about, fit places finde,
> Such Formes as best agree, make every kinde.
> For when we build a house of Bricke, and Stone,
> We lay them even, every one by one:
> And when we finde a gap that's big, or small,
> We seeke out Stones, to fit that place withall.

And so it goes on. As I say, this is one of her *atomic poems* and it is quite remarkable. The reason it's remarkable is she doesn't quite work out the conceit, but she does extremely well. John Donne could probably have done it better, but, nonetheless, she does it well. But what's interesting about this is this poem identifies her as not merely the first career poetess—an ugly word, but one has to use it—in the annals of English literature, but also, and this is as important, the first *bluestocking*, that's to say, female intellectual in those annals of English literature.

And it's a line which we'll follow through via such figures as George Eliot to Iris Murdoch in the present day. So, she's interesting, make what you will of her poetry, but it is remarkably interesting poetry.

I want to move on now in this review, flipping through these kind of women poets, these private women poets, to Katherine Philips, who's also known by her nom de plume, the Matchless Orinda. Her dates are 1631 to 1664. She's born in London, the daughter of a merchant and a nonconformist. And the household was excessively pious. Katherine is recorded as having read the Bible from cover to cover before she was five years old, and to have learned several languages in her childhood.

Such prodigious feats are often recorded of girls because they were denied, as they were, any formal institutional education, and they had to overachieve to be taken notice of. And she certainly was. In her teens, she turned royalist, probably in a spirit of rebellion. It was kind of adolescent rebellion, if you like. At 16, she married a Welsh MP, James Philips, who was almost 40 years older than her, and they moved to Wales.

It wasn't, on the face of it, a propitious preparation for a career in poetry, but in Wales, she set up a salon, a group of like-minded people, like-minded writers, women, earning herself the nom de plume, as I say, of Orinda, a pen name. She was a notably virtuous woman, unlike Behn, with whom she was often contrasted, her contemporary, who was, of course, famously immoral, as people thought.

And Philips earned a reputation for herself as a writer from her Welsh literary base. And there's some speculation about some of her poems which are addressed to fellow females, which may be thought, under their veneer of literary affectation, to be Sapphic or lesbian.

For example, this poem called "A Retir'd Friendship":

> Come, my Ardelia, to this bowre,
> Where kindly mingling Souls a while,
> Let's innocently spend an houre,
> And at all serious follys smile
>
> Here is no quarrelling for Crowns,
> Nor fear of changes in our fate;
> No trembling at the Great ones frowns
> Nor any slavery of state.
>
> Here's no disguise, nor treachery
> Nor any deep conceal'd design;
> From blood and plots this place is free,
> And calm as are those looks of thine.

And so it goes on. Bowers, of course, are where lovers enjoy their bliss, but Phillips here insists on innocence, or is that merely a convenient mask or disguise?

What's genuinely interesting in poems like the above by Orinda is, I think, the sly use of male lover conventions. Whether it's innocent or not, who can say? But if we have to ask the question, then the poet has us hooked.

High in this female poetic company is another aristocrat, Anne Finch, Countess of Winchilsea, whose dates are 1661 to 1720, slightly later, one of the first women poets to make it under her own name, or, at least, her husband's name, actually, into print. The high born always had it easier. They had friends.

But she was unusual in other ways than being a published woman writer. Her father, Sir William Kingsmill, had the very unusual belief at the time that women should be educated. And her poetry, like Cavendish's, is clever, witty, and, I think, better controlled. For example, there's a poem I want to read out, which is called, enigmatically, "Glass." Now, glass is an object which is traditionally associated with woman's vanity. It's something, paradoxically, which you look into to see your own reflection and look through to see the world outside.

This, in fact, is a conceit. Finch, as we gather, is addressing both the window in her living room and, at the same time, alluding to the looking glass in her boudoir.

This is the poem. "O Man!" What an interesting way for a poem by a woman to start:

> O Man! what Inspiration was thy Guide,
> Who taught thee Light and Air thus to divide;

As the window does.

> To let in all the useful Beams of Day,
> Yet force, as subtil Winds, without thy Shash to stay;
> T'extract from Embers by a strange Device,
> Then polish fair these Flakes of solid Ice;

Using the glass as a magnifying glass, and a burning glass.

> Which, silver'd o'er, redouble all in place,
> And give thee back thy well or ill-complexion'd Face.

And so it goes on. She goes through the range of things which you can do with glass. It's a very witty poem, but it's also a poem which deals, of course, with household objects, the things which a woman would see about her every day: a mirror, a window, a vase, a glass vase.

"Had we but world enough, and time"—you'll remember that quotation from Andrew Marvell, who's very appropriate, I think, in this company— one could look at other poetesses, such as Anna Laetitia Barbauld, wonderful name, Joanna Baillie, Hannah More. And there are many, many more than our literary histories customarily make room for, but I hope that in this lecture, we've actually reviewed enough to make an important point.

However repressed, in a general sense, women may have been, nonetheless, literature, specifically a characteristic kind of poetry, forced its way through the barriers, the things that were holding women down. And if we listen, there are always women's voices. They might be on the edge, we might have to cock an ear to catch them, and those women's voices are interestingly and differently, and this is the key word, womanly. It's a very fine anthology which we can put together of what I've called private women's poetry. And one should really visit it. It should not be excluded, to go back to what I was talking about at the beginning.

Wollstonecraft—"First of a New Genus"
Lecture 23

> She [Mary Wollstonecraft] calls her great work ... *A Vindication*, and that term, I think, implies combat. ... She's going out to do battle. ... She is taking it to the men—men who, as with Thomas Paine's universally read *The Rights of Man*, assume in that title that half the human race have no rights at all.

In the last lecture, we looked at the quieter female voice as it was expressed in essentially private poetry. In other lectures, female characters have also spoken "soft, Gentle and low," but Mary Wollstonecraft (1759–1797) speaks loud, clear, publicly, and wholly unmuzzled. Few writers of her time have spoken across the centuries to our time as clearly as she does, mainly, in Mary's case, to other women. Her voice carries wonderfully and with undiminished potency across the years. The title of her great work, *A Vindication of the Rights of Woman*, implies combat. She is not defending her position but vindicating it. Further, her writing is directed toward men, those readers of Thomas Paine's *The Rights of Man*, for example, who might assume, as the title of Paine's work seems to, that half the human race has no rights at all.

The works of Mary Wollstonecraft warrant consideration as literature on two counts: First, they are powerfully written. It was a matter of pride to this author to write as well as or better than any man. Second, Wollstonecraft's works are instrumental in clearing a space in the arena of literature in which women could operate. Her own daughter, Mary Shelley, could never have written *Frankenstein* had her mother not paved the way for that novel.

Let's look at the life of this remarkable woman. Mary Wollstonecraft lived a brief 39 years. She died of an infection contracted while bringing her daughter into the world. She never lived to see the outcome of the French Revolution, the greatest social experiment in history and an event about which she had written a history. Mary saw herself as a revolutionary, a woman of the barricades, as much as a social philosopher.

The main argument of *A Vindication of the Rights of Woman* is simple: Women are not genetically inferior to men. They are made inferior to man by being denied, principally, education. It is "circumstances" that make woman the inferior sex. They are genetically or naturally as rational, as intelligent, and as creative as men or potentially so.

Wollstonecraft was born in London, the daughter of an investor. The family's condition, which was initially prosperous, declined precipitously as she was growing up. As she entered womanhood, Mary's expectations, particularly her financial expectations (which were important if she wanted to make a good marriage) diminished catastrophically.

> **Mary resolved, as she told her sister Everina in 1787, to make herself "the first of a new genus"; she would be a pioneer woman author.**

Mary had more than one reason for harboring resentment against the father who, by injudicious speculation, had ruined her financial prospects. He was in other ways unreliable, as well as a drunk and a wife beater, and Mary seems to have learned well the lesson that men were not to be trusted. This view was confirmed by the domestic crisis of her sister, Eliza, whom Mary helped to escape from an unhappy marriage. Unfortunately for Eliza, freedom proved to be as unhappy as marriage. Alternatives were few for women seeking refuge or alternative lifestyles at this time.

Mary's most formative early friendships were with other women of an intellectual bent. These women would read and hold intelligent discussions. They attended lectures on natural philosophy and history. They educated themselves because there were no institutions offering education to women. One such friend of Mary's, Fanny Blood, was particularly influential. Although only two years older than Mary, Fanny, who was cultivated in the fine arts, served as her mentor. One of Mary's great themes would be that women could help women; they did not need to be dependent on men. She enlarged on this theme in her later treatise *Thoughts on the Education of Daughters*. Even in her early relationship with Fanny Blood, Mary exhibited signs of a volatile, self-destructive personality, which may have been indivisible from the energies that drove her intellectually.

At 19, Mary took a job as a lady's companion in Bath, a sort of wealthy retirement community. She was not by nature submissive, and her two years in Bath were unhappy. She returned home to care for her ailing mother, who died shortly thereafter, and Mary left home for good.

Mary went to live with Fanny Blood in the Blood household, but as close as the women were, this arrangement didn't work out. Inevitably, some modern critics have inquired as to whether there was a lesbian aspect to the relationship. It seems more likely to have been a kind of feminist utopianism, an experiment in a monosexual society. After an unsuccessful attempt at setting up a school together, the relationship between Fanny and Mary cooled, and Fanny left to marry. Her health, never strong, had been undermined by tuberculosis. The friendship between the two was renewed when Mary returned to nurse Fanny, who later died as a consequence of pregnancy. Mary's experience of taking care of her friend fed into her first novel, *Mary*. Into this short, rather amateurish novel, Mary poured the strong emotions that had been generated by the deaths of her mother, her father, and Fanny. The novel is interesting primarily for its conclusion, which contradicts the conventional happy ending in which the heroine marries.

With Fanny gone, Mary took a position as a governess in Ireland. Although she was good at the job, it was beneath her abilities. Out of this experience, she wrote a children's book.

At this stage of her life, Mary was without financial resources, but she had by now made contacts in the London literary world. The publisher Joseph Johnson, who was a big player among radical thinkers of the time, particularly liked her work and liked her personally. Astutely, Johnson realized that there was a market for Mary's writings, and he cultivated her.

Mary resolved, as she told her sister Everina in 1787, to make herself "the first of a new genus"; she would be a pioneer woman author. She trained herself for this career by the traditional writer's apprenticeship of hackwork, but at the same time, she educated herself. She became proficient in French and German and did translation commissions. Among the works Mary translated were philosophical treatises of the Enlightenment, through which she picked up interesting ideas and ways of communicating ideas. Mary also did a good bit of reviewing, particularly for Johnson's house magazine, *Analytical Review*. Through this work, she was learning the tricks of the writing trade, and through Johnson, she also met the leading radical philosophers of the day in England, Thomas Paine, author of *The Rights of Man*, and William Godwin.

Mary would later marry Godwin, but their initial contact wasn't particularly friendly. At the time, Mary was in a tempestuous relationship with the Swiss artist Henry Fuseli. The fact that Fuseli was married did not deter Mary, who saw no reason to respect the institution she despised by any kind of self-denial. This was also the period when Mary was beginning to write her great work, *A Vindication*, which was published in 1790.

Fuseli ultimately broke off the relationship, and Mary traveled to France to join in the revolution. The work that brought her fame was, paradoxically, not her work on the rights of women but a polemic she wrote at this time, *A Vindication of the Rights of Men*, in response to Edmund Burke's criticism of the French Revolution.

In the 1790s, Mary was resident in France during the most enthusiastic and turbulent phase of the revolution. There, she embarked on a passionate relationship with an American, Gilbert Imlay. Their love affair ran against the Wollstonecraftian theory of male/female relationships outlined in *A Vindication*. There, Mary insists that men and women ought not to "love each other with passion"; instead, reason should be sovereign in all things. Mary became pregnant, but she and Imlay did not marry. In 1794, Mary gave birth to her first child, a daughter named Fanny.

Now, the revolution turned ugly; Britain had declared war on France and was fearful that the revolutionary virus would spread across the Channel. Disguising herself as Mrs. Imlay, Mary was obliged to leave France. Although he returned to London with her, Imlay was in the process of detaching himself emotionally from Mary.

Back in England in early 1795, Mary attempted suicide. She credited Imlay with saving her life after she'd taken an overdose of opium, but the relationship was doomed. She attempted suicide again, leaving a note for her lover, before jumping into the river Thames. This time, she was saved by a passerby. Mary had been wronged by Imlay, but her attempts at self-destruction worked against the ideals of fortitude and rational independence advocated in her writing.

Mary gradually recovered her spirits and rejoined the London literary world, where she was by now a prominent and respected ornament. At this point, she renewed her acquaintance with William Godwin, a leading social philosopher and radical. The two fell in love, and this time the union was of the mind, of political sentiment, as much as it was physical.

Mary found herself pregnant again, and despite the couple's free-thinking doctrines, they resolved to marry for the sake of the child. The two lived separately in adjoining houses. Sadly, the marriage would be short. After the birth of her second child, who would later become Mary Shelley, Wollstonecraft died of postpartum complications.

In a memoir, Godwin revealed many details of Mary's dramatic life, which was thought scandalous at the time. After all, a woman writing was one thing; a woman sympathizing with French revolutionaries and bearing illegitimate children was something quite different.

In the 1960s, Wollstonecraft was elevated to the highest of plinths of the feminist movement in Britain and America. Feminists see in her work a pugnacity and, at times, a ferocity that is sometimes perceived as necessary if chains are to be broken.

One cannot win independence by simply suffering. In the final stanza of "The Masque of Anarchy," Percy Bysshe Shelley says that if enlightenment is spread, the chains that hold oppressed people down will drop away like the "morning dew." History demonstrates, however, that they don't. As Rousseau, one of Mary's idols, said, "Man is born free, and everywhere he is in chains." Mary believed the same of women: They were enchained, and the enchained or incarcerated female, particularly the wife, is one of her recurrent images.

It's important to note that there is much more in the writing of Mary Wollstonecraft than in-the-male-face polemic. It is, perhaps, the good sense that shines through *A Vindication* that impresses us most. For example, she advocates exercise for young girls and encouragement to be brave. This is the keynote of *A Vindication*: common sense, uncommonly well expressed. ∎

Suggested Reading

Craciun, *Mary Wollstonecraft's A Vindication of the Rights of Woman: A Sourcebook.*

Johnson, ed., *The Cambridge Companion to Mary Wollstonecraft.*

Taylor, *Mary Wollstonecraft and the Feminist Imagination.*

Tomalin, *The Life and Death of Mary Wollstonecraft.*

Questions to Consider

1. In what sense is Mary Wollstonecraft writing "literature" in her great Vindication?

2. In what ways does Wollstonecraft redraw the cultural map of England?

Wollstonecraft—"First of a New Genus"
Lecture 23—Transcript

In the last lecture, we looked at what I call the quieter female voice as it expressed itself in essentially private poetry. What was it that King Lear said of his beloved daughter, Cordelia, as he held her dead body in his arms? "Her voice was ever soft, Gentle and low, an excellent thing in woman."

In that other Shakespeare play we looked at, *The Taming of the Shrew*, the main lesson that Kate learned, shrew that she was, as her lord and master tamed her, was to keep a quiet tongue in her head, to speak "soft, Gentle and low."

The subject of this lecture, Mary Wollstonecraft, speaks loud, clear, publicly and wholly unmuzzled. I mean sometimes she shrieks. No low voice for her, however excellent the fathers, brothers and husbands of the world may think such a thing. Call her shrew if you will, but hear her, you must. That's Mary Wollstonecraft.

And few writers of her time have spoken across the centuries to our time as clearly and as loudly as she does, mainly, in Mary's case, to women like herself, her own sex. Her voice, we may say, carries wonderfully and with undiminished potency across the years.

She calls her great work not *A Defense of the Rights of Woman*, but *A Vindication*, and that term, I think, implies combat. She's a vindicator, not a defender. She's going out to do battle. She was not persuading her fellow woman, who needs no persuasion on the point, she is taking it to the men. Men, who, as with Thomas Paine's universally read *The Rights of Man*, assume in that title that half the human race have no rights at all. What about the rights of woman? No one, I think, actually now looking at Paine's book has that uneasy echo thrown back at them.

By way of preface to what we'll be looking at later in Mary Wollstonecraft, let's start by remarking that her principal works—notably *A Vindication*, are feminist polemic, fighting talk—warrant consideration as literature on two counts: first, they're very powerfully written. Rhetorically, they're strong.

They have style. It was a matter of pride to this author to write as well, or better, than any man. Secondly, Wollstonecraft's works are instrumental in clearing a space, a large space in the arena of literature for women to operate and write in. She, to some extent, wedges open a kind of room in literature in which women can henceforward be respectable, equal status authors.

To take one example relevant to this course, Mary Wollstonecraft's daughter, Mary Shelley, whom, tragically, the older Mary would never be permitted to know, could never have written or have got into print her novel *Frankenstein* had not her mother, Mary Wollstonecraft, cleared that space which I've just been talking about.

Let's now look briefly at the life of this remarkable woman before moving on to her great work, *A Vindication*. Mary Wollstonecraft lived a brief 39 years, from 1759 to 1797. She was actually, and this is ironic and poignant, killed by being a woman, specifically by motherhood, dying, as she did, of postnatal infection, contracted while bringing that other Mary, the author of *Frankenstein*, into the world.

Alas, Wollstonecraft never lived, as she desperately wanted to, to see how the French Revolution—the big event of her adult life, the greatest social experiment in the history of the world—was working out, how it would end. She might have been very depressed had she done so, but as she lay there on her deathbed, it must have been one of the many regrets of her prematurely terminated existence.

And she, incidentally, wrote a history of the French Revolution, which was necessarily incomplete. She was fascinated by it. And Mary saw herself as a revolutionary, a woman of the barricades, as much as a social philosopher or, this tame word in the context of her work, a reformer. She rather despised that notion that you reformed things. In her view, by force, you had to change things.

The main argument of *A Vindication of the Rights of Woman* is simple: women are not naturally, genetically, inferior to men. They are made inferior to man by being denied, principally, education. It is "circumstances," which was a favorite word of Mary Wollstonecraft's husband, William

Godwin. It is circumstances which make woman the inferior sex. They are genetically or naturally as rational, as intelligent, and as creative as men, or potentially so.

Wollstonecraft was born in London, the daughter of what we would call an investor, then called a speculator, someone, in fact, who put his money in different places in the hope that he'd get a good return on it. The family's condition, which was initially prosperous, declined precipitously and disastrously as she was growing up. It was a very unstable domestic environment.

And as she entered womanhood, Mary's expectations, particularly her financial expectations, which were crucially important if she wanted to make a good marriage, diminished catastrophically. She had no money, in other words, with which to put herself forward as a potential woman on the marriage market, which was an important consideration in these times. But Mary Wollstonecraft did not, as her later career made clear, want the conventional destiny of women of her class at that period of history.

She would not, that is, be what was then thought a good woman. There was more than one reason for Mary's harboring resentment against the father who, by injudicious speculation, had ruined her financial prospects. He was in other ways unreliable. He was not to be depended on, and this seems to be a lesson about men which caused the iron to enter her soul. Men were not to be trusted. This, in fact, was one thing that she took from what was otherwise a very unhappy relationship with her parent.

Her father was also, it seems, violent, drunken, a wife batterer. A husband at that period, of course, could beat his spouse as unconcernedly as he could whip his horse or kick his dog. She was his. He could do what he liked with her. And male heads of households were, in the term favored at that time, despots.

In her formative years, Mary had few reasons to admire the despotic sex, man, and this view of things was confirmed by the domestic crises of her immediate family. Her favorite sister, Eliza, had a very unhappy marriage, and Mary helped her escape from it, helped her run away, but that freedom proved to be, for Eliza, as unhappy as the marriage. Alternatives were very bleak for women seeking refuge or seeking alternative lifestyles at this time. Very few doors were open to them, other than what society held open for them: a conventional marriage or conventional spinsterhood.

Mary's most formative early friendships were with congenial women like her, intellectual women whose domestic circumstances in some cases were rather happier than her own, than those that Mr. Wollstonecraft had set up for his daughter. We know quite a lot about these friendships, which are so important in Mary's early life.

The ladies would read and talk and discuss together in a kind of *bluestocking* way. It wasn't just gossip over the tea cups about who was doing what, who was wearing what kind of bonnet, but discourse. They talked intelligently. They made conversation. They attended lectures on natural philosophy, on history. They educated themselves. A woman needed to pick up education where she could. It was not, as it was for young men, freely on offer. There were no institutions, as such, for them to be educated in.

One such intimate woman friend of Mary's, the magnificently named Fanny Blood, was particularly influential. She was her mentor, Mary's mentor, although she was only two years older. But she was cultivated in the fine arts, as they were called. At this time, women helped women. That would be one of Mary's great themes. They did not need to be dependent on men. They could actually assist each other.

And it's a theme which she enlarged on in her later treatise, *Thoughts on the Education of Daughters*, wonderful title. And her titles are always straightforward. She never minced her words. The book, incidentally, came out in 1787. There's another of her novels which I love the title of, *Maria: or the Wrongs of Woman*. And there's no mystery there as to what the reader's going to find in that volume, sort of up with women, down with men.

Already, in this early kind of relationship with Fanny Blood, Mary was exhibiting signs of a volatile, self-destructively emotional personality, which I think was indivisible from the energies which drove her intellectually, but they were dangerous and potentially, as I say, self-destructive. Things did not look good for her because she, in fact, was emotionally, powerfully unstable. But who could be stable in the world into which she was born?

It was clear from early on to those close to her that she would never have an easy path through life, and nor did she. Personal relationships, particularly, would be fraught things for her. But initially, personal independence was the issue in her life. And at 19, Mary took a job as a lady's companion in Bath, which was a place where ladies retired to and gentlemen retired to when they had money. It wasn't a happy two years that followed. Mary Wollstonecraft was not by nature submissive, and her mistress was haughty. And women too could be despots. This was a fact of life.

Mary returned home to care for her ailing mother. This mother shortly died and Mary then left home for good. There was nothing to keep her there. And she went to live with Fanny Blood in the Blood household. Close as women were and could be, intimate as they could be, this didn't work out. Female friendship could, Mary discovered, only go so far, at least for her. Inevitably, some modern critics have inquired as to whether there was a lesbian aspect to the relationship. It seems more likely to have been a kind of feminist utopianism, an experiment in a monosexual society.

Anyway, whatever it was, after an unsuccessful attempt at setting up a school together, the relationship went cool. Fanny left to marry. Her health had been undermined by tuberculosis. It was never strong and she died as a consequence of pregnancy. Mary returned to nurse her friend. Their friendship was powerfully renewed during this last period as Fanny died. It was a devastating experience, which fed into Mary's first novel, *Mary*. And it's interesting that she chose her own name for this novel.

Into this short, briskly written, and to be honest, rather amateurish novel, there's a death bed in virtually every chapter, by the way, Mary poured the strong emotions which had been generated by her mother, her father, and Fanny's death, all the things that had come together to make her life unhappy. And it ends with the heroine, Mary, whom all the deaths around her has left entirely bereft of human companionship, looking forward glumly to her own end, with whatever kind of philosophical consolation she can find.

The novel ends:

> Her delicate state of health did not promise long life. In moments of solitary sadness, a gleam of joy would dart across her mind— she thought she was hastening to that world where there is neither marrying—nor giving in marriage.

That, in fact, is a direct contradiction of the conventional happy ever after. As I say, it contradicts the conventional happy ending of fiction with its peal of wedding bells. It's interesting in that respect and the novel is otherwise not all that wonderful. But symptomatically, insofar as what it tells us about Mary, it's both informative and interesting.

With Fanny gone, Mary took a position as a governess in Ireland. And she was very good at the job. She liked children, particularly young girls, and interacted well with them, but it was beneath her already startlingly evident abilities. There was much more in life that she could have done than actually educating young girls.

But out of this experience, she wrote a children's book, and children's books was a genre, like fiction, which was open to the female pen. It's a pretty good children's book, but it's not what one chooses to remember Mary Wollstonecraft by.

She was, at this stage of her life, without financial resources, penniless, if you want to put it that way. But she had by now made contacts in the London literary world. She was very good at social relationships, and more usefully, she'd made contacts in the capital's book trade. And the publisher Joseph Johnson, who was a big player among radical circles and thinkers of the time, particularly liked her work, and liked her personally. This, in fact, was very useful to Mary and was one of the stepping stones to her later achievements. So at this point in her life, she did need men, but it was a very congenial man in this particular case.

Astutely, Johnson realized there was a market for the kinds of things that Mary Wollstonecraft had in her as an author, and he cultivated her. She resolved, as she told her sister Everina in 1787, to make herself "the first of a new genus," the first of a new species, a new time. She would be a pioneer woman author. Authorship was a realm almost, if not quite, as closed to the female sex at the time as the army or the navy. She might as well have said, "I'm going to be a great woman general." In a sense, it would have seemed as preposterous to many males of that particular period, at the end of the 18th century.

Mary trained herself for this career as the "new genus," woman author, by the traditional writer's apprenticeship of hack work. She grubbed along in Grub Street. At the same time, she educated herself. Higher education was, in fact, one of the projects of her life and one of the things that she thought women should have. And she made herself proficient in French and German and did translation commissions.

Among the works she translated were works of enlightenment, philosophical enlightenment, which in fact, were current on the Continent, for which there was market in England. So to some extent, it was hack work. I mean she was actually Englishing things, taking foreign text and making them English, but at the same time, she was picking up all sorts of interesting ideas and interesting ways of communicating those ideas and articulating those ideas.

The thing about translators was that they were required to work fast while the product was still oven-fresh, and since there was no copyright, before some other publisher got it out. So accuracy wasn't always the priority, but speed was. And she had a very "fast aisle" pen; she could write fast. And it was very good training for a writer, this. Having to write under pressure is, in fact, a good way to learn how to write well.

She did a lot of reviewing. Johnson had a house magazine called *Analytical* magazine and she did reviews for them. They were anonymous, but, again, she was learning tricks of a very, very complex trade in this period. And, momentously, through the publisher Johnson, she met the leading radical philosophers of the day in England, Thomas Paine, author of *The Rights of Man*, and William Godwin.

She would later marry Godwin, but at the moment, their initial contact wasn't all that friendly and she was meanwhile in a tempestuous relationship with the artist Henry Fuseli. He's a leading figure in art circles of the time. He was foreign, Swiss. He was highly unorthodox in his visual designs. He's sometimes seen as the father of surrealism, and his painting, *The Nightmare*, is a very vivid description of a terrible dream with a monster sitting on the sleeper's chest. He was interesting, and he had a very strong influence, incidentally, on William Blake, who we'll be looking at later. The fact that Fuseli was married did not deter Mary at all, who saw no reason to respect that worthless institution by any kind of self-denial. She despised marriage. Fuseli, under pressure from Mrs. Fuseli, eventually broke the relationship off. And this was the period in which Mary was beginning to write her great work, *A Vindication*, which was published in 1790.

After Fuseli had spurned her, she traveled to France to join in the Revolution, a very amazingly sort of brave thing to do. This is a woman, remember. It was, paradoxically, not her work on the rights of woman, but a polemic which she wrote at this time in response to Edmund Burke's criticism of the French Revolution, which was called *A Vindication of the Rights of Men*, which brought her fame. That's what she calls it, *A Vindication of the Rights of Men*, which was written against Burke. And it took off and it earned her notoriety, and, most importantly, money. Money meant that she could travel, that she no longer had, as it were, to keep the wolf from the door by hack work.

Wollstonecraft—it's the 1790s—was now resident in France at the most enthusiastic and turbulent phase of the Revolution. And one can't exaggerate the impact this had on the watching world. The whole world was looking at France in amazement and terror. Was their world, too, about to explode, they wondered, particularly in England, which is a next-door neighbor?

In France, Mary embarked on a passionate relationship with an American—he was similarly excited by the Revolution—Gilbert Imlay. And their love affair, *amour fou*, "wild love," as the French call it, ran against the Wollstonecraftian theory of male/female relationship. In *A Vindication*, Mary insists that men and women ought not to "love each other with passion."

What she wrote was:

> I mean to say, that they ought not to indulge those emotions which disturb the order of society, and engross the thoughts that should be otherwise employed. The mind that has never been engrossed by one object wants vigour—if it can long be so, it is weak.

What she meant by that was love is irrational. Who'd disagree with that? And reason is sovereign in all things. Not everyone would agree with that proposition. Indeed, Mary's own relationship with Imlay contradicts the notion that you can always be governed by reason.

The relationship was wildly sexual. Mary became pregnant. Imlay, true to his radical principles, had no intention of marrying her, and in 1794, Mary gave birth to her first child, a daughter named Fanny, after the other great love in her life, Fanny Blood. She was still in France, writing enthusiastically. Imlay was in her life, but not in any legal way attached to her or to their daughter.

And the Revolution at this period was turning very ugly. Britain had declared war on France, and it was fearful of the spread of the revolutionary virus across the Channel. Disguising herself as Mrs. Imlay, and thus protected by his nationality, Mary was obliged to leave France. And Imlay had, in fact, detached himself, or was in the process of detaching himself emotionally, although he returned to London with her.

Wollstonecraft and her daughter were back in England in early 1795, and it was a very bad time for her. On her return, she attempted suicide. She credited Imlay with reviving her after she'd taken an overdose of opium, and saving her life. But the relationship was doomed. She attempted suicide again, leaving a note for her lover, before jumping into the river Thames, which was the standard way in which women destroyed themselves because their skirts were so heavy, they would be quickly dragged down. And of course, no one taught women to swim in those days.

She wrote a very powerful farewell note to Imlay, the rat:

> Let my wrongs sleep with me! Soon, very soon, I shall be at peace. When you receive this, my burning head will be cold. ... I shall plunge into the Thames where there is least chance of my being snatched from the death I seek. God bless you! May you never know by experience what you have made me endure. Should your sensibility ever awake, remorse will find its way to your heart; and, in the midst of business and sensual pleasure, I shall appear before you, the victim of your deviation from rectitude.

She was actually saved by a passerby. As a woman, she'd been wronged, but her attempts at self-destruction rather worked against the ideals of fortitude and rational independence which her work advocated. And what one deduces from that is that living life is much harder than writing about it.

Wollstonecraft, one's glad to say, gradually recovered her spirits, and rejoined the London literary world, where she was by now a prominent ornament. People respected and read her carefully. And at this point, she renewed her acquaintance with William Godwin. Godwin was the leading social philosopher, and with Thomas Paine, the leading radical of the age.

They fell in love, but now it was a union of mind, of political sentiment, as much as it was physical, but the physical side was evidently there from the beginning. Again, Mary found herself pregnant out of wedlock. Despite their free-thinking doctrines, and Godwin had actually argued that marriage as an institution should be abolished for the good of society, they resolved to marry for the sake of the child. They went against their principles, but for good reasons. This was 1797. The Revolution is still going on in France.

One never talks about her as Mary Godwin, by the way, always as Mary Wollstonecraft. I think that's interesting. But true to their principles, they lived together, but separately in adjoining houses. Rather sweetly, they would actually come together in a kind of common space. That marriage would be short. After the birth of her second child, Mary, later to be Mary Shelley, author of *Frankenstein*, Wollstonecraft died of postnatal complications.

Their life was highly dramatic. Godwin revealed many of its details, which were thought scandalous at the time, in a memoir of Mary. A woman writing was one thing. A woman sympathizing with French revolutionaries and bearing illegitimate children without any sense of shame was something quite different.

In her own day, as I say, she was a scandalous figure, but famously, Wollstonecraft has been elevated to the highest of plinths by the feminist movement of the 1960s and after, particularly in Britain and America. And the members of this kind of movement see in her work a pugnacity and at times a ferocity, which is sometimes perceived to be necessary if fetters and chains are ever to be broken. You cannot win through to independence, to freedom, by simply suffering.

It was all very well for Percy Bysshe Shelley to say in the final stanza of "The Masque of Anarchy" that if you spread enlightenment, those chains which hold the oppressed people down, whether they're women or whether they're the lower classes, those chains drop away like the "morning dew." They manifestly, history demonstrates, don't.

As Rousseau, one of Mary's idols put it, "Man is born free, and everywhere he is in chains." Mary believed the same of women: they were enchained, and the enchained or incarcerated female, particularly the wife, is one of her recurrent images.

For instance, this is how she describes the condition of womanhood: "Taught from their infancy that beauty is woman's sceptre, the mind shapes itself to the body, and, roaming round its gilt cage, only seeks to adorn its prison."

And that's the lot of woman. They're birds in a gilded cage. Mary wanted much more than that for her sex. There's more, there's much more in the writing of Mary Wollstonecraft than "in the male face" polemic. It is, I think, above all, as I read it, the good sense which shines through *A Vindication* which impresses us most.

Why, for example, asks Mary, are girls always admired as "little girls"? "Thank 'eavens for leetle girls," sang Maurice Chevalier. And if that French chanteur had met Mary Wollstonecraft, she would, I think, have cut him up into steak tartare.

This is what Mary wrote about, that particular male affectation:

> I am fully persuaded that we should hear of none of these infantine airs, if girls were allowed to take sufficient exercise, and not confined in close rooms till their muscles are relaxed, and their powers of digestion destroyed.

It's very sensible advice, this.

> To carry the remark still further, if fear in girls, instead of being cherished, perhaps created, were treated in the same manner as cowardice in boys, we should quickly see women with more dignified aspects. It is true, they could not then with equal propriety be termed the sweet flowers that smile in the walk of man; but they would be more respectable members of society, and discharge the important duties of life by the light of their own reason.

That, it strikes me, is the keynote of *A Vindication*: commonsense, uncommonly well expressed. That, I think, is the essence of this remarkable woman's writing and what she has left us. Above all, in her great *Vindication*, she does, indeed, I think, vindicate. She does go out to battle, and she does win.

Blake—Mythic Universes and Poetry
Lecture 24

If there is one statement which sums up the achievement of William Blake ... that statement is "I must create my own system or be enslaved by another man's." ... What Blake is laying out for himself here is the creation or the invention of a whole new method of poetry. Not a new style, every major writer does that, but ... an as yet undreamed-of, uninvented system.

For William Blake (1757–1827), the entirely new method of poetry that he was laying out would involve the creation of mythic universes. In more practical, materialistic aspects, it would involve the making of an entirely new form of illustrated poetry book. To read Blake requires, first of all, to learn how to read Blake; once that trick is mastered, few writers in English literature are so rewarding.

Blake's life tells us much about his work. He was born in 1757, which puts him in the first generation of the Romantic Revival. Like John Keats, Blake was a cockney, and the son of a humble but decent tradesman, a draper, in central London. The influence of social rank can be important in studying literature. Some Romantics, such as Lord Byron and Percy Bysshe Shelley, came from the upper tiers of society; William Wordsworth, Sir Walter Scott, and Samuel Taylor Coleridge were born into families of the respectable, professional middle classes. Keats and Blake were on the lowest respectable rung. Beneath them, amid the working classes, was a place where no poetry was possible.

Blake had minimal schooling, but by the age of 11, his extraordinary artistic skills were already recognized, and he had three years of training at a drawing school. At the age of 14, he was apprenticed to a London engraving firm that produced illustrations for books and pictures to decorate middle class homes.

At the time, printers were notoriously radical. They were literate and politically aware and saw a good deal of radical literature as it passed under their professional eyes. From his teens onward, Blake was imbued with revolutionary spirit. He admiringly observed both the French and the American revolutions. In later life, he would write majestically prophetic poems about those earthshaking events.

Blake was, at the same time, enthusiastically religious, although nonconformist. Here, as elsewhere, he made his own systems. He was influenced by Unitarianism and excited by the way in which it freed the Christian system from the Anglican Church.

In his 20s, Blake set up his own shop in London, which failed. By now, however, he was moving in radical circles and was influenced by the thinking of William Godwin, Thomas Paine, and Mary Wollstonecraft.

The strands of Blake's artistic, philosophical, and metaphysical life came together in a novel series of books of poetry. Blake made these books by means of illustration and invention of new systems of religious allegory; he then merged the pieces into a highly innovative ensemble. In this early, most accessible period of his poetic career, a period when the French Revolution was at its most idealistically revolutionary, Blake produced the *Songs of Innocence and Experience* and *The Marriage of Heaven and Hell*. English literature had seen nothing like them.

These two works were followed by the first of the great prophetic books—vast, symbolic poems and interlinked designs—*The French Revolution* (1791), *America: A Prophecy* (1793), and *Visions of the Daughters of Albion* (1793). These are geopolitical works and difficult to understand, unless one understands the Blakean system.

Blake continued to write, design, and agitate. At one low point in his life, he was even tried for treason. Few of his contemporaries, least of all contemporary poets, were aware of him. His paintings did not sell, and his books were produced only in small batches.

Blake lived obscurely for much of his time in Soho, where a broken plaque among the city's brothels and drinking dens commemorates his residence. He died in 1827 and is buried in an unmarked grave.

As we've just seen, Blake's was a life without educational or social advantage. The Bible, Shakespeare, Milton, and the engraver's tools were placed in his hands, together with the most exciting political ideas of his time, and out of this mix, animated by his genius, he made poetry.

Let's now turn to two of Blake's works that may give us the key to the Blakean system. The first of these is *The Songs of Innocence and Experience* and the second is *The Marriage of Heaven and Hell*.

The titles of these works alone tell us much about the essential dynamic of Blake's poetry, which can be summed up in the word "dialectic," meaning two forces coming together in conflict to produce a third, higher force. Blake gives us a classic definition of dialectic in *The Marriage of Heaven and Hell*. As he says, "Without Contraries is no progression." He can be seen, along with Hegel, as one of the fathers of Marxism, a political theory founded on the dialectical triad of thesis, antithesis, and synthesis.

Blake's poetry ... can be summed up in the word "dialectic," meaning two forces coming together in conflict to produce a third, higher force.

Innocence and experience are, clearly, moral contraries. In the two collections of *Songs*, Blake opposes examples of innocence and experience from natural creation, from history, and from society. His question is: Can an individual who is innocent (inexperienced) be truly good, or does the achievement of goodness require experience? If we believe that someone who is innocent is truly good and if we believe that only the good go to heaven, we would rejoice when a baby, the incarnation of innocence, dies at birth. We don't because there is more than blank purity to life. This is one of the points stressed by Blake, although he doesn't argue it as a philosopher might.

To demonstrate how this complexity operates in Blake, let's consider two opposed lyrics. The first is "The Lamb" from *Songs of Innocence*. The poem is as simple as a nursery rhyme, a token of childlike, lamblike innocence. As indicated, the lamb is one of the conventional symbols of Christ. It is also innocent of sex. However, the mature ram is sexual. Blake was well aware of the complications of carnal desire, which he discusses frequently in his poetry. The poem is pivoted on a question, but the larger question is unanswered: God made the lamb, but why did the innocent lamb have to be sacrificed? Think of Abraham and Isaac and the ritual sacrifices of lambs in many of the world's great religions.

The partnering poem in *Songs of Experience* is "The Tyger." The text here is not as simple as in "The Lamb." The tiger is, of course, the antitype of the lamb. In the design he made for this poem, Blake has an image of the tiger smiling as if it has eaten a lamb for lunch. Where the force of destruction is involved, the answer is not as simple as "Did he who made the Lamb, make thee?" The answer, yes or no, is not forthcoming. The answer Blake hints at is that without the destructive tiger—without crucifixion, to allegorize it in Christian terms—the innocence of the lamb would be nothing. It would be literally bloodless. And it is the blood of the lamb, not the innocence of the lamb, that the Christian William Blake believes will save us.

Blake's poetry takes us into strange territories, and typically, we emerge less certain of things than we were when we entered. Always in his poetry, it is the unanswered questions that are, mysteriously, the pathways to higher understanding.

We see an example in a short, simple poem, "The Sick Rose," from *The Songs of Experience*. As we know, roses wither and die, but the rose in this poem is not merely conforming to the eternal laws of vegetation and decay; it is sick. What is the nature of that sickness? What's killing the rose is a worm, and in the Bible, the worm is an image of Satan. It's also a phallic image. The crucial word in this poem is secret: "his dark secret love / Does thy life destroy." How different would the poem be if it read "Its insatiable love / Does thy life destroy"? Blake, we must remember, was a sexual anarchist. He believed that love destroys only when it is furtive and ashamed of itself, not if it is open. This is the nature of the sickness. One can agree or disagree with that proposition, but it is one of the foundational elements in the poet's idiosyncratic system.

Blake was also attracted to, and fascinated by, the poetry of Milton, specifically, *Paradise Lost*. As you recall, that poem was founded on a great opposition between two mighty adversaries, God and Satan. But Milton, as Blake believed, wrote "in fetters." His imagination perceived something that his reason would not fully let him know. Blake was the first to make the much-repeated critical observation about the moral contradiction at the core of *Paradise Lost*. As he wrote, "The reason Milton wrote in fetters when he wrote of Angels & God, and at liberty when of Devils & Hell, is because he was a true Poet and of the Devils party without knowing it." Blake didn't mean that Milton was a Satanist. He meant that a part of Milton understood that Adam and Eve could never have fulfilled their destiny without Satan, without the fall, and without the responsibility of regaining paradise. Without contraries, that progression would never have been possible. Therefore, and perversely, Satan was the instrument of religious progress. Satan was a necessary component in Blake's system and in Milton's, too, but the earlier poet could not write what he inwardly knew because the fetters of Puritanism were too strong at the time. Blake wrote and rewrote *Paradise Lost*, although he didn't call his poems that, throughout his career. Time and again, he revisits the questions that Milton's poem posed. Despite the ferociously authoritarian voice tone of his poems, Blake never quite worked out the answer to the Milton problem, but the problem itself is both clearer and more beautiful for his investigation of it.

The Marriage of Heaven and Hell is another early work of Blake that offers us a gateway into his system. Here, he uses the term "marriage" as a synonym for synthesis; the work is about the fusion of the two contraries. The section titled "The Marriage" does not strike us as a poem at all; it seems to be a grab bag of manifesto, proverbs, blank verse, and epigrams. Much of it is in prose, and it seems to contain hundreds of Mosaic commandments. One section states the devil's philosophy as a series of truths, and here again we see that Satan is a vessel of truth. A particularly revealing trove of Blakean truth is found elsewhere in the poem, in the section called the "Proverbs of Hell." The allusion, of course, is to the Book of Proverbs in the Bible. Examples of these hellish proverbs include: "The road of excess leads to the palace of wisdom" and "A fool sees not the same tree that a wise man sees." Blake wrote *The Marriage of Heaven and Hell* at a time when he was most intensely under the influence of the radical theologian Swedenborg. Although he outgrew that phase, members of the sect still regard him as one of their most important prophets.

433

Over the next 15 years of his life, Blake progressed further down his own idiosyncratic path. He remained deeply connected to the traditions of English literature. For him, the Bible was the greatest of literary books, as well as a vessel of divine truth, as was poetry.

Unlike Wordsworth, Blake never compromised with his early radical, republican, revolutionary beliefs. He is also probably the most misread or misunderstood poet in the language, and nowhere more so than in the poem "Jerusalem." The poem alludes to the legend that, in the lost years of Christ between his childhood and his 30th year, the savior visited England and preached at Glastonbury. The poem, as it has been popularized, is an extravagantly chauvinistic patriotic anthem, but that sentiment is not at all what Blake had in mind when he wrote it. The "dark Satanic Mills" are not, as is often asserted, the new and exploitative textile factories of the early Industrial Revolution but, more probably, the established churches, which Blake loathed as prisons of the soul and mind. His "arrows of desire" refers to sexual desire. In short, this poem isn't a celebration of traditional England, a "green and pleasant Land," but a vision of the Blakean anarchist utopia, a place of complete freedom of belief and free love.

Although the poem is widely misunderstood, the popularity of "Jerusalem" has installed Blake where he never was during his life, at the center of English life and culture. He is arguably one of the giants of the Romantics. And if he demands that we learn his system in order to appreciate his achievement, we should do him that service. ∎

Suggested Reading

Blake, *The Complete Poems.*

Eaves, ed., *The Cambridge Companion to William Blake.*

1. Why was Blake so unappreciated in his own time?

2. What does Blake understand by the terms "innocence" and "experience"?

Blake—Mythic Universes and Poetry
Lecture 24—Transcript

If there is one statement which sums up the achievement of William Blake, the poet we'll be looking at in this lecture, that statement is "I must create my own system or be enslaved by another man's." It's Blake himself speaking, of course, here, and it's a proclamation of the extremest individualism. What Blake is laying out for himself here is the creation or the invention of a whole new method of poetry. Not a new style, every major writer does that, but, as Blake says, an as yet undreamed-of, uninvented system.

For Blake, this new system would involve the creation of whole mythic universes. In more practical materialistic aspects, it would involve the making of a new form of illustrated poetry book, for which we still have no adequate name, and which his own time was wholly unequipped to make sense of.

Shelley, a Romantic contemporary of Blake's, famously decreed that the poet was the "unacknowledged legislator" of mankind. The poet was to mankind, that is, what Washington was, for example, to the new United States of America. Presidential power, or its equivalent, was not enough for William Blake, however. For him, the poet must be something even more than that, must be a kind of god, a creator.

To read Blake requires, I think, first of all, to learn how to read Blake, and once that trick is mastered, few writers in English literature are so rewarding. That proposition may be questioned by those who find themselves immune— and there are such—to his arguably excessive claims on the reader. Why, they may ask, should we be "enslaved," to use his own formulation, by Blake's system?

But one thing is incontrovertible, even by Blake skeptics: no writer is as original or as innovative as William Blake is. Before putting some flesh on those bones, which, in fact, are very large observations, let's look at the man himself and his life, and that life will tell us much about his work.

Where, literally, was William Blake, as we say, coming from? Well, he was born in 1757, which puts him in the first generation or wave of what we call the Romantic Revival. He was the son of a draper or a tailor in central London. Like Keats, another great innovator whom we'll be looking at shortly, Blake was a cockney, and the son of a humble, but decent metropolitan tradesman.

Other ranks of life produced writers at this time, and the Romantics, whom we're looking at, often came from the upper tiers of society. And it's important to be aware of social ranks when one looks at these writers because they affect, they infect, even, the poetry. Byron, Lord Byron, was born into the purple, the aristocracy. He was the friend of princes and kings. Shelley was born in the upper classes. Wordsworth, Scott, and Coleridge, all writers we'll be looking at, were born in the respectable, professional middle classes, the rank of life occupied by lawyers, doctors, and clergyman.

Keats and Blake were on the lowest respectable rung. Beneath them was the abyss, a place where no poetry was possible, the lower ranks of society, the working classes. Blake had a minimal schooling, but by the age of 11, his extraordinary artistic skills were already recognized, and he had three years' training at a drawing school. It was a humble place, not the Royal Academy, the established art institution for which he, incidentally, would have a lifelong scorn.

At the age of 14, young William was apprenticed to a London engraver, in a firm which was largely making illustrations for books but also easily reproduced pictures to decorate middle class homes. There was a rage for illustration at this time, a huge visual appetite, and techniques and processes had evolved to the point that the market for this appetite, this trade, this market, could be supplied cheaply. The same thing would happen with photography a century later.

Printers, as Benjamin Franklin, who was also for a period a London printer, were notorious. Franklin confirms this. Printers were notoriously radical. Why? Well, because they were necessarily literate. They were probably the most literate profession in the land, actually. Obviously composing was done by hand at this time and a lot of radical literature passed under their professional eye. They knew what was going on, politically. They read it. They had to read it. It was their trade.

From his teens onward, Blake was imbued with revolutionary spirit and sentiment. Well now, it was, of course, the age of revolutions. Blake admiringly observed both the French and the American revolutions and, in later life, would write majestically prophetic long poems about those earthshaking events.

But while politically radical, Blake was at the same time enthusiastically religious, but very nonconformist in his faith. Here, as everywhere else, he made his own systems. He was very early influenced by Unitarianism and excited by the way in which it, as he would say, remade the Christian system, so as to free it from the established Anglican Church. One could, if you were a Unitarian, be a devout Christian and still be a rebel.

In his 20s, Blake was skilled enough to set up his own shop in London's Soho, which is the bohemian artistic heart of the capital, even today. That business, alas, failed, but by now, Blake was moving in advanced radical circles and was directly influenced by the thinking of William Godwin, the political revolutionary, by Thomas Paine, and by the feminist we've just been looking at, Mary Wollstonecraft.

And the strands of his artistic, philosophical, metaphysical life come together—they're bound together—in a novel series of books of poetry, which he made as much as wrote. He made them by means of illustration, by means of inventing new systems of religious allegory, and merging the whole thing into some new ensemble, which was startlingly new then, and still strikes us as highly innovative.

In this early, most accessible period of his poetic career, at a period when the French Revolution was at its most idealistically revolutionary, Blake produced the *Songs of Innocence and Experience*, and *The Marriage of Heaven and Hell*. English literature had seen nothing like them before. They were followed by the first of the great prophetic books, vast, symbolic poems and interlinked designs, *The French Revolution* in 1791, *America: a Prophecy* in 1793, *Visions of the Daughters of Albion*, 1793. Albion is England, of course. It's all geopolitical stuff and dauntingly hard to understand, unless, that is, one also understands the Blakean system.

Blake continued to write, to design and to agitate. At one low point in his life, he was even tried for treason. It wasn't a safe time to be revolutionary in England, or anywhere. Few of his contemporaries, least of all his contemporary poets, were aware of him. They didn't know he existed, or of his remarkable achievements. They were just beneath the radar.

His paintings did not sell. His prophetic books were produced in batches of a few score. Pitiably few survive and there's a scramble in any auction houses nowadays when they come on the market. In a mint condition, *Songs of Innocence* can fetch hundreds of thousands of dollars.

Blake lived obscurely for much of his time in Soho, where a broken plaque, symbolically in Marshall Street, among the city's brothels and drinking dens still there, commemorates his residence. He died in 1827 and is buried in an unmarked grave. No pilgrimage is possible to his tomb, as it is to those of the other great Romantics. He died obscure. He never knew, during his life, that he would, after death, quite a long time after his death, be world famous. And William Blake, to be honest, probably would not have cared that much.

Blake's, as I say, is a life without any privilege, educational or social advantage whatsoever. The Bible, Shakespeare, Milton, and the engraver's tools were placed in his hands, together with the most exciting political ideas of his time, and out of this mix, animated by his genius, he made his poetry.

I want to concentrate on two of Blake's works, which may, I think, be taken as the gateways to the great prophetic books. They're works which give us the key to that Blakean system which I've been talking about. The first of those is *The Songs of Innocence and Experience* and the second, *The Marriage of Heaven and Hell*.

Without going a syllable further than those titles, we can learn much about the essential dynamic of Blake's poetry. In a word, that dynamic is "dialectic." What does that word *dialectic* mean? Literally, two forces coming together in conflict to produce a third thing and a higher thing.

Blake himself gives us a classic definition of dialectic in one of his proverbial utterances in *The Marriage of Heaven and Hell*. Note particularly the opening statement when I read it, about "Contraries":

> Without Contraries is no progression. Attraction and Repulsion, Reason and Energy, Love and Hate, are necessary to Human existence. From these contraries spring what the religious call Good & Evil. Good is the passive that obeys Reason. Evil is the active springing from Energy. Good is Heaven. Evil is Hell.

Blake can be seen, along with Hegel, as one of the fathers of Marxism, a political theory founded on the dialectical triad of thesis, antithesis, synthesis, those two things coming together and producing a third thing, contraries.

Let's move away from politics to our proper concern in these lectures: poetry. Innocence and experience are, clearly, moral contraries. In the two collections of *Songs*, Blake suggestively opposes examples of innocence and experience from natural creation, from history and from society. And the big question is "Can a person who is innocent, that is, inexperienced, be truly good, or does that achievement, goodness, require experience?"

If we believed that and also believed that only the good go to heaven, we'd rejoice more when a baby, the incarnation of innocence, dies at birth, rather than grieving when it dies. But we don't because there is more than blank purity to life. This is one of the points which Blake is stressing.

Blake does not attempt to argue this through, as a philosopher might. He's not a philosopher, he's a poet. Poetry, as Keats points out, at least, the kind of poetry that Keats and Blake valued, does not work in this way. It "nothing affirmeth," as Keats [*sic*] says. It merely depicts things in their maximum complexity, using all the tools that language raised to its highest level, the level that we call literary, allows.

To demonstrate how this complexity operates in Blake, consider two opposed lyrics. The first is from *The Songs of Innocence* and is called "The Lamb":

> Little Lamb, who made thee?
> Dost thou know who made thee?
> Gave thee life, & bid thee feed
> By the stream & o'er the mead;
> Gave thee clothing of delight;
> Softest clothing, wooly, bright;
> Gave thee such a tender voice,
> Making all the vales rejoice?
> Little Lamb, who made thee?
> Dost thou know who made thee?

It's like a nursery rhyme. It's consciously so.

> Little Lamb, I'll tell thee,
> Little Lamb, I'll tell thee:
> He is called by thy name,
> For he calls himself a Lamb.
> He is meek, & he is mild;
> He became a little child.
> I a child, & thou a lamb,
> We are called by his name.
> Little Lamb, God bless thee!
> Little Lamb, God bless thee!

As the poem indicates, the lamb is one of the conventional symbols of Christ. And the poem itself is, as I say, nursery-rhyme simple. It's a token of childlike, lamblike innocence. But the mature ram, when the lamb grows up, is sexual. The lamb is innocent of sex. Blake was well aware of the complications of carnal desire, and he discusses it frequently in his poetry. God made the lamb, but why then did the innocent lamb have to be sacrificed? Think of Abraham and Isaac and the ritual sacrifices of lambs in many of the world's great religions.

The poem, you'll notice, is pivoted on a question, but the larger question is unanswered. It hovers. Consider the equivalent partnering poem in *The Songs of Experience*. It's a famous, much quoted lyric, but it merits contextual examination, alongside our lamb, I mean. It is not, I would suggest, as simple a text as "The Lamb" poem is. It's "The Tyger." You probably know it well.

> Tyger! Tyger! burning bright,
> In the forests of the night,
> What immortal hand or eye
> Could frame thy fearful symmetry?
>
> In what distant deeps or skies
> Burnt the fire in thine eyes?
> On what wings dare he aspire?
> What the hand dare seize the fire?
>
> And what shoulder, and what art?
> Could twist the sinews of thy heart?
> And when thy heart began to beat,
> What dread hand, and what dread feet?
>
> What the hammer? What the chain?
> In what furnace was thy brain?
> What the anvil? What dread grasp
> Dare its deadly terrors clasp?
>
> When the stars threw down their spears,
> And watered heaven with their tears,
> Did he smile his work to see?
> Did he who made the Lamb, make thee?
>
> Tyger! Tyger! burning bright,
> In the forests of the night,
> What immortal hand or eye
> Dare frame thy fearful symmetry?

The tiger is, of course, the antitype of the lamb. Tigers kill and eat lambs if they come across them. It's not cruelty, it's their nature. In the design he made for this poem, Blake has an image of the tiger smiling—it's very strange—like it had lamb for lunch.

Where the force of destruction is involved, the answer is not as simple as "Did he who made the Lamb, make thee?" The answer, yes or no, is not forthcoming. As I say, it hovers. The two poems stare across the volumes at each other. They are, in Blake's terms, contraries.

And the hinted answer to that big, hovering question is that without the destructive tiger, without crucifixion, to allegorize it in Christian terms, the innocence of the Lamb would be nothing. It would be empty. It would be, literally, bloodless. And it is the blood of the lamb, not the innocence of the lamb, which the Christian William Blake believes will save us, and us, who are anything but innocent.

As I say, it's worth looking at the design which Blake put together when he made the original engraving for that poem, "The Tyger."

Let's move on. Blake's poetry, in short, takes us into exciting mysteries, strange territories, and typically, we emerge from his poetry less certain of things than we were when we entered. He disturbs us. And always in his poetry, it is the unanswered questions which are, mysteriously, the pathways to higher understanding, even if we struggle to make sense, as a rationalist might say, of that understanding.

Let me give one other example, a very short one, from *The Songs of Experience*. The poem is called "The Sick Rose," a very beautiful poem, very short and very simple:

> O Rose, thou art sick!
> The Invisible worm,
> That flies in the night,
> In the howling storm,

Has found out thy bed
Of Crimson joy;
And his dark secret love
Does thy life destroy.

Roses wither and die. Poets have always known that, and written about it. But this rose is not merely conforming to the eternal law of mutability, vegetation and decay: it is sick. But this is the big question in this little poem, "What is the nature of that sickness? What, precisely, is killing the rose?"

Well, it's a worm, but it's not the kind of parasite which the off-the-shelf weed killer will cure. The worm, of course, is, in the Bible, an image of Satan. It's also phallic. The crucial word in this poem, and it's a minute or two, I think, until we realize the fact, is secret: "his dark secret love / Does thy life destroy."

How different would the poem be if it read "Its insatiable love / Does thy life destroy"? Blake, we must remember, was a sexual anarchist, a philosophy which he found justified in the writings of William Godwin. Love does not destroy if it is open. It is only when it is furtive and ashamed of itself that it destroys. This is the nature of the sickness, that it is secret love.

One can agree or disagree with that proposition. Obviously everyone in their life has to make a decision on that point, but it's one of the foundation elements in the poet's idiosyncratic system. And we shall never comprehend Blake's poetry unless we take it and similarly radical, passionately held beliefs of his on board. We don't have to agree with them, but we have to know about them.

Blake was particularly attracted to and fascinated by the poetry of Milton, specifically, *Paradise Lost*. Now, remember that poem. It founded on that great opposition between two mighty adversaries or contraries, God and Satan. But Milton, as Blake believed, wrote "in fetters." His imagination perceived something that his reason would not fully let him know.

This is how Blake puts it, and he was the first to make this much repeated critical observation about *Paradise Lost* and the moral contradiction at that poem's core. What Blake wrote was the following: "The reason Milton wrote in fetters when he wrote of Angels & God, and at liberty when of Devils & Hell, is because he was a true Poet and of the Devils party without knowing it."

The last three words are devastating. He didn't mean by this, of course, that Milton was a Satanist. What he meant was that a part of Milton understood that Adam and Eve could never have fulfilled their destiny without Satan, without the Fall, without the crushing responsibility of regaining paradise, which they had lost. Without contraries, without Satan, that progression would never have been possible. Therefore, and perversely, Satan was the instrument of religious progress.

He was, in Blake's system, the necessary component, and in Milton's too, if the earlier poet had but known it, and trusted what he inwardly, intuitively knew, but could not write because the fetters of Puritanism, of orthodoxy were too strong at that time. Now, it's a pretty thought to visualize Blake and Milton arguing this point in poets' heaven.

Blake wrote and rewrote *Paradise Lost*, although he didn't call his poems that, throughout his career. Time and again, he revisits the questions that Milton's poem posed. It was an obsession with him. And as the latent contradictions in Genesis, as we discussed earlier, were an obsession with Milton, so Milton was an obsession with Blake.

Despite the ferociously authoritarian voice tone of Blake's poems, which bark out truths, daring the reader to disagree, Blake never quite worked out the answer to the Milton problem, but the problem itself is both clearer and more beautiful for his investigation of it.

With this in mind, let's turn to the other of those early gateway poems, as I've called them, *The Marriage of Heaven and Hell*. If ever there were a divorced couple in the realm of metaphysics, one would think it was these two. But dialectician that he is, Blake is using the term "marriage" as a synonym for synthesis, as the Marxist would say. So he's talking, not about a marriage in the sense of a marriage ceremony, but, to some extent, the fusion of those contraries, which are omnipresent in his work.

"The Marriage," as it presents itself on the page, will probably not strike the reader's eye as a poem at all, but it seems to be a grab bag of manifesto, proverbs, blank verse, epigrams. Much of it's in prose and it has much of what look like Mosaic commandments, hundreds of them, not just ten.

Take, for instance, the section which states the devil's philosophy as a series of truths. This is the third of those truths:

> Energy is Eternal Delight. Those who restrain desire, do so because theirs is weak enough to be restrained; and the restrainer or reason usurps its place & governs the unwilling.
>
> And being restrain'd it by degrees becomes passive till it is only the shadow of desire.
>
> The history of this is written in Paradise Lost, & the Governor or Reason is call'd Messiah.

It's an extraordinary, contradictory, and difficult passage, that, but again, one sees it is Satan who, although the universal mischief maker, is the vessel of truth as well.

A particularly revealing trove of Blakean truth is found elsewhere in the poem, in the section called the "Proverbs of Hell," and the allusion, of course, is to the Book of Proverbs in the Bible. Now, let me just give some samples of these hellish proverbs, as Blake sees them:

> The road of excess leads to the palace of wisdom.
> Prudence is a rich ugly old maid courted by Incapacity.
> He who desires but acts not, breeds pestilence.
> A fool sees not the same tree that a wise man sees.
> He whose face gives no light, shall never become a star.
> The hours of folly are measur'd by the clock, but of wisdom: no clock can measure.
> If the fool would persist in his folly he would become wise.

Every one of those could be a text for a whole Victorian novel. One could have a three-hour discussion on Blake taking any one those proverbs, but the truest of them all, I believe, is "A fool sees not the same tree that a wise man sees," which I would adapt as "The fool reads not the same poem that a wise person reads." And it's a truth, I think, which is particularly appropriate to Blake.

Blake wrote *The Marriage of Heaven and Hell* in what is seen as his most Swedenborgian phase, when, that is, he was most intensely under the influence of the radical theologian, Swedenborg. He outgrew that phase, although that sect still regard him as one of their most important prophets, and his poem *The Marriage of Heaven and Hell* as one of the most eloquent expositions of Swedenborgianism.

Blake, over the next 15 years of his life, progressed further down his own idiosyncratic path. And those who accompany him can often lose their way. The prophetic books are like James Joyce's later works. They're not for amateurs or the faint of heart or for those disinclined to spend many hours' preparation reading them and coming to them.

He remained always, however, deeply connected to the traditions of English literature, as he valued it. He rewrote, for example, Chaucer. For him, the Bible was the greatest of literary books, as well as a vessel of divine truth, as was poetry. And much of his work, particularly his pictorial designs, rewrite or re-picture, recycle, as one might say, the Bible.

Unlike Wordsworth, whom we'll be looking at shortly, Blake never compromised with his early radical, republican, revolutionary beliefs. He is probably the most misread or misunderstood poet in the language, and nowhere more than in that poem which is ritually chanted out in international soccer matches nowadays, and at party political broadcasts, and conferences. I'm referring, of course, to "Jerusalem," as that poem of Blake's was put to music by Hubert Parry during the darkest days of World War I.

Blake's poem alludes to the legend that, in the lost years of Christ between his childhood and where the Gospels pick up his 30th year, the savior visited England, that he preached at Glastonbury, specifically, where the country's biggest pop music festival is held annually, and where, inevitably, the poem is sung out every year.

This is the poem, "Jerusalem":

> And did those feet in ancient time
> walk upon England's mountains green?
> And was the holy Lamb of God
> on England's pleasant pastures seen?
> And did the countenance divine
> shine forth upon our clouded hills?
> And was Jerusalem builded here
> among these dark Satanic Mills?
>
> Bring me my bow of burning gold!
> Bring me my arrows of desire!
> Bring me my spear! O clouds, unfold!
> Bring me my chariot of fire!
> I will not cease from mental fight,
> nor shall my sword sleep in my hand,
> till we have built Jerusalem
> In England's green and pleasant Land.

You probably know the song, a very good tune. The poem, as it's been popularized, I'm sorry to say, is an extravagantly, not to say disgusting, chauvinistic patriotic anthem. That's how it's misread. It's not at all what Blake had in mind when he wrote it.

The "dark Satanic Mills" are not, as is often asserted, the new and exploitative textile factories of the early Industrial Revolution, but more probably they're the established churches, which Blake loathed as prisons of the soul and mind.

His "arrows of desire" which he talks about are, frankly, sexual desire. In short, this isn't traditional England, a "green and pleasant Land," Tory England, which he's celebrating, but a vision of the Blakean anarchist utopia, a place of complete freedom of belief and free love.

448

This is not, one can be sure, what the many see when they bellow it out at football matches, but it's an ill wind that blows no good, and at the very least, the popularity of "Jerusalem" has installed Blake where he never was during his life, at the very center of English life and culture. It is, however one reads or misreads him, where William Blake deserves to be.

He is, arguably, in that very sort of impressive company of Romantics, one of the giants. And if he demands that we learn his system in order to appreciate his gigantic achievement, we should do him that service and learn his system. And it's very rewarding, too.

Timeline

c. 350 B.C. .... Aristotle, *Poetics*.

c. 700–800 .... Oral version of *Beowulf* arrives, with immigrants, from Europe.

991 .... Battle of Maldon.

c. 1000 .... First extant manuscript of *Beowulf*.

1066 .... Norman invasion and conquest of England.

1337 .... Hundred Years' War with France.

c. 1343 .... Geoffrey Chaucer born.

c. 1350–1352 .... Boccaccio, *Decameron*.

c. 1367–1377 .... William Langland, *Piers Plowman*.

c. 1380 .... First translation of the Bible into vernacular English (Wyclif).

c. 1385 .... Chaucer, *Troilus and Criseyde*.

c. 1387–1400 .... Chaucer, *The Canterbury Tales*.

c. 1400 .... *Sir Gawain and the Green Knight*.

1400 .... Chaucer dies.

1476 .... Caxton publishes a printed *Canterbury Tales*.

1525.. William Tyndale's New Testament
                                                                published in Germany.

1533.. Elizabeth I born.

1536.. Tyndale executed.

1558.. Elizabeth I comes to the throne.

1564.. William Shakespeare born; Christopher
                                                                Marlowe baptized.

1572.. John Donne born.

1588.. Defeat of Spanish Armada;
                                                                Hobbes born.

1590.. Marlowe, *Tamburlaine;* Spenser, *The
                                                                Faerie Queene*, books I–III.

1590–1592.. Shakespeare's *Henry VI* history plays.

c. 1591.. Shakespeare, *Richard III.*

c. 1592.. Shakespeare, *The Taming of the Shrew.*

1593.. George Herbert born; Marlowe dies.

1596.. Shakespeare, *The Merchant of Venice.*

1599.. Shakespeare, *Henry V;* Globe
                                                                Theatre opens.

1601.. Jonson, *Every Man in his Humour.*

1602.. Shakespeare, *Othello.*

1603... Elizabeth I dies, King James I accedes to the throne.

1604... Shakespeare, *Measure for Measure* and *King Lear*; Hampton Court conference on a new English Bible.

1606... Shakespeare, *Macbeth*.

1607... Jonson, *Volpone*.

1608... John Milton born.

1611... Shakespeare, *The Tempest*.

1612... Jonson, *The Alchemist;* Webster, *The White Devil*.

1616... Shakespeare dies.

1621... Andrew Marvell born.

1623... First (folio) printing of Shakespeare's plays; *The Duchess of Malfi* published.

1631... Donne dies, his *Poems* published 1632; Dryden born.

1633... George Herbert dies; *The Temple* published.

1638... Milton's *Lycidas*.

1640... Donne's sermons published; Aphra Behn born.

1642–1647....................................... First English Civil War.

1647 .... John Wilmot, Earl of Rochester, born.

1649 .... Execution of Charles I.

1651 .... Hobbes's *Leviathan* published.

1652 .... Cromwell becomes Protector.

1660 .... The Restoration (Charles II King); John Bunyan imprisoned; Daniel Defoe born.

1665 .... The Great Plague in London.

1665–1667 .... War with the Dutch.

1667 .... *Paradise Lost* published (two later books published in 1674); Jonathan Swift born.

1673 .... Behn's play, *The Dutch Lover*.

1674 .... Milton dies.

1677 .... Behn, *The Rover*.

1678 .... Bunyan's *The Pilgrim's Progress* published (second part published 1684); Hobbes dies; Marvell dies, his poems published three years later.

1680 .... Earl of Rochester dies.

1682 .... Dryden's *MacFlecknoe* published.

1685 .... James II accedes to the throne.

1688.. The Glorious Revolution. James II abdicates; Bunyan dies; Alexander Pope born.

1689.. William and Mary accede to the throne; Behn dies; Samuel Richardson born.

1700.. Dryden dies.

1701.. War of Spanish Accession; Queen Anne accedes to the throne.

1704.. Swift, *The Battle of the Books*.

1707.. Henry Fielding born.

1709.. Samuel Johnson born; first ("Queen Anne") copyright act.

1713.. Laurence Sterne born.

1714.. Pope, *The Rape of the Lock*; George I accedes to the throne.

1719 ....Defoe's *Robinson Crusoe* published.

1722.. Defoe, *Moll Flanders*.

1726.. Swift, *Gulliver's Travels*.

1727.. George II accedes to the throne.

1728.. Pope's *The Dunciad* (first version).

1729.. Swift, *A Modest Proposal*.

1731.. Defoe dies.

1735	Pope, "Epistle to Dr. Arbuthnot."
1737	Edward Gibbon born.
1740	Samuel Richardson, *Pamela*.
1742	Fielding, *Joseph Andrews*.
1744	Pope dies.
1745	Swift dies.
1747	Johnson's "Plan" for his Dictionary; Richardson's *Clarissa*.
1749	Fielding, *Tom Jones*; Johnson, *The Vanity of Human Wishes*.
1754	Fielding dies.
1757	William Blake born.
1759	Mary Wollstonecraft born; Robert Burns born; first volumes of *Tristram Shandy* published.
1760	George III accedes to the throne.
1761	Richardson dies.
1763	Johnson meets James Boswell.
1764	Ann Radcliffe born.
1768	Sterne dies.
1769	Napoleon born.

1770.. William Wordsworth born.

1771.. Walter Scott born.

1772.. Samuel Taylor Coleridge born.

1775.. Jane Austen born.

1786.. Burns, *Poems Chiefly in the Scottish Dialect*.

1788.. Byron born.

1789.. Blake, *Songs of Innocence*.

1791.. Boswell's *Life of Samuel Johnson*.

1792.. Wollstonecraft, *A Vindication of the Rights of Woman*; Percy Bysshe Shelley born.

1794.. Blake, *Songs of Experience*; Radcliffe, *The Mysteries of Udolpho*.

1795.. Thomas Chatterton, *Poetical Works*; John Keats born.

1796.. Matthew Lewis, *The Monk*; Burns dies.

1797.. Radcliffe, *The Italian*; Mary Shelley born.

1798.. Coleridge and Wordsworth, *Lyrical Ballads*.

1800.. *Lyrical Ballads* revised and enlarged.

1804.. Napoleon crowned emperor, Benjamin Disraeli born.

1804.. Scott, *The Lay of the Last Minstrel.*

1806.. Elizabeth Barrett born.

1807.. Byron, *Hours of Idleness.*

1809.. Tennyson born.

1810.. Scott, *The Lady of the Lake*; Elizabeth Gaskell born.

1811.. William Makepeace Thackeray born.

1812.. Robert Browning born; Charles Dickens born; Byron's *Childe Harold, Books I and II.*

1813.. Austen, *Pride and Prejudice.*

1814.. Austen, *Mansfield Park;* Scott, *Waverley.*

1815.. Battle of Waterloo; Austen, *Emma.*

1816.. Coleridge, *Kubla Khan*; Charlotte Brontë born; Mary Shelley writes *Frankenstein.*

1817.. Keats, *Poems*; Jane Austen dies.

1818.. Austen, *Northanger Abbey*; Emily Brontë born.

1819.. Scott's *Ivanhoe*; Byron's *Don Juan, Books I and II*; George Eliot born; Victoria born.

1820.. George IV accedes to the throne; Keats, *Hyperion*; Ann Brontë born.

1821.. Keats dies, Napoleon dies.

1822.. Percy Bysshe Shelley dies.

1824.. Byron dies.

1827.. Blake dies.

1828.. Henrik Ibsen born.

1830.. Tennyson's *Poems, Chiefly Lyrical*.

1832.. Scott dies.

1834.. Coleridge dies.

1836–1837.. Dickens, *The Pickwick Papers*.

1837.. Dickens, *Oliver Twist*; Victoria accedes to the throne.

1840.. Browning, *Sordello*; Thomas Hardy born.

1842.. Dickens, *American Notes*; Tennyson, *Poems*.

1843.. Wordsworth named Poet Laureate; Dickens, *A Christmas Carol*; Henry James born.

1844...Elizabeth Barrett, *Poems;* Gerard
Manley Hopkins born.

1845...Disraeli, *Sybil.*

1846...Marriage of Robert Browning and
Elizabeth Barrett.

1846–1848......................................Dickens, *Dombey and Son.*

1847–1848......................................Thackeray, *Vanity Fair*; Anne Brontë,
Agnes Grey; Charlotte Brontë, *Jane
Eyre*; Emily Brontë *Wuthering Heights.*

1848...Gaskell, *Mary Barton.*

1848...Emily Brontë dies.

1849...Anne Brontë dies; Dickens,
David Copperfield.

1850 ....Tennyson, *In Memoriam*;
Wordsworth dies.

1851...The Great Exhibition.

1852–1853......................................Dickens, *Bleak House.*

1854...Crimean War; Tennyson, *Charge of the
Light Brigade;* Oscar Wilde born.

1855...Charlotte Brontë dies.

1856...George Bernard Shaw born.

1857...Joseph Conrad born.

1859 .... Arthur Conan Doyle born.

1861 .... Elizabeth Barrett Browning dies.

1863 .... Thackeray dies.

1865 .... Mrs. Gaskell dies; Rudyard Kipling born; William Butler Yeats born.

1866 .... H. G. Wells born.

1870 .... Dickens dies.

1871–1872 .... *Middlemarch* serialized.

1871 .... Hardy's first novel, *Desperate Remedies*, published.

1877 .... James, *The American*.

1879 .... E. M. Forster born.

1880 .... Eliot dies.

1881 .... Wilde, *Poems*.

1882 .... James Joyce born; Virginia Woolf born.

1885 .... D. H. Lawrence born; Ezra Pound born.

1886 .... Siegfried Sassoon born.

1887 .... Rupert Brooke born.

1888 .... T. S. Eliot born.

Timeline

1889	Doyle, *The Sign of Four*; Robert Browning dies; Hopkins dies.
1891	Doyle, *The Adventures of Sherlock Holmes*; Wilde, *The Picture of Dorian Gray*.
1892	Tennyson dies; Kipling's *Barrack-Room Ballads*.
1893	Wilfred Owen born.
1894	Yeats, *The Land of Heart's Desire*.
1895	Hardy, *Jude the Obscure*; H. G. Wells, *The Time Machine*; Wilde, *The Importance of Being Earnest*.
1897	Wells, *The Invisible Man*.
1898	Hardy, *Wessex Poems*; Wilde, *The Ballad of Reading Gaol*.
1899	Boer War; Noel Coward born.
1900	Conrad, *Lord Jim;* Wilde dies.
1901	Queen Victoria dies; Edward VII accedes to the throne.
1902	Conrad, *Heart of Darkness*; Doyle, *The Hound of the Baskervilles*.
1903	George Orwell born; Evelyn Waugh born.
1904	Graham Greene born.

1905.. Doyle, *The Return of Sherlock Holmes*.

1906.. Samuel Beckett born; Ibsen dies.

1907.. W. H. Auden born; Kipling awarded Nobel Prize.

1910.. George V accedes to the throne; Forster, *Howards End*.

1911.. William Golding born; Terence Rattigan born.

1913.. Lawrence, *Sons and Lovers*.

1914.. Joyce, *Dubliners*; World War I begins.

1915.. Brooke dies; Lawrence, *The Rainbow*; Woolf, *The Voyage Out*.

1916.. James dies; Easter Rising in Dublin; Shaw's *Pygmalion*.

1917.. T. S. Eliot's *Prufrock*; Russian Revolution.

1918.. World War I ends; Owen killed; Hopkins, *Poems*; Sassoon, *Counter-Attack*.

1919.. Hardy, *Collected Poems*.

1920.. Lawrence, *Women in Love*.

1921.. Irish Free State established; Shaw, *Back to Methuselah*.

Timeline

1922...Eliot, *The Waste Land*; Joyce, *Ulysses*;
Yeats, *Later Poems*; Philip Larkin born.

1923...Yeats awarded Nobel Prize.

1924...Forster, *A Passage to India*; Coward,
The Vortex; Conrad dies.

1925...Woolf, *Mrs. Dalloway*; Shaw awarded
Nobel Prize.

1926...General Strike cripples Britain.

1927...Woolf, *To the Lighthouse*.

1928...Hardy dies; Lawrence publishes *Lady
Chatterley's Lover*.

1929...John Osborne born; Woolf publishes *A
Room of One's Own*.

1930...Auden publishes *Poems*; D. H.
Lawrence dies; Conan Doyle dies;
Harold Pinter born.

1932...Waugh, *Black Mischief*.

1933...Orwell, *Down and Out in Paris and
London*; Yeats, *Collected Poems*; Hitler
becomes German Chancellor.

1934...Waugh, *A Handful of Dust*.

1935...Eliot, *Murder in the Cathedral*.

1936...George VI accedes to throne; Kipling
dies; Spanish Civil War breaks out.

1937...Tom Stoppard born.

1938...Orwell, *Homage to Catalonia*.

1939...Joyce publishes *Finnegans Wake*; Yeats dies; World War II breaks out; Seamus Heaney born.

1940...Greene, *The Power and the Glory*.

1941...Woolf dies; Joyce dies.

1943...T. S. Eliot, *Four Quartets*.

1945...Orwell, *Animal Farm*; Waugh, *Brideshead Revisited*; World War ends.

1946...Wells dies.

1947...India and Pakistan gain independence; Salman Rushdie born.

1948...Greene, *The Heart of the Matter*; T. S. Eliot awarded Nobel Prize.

1949...Orwell, *1984*.

1950...Shaw dies; Orwell dies.

1951...Greene, *The End of the Affair*.

1952...Elizabeth II accedes to the throne; Waugh, *Men at Arms*.

1954...Kingsley Amis, *Lucky Jim*; Terence Rattigan, *Separate Tables*; Golding, *Lord of the Flies*.

1955	Larkin, *The Less Deceived*; Waugh, *Officers and Gentlemen*.
1956	Osborne, *Look back in Anger*; Suez Crisis.
1957	Osborne, *The Entertainer*.
1958	Pinter, *The Birthday Party*.
1960	Lawrence's *Lady Chatterley's Lover* cleared for publication in the UK; Pinter, *The Caretaker*.
1964	Larkin, *The Whitsun Weddings*.
1965	T. S. Eliot dies.
1966	Waugh dies.
1967	Stoppard, *Rosencrantz and Guildenstern are Dead*.
1969	Beckett awarded Nobel Prize.
1970	Forster dies.
1972	Heaney, *Wintering Out*; Stoppard, *Jumpers*.
1974	Larkin, *High Windows*.
1977	Rattigan dies.
1978	Greene, *The Human Factor*.
1979	Golding, *Darkness Visible*.

1981.. Rushdie, *Midnight's Children* (Booker Prize for fiction).

1983.. Golding awarded Nobel Prize.

1985.. Larkin dies.

1988.. Rushdie, *The Satanic Verses*.

1989.. Ayatollah Khomeini issues *fatwa* against Rushdie; Samuel Beckett dies.

1991.. Greene dies.

1993.. Golding dies; Stoppard, *Arcadia*.

1994.. Osborne dies; Rushdie, *East, West*.

1995.. Heaney awarded the Nobel Prize in Literature.

2005.. Pinter awarded the Nobel Prize in Literature.

Glossary

absurd(ity): The term is borrowed from the French Existentialist philosopher, Albert Camus (1913–1960), to describe the only rational description of a universe without meaning. It became current in literary critical circles to describe the theater which, following Beckett, took off in the 1950s.

apocalyptic: Describes a premonition of the imminent, and unavoidable, end of the world. Derived from the "signs of the apocalypse", or the coming final judgment, in the book of Revelation. It also implies a power of reading those signs. Whole schools of literary activity (Jacobean tragedy, for example) can be tinged with apocalypticism.

aubade: From the French, a poem celebrating the arrival of the dawn. Antithetical to "nocturne."

Augustan: Term borrowed, principally, by writers in the 18th century to describe their work—presuming that it rivaled that of the golden era of Rome, under the emperor Augustus, which could boast Vergil, Ovid, and Horace.

Baroque: Lavish or extravagantly ornate in style—often opposed to "chaste."

bathos (adj. **bathetic**): A lapse or drop in tone, for artistic or comic effect. Often used in 18th-century mock-heroic verse. Pope is a master of bathos.

belles-lettres (**English, belleletrism**): French for "fine writing." Often used as a term of deprecation.

Bildungsroman: German loan word for a biographical novel, which follows a hero/heroine from childhood through youth to adulthood. Dickens's *David Copperfield* is an example.

blank verse: Characteristically English poetic meter: unrhymed iambic pentameter (i.e., 10 syllables, alternately strongly and weakly stressed).

Bloomsbury group: Also known as the "Bloomsberries." A coterie of writers and thinkers (notably Virginia Woolf, Lytton Strachey, E. M. Forster, the economist Maynard Keynes) based in the area around Bloomsbury in central London, where Woolf lived. They were notable for the Liberal values they espoused on life, literature, and ethical philosophy.

burlesque: Broad comic parody of a higher literary form. Henry Fielding's *Shamela*, for example, burlesques Samuel Richardson's novel *Pamela*.

cadence: The rising or falling "lilt" of a line, or part of a line, of poetry.

caesura: Latin term for cut, or break, which creates a silent stress, or gap, in the middle of a line of poetry.

canto: Italian for "song," used to indicate a subdivision in, typically, long narrative poems such as Spenser's *The Faerie Queene*.

carpe diem: Latin for "seize the day"—used to indicate poetry (usually) which meditates the shortness of human life and the mutability of human affairs.

catharsis: From the Greek, in Aristotle's *Poetics*. It describes the final "purging" effect of tragedy on the audience.

chronicle: Narrative which strictly follows the order of time—as, for example, in Shakespeare's history plays.

coda: End piece or, in narrative, epilogue.

codex (plural, codices): Book-form printed, or manuscript material (unlike, say, the papyrus, or vellum, scroll).

collage: From the French. Work composed of scraps of other works.

comic relief: Therapeutic intrusion of comic, or light, material into serious literature. Typically used about drama.

consonance (consonantal): Repetition of the same, or similar, consonants for effect in poetry (usually).

coup de théâtre: French for "stroke of drama"—a surprise effect in a play.

courtly love: The elaborate codes of love, and lovemaking, in medieval romance—as, for example, the relationship of Troilus and Criseyde in Chaucer's poem.

deconstruction: Modern school of criticism which explores the infinite indeterminacy or "ambiguity" of literary expression.

demotic: Greek—"of the people"; medieval "mystery" plays are an example.

dialectic: Of the same Greek root as "dialogue," indicating the clash, or merging, of two forces, ideas, or arguments.

diction: Words specifically fitted to literature—as in, for example, "poetic diction" (i.e., language which would normally be found only in poetry).

dirge: Song of lamentation.

dissonance (dissonant): Harsh clash of sound, especially in poetry.

double entendre: French for "double meaning" or "pun."

dystopia (dystopian): Opposite of "utopia," or idealized future state. Orwell's *1984* is a dystopia.

elegy: Poem lamenting the death of (usually) a friend, relative, or admired personage. Milton's *Lycidas* is an elegy for his drowned fellow poet, Edward King.

ellipsis (elliptical): From the Greek, indicating a word, phrase, or passage which is missing. Elliptical denotes a terse style of writing.

encomium: Work of praise, or eulogy. Dryden's "MacFlecknoe" is a mock encomium of Thomas Shadwell. Spenser's *The Faerie Queene* is a genuine encomium of Queen Elizabeth.

enjambment: From the French. It describes two lines of poetry, in which the sense runs over from one to the other without any punctuation.

epic: Long, typically ancient poem commemorating the acts of heroes. Loosely used in modern critical discourse to describe something grand, large, or impressive.

epigram: Short pithy poem or statement.

epigraph: Meaningful quotation placed at the head of a work of literature.

epistolary novel: Novel written in the form of letters, or exchange of letters.

epitaph: Literally the inscription on a tomb—extended to mean poetry suitable for that purpose.

epithet: Adjectival term used to typically describe a hero or thing; e.g., Othello's (ironic) repeated use of the term "noble Iago."

euphuism (euphuistic): Elaborately ornate style of writing.

exposition: Opening section of a narrative, giving the reader (or audience) the necessary information to understand what follows.

fabliau: From the medieval French—bawdy tale in verse. Much favored by Chaucer.

fin-de-siécle: From the French, meaning "end of century"—invariably the 19th century.

flyting: Abusive exchanges of verse (medieval).

folio: From the Italian, meaning "leaf." A large sheet of paper indicating a similarly large book. "Quarto" (i.e., a sheet of paper folded into four), "octavo" (eight) and "duodecimo" (12) indicate progressively smaller sizes of paper and book.

free verse: Translation of the French *vers libre*; poetry that does not conform to the rules of rhyme and conventional meter. Favored in the 20th century.

genre: From the French: a style, or form of literature—often within a larger form. Thus "science fiction" is a genre within the larger domain of the novel.

Gothic fiction: Fictional romance with dominant element of "terror" and "suspense."

Grub Street: Metaphorical term (originally an actual London street name) for writing of a low, journalistic kind. Current in the 18th century (viz., Alexander Pope's *The Dunciad*).

Hellenistic: A term derived from classical Greek literature, describing literature which aspires to that quality.

hermeneutics (hermeneutic): The theory and practice of literary interpretation.

heroic couplet: A pair of lines in poetry, of regular 10-foot meter, ending in a strong rhyme, with an implication of closure at the end of the second line. Current principally in the 18th century.

hubris: Greek term for overweening pride, often associated with tragic heroes, impelling their fall.

humours: Originally applied to the four physiological elements believed to combine in the body to create personality or temperament.

icon (iconic): Literally an image or object which attracts, or demands, admiration or adoration. (Hence "iconoclastic"—literally the breaking of images; literature which is contrarian or controversial.)

idiolect: The language, or style of language, used by a particular individual and no one else.

in media res: From the Latin meaning "in the middle of things," describing narrative that jumps into the story (e.g., *Paradise Lost*).

intertextuality: A modern term describing the relationship which literary texts have with other texts (e.g., *Paradise Lost* and the *Odyssey*).

Jacobean: As in "Jacobean tragedy," a term indicating work produced during the reign of James I of England (1603–1625).

jeremiad: A lamentation, often of an exaggerated kind.

jeu d'esprit: French term literally a "game of the mind"; i.e., a playful work of literature.

juvenilia: From the Latin, indicating work produced by an author during their youth.

kenning: In Old English verse, a poetic compound which in modern usage would require a number of words: e.g., *geardagum*/"days of yore."

lacuna: From the Latin, "gap" or "vacancy" in a text or narrative.

lampoon: Insulting personal attack.

leitmotif: From the German; a repeated phrase, or theme, introduced meaningfully at intervals.

literati: Literary or educated people. Often used contemptuously.

litotes: Literary effect which depends on deliberate understatement.

lyric: Originally (via the instrument the lyre) meaning something musical. In modern poetry, it has come to mean the short poem.

Machiavel: Used in Renaissance tragedy to indicate a ruthless villain, supposedly inspired in his villainy by the Italian political writer, Niccolo Machiavelli.

magic realism: A 20th-century term describing fictional narrative which embeds fantastic elements in an otherwise literary narrative.

melodrama (melodramatic): Originally drama dependent on song, but now meaning literature which is extravagantly emotional or sentimental.

metonymy: A device by which the part stands for the whole; e.g., "all hands on deck."

mimesis: From the Greek, meaning "imitation". According to Aristotle, in *The Poetics*, the starting point of all literature.

mise en scène: French meaning the "set up," or initial staging in drama, or narrative.

mock-heroic: Literature whose principal effect is the parody of epic ("mock epic") or heroic works. Current in the 18th century.

motif: Meaningful feature, common to a number of works, styles, or literatures.

mystery play: Medieval street theater, or pageants, sponsored by guilds.

mythopoeia (mythopoeiac): The making, or invention, of new myths in literature.

Naturalism: "Tough" realism, typically applied to a school of 20th-century fiction.

Neoclassicism: The adoption of antique classical styles in modern literature. Current in the 18th century.

Neologism: Newly invented word or term.

nom de plume: French for "pen name" (e.g., "Boz"/Charles Dickens).

novella: Work which is midway in length between a short story and a novel proper. Not to be confused with "novelette"—a short novel of a worthless kind.

occasional verse (or **poem**): A work inspired by a particular occasion (e.g. Byron's *Vision of Judgment*, inspired by the death of George III).

ode: A poem ostensibly spontaneous, and deeply felt, in origin.

oeuvre: From the French, meaning an author's whole body of lifetime work.

ottava rima: From the Italian, 8-line stanza (or verse) poetry. Favored by, among others of the period, Byron.

parataxis (paratactic): Poetry, usually, in which the usual connections of syntax are missing.

pastiche: From the French, stylistic imitation of another work—often, but not always, for comic effect.

pathetic fallacy: The notion that nature has feelings, and can respond intelligently to us and our feelings.

pentameter: As in iambic pentameter; a 10-syllable line with five strong stresses in it.

peripeteia: Term used by Aristotle, in *The Poetics*, to describe the downfall of a tragic hero: e.g., King Lear reduced to vagrancy on the heath.

picaresque: Originally a term from the Spanish, for literature with a rogue or scapegrace hero. Often extended to mean a narrative with loose, wide-ranging action.

polyvalence: Like "ambiguity," multiple meaning.

Postmodernism: Literature that consciously moves forward from 20th-century avant-garde styles.

prosody: The study of versification, particularly meter.

quatrain: Stanza, or verse, of four lines only.

Renaissance: Now more often termed the "early modern period," the centuries in which ancient learning and literature was rediscovered, leading to a cultural "rebirth" in Europe.

Restoration literature: Literature produced in the late 17th century, after the downfall of the Commonwealth (i.e., English Republic) and the restoration of the king of England, in 1660.

rhetoric (rhetorical): Language used to produce a particular response from the reader/listener. Opposed to the "expressive" use of language, in which response is not a paramount concern.

roman à clef: A French term for fiction which has a thinly veiled reference to real, or historical, situations and characters.

roman à thèse: French term for "fiction with a purpose."

Romanticism: As a period term, literature produced from the late 18th century through the 19th century. It also indicates literature of that period strongly conscious that it was breaking away from old styles of literature.

satire: Literature that sets out to correct vice (often by holding it up to ridicule) and commend virtue.

scald (or *scop*): Old English term for minstrel or poet.

semantics: The study of the meaning of words.

sensibility: The capacity to respond, sensitively, to the world around oneself, and the feelings of others. Much cultivated in literature of the 19ᵗʰ century, and by the Romantics.

Shavian: Pertaining to the works, styles, and wit of the dramatist George Bernard Shaw (1856–1950).

soliloquy: A character's speech, aloud, ostensibly to himself with no auditor.

Spenserian stanza: Pioneered by Edmund Spenser in *The Faerie Queene*, a verse of nine, intricately rhymed, iambic lines. Much used by Keats and Byron, among others.

stream of consciousness: Applied to fiction (of Virginia Woolf, or James Joyce, for example) that sets out to convey the thoughts of characters, in all their randomness and spontaneity.

tragic flaw: The character quality, or defect, which brings down a tragic hero (e.g., ambition in *Macbeth*).

unities, the: In Aristotle, the dimensions of time, place, and action to which, ideally, drama should adhere. Much followed in the 18ᵗʰ century.

verisimilitude: The aim of creating likeness to life in literature.

Zeitgeist: From the German, "the spirit of the age."

Glossary

Biographical Notes

Aristotle (384–322 B.C.): Born in Macedonia, he studied under Plato, in Athens, for 20 years, developing his own (in some ways anti-Platonic) philosophy. He was tutor to the young prince who later became Alexander the Great. His "peripatetic" (i.e. teaching while walking around) method favored debate, discussion, and argument over dictatorial instruction. Aristotle's works, which cover logic, rhetoric, aesthetics, and ethics were, as they have come down to us, probably lecture and seminar notes. His *Poetics*—of which only the coverage of tragedy survives—remains the finest short treatise on how literature works, and how the "fictional" can be "real." With the European Renaissance, "neo-Aristotelianism" was a major force in the aesthetic theory of that period. His thinking remains as relevant today as it was in Periclean Athens.

Beowulf Poet: Neither the author(s) of the original oral epic (usually dated around the 8th century), nor the (presumably) monastic, or clerical, scholar who transcribed the text of the work in the 10th century (presumably), interpolating Christian elements, can be identified. Nor can the anonymous *scops* and reciters who, over the centuries, added their own improvements. A recent scholar, Richard North, in his monograph *The Origins of Beowulf* suggests that the epic "was composed in the winter of 826–827 as a requiem for King Beornwulf of Mercia on behalf of Wiglaf, the ealdorman who succeeded him." The place of composition, North suggests, is "the minster of Breedon on the Hill in Leicestershire" and the poet is identified as the abbot, Eanmund. North's thesis has been found controversial, but it indicates how speculative identification of the *Beowulf* poet necessarily is, and how fascinating it is, as well. We hear a voice in the poem—but whose?

William Caxton (c. 1422–1491): Pioneer English printer, publisher, and bookseller. Born in Kent, Caxton served his apprenticeship in London, before spending 30 years trading in the Low Countries (modern Holland and Belgium) where he picked up the new art of printing. Caxton set up the first English press, in Westminster (outside the abbey) in 1476. He published, among other primal texts in English literature, the works of Chaucer and Malory.

Geoffrey Chaucer (c. 1343–1400): The son of a London wine-merchant, of distantly French origin, Chaucer—after trying out the various careers open to a clever young man like himself—served as a soldier. He was with Edward III's invading English army in France, in 1359, where he was taken prisoner and ransomed. On his return from the wars, he married (probably in 1366) Philippa, the high-born daughter of Sir Paon Roet. This union brought useful patronage in his subsequent careers. Those careers were diverse. He served the king in a number of capacities and travelled abroad as a diplomat. On his travels, he may have met French and Italian men of letters, such as Boccaccio and Petrarch: Both of whom would be influential on his own writing. In 1374, Chaucer was appointed controller of customs in the Port of London. He was a "knight of the shire" in Kent in the mid-1380s, and spent his last years in that county (whose county town is Canterbury). Chaucer's earlier literary works (all of which were intended for recitation and manuscript circulation) include *The House of Fame*, in the 1370s, and *Troilus and Criseyde*, in the mid-1380s. It was in Kentish retirement and relative obscurity (his star having waned at court and his patrons no longer smiling on him) that he wrote what is considered his greatest work, *The Canterbury Tales*. Chaucer is buried in Westminster Abbey, the first occupant, of many, in that holy place's Poets' Corner over which he has always, rightfully, presided as the father of English poetry.

John Donne (1572–1631): Donne was born into a devout Catholic family, a distant descendant of the Catholic martyr, Sir Thomas More. His father, a leading merchant in the City of London, died when John (one of six children) was four. Hardship and persecution (for the Donnes' Catholic belief) made his childhood difficult. As a small child he was educated by Jesuits. Donne's inwardness with the subtleties of theology would assist him both in his later career as churchman, and poet. He went on to study at both Oxford and Cambridge universities but could not, given the religious oaths required, graduate from those Anglican institutions. In 1592, he enrolled at Lincoln's Inn, to study law. The following year his brother Henry died in prison, having been arrested for harboring a Catholic priest. The next few years are largely blank—other than that we know Donne began questioning, and gradually recanting, his Catholicism. He saw active military service with the Earl of Essex and Sir Walter Raleigh in Spain. In his mid-20s, Donne evidently sought a career in diplomacy and acquired useful positions with patrons. This plan encountered a total set-back when he secretly married his principal patron's very young niece, Anne. It provoked his witty observation: "John Donne, Anne Donne, Undone." It was no overstatement. Donne was briefly imprisoned for his marital imprudence. He and his wife lived quietly for some years thereafter, he working as a lawyer for small fees. The family needed income. Anne would bear him eleven children, before dying in her early 30s. Donne had evidently been writing poetry, much of it wittily erotic, all of it daringly "Metaphysical," throughout his young manhood. In the early 1600s, his fortune gradually improved. Patrons, impressed with his verse (privately circulated in manuscript), were inclined to help him. He was elected a Member of Parliament in 1602. By 1610, he was rigorously and publicly anti-Catholic. King James urged him to become a churchman. Eventually he did so, in 1615. This, and the death of Anne in 1617, ushered in the second great phase of his writing career—the Divine Poems (notably the "Holy Sonnets") and his sermons. Donne was regarded as the best preacher of his age, and his prose is as distinguished, in literary terms, as his verse. By 1621, Donne was dean of Saint Paul's, in London—a senior post in the church. He was later chaplain to Charles I. He had his portrait drawn, as he was dying, in his burial shroud—the image, as he expected, of his resurrected self. His last sermon, "Death's Duel" (as he himself was fighting death) is among his most famous. Donne died, as he had lived, dramatically. Underrated at the time, and for centuries after, his reputation soared in the 20th century, as did that of the whole Metaphysical School, of whom he is the acknowledged leader.

George Herbert (1593–1633): Born into a Welsh family with aristocratic connections (and, through his mother, friendship with John Donne), Herbert was educated at Westminster School and at Cambridge University. He was publishing accomplished poems, in Latin and English, in his early teens, and was regarded as a rising scholar at the university, where he was appointed orator. In the early 1620s he was elected to Parliament and may have toyed with a political career. He was a favorite of King James, in that monarch's last years. But in the mid-1620s (and after the king's death in 1625), Herbert settled on the Anglican Church as his vocation. He had inherited wealth and used it to restore the church where he was, for the rest of his short life, a rector (a lowly post), near Salisbury. He died of consumption only three years after taking orders. Herbert wrote religious, or "divine," poetry of crystal clarity and simplicity, but using the full resource of Metaphysical Wit. The most modest of poets, he left his major collection of verse, *The Temple*, to be published if it might be of help to any "dejected soul." It survives as one of the greatest poetry collections of the century.

Ben Jonson (c. 1572–1637): The son of a clergyman (who died before his son was born) Jonson was educated at Westminster School. The school gave him an excellent education, and steeped him in the classics. On leaving school, he was for a time a manual laborer in his step-father's employment. He then turned soldier, and saw active service in Flanders. He subsequently took to the stage, as an actor, playing star roles in such hits of the 1590s as Thomas Kyd's *The Spanish Tragedy* (a play which had a strong influence on Shakespeare's *Hamlet*). In 1598, Jonson killed a fellow actor in a duel, and was for a while imprisoned. During this period he temporarily converted to Catholicism. He began producing his comedies in the late 1590s: works such as *Every Man Out of His Humour* were hugely popular (the "comedy of humors" would be Jonson's trademark). Over the period 1605 to 1610 he produced what are considered his major works, *Volpone*, *The Alchemist*, and *Bartholomew Fair*. Convivial (and famously bibulous) by nature, Jonson was a friend of Shakespeare, and it is through him that one knows most about what the other dramatist was like in life. Jonson received honors in later life (including a degree from Oxford), and was (unofficially) the first poet laureate—in the service of the monarch, James I. His later stage works, "masques" or pageants, were much admired at the time (not least by King James). In his later years, as a poet and man of letters, Jonson gathered around him a group of disciples, the so-called "tribe of Ben". His influence on drama of the late 17th century is profound. He is buried in Westminster Abbey, his gravestone reading: "O rare Ben Jonson."

Thomas Malory (d. 1471): Very little is known of Malory's life: not even if he was, actually, the author of the hugely and perennially influential Arthurian Cycle work, *Le Mort d'Arthur*. It is, however, probable that Malory wrote this seminal work in prison, having been convicted of robbery and rape (hardly Camelot). The work, as the title suggests, may have had a lost French original. Who Malory actually was, and what he did in his life, is one of the great conundrums of English Literature.

Christopher Marlowe ("Kit," 1564–1593): Marlowe was born the son of a shoemaker in Canterbury and attended school in that city before going on to Cambridge University. At university, he may have converted to Catholicism—one of the many antiauthoritarian acts in his short and rebellious life. Even at this early stage of his life he may have been a spy in the service of the government. Marlowe was already writing proficient verse at university, and consorting with leading literary figures. His first, and sensationally successful, play for the London theater was *Tamburlaine the Great* in 1587. This tragedy patented, in precocious maturity, Marlowe's mastery of blank verse—the so-called "mighty line", which would be the main literary vehicle for the great dramatists who succeeded him. *Tamburlaine* (particularly the second part) also introduced his "overreacher" theme: the heretical proposition that men could challenge the gods, and defy religion. The order in which Marlowe's other plays were composed is uncertain, but the most mature of them are taken to be *Edward II* (a play which introduces frank homosexuality into the downfall of the monarch) and *Doctor Faustus.* Unfortunately no complete text of this last work survives, although enough does survive to establish Marlowe's genius. His later years are shrouded in mystery, much of it sensational. He was arrested in 1592, in Holland, for counterfeiting coins. No charge resulted. He was murdered in 1593, in a tavern brawl. It may have been a squalid crime, fuelled by drink and sexual jealousy or—it is suggested—Marlowe may have been assassinated on government orders, although for what reason is obscure. He was in trouble with the Privy Council, and his atheism (and plays) had rendered him notorious and, arguably, an enemy of the state. He was buried in an unmarked grave, in Deptford, on the South Bank of the Thames, not far from the playhouses where his work had been so successfully given to the world.

Andrew Marvell (1621–1678): Marvell was born in Yorkshire, the son of an Anglican churchman. The family was well off, and after graduating from Cambridge University in 1639, and his father's death in 1641, Andrew's education was finished with four years in Europe. This was the period of the Civil War (1642–1647), and Marvell may have remained abroad to avoid the worst of it. He had divided loyalties, and it is not clear whether his heart was with the Royalists or the Commonwealth (this uncertainty permeates the greatest of his political poems, "An Horatian Ode upon Cromwell's Return from Ireland"). On his return from Europe, Marvell took employment as a personal tutor in York. His affiliation was to the Parliamentarians, under Cromwell (although many of his friends were of the other party). This period saw the publication of the complex poem, "Upon Appleton House" (essentially a meditation on England). It was also at this period he wrote his best known work, the erotic love poem, "To His Coy Mistress". Marvell subsequently took a number of official positions, carefully negotiating his positions between opposing political forces. In the late 1650s, he was helpful to the now blind John Milton in the years of his greatest distress. In 1659, Marvell was elected to Parliament for a constituency in his native Yorkshire. It was a post he held, conscientiously, until his death. Known in his own time as, principally, a writer of polemical prose and satire, it is Marvell's lyrical Metaphysical poetry which posterity has seen as his great achievement.

John Milton (1608–1674): Milton was born in London, the son of a scrivener (i.e., clerk) and musician. He was educated locally at Saint Paul's school, and thereafter at Cambridge, graduating in 1632. While at university he began to write verse in Latin and in English (the two languages would mix, creatively, in the poetry of his mature period). On leaving Cambridge, and taking up residence again in his father's house, Milton dedicated himself to a career in poetry; although he may also have thought of eventually taking holy orders. For six years he read widely and intensely, mastering half-a-dozen languages, always aiming to perfect his extraordinary literary talent. His elegiac poem, *Lycidas,* expresses his aspiration to be the English Homer. In the late 1630s, Milton traveled—notably to Italy. Contact with the literature of that country would have a profound effect on his own composition. As the Civil War broke out, in 1642, Milton pamphleteered on the side of the Parliamentarians, and Cromwell. In the same year, 1642, he married 16-year-old Mary Powell. The marriage temporarily broke down, inspiring Milton's powerful tracts on the legitimacy of divorce. The furore they provoked led to his even more famous tract against censorship, *Areopagitica.* During the period of the Commonwealth, Milton enjoyed privileges and occupied official positions with Cromwell's administration. By 1654, however, his eyes—afflicted with glaucoma—had failed. He was now like Homer in more than one way.

Among his amanuenses, to whom he dictated prose and poetry, was Andrew Marvell. After Cromwell's death, in 1658, and the imminent Restoration in 1660, Milton refused to trim his now dangerous political beliefs. He was forced into hiding, and his writings were burned. Marvell again helped him. The twice widowed, wholly blind, Milton now married for a third time, and in the relative peace of his final years published *Paradise Lost*, in 1667. Indifferent to wealth, or anything but literary fame, he sold the copyright for £10. Other major poems followed (*Samson Agonistes*, *Paradise Regained*) before his death in 1674.

William Shakespeare (1564–1616): Shakespeare was born in Stratford-on-Avon (Avon being the river running through the Warwickshire town), the son of a glover and local merchant. His father, John, may also have been a Catholic at a period in history when it was unsafe to profess that faith. William's relationship to Catholicism is much debated and argued over. Shakespeare's mother, Mary, was of higher social standing than her husband, and may have inspired her eldest son to rise in life above the station of a glover. He was educated at the local grammar school and, as is evident from his drama, exceptionally well educated there. What he did in his late teens, after leaving school, is not known. He may have been in trouble from the law, for poaching. What is clear is that he had access to the best books available at that period. In 1582, aged 18, he married a local woman, Anne Hathaway, eight years his senior and pregnant at the time of the ceremony. The couple had a daughter, Susanna, shortly after marriage, and twins, Hamnet and Judith in 1585. Thereafter come what are known as "the lost years." What Shakespeare was doing in the years immediately following his marriage, and his first making his mark on the London stage, in the late 1580s, is not known. He may have been a country schoolmaster. He may have been a tutor in a Catholic household, in the north of England. He may have been a traveling player, in a theatrical company. The relationship with Anne is the subject of much speculation. Whether or not he was happily married, will never be known. The sonnet sequence, written in the mid-1590s, suggests bisexuality. From the late 1580s onwards, with his first cycle of history plays, Shakespeare was a rising star in the London theater, principally associated as he was with the Globe playhouse and Lord Chamberlain's company of players. His family, in his most active decade artistically, the 1590s, remained in Stratford. In addition to his stage work (which may have included acting and directing) Shakespeare speculated in various commodities, establishing himself as a wealthy and successful citizen. His only son, Hamnet, died in 1596—arguably inspiring the tragedies of which the greatest is *Hamlet*. Although precise dates are unascertainable, Shakespeare moved through a series of modes, or genres exhausting their literary potential as he went: history plays, comedies, problem plays, Roman plays, romances, tragedies, tragi-comedies. He mastered each and all. Shakespeare's was not merely the greatest genius in English literature, but also one of the most restless. Over the years of his London triumph, and particularly after the death of his father in 1601, he was buying land in Stratford. He retired and died in his home town, prematurely: from typhoid probably. He had, at the time of his death, achieved his aim of becoming a member of the English landed gentry: this may well have meant more to him than his literary achievements.

Sophocles (496–406 B.C.): One of the three greatest tragedians ancient Athens produced (the others being Aeschylus and Euripides) little is known of his life. Seven of his works survive. Sophocles's most famous tragedy, *Oedipus Rex* is the main example Aristotle draws on, in his *Poetics* and the play's influence is formative on Shakespeare's *King Lear*.

Edmund Spenser (c. 1522–1599): Born into a family enriched in the cloth trade, Spenser was born (probably) in London, and educated at the Merchant Taylors' school, and at Cambridge University. He began writing poetry in his undergraduate years, influenced principally, by the Italian poet, Petrarch. Little is known of Spenser in his early 20s: other than that he was a supplicant for, and the recipient of, patronage of various kinds, serving as he did in various capacities in various noble households. Among his early acquaintance was the sonneteer Sir Philip Sidney (to whom Spenser would dedicate his pastoral poem, the *Shephearde's Calendar*, 1579). Spenser married, probably in 1579, and in the same year began writing *The Faerie Queene*. In 1580, he was posted to Ireland as Lord Deputy, acquiring for himself a castle in County Cork. In Ireland, he began writing in earnest, whilst administering the severe colonial discipline on the local populace expected from servants of the English crown. The first three (of a projected 12) books of *The Faerie Queene* were published in London, in 1589. They were very successful with readers, and did Spenser no harm at Elizabeth's court, although he would never receive the patronage from the monarch that he evidently aimed for with this hugely complimentary work. The following three books of his (forever incomplete) poem were published (alongside much else in this decade) in 1596. His star had waned in London, and in 1596 (or possibly the following year) his castle was burned in Ireland, in a general uprising by natives in the region. Spenser was obliged to flee, with his family. He died in London, in financial hardship. He is buried alongside Chaucer, in Poets' Corner, in Westminster Abbey.

William Tyndale (c. 1490–1536): More is known about Tyndale's death than about his life. Even his surname is uncertain (it may have been "Hitchins"). He was born in Dursley, Gloucestershire. The family was well off and respectable and William attended Oxford University, graduating in 1512, before being ordained a priest. He studied theology, at both Oxford and Cambridge universities, and became fascinated by scripture—its status and its accessibility. Printing had made books, even the Bible, readily acquired commodities. But the Bible in Latin was beyond most English citizens' understanding, even if it was within their means to buy it. A phenomenally gifted linguist, Tyndale was able to read Hebrew as readily as Latin and Greek, and eminently capable of translating Holy Writ into his native English. His conviction that the Bible should be "Englished" brought him, inevitably, into conflict with the authorities, clerical and secular—and most particularly with Rome and the pope. In Germany in the 1520s, as an acknowledged disciple of Martin Luther, he embarked on his great work of translating the New Testament into English. On the publication of this work he was proclaimed a heretic, by Cardinal Wolsey, Henry VIII's plenipotentiary. Tyndale further vexed the monarch by criticizing, on religious grounds, his royal (but unreligious) divorces. Unwisely having returned to England, Tyndale was tried for heresy in 1536, found guilty, and burned at the stake. His last words were, reportedly, "Oh Lord, open the King of England's eyes." His translation supplies the basis of the subsequent King James, or "Authorized" version. Tyndale's version, alas, was tragically unauthorized.

Wakefield Master, The: This is the only identity we can ascribe to the unknown, now forever unknowable, genius who, in the early 15th century (at some point between 1400 and 1450), wrote seven of the plays in the Wakefield cycle, most famously the *Second Shepherd's Play*. He may well have been a churchman. That a single author produced these early masterpieces is deduced from stylistic characteristics—notably his use of stanza, rhyme, proverb and comic effect. Others of the Mystery Plays were probably the production of many hands, and many contributions from players over the generations.

John Webster (c. 1578–c. 1634): Little is known of Webster's life. His father was a prosperous London coachmaker. John evidently had a good school education, and trained as a lawyer in one of the London Inns of Court. These were institutions in which drama was relished, and often performed. Webster married a very young woman (evidently pregnant by him) in 1606. Thereafter, he was a man of the theater. He worked in collaboration with many of the leading playwrights of the time. His own, single-authored, major works, *The White Devil* and *The Duchess of Malfi,* were, evidently, written and staged around 1610. They establish this shadowy dramatist as one of the greatest of Shakespeare's late contemporaries.

Lectures 13–24

Aphra Behn (c. 1640–1689): Little is known of Aphra (sometimes "Afra," or "Eaffry") Behn's life, and the little we do know is tantalizing, and, if true, highly dramatic. The woman destined to be the first professional writer among her sex in England was born Aphra Johnson in Kent, where her father was a barber. She may have been Catholic. It seems likely, although not certain, that she went with her family (the circumstances are mysterious), in her early 20s, to the island of Surinam, near Venezeula, then a British colony, and stayed there around a year. This supplies the narrative to her most famous work, the novel (perhaps the first novel in English) *Oroonoko*. The Restoration of the monarchy, with Charles II, in 1660, confirmed her Tory, Royalist sympathies. It seems likely that, in her mid-20s, she married a German merchant, called "Johah Behn". The marriage was short-lived: he may have died. (Or, some speculate, Mr. Behn may never have existed.) In her late 20s, Behn (as she now was) served as a spy in the Low Countries for the King (England and Holland were intermittently at war). It did not profit her. By a series of misadventures, she ended up in debtors' prison at the end of the 1660s. In the 1670s, she turned her hand very profitably to drama (principally Restoration Comedy) and prose fiction. Such was her reputation, that she is buried in Westminster Abbey. Another first for womanhood. She is celebrated as a pioneer by, among many others in the 20th century, Virginia Woolf, whose epitaph for Behn is: "All women together, ought to let flowers fall upon the grave of Aphra Behn ... for it was she who earned them the right to speak their minds." And, one might add, keep their private lives very private.

William Blake (1757–1827): Blake was born, of humble stock, in London, the son of a hosier (trouser maker). His education was basic—but ran, momentously for English literature, to formal training at a local drawing school. His talent in this direction enabled him to escape his class destiny: apprenticeship, making clothes, in his father's shop or some other tailor's. William was, instead, apprenticed to a local engraver. The picture industry, for domestic decoration, was booming at this period. Having served his time, Blake set up as an independent engraver in his early 20s. In his mid-20s, he married Catherine Sophia Boucher, who assisted him in his subsequent literary and artistic activities. Blake's early collections, the self-illustrated *Songs of Innocence and Experience* were never recognized for the major works they are until long after his death; that, indeed, is the case with all Blake's work, particularly with the so-called "prophetic" poems, in which he set out to create literature on the scale of Milton, Shakespeare and—most ambitiously—the Bible. He was too big, too original and (it has to be said) too "low" for his own age. His income came mainly from commissioned work. At a period of historical unrest, Blake was "radical," and imprudently so. The authorities had marked him as a dangerous. He was tried, and cleared, of treason. But his poems continued to applaud the revolutions in France and America, and to welcome something similar in England. Blake died in 1827 and is buried in an unknown grave. It is a symbolism that would have pleased his genius, which was as subversive as it was original.

Anne Bradstreet (c. 1612–1672): Variously labeled the first Metaphysical woman poet in English Literature, and the first considerable writer in American Literature, she was born in England. Her father, Thomas Dudley, a former soldier, was a nonconformist. In 1630, the family sailed for Massachusetts, in search of religious tolerance and trading opportunities. Traveling with the family was Simon Bradstreet, whom Anne had earlier married. Anne, as was commoner with nonconformists, had been well educated. Life in New England was harder than it had been in the Old Country (where, for example,

Anne had enjoyed the run of a fine library). The physical conditions were primitive, the religious discipline strong. Little is known about her life in Massachusetts—other than that she moved house several times (on one occasion because of fire) and that she had eight children and grandchildren, some of whom she outlived. And, most significantly for literature, that she wrote poetry. Her brother-in-law had her first volume of poetry published in England, in 1650. Her shorter, much more admired, poems were published posthumously.

John Bunyan (1628–1688): Bunyan was born on the outskirts of Bedford—a small town in the Midlands of England, whose laureate he will forever be. He was the son of a tinker: the humblest of trades (mending and selling kitchenware was the principal tinker's activity). One book, the Geneva Bible, gave him most of the education, and literary wherewithal, that he would need in his later life as the greatest Puritan writer of his time. Bunyan fought with Cromwell's Parliamentarians, in the Civil War. Their uncompromising, "leveling" Puritan values, sense of constant persecution, and severe theology, would sustain him through much subsequent hardship. He married twice. According to his spiritual autobiography, *Grace Abounding*, he was wild and sinful in his early days, before mending his ways. After the war, he turned preacher. There was, however, no peace for John Bunyan. With the Restoration, times were hard for hardliners like himself. He flagrantly disobeyed Royalist prohibitions on preaching, and was jailed, at Bedford, from 1660 to 1672. The conditions of his incarceration were not stringent. It was during this period that he conceived and wrote his great work, the *Pilgrim's Progress*. It would be published in 1678 and establish itself as the most popular work of English fiction, for those of a religious bent, for centuries to come. Bunyan, who never recanted his views, was released, by act of Royal clemency—and promptly imprisoned again in 1673, for four more years. Bunyan used his enforced leisure to write some 40 books, before dying in 1688. He is buried in London.

Margaret Cavendish (the Duchess of Newcastle, 1623–1673): Born Margaret Lucas in Colchester, Essex, she emigrated with her sisters to France, in 1640, to escape the Civil War. She was a courtier of the Queen in exile, and met her husband, William Cavendish, the Duke of Newcastle, in Paris. They married in 1645. Her first volume of poetry, *Poems and Fancies,* was published in 1653. It reveals her lively interest in science—and her consciousness of how unusual such an interest in one of her sex: a woman, moreover, who writes and publishes poetry. The book caused something of a sensation. It also attracted some ridicule. She went on to write prolifically, and often aggressively, against the prejudice of her time. She died, prematurely, aged 50.

Daniel Defoe (c. 1660–1731): Daniel Defoe (or "Foe"—the upper-class prefix was added later) was born in London, the son of a tallow chandler (maker of candles). His family background was "dissenting" (that is, the Foes did not subscribe to the doctrines of Anglicanism). His early childhood saw a near invasion of London, a London which had been ravaged by the Great Fire of 1666 and a catastrophic outbreak of plague. He would reconstruct, in vivid journalistic style, those events in later life. Defoe in early adult life seems to have been a merchant; trading moderately prosperously; although throughout life, he was never clear of debt and sometimes bankrupt. He married in 1684, and had a large family. After a particularly severe financial crisis in 1692, he seems to have traveled abroad, dealing principally in wine and other commodities. He began writing and publishing seriously, well on in life, in the late 1690s. Defoe produced more pamphlets, political journalism, books, and anonymous material than have ever been identified. Late as he may have started, he is one of the most prolific authors of the time. His pamphleteering was very effective and got him, occasionally, into hot water with the authorities. He was placed in the pillory (publicly shackled by the neck) in 1703, for his attacks on the ruling Tories—although he switched allegiance strategically, and cynically, as the political wind blew. It was very late in life, beginning with *Robinson Crusoe* in 1719, that Defoe began writing the novels for which he is now principally remembered. At the same late period, he wrote his great survey, *A tour thro' the Whole Island of Great Britain.* He died in London, as he lived, in debt taking refuge from his numerous creditors.

John Dryden (1631–1700): Dryden was born in the Midlands county of Northamptonshire, into the gentry class, on the fringe of the aristocracy (a position he would cultivate in his later writing career). Jonathan Swift was a distant relative. Dryden was educated at one of the country's best schools, Westminster, in London and thereafter at Cambridge University. He came into adulthood during Cromwell's Protectorate. His religious views were flexible and pragmatic, throughout life, and expressed fluently, and often ambivalently, in his poetry. As his later career demonstrated, John Dryden could survive, and thrive, under both the Protector, and the restored monarch. In 1654 he graduated and, on the death of his father, came into a small inheritance. It was not sufficient to live on, and thereafter Dryden would be a professional writer, dependent on patronage and royal favor in his verse, and the box-office in his dramatic work. In the first instance, however, he gained employment with Cromwell's administration. He went on (after Cromwell's funeral, in 1658, which he attended) to celebrate Charles II's return to the English throne with a panegyric poem of praise. Thereafter he turned his hand to many forms of literary work: criticism, satire, drama, translation. He can claim to be one of the greatest Restoration exponents of each of these genres. He was established Poet Laureate in 1688—versifier to the king. About the same time, he converted to Catholicism, commemorating the fact with a reflective poem on faith: *The Hind and the Panther*. He himself expected that such grand ventures as his translation of Vergil would establish him alongside Shakespeare and Chaucer (both of whom he "modernized") as one of the great figures in English Literature. Posterity, perversely, has preferred his incidental, lighter satires, his poems on "Affairs of State," and mock-epic ventures, such as *MacFlecknoe*. He died in 1700, and is buried in Westminster Abbey alongside Chaucer—company John Dryden would see as fit to accompany him into eternity.

Olaudah Equiano (c. 1745–1797): Equiano was born in the Eboe (the spelling varies) province of what is now southern Nigeria. The only account we have of his early life in Africa is what he provides in his *Interesting Narrative*. He was, he informs us, kidnapped by slavers, aged 11. He was sold on, by traders, eventually finding himself first in the West Indies, and then in Virginia (both British possessions). His experiences in the first months of his slavery constitute the most horrifying passages in his narrative. This autobiographical version of Equiano's early years has, however, been questioned: he may, other sources suggest, have been born in America. Accounts of his later life are more reliable. An intellectually able, but physically slight, man, he was able to ingratiate himself with various masters, and preserve himself from the destructive manual labor of black slavery. In Virginia, he became the personal slave to a British Royal Navy officer—something which enabled him to educate himself by stealth. His master renamed him "Gustavus Vassa" (a royal Swedish name, bizarrely). He was baptized a Christian. Equiano remained in this servitude for eight years, traveling widely. Now a valuable property—literate and numerate—Equiano was sold on to a merchant. After three years, he was able to buy his freedom. He subsequently traveled widely, making good use of the commercial skills he had picked up. Few writers of the time had seen as much of the world as Olaudah Equiano/Gustavus Vassa. In the mid-1780s, he settled in England and associated himself with the abolition movement, becoming a prominent speaker and lobbyist. This led to the publication of his *Interesting Narrative*, in 1789. The book was hugely successful. In 1792, Equiano married an Englishwoman, Susanna Cullen. The couple had two daughters. He died in 1797. His grave is unmarked and it was not until the second half of the 20th century that his remarkable literary achievement was fully recognized.

Henry Fielding (1707–1754): Fielding was born into the landed gentry class of England, in the county of Somerset. His family had aristocratic connections—something that would make Henry's way through the world relatively easy. He had his early education at Eton—the best school in the country. Here it was he picked up his lifelong love of, and familiarity with, the classics. A relative, the writer Lady Mary Wortley Montagu, encouraged his early ambition to write. Initially, his interest was the London stage and he enjoyed considerable success with his comic burlesque, *Tom Thumb* (1730). Fielding was both writing for the stage and managing a theater at this time of his life. His satire of the government, however, led to the censoring of his activities (and the stage generally). Fielding was obliged to undertake a career change (one can thank the vindictive prime minister, Sir Robert Walpole, for *Tom Jones*—without his philistine persecution, Fielding would never have taken to fiction). After attempts at magazine editorship, and the law, he turned to the novel. His contemporary, Samuel Richardson, provoked Fielding's ire and his first serious effort in fiction was *Joseph Andrews*, a satirical burlesque on the other novelist's *Pamela*. His generous, man-of-the-world morality was displayed at greater length in his most popular work, *The History of Tom Jones: A Foundling* (1749) which, despite its anti-Richardsonian line on what constitutes "virtue" went well beyond satire. Fielding had married in 1734, and his wife, Sophia (a favorite name with him) is portrayed as the heroine in *Amelia*. She died in 1744.

Fielding remarried his wife's maid, provoking scandal among friends of his own, upper class. He had often been short of money, but his later years were relieved by his being appointed a Justice of the Peace (local judge) in 1748. In this role, Fielding interested himself in the establishment of an efficient London police force. He was regarded as an eminently good JP, and became something of a London institution in the most famous of the capital's local courts, in Bow Street, by Covent Garden. He died in Lisbon, where he had gone with his wife and family for health reasons. His last book, published posthumously, is an account of the voyage. It is, like everything he wrote, exquisitely well written and humorous.

Anne Finch (Countess of Winchilsea, 1661–1720): Born Anne Kingsmill, she was the daughter of Sir William Kingsmill, who died very shortly after her birth. In her early 20s, she served in the royal household as a maid of honor to the Duchess of York. As someone able to move in public life, she was the friend of, among others, Alexander Pope and Jonathan Swift. She married a fellow courtier, Colonel Heneage Finch. Both lost their posts at court with the deposition of King James II. Thereafter they lived quietly in the countryside, from where she published a volume of verse, *Miscellany Poems on Several Occasions* (1713).

Edward Gibbon (1737–1794): England's greatest historian was born in London, into a family enriched by trade. In poor health all his life (something that, he records, made him an unnaturally bookish child) he attended Westminster School and Oxford University. The formative influence on his intellectual development, however, was a trip taken, in his late teens, to Switzerland, where he imbibed the principles, practices, and skeptical attitudes of the European Enlightenment—"free thinking," as it was called. It was on this trip, that Gibbon relinquished the Catholicism he had temporarily embraced—remaining open-minded about religion for the remainder of his life (something that permeates his historical thinking). Although the episode is murky, it was in Switzerland that the young student fell in love. It ended unhappily, and Gibbon would remain a lifelong bachelor—and sternly unromantic. In affairs of the heart, as everything else, he was a rationalist. Gibbon's first book—a stylish essay on literature—was published when he was only 23. In 1763, he embarked on a Grand Tour of Europe (the finishing touch to an English gentleman's education). It was to have a momentous influence on him, bringing him as it did to Rome in October 1774. Seated in the ruins of the "Eternal City," he conceived the germ of what was to become his life's project: how did the greatest empire the world had known become this heap of tumbled stones? Gibbon's father, with whom he had a difficult relationship, died in 1770—allowing him full financial independence. He moved to London, enjoying to the full the clubman-scholar's life in the capital. Dr Johnson was among his acquaintance. He served, unenergetically, as a Member of Parliament (the best club in London, as it was known). All the while he was researching and drafting his great "history." The first volume of *The History of the Decline and Fall of the Roman Empire* was published in 1776 and proved a bestseller. The final sixth volume was published in 1788. Never physically strong, exhausted by his scholarly labors, and prey to organic weakness, Edward Gibbon died prematurely aged 56.

Thomas Hobbes (1588–1679): Hobbes was born in the year of the defeat of the Great Spanish Armada—an ill-fated invasion attempt on England. War would be the conditioning fact over his long life. His father was a parson, although it was an uncle who made provision for the young Thomas's education. An exceptionally clever child—with a precocious mastery of the classics and mathematics—he excelled in his studies at the University of Oxford (also, at the turn of the century, a hotbed of political activity). His intellectual prowess brought him patronage and a close connection with the royal court. When that court was imperiled by the Civil War (1642–1651) Hobbes, like the king and his followers, took refuge in France. There, he immersed himself in the intellectual and philosophical debates which were fomenting in that country. But the English Civil War was principally formative on Hobbes's political thought, as expressed in his great treatise on government and society, *Leviathan*. On the monarch's return to England, in 1660, Hobbes was awarded a pension, which allowed him to pursue his studies. A polymath, he attracted fame over the following decades as a methapysician, a translator of the classics, a legal theorist, and a mathematician. His was a genius without compartments. Nor, happily, was his life "solitary, poor, nasty, brutish and short."

Samuel Johnson (1709–1784): Johnson was born in the small midlands town of Lichfield, in the county of Staffordshire. His father was a bookseller, of advanced years. Being born into a bookish environment was influential on the young Johnson, as was chronically poor health (he was, from babyhood, blind in one eye, had imperfect hearing, and scarred by scrofula). He attended the local grammar school, and went on to Oxford. The family, however, could not afford to keep him there. After a year, he was obliged to leave, although his remarkable intellectual powers were already evident. So, too, was his temperamental inclination to melancholy and what contemporary medicine would label depression. For a while, he was employed as a school teacher. His financial affairs improved with marriage, in 1735, to a woman of property, a widow over 20 years his senior. This enabled him to set up a private school. The venture was unsuccessful and two years later he settled himself in London—at which point his outstanding intellectual talents enabled him to rise in the world. He did so, momentously for English literature, without the aid of aristocratic, or state, patronage. Among his other achievements, he established writing as a dignified profession. Initially Johnson worked as magazine journalist and took on any Grub Street hackwork that came his way. His two verse satires *London* (1738) and the later, majestic, *The Vanity of Human Wishes* (1749)—the first work to be published under his own name—established him as a major voice in the Augustan Revival of English literature. Poetry, however, was not his main outlet. In 1750, he launched his own journal, *The Rambler*, which would be the outlet for many of his finest essays, all written in a distinctly "Johnsonian" style. In the 1750s he was also working on his magnum opus, the *Dictionary*. Despite his depiction of himself as an "idler," his literary output was vast. He edited Shakespeare and wrote the first extensive work of English literary history, *The Lives of the English Poets*. In 1763, he met the young Scot, James Boswell, to whom posterity is indebted for the greatest biography (and most vivid pen-portrait) of a literary man in the English language. In 1762, Johnson received a Crown Pension of £300 a year, which relieved his later years. Widowed in 1752 (and having given up alcohol, for which he had an early weakness) he lived a sociable domestic life with friends, establishing himself as—among all his other achievements—the greatest conversationalist of his age. Thanks to Boswell, we have a full record of that conversation.

Katherine Philips (1631–1664): Born Katherine Fowler, her father was a nonconformist in London. She was well educated at local schools, and cultivated friendships there which would be lifelong. In 1639, her father died and her mother remarried a Welsh nobleman. The family resettled in Wales. Katherine married a relative of her stepfather, James Philips, in 1648. He was almost 40 years older than his 16-year-old bride. As a married woman, under the pen-name "the Matchless Orinda" Katherine began to write poetry. Her first poems, Metaphysical in style, were published in 1651. Her collected poems were published in the year of her death. Like many of her contemporaries, Katherine Philips was conflicted by the Civil War, and seems to have had somewhat divided loyalties (unlike her husband, who actually signed the death warrant of Charles I). She died, prematurely, of small pox. The most respectable of women writers of her time, her character was conventionally opposed to that of the more scandalous Aphra Behn—who is, nonetheless, the greater writer.

Alexander Pope (1688–1744): Pope was born a Roman Catholic at a time when members of that faith encountered difficulties verging on persecution. This, and serious health difficulties (principally spinal), resulting in lifelong disability, led to young Alexander's being privately tutored. His father, a prosperous London linen-draper, encouraged his son's extraordinarily precocious poetic talent. At the age of 16, he was publishing verse which brought him to the attention of discriminating readers and critics. He was also immersing himself in literature of the past, and of other European cultures, framing the principles and practice of Augustan verse—of which he would be the principal exponent. Pope's subsequent life was one of literary creativity, interspersed with literary warfare against those opponents whom he regarded as witless dullards. This belligerence inspired his greatest satirical project, *The Dunciad*, first published in 1728. This mock-epic (a form in which Pope excelled) was reissued with new targeting of dunces of the day during the next 15 years. Pope secured his financial independence with Augustanizing translations (effectively "modernizations") of Vergil and Homer. His Horatian "epistles" are, among his varied poetic output, the works which have found greatest favor with modern readers. He was a friend of those great writers of his day who were congenial (notably Jonathan Swift) although he had an unfortunate tendency to fall out with friends (most bitterly with the blue-stocking author, Lady Wortley Montagu). He never married, and died, prematurely, in his mid-50s.

Samuel Richardson (1689–1761): Richardson was born near Derby, in the north of England, the son of a joiner (a skilled worker in wood). His formal education did not extend beyond his school years, although, as his later career witnesses, young Samuel must have been a remarkably apt pupil. From an early age, he is recorded as being used by friends to write their love letters. He was apprenticed in London as a printer in 1706, and in 1721 was able to set up in business for himself as a printer, publisher, and bookseller. He married the same year. His business thrived (he would eventually be a leader in the book trade), but Richardson's family history was tragic. By 1731, his wife and six children had all died. He married again in 1733, although his earlier marital suffering left a wound which never healed, and left him prey to melancholy. Richardson liked to write—particularly instructional materials ("conduct manuals") for women. In 1740, he published his first (huge) novel, *Pamela*, which enjoyed sensational popularity, particularly among women readers. It also attracted the satire of Henry Fielding, for its simple (as Fielding thought) morality, leading to one of the most entertaining, and productive, feuds in English literature. Richardson's equally massive, but more complex, novel (also narrated in epistolary, or "familiar letter" form), *Clarissa*, was published in 1747. He tried his hand at a male leading character in his last great effort in fiction, *Sir Charles Grandison* (1754).

Laurence Sterne (1713–1768): Sterne was born in Ireland, where his father was a serving English army officer. Shortly after his birth, the family removed to Yorkshire—the northern county which would be Sterne's lifelong home, and the setting of his major fiction. After a gentleman's school education, Laurence took his degree at Cambridge University. A number of members of his family had been eminent churchmen, and that was the profession which Laurence followed. Alongside his literary achievements, he would, in later life, be recognized as one of the great Anglican preachers of his age. Sterne married in 1741. Both he and his wife Elizabeth were afflicted with consumption—something that he mentions, in passing and poignantly, in his fiction. The skull, as he said, was always on his desk as a *memento mori*, adding a dark tinge to Shandean comedy. The duties of an Anglican clergyman in Yorkshire were not onerous, and Sterne was able to begin publishing the first volumes of his great comic work, *The Life and Opinions of Tristram Shandy, Gentleman* in 1759. It was a hit with the reading public, and made him something of a London celebrity—if always suspicious in the eyes of his church, given the work's impropriety. *Tristram Shandy* continued to appear, volume by volume, until 1767. It was followed by the journal novel, *A Sentimental Journey through France and Italy*, in 1768. Sterne died, soon after, of the tuberculosis which had afflicted him throughout life.

Jonathan Swift (1667–1745): The greatest prose satirist in English literature (and only half English, given his Irish connections) Swift was born in Ireland. His parents were Protestants and members of the so-called "Ascendancy," or Irish upper-class establishment. His father died early; his mother left for England. Swift was left to be educated at school and university in Dublin. In 1688, after the Glorious Revolution—which led to the Protestant William of Orange (i.e., Holland) acceding to the throne of England—Swift took up residence in London. He intended eventually to enter the church. In England, he found aristocratic patrons, and began a Platonic romance with the woman he called "Stella" (Esther Johnson). At the same period, the ailments which would torment his later life began to manifest themselves. In 1795, Swift was ordained a Church of Ireland priest—it being, despite the name, the Anglican Church in Ireland (then an English colonial possession). In the late 1690s, Swift began publishing the satires for which he would later become famous, beginning with *A Tale of a Tub* and *The Battle of the Books*. In both these works, his arch-conservative views are trenchantly, and hilariously, expounded. In 1700, Swift had established himself back in Ireland. His relationship with the English power elite never brought him the favors, or preferment, his talents deserved: and disfavor embittered him. In the early 1700s, he began another, mainly epistolary, romance with the woman he called "Vanessa" (Esther Vanhomrigh). His writing suggests incorrigible phobia about physical sexuality, and what romantic impulses he had were distilled into exquisite prose. By 1710, Swift had allied himself with other, congenial, men of letters in England—such as Addison, Steele, Congreve, and Pope. In 1713, he was appointed Dean of Saint Patrick's Cathedral in Dublin (he had hoped for much more). He began writing, aggressively, on the unfairness meted out to Ireland by its English masters. He began work on *Gulliver's Travels* in 1720, and the great satire was published six years later. He died—if not quite, as Dr. Johnson said, "a driveller and a show"—sadly afflicted with mental disorder. He may possibly have married "Stella," alongside whose tomb, in Saint Patrick's, he chose to be buried.

John Wilmot (second Earl of Rochester, 1647–1680): The most famous libertine writer in English literature, at a period when there were many such, Rochester (as he is commonly referred to) was born in Oxfordshire. His father had been ennobled for services to the monarch, Charles II, while in exile in France. Born as the Civil Wars were ending, young Rochester would be flagrantly anti-Puritanical in his life and writing. He also inherited from his father a propensity for license and dissoluteness which went well beyond the cavalier into the frankly depraved. He inherited his title early in life. After a perfunctory period at Oxford University (he graduated at 14) Rochester undertook the Grand Tour, before taking up residence in London. He fought gallantly for his country against the Dutch, before marrying an heiress, in 1667. He kept a domestic establishment in the country, and cut a dash at Court. In town, he was notoriously drunk, adulterous, and "profligate" (as the current term was), along with other wild, aristocratic comrades. He wrote scurrilous verse, prose and drama (his most famous work in this line is aptly entitled *Sodom: Or the Quintessence of Debauchery*). His literary irresponsibility led to him being exiled even from Court on one occasion. He died, of syphilis it is assumed, in his early 30s. He repented his wicked ways on his deathbed, leaving a quantity of wholly unrepentant verse behind him. Almost all of it was circulated in manuscript.

Mary Wollstonecraft (1759–1797): Mary Wollstonecraft (her married surname, "Godwin", is rarely used) was born in London. Her father, whom she called a "despot," created for her, her mother, and her siblings a desperately unhappy and improvident family background. Aged 19, Mary set out to make her own way in the world. Her father, Edward John Wollstonecraft, had wasted what money he inherited and she was obliged to live by her wits. With her sister Eliza, a refugee from an unhappy and brutal marriage, she set up a school, in London. Mary would later go on to write, shrewdly, on *The Education of Daughters* (1787). Subsequently, as was the destiny of other well-educated but unmoneyed, young women, she took up work as a governess. By the late 1780s, she was settled in London, living by her pen. She was helped by a congenial publisher, Joseph Johnson. A radical, Johnson was instrumental in politicizing his young assistant. She was also strongly (and sympathetically) affected by the Revolution which was currently transforming France. In 1792, she produced her momentous feminist tract, *A Vindication of the Rights of Woman*. In the same year, she went to Paris where she met, and fell in love with, the American writer and merchant, Gilbert Imlay. The relationship was intense and unhappy, so much so that Mary twice attempted suicide. A daughter, Fanny, was born in 1794. Having written a book on the Revolution, Wollstonecraft returned to England in 1795. Through Johnson, she had met the most influential radical philosopher of the time, William Godwin, whom she married in 1797. In the same year, she died having just given birth to a daughter, Mary— subsequently Mary Shelley, the author of *Frankenstein.*

Lectures 25–36

Jane Austen (1775–1817): Jane Austen was born into the large family of a Church of England clergyman, in Hampshire. She was the seventh child in a family of eight (all of whom survived childhood—rare at the time). Jane grew up, happily, in a rural-small town setting, something that left an indelible mark on her later fiction, as did occasional visits to fashionable watering places (i.e. where visitors would drink the supposedly healthful spring waters) such as Bath, and even more occasional visits to London. Being a girl, she was educated mainly at home, and learned music as well as foreign languages. Her brothers were in the navy, or in business, and she evidently knew much more about the world than she chose to display in her fiction. She was also allowed access to a large supply of reading matter: through her father's books, and circulating (i.e. lending) libraries. Her first compositions were for the amusement and admiration of her immediate family, who encouraged further efforts, and evidently offered useful advice. Her father, for example, bought her a writing desk (such as Catherine Morland buys, with the money her father gives her, in *Northanger Abbey*). After her father's death, in 1805, Austen lived with her widowed mother and sister. She received at least one proposal of marriage which, after a temporary acceptance, she declined. It was, evidently, her choice to be single. Details of her personal life were jealously protected, after her death, by her brothers and sister, Cassandra. We shall never know Jane Austen intimately. The publication dates of her novels do not give much indication of when they were actually composed, revised, and (in many cases) rewritten. Nor do any of them reflect, in any detail, the turbulence of the world around her in the early years of the 19th century. *Sense and Sensibility* (1811) was the first of her major novels to see print, although the ideas, and first writing of the narrative, may date from a decade earlier. Her novels were popular during her lifetime, but in no sense were they bestsellers to rank with the fiction of Walter Scott (who admired her) or Mrs.

Radcliffe (whom Austen herself enjoyed reading, although she satirized the Gothic novelist mercilessly in *Northanger Abbey*). Her fiction was published anonymously, "by a Lady." That she certainly was. Austen died, prematurely, of an organic ailment which has not been positively identified. She is buried in Winchester Cathedral. It was a hundred years before her stature, as one of the very greatest writers in English literature, was established. That opinion is unlikely to be revised.

The Brontës (Charlotte, 1816–1855; Emily, 1818–1848; Anne, 1820–1849): The most renowned writing sisterhood in English literature. Their father was born into the peasant class in Ireland. Gifted, he raised himself in life, eventually graduating from Cambridge University (by which point he had changed his name from "Prontey" to something less obviously Irish). Patrick Brontë took religious orders, married well, choosing an English heiress as his bride. He earned for himself a comfortable living (i.e., church position) in Haworth, Yorkshire. His wife, however, died in 1821 and the young Brontë children were brought up by relatives and housekeepers. It was predominantly a female family, there being five daughters, of whom three survived into (short) adulthood. The one son, Branwell, also had outstanding gifts—but not as lavish, or as well-disciplined, as those of his three writing sisters. All of them were destined to live short—if intense—lives. Charlotte and Emily were sent, for a short period, to the brutal boarding school described as "Lowick" in *Jane Eyre*. Thereafter, the Rev. Brontë resolved to educate his children himself (with the exception of Branwell who, being the son and heir, merited more professional treatment). Emily and Charlotte spent some time in Belgium, teaching at a boarding school for girls and learning something of the world. It had a formative effect, particularly on Charlotte, who fell in love with the married proprietor of the institute (in a transformed state, M. Heger returns as the hero of at least two of her subsequent novels). Emily was never happy outside Yorkshire, away from her native moors. All three of the sisters tried governessing, with the long-term ambition of setting up a school. The family mood was darkened not merely by the omnipresent sickness and death, but by Branwell's dissipation and increasing moral degeneration (about which Anne was the most vivid in her later fiction). The Brontë children (including Branwell), as soon as they could write, were composing long, fantastical narratives, and whole worlds ("Gondal," "Angria") in which their stories could be set. Their first attempts were in poetry, and wholly unsuccessful. Fame struck when Charlotte sent a sample of her work to the London publisher George Smith, an approach which led to the publication of *Jane Eyre* in 1847. Less luckily, Anne and Emily entrusted their first novels (*Agnes Grey*, *Wuthering Heights*) to the least trustworthy publisher in London. As a result, neither received the acclaim they deserved, and that *Jane Eyre* won for its (pseudonymous) author, "Currer Bell." Thereafter, all three sisters' lives were tragically curtailed. Emily and Anne died from consumption; Branwell, in the same year as Emily (1848), from drink. Charlotte lived on to marry her father's assistant, the Rev. Arthur Nichols. She died, soon after, from complications in her first pregnancy. The Rev. Brontë, now childless, lived on at Haworth for many years.

Robert Browning (1812–1889): Unlike his great coeval in Victorian poetry, Tennyson, Browning was never laureate, never ennobled, and spent his most productive years well away from England. Yet his influence on the poetry of his time, and his reputation—contemporary and posthumous—are fully as great as the other poet's. Browning was born in London, the son of a senior official at the Bank of England. Robert would never know poverty. The Browning household was prosperous, and highly cultivated. Robert wrote poetry from childhood onwards and picked up modern languages with great facility. A post-Romantic, if not as obviously as Tennyson, he was more influenced by Shelley and Byron. He, like them, would be an intellectual radical, and a "pilgrim" more at home abroad than in England. After a brief flirtation with higher education at London University he undertook to educate himself. Over the 1830s he tried his hand at drama (unsuccessfully) and developed (successfully) what would be his principal instrument in poetry, the "dramatic monologue"—a form which required the creation of character and situation. His early long poems *Paracelsus* (1835) and—particularly— *Sordello* (1840) were found to be excessively difficult by his contemporaries(something else which differentiated him from the more easily accessible Tennsyon). Browning's career took a dramatic turn in 1845. Having come across the poems of Elizabeth Barrett, he arranged to meet her. The two poets fell in love and—despite fierce opposition from her disciplinarian father (she was a chronic invalid)—they married and eloped to Italy: an environment more congenial to both of them (and kinder to her health) than England. They produced, in the next few years, the works for which they are famous:

Elizabeth's *Sonnets from the Portuguese*, and his *Men and Women*, a volume which displays his mature mastery of the dramatic monologue form. She, never strong, died early: He lived long. He is buried in Westminster Abbey's Poets' Corner: she is not.

Robert Burns (1759–1796): "The poet who followed the plough" (and "liked his drop," not to mention the lassies) was born in Ayrshire, in the south west of Scotland—the "Lowlands" (i.e. south of the barrier of mountains beyond which, to the north, are the Highlands, clans, and kilts). "Rabbie" was the eldest of seven children of a tenant farmer (a "sharecropper," in American terminology). As was the fate of male children, he was put to work early in the fields. In addition to what education he could pick up there was, in the late 18th century, a rich oral tradition to be picked up there, particularly of dialect balladry. It was a woman friend, Nelly Kilpatrick, who inspired him to take advantage of his manifest singing and writing skills. Robert was also attracted (to his father's stern displeasure) to dancing. He proposed marriage to a lady who wisely, given his meagre resources and wild ways, rejected him. After a brief attempt at work away from home, in 1781, Burns continued to live and labor at the home farm (now a different one from that in which he was born). He was also beginning to write and compose. Burns's life changed with his father's death, in 1784. Without its patriarch, the farm failed, and the family was obliged to move on. Burns already had a reputation (in a community which strongly disapproved of such things) as a womaniser. His first illegitimate child (of many) was born around this period. He eventually married the mother of two of his children, Jean Armour, in 1788. It was increasingly clear that Burns could not support himself by his father's trade. He toyed with the idea of emigration. But his fortunes took a turn to the literary with his first collection of verse *Poems, Chiefly in the Scottish Dialect* (1786). Initially published locally, it was hugely successful. It contains many of Burns's most loved poems ("To a Mouse," for example). This was the period of the so-called "ballad revival"—and Burns, a genuine balladeer of the people—found himself, quite unexpectedly, at the head of a literary school. He enjoyed to the full his celebrity in Edinburgh ("the Athens of the North"), mixing with the capital's luminaries. He continued to publish in dialect and much less successfully so, in the King's English. Despite his fame, he carried on farming, until the early 1790s, after which his principal source of income was as an exciseman (i.e., an official in the customs office).

He settled with his family in the small town of Dumfries, not far from where he had been born and brought up. In 1790, Burns produced what is probably his best known poem, *Tam O'Shanter*. At a period when France was in Revolution, Burns's sentiments—reflected in his verse—were republican and radical: something that has always endeared him to Scottish Nationalists, whose laureate he is. Always prone to dissipation—drink, that is—Burns died at the tragically young age of 37. He enjoys the unique honor, among literary authors, of being commemorated annually round the English-speaking world (with haggis, whisky, and pipes) on "Burns Night," 25 January.

Lord Byron (George Gordon Byron, 6th Baron Byron, 1788–1824): Byron was born in London. His family background was famously disordered. He feuded, from childhood on, with his mother. His scapegrace father, nicknamed "mad Jack Byron" passed on to his son a natural rebelliousness. "Gordon" would grow up, famously, as "mad, bad, and dangerous to know." But a genius. He inherited his family's title ("Lord"), aged only 10. Few writers have been more lordly. Byron attended one of the country's best public schools, Harrow, and Cambridge University. While still a student, he was publishing verse (in a volume entitled, mischievously, *Hours of Idleness*) and provoking savage criticism from unsympathetic reviewers: attacks which he relished. Bisexual, Byron was a lifelong outlaw in his private life—something in which his later poetry (notably *Don Juan*) glories. In his early 20s, Byron undertook the Grand Tour. Europe at the time was ravaged by the Napoleonic Wars, and he spent time in the East, whose relaxed manners, morals and exoticism had a profound effect on him. Already he had cultivated the Anglophobia which was to condition his later writing: he was an inveterate foe of English morality, the English middle classes, and English insular provinciality (as he saw it). He, by contrast, was worldly, insubordinate, and cosmopolitan. This was the essence of what would become known as "Byronism." Despite his aristocratic heritage (and the parliamentary seat that went with it), he was notably radical in his politics—especially on the issue of national liberation. In 1812, the first books of *Childe Harold's Pilgrimage* (his Grand Tour poeticized) made him, overnight, the most celebrated writer in England. Exile, however, rather than pilgrimage, would mark his subsequent career. A series of newsworthy sexual scandals, ugly divorce, suspicions of incest, and the furious indignation of the English bourgeoisie led to his leaving England in 1816 (in the company of Shelley, and Shelley's new partner, Mary Godwin, themselves fugitives from English morality), never to return. Resident mainly in Italy, he produced his major work, the long-running satire on England, sexual mores, and the battle of the sexes, *Don Juan*. It was begun in 1819, published serially in England by his friend, John Murray, and was unfinished at the time of his death. Nor is it easy to see how the picaresque narrative of this intrepid sexual adventurer could ever be finished. Byron died (of fever) at Missolonghi, in Greece, where he had joined the forces fighting for liberation from Turkish colonial occupation. A hero in Greece he was the "bad Lord Byron" in his own country. Westminster Abbey refused his body for interment in Poets' Corner.

Samuel Taylor Coleridge (1772–1834): Coleridge was born in Devon, the son of an Anglican country parson. After his father's death, he was sent to school in London, and to Cambridge University. From his earliest years, his reading was extensive and eccentric. On leaving Cambridge, in 1794, he briefly served in the army. At Cambridge he had made the acquaintance of another, future "Lake Poet" (as the Wordsworth—Coleridge circle would be later called), Robert Southey. A romantic idealist in life, as much as in literature, he and Southey planned a utopian community—a "pantisocracy"—which came to nothing. As did much in Coleridge's life. More practically, Southey introduced him to the woman he made his wife, Sara Fricker, in 1795. The marriage would prove unhappy. In the later years of the 1790s, Coleridge was publishing poetry, and was active, although never successful, in political journalism. As would be the case throughout his career, he had great difficulty in seeing through, or finishing, anything that he started. Like all liberally inclined intellectuals of the time, he was excited by the French Revolution and had become an object of interest to the English authorities. At the same period, in the hectic mid-1790s, Coleridge formed his friendship, and literary alliance, with William Wordsworth (and Wordsworth's sister, Dorothy, an important figure in both their lives). It introduced a welcome stability into Coleridge's career. The result was the collection, *Lyrical Ballads*, arguably the most revolutionary single volume in English literary history. The democratic idea of the "ballad"—the poem of the people, written in the language of the people—was at the heart of the venture. Coleridge's life was made easier with a lifelong pension, of £150 a year, from the Wedgwood family (enriched by the manufacture of domestic pottery). It enabled him to travel to Germany, and pursue his interest in the philosophy (particularly that of Immanuel Kant) and the Romantic literature of that country: It was from Germany he took his ideas, and from France his politics. Through Wordsworth he met, and fell in love, with Sara Hutchinson, in 1799—precipitating what would be a long-running and insoluble crisis in his married life. His relationship with Wordsworth (a much steadier man, morally) deteriorated in the early 19th century. Coleridge, despite an addiction to opium (about which he writes, in the preface to one of his unfinished poems, "Kubla Khan") remained active on a number of fronts: as a poet, a journalist, a critic, a lecturer (on Shakespeare, notably), and as a political and social philosopher. His later life was socially reclusive. He published a writer's autobiography, *Biographia Literaria* in 1817. Extraordinary as his achievements were, his career is one of supreme genius—tantalizingly unfulfilled. Increasingly addicted to opium, he died in London, and is buried there.

Charles Dickens (1812–1870): Dickens was born in Portsea, on the English coast, the son of a shiftless naval clerk. Of his nine siblings, only four survived childhood. Charles was the eldest son. As a result of his father's financial difficulties, the family's circumstances were chronically unsettled. It was a disturbed childhood. The Dickenses moved to London where, in 1824, John Dickens was declared bankrupt, and was imprisoned for debt (Dickens would recall these disasters in his later, and "darkest," novel, *Little Dorritt*). At the age of 12, young Charles was sent to work in a factory alongside the Thames. Although the experience was brief, it scarred him for life leaving what he called "a secret agony of my soul" (the wound resurfaces, fictionalized, in the early chapters of *David Copperfield*). Dickens was first articled (i.e. apprenticed) as a solicitor (lawyer). But he hated the law, and was attracted to journalism and the theater, where he could display his talents to applause. His first newspaper article was published in 1833. Three years later, he was earning enough from this line of work to marry Catherine Hogarth (his then editor's daughter). His career took off like a rocket (as he put it) with the serialized novel, *Pickwick Papers*, in 1836. For this work, he assumed the pen-name "Boz." The comic chronicle of amiable Sam Pickwick took the reading public by storm. It led to a stream of offers—notably from the publisher Richard Bentley, who commissioned (for his new magazine, of which Dickens was to be the editor) the serial *Oliver Twist* (1837), the first "social problem" novel of the Victorian era. Over the next 10 years (which included a highly contentious trip to America, in 1842) Dickens established himself as the leading writer of his time, and a Great Victorian Institution. Astonishingly innovative, he pioneered the "Christmas Book," in 1843, with *A Christmas Carol*. In the mid-1840s, a darker tone and more careful construction can be detected in his work. The threshold novel is *Dombey and Son* (1846–1848) which, like most of his fiction, was serialized in his favorite monthly installment form. Among his other innovations, Dickens can be said to have invented the detective novel, with *Bleak House* (1852–1853). At the same period, Dickens cemented his relationship with the British public with his tuppenny (two-pence) weekly journal, *Household Words*. The title could apply to almost everything he wrote. No writer has ever glorified the family more than Dickens. Ever practical and incorrigibly determined to make the world better, in the 1850s he set up (with the rich heiress Angela Burdett-Coutts) a reformatory for "fallen women." Like everything he turned his hand to, it was successful. By the end of the decade, Dickens was earning up to £10,000 a novel, and supplementing his vast income with highly successful lecture tours. His private life was less triumphant. In the late 1850s, he fell in love with a young woman, Ellen Ternan. He separated, amid some scandal, from his wife (who had borne him 10 children). His relationship with Ternan, "the Invisible Woman," is mysterious. There may have been an illegitimate child. Dickens's second visit to America in 1867–1868, a lecture tour, was hugely successful and remunerative. But it took a huge toll on his health as did his furious work-rate. A third of the way through the serialization of his last novel, *The Mystery of Edwin Drood* (whose unwritten conclusion has always baffled Dickensians), the author suffered a fatal aneurysm, and died at his country house at Rochester, in Kent. He is buried in Westminster Abbey. There is no "Novelists' Corner," but if there were, Charles Dickens would have first place in it.

Benjamin Disraeli (1804–1881): The future prime minister of England (and the only prime minister to have practiced fiction) was born in London, the son of the antiquarian scholar, Isaad D'Israeli. The family was Jewish, but Benjamin was baptized into the Church of England, in 1817. He retained throughout life, however, an idealistic attachment to Zionism. In young manhood, he tried various careers—law and journalism, among others—before enjoying success, in the 1820s, with "fashionable novels." They celebrated youth, energy, and arrant Byronism ("coxcombry," as indignant contemporaries called it). Disraeli's course in life took its definitive direction when (after some strategic changes of party affiliation) he entered Parliament, in 1837. In the 1840s, Disraeli used fiction to propagate his distinctive "One Nation" brand of Conservatism, in the so-called "Young England" trilogy of novels. In the 1850s and 1860s, he occupied a series of increasingly high political offices, culminating in the premiership, in 1868. He continued writing "political" fiction throughout his life, in the intervals in which he was out of office. His last work of fiction, *Endymion*, for which he received a record-setting £10,000, was published in the year before his death.

Elizabeth Gaskell (1810–1865): The novelist universally known to her contemporaries as "Mrs. Gaskell" was born Elizabeth Stevenson in London of Unitarian parents. Her father was a civil servant (government administrator)—formerly an Anglican minister who had lost his faith. "Doubt" was epidemic at this period. As was usual with Unitarians, the young girl was as well educated as a boy would have been. The formative incident in Elizabeth's life, however, was the death of her mother in her early childhood, and the young girl's removal from London, to the North of England—specifically Knutsford (later immortalized as "Cranford"), a village near the urban powerhouse of the industrial revolution, Manchester. The dichotomy between "North and South" (the title of Gaskell's 1855 novel), and the perennial misunderstandings between the two great regions of England, would furnish her principal theme as an author. In 1832, Elizabeth married a Unitarian minister, William Gaskell, based in Manchester. The marriage was happy. The inexhaustibly philanthropic Mrs. Gaskell was the model of a minister's wife. In 1845, after the death of her only son from scarlet fever, her husband advised her to take up writing, as a kind of grief therapy. The "hungry 1840s" were a period of terrible distress among Lancashire textile workers. Mrs. Gaskell wrote a social-problem novel, on the Dickensian model, *Mary Barton* (1848). Subtitled *A Tale of Manchester Life* the novel was successful. The depiction of the heroine's father, an unemployed mill-worker driven to desperate measures, attracted sympathy for the currently distressed working class; which was precisely what the novelist desired. Mrs. Gaskell attracted the favorable interest of Dickens, who employed her as a serial novelist in his journals, and encouraged her talent (although he always paid her less than his male serialists). In addition to hard hitting industrial fiction, Mrs. Gaskell penned the charmingly idyllic

Cranford (1853), depicting a society entirely made up of maidens, spinsters, and widows—"Amazons," she ironically called them. In addition to fiction, Mrs. Gaskell published the definitive biography of her friend, *The Life of Charlotte Brontë*, in 1857. Mrs. Gaskell died of a heart attack while visiting the house she had just bought with the proceeds of her last novel, surrounded by her three daughters. She is buried at Knutsford.

John Keats (1795–1821): Keats was born into the lower classes of English society, in London. His father was an ostler (i.e., he looked after patrons' horses, at a public house). John Keats Sr. was killed in an accident, when John was nine, and family life, thereafter, was unsettled—although John was sustained by a close relationship with his brother, Tom. Both of them would go on to be afflicted with the family ailment, consumption. Keats was largely brought up by his grandfather. A child of astonishing precocity and native genius, he picked up a school education (effectively self-education) before enrolling as a student at Guy's Hospital. He was not cut out to be a surgeon or an apothecary. Under the patronage of the progressive magazine editor, Leigh Hunt, Keats published his first poems when he had just turned 20. *Endymion*, published in 1817, attracted savage scorn from the critical establishment. Keats was lampooned as the "Cockney Poet." Hunt's radicalism did not help Keats's reputation. Although morbidly sensitive to criticism, he continued to write and in 1819—the so-called "Living Year"—he produced a series of masterpieces in poetry, including the famous "Odes." At this period, although the circumstances are elusive, he was involved with the love of his life, Fanny Brawne. Keats's most ambitious work, *Hyperion*, was destined to be unfinished as, indeed, was what promised to be one of the most glorious careers in English literature. As his health deteriorated, friends arranged for him to travel to Italy, for the sake of his lungs. He did not recover, and died and is buried in Rome. At his request, the epitaph "Here lies one whose name was writ in water" was inscribed on his tombstone.

Ann Radcliffe (1764–1823): Little is known of Radcliffe's life. She was born, Ann Ward, in London. Aged 22, she married a journalist and newspaper proprietor, William Radcliffe—and it was as "Mrs. Radcliffe" that she wrote and published her fiction. Legend has it that she was encouraged by her husband to write, in the absence of the couple having children. Writing in the florid, highly melodramatic, Gothic style, for which popular circulating libraries had created a huge demand, she produced her first novel in 1789. But it was with *The Mysteries of Udolpho* (1794) and *The Italian* (1796) that she became sensationally popular, earning the highest prices ever hitherto paid a novelist. Despite the huge readership she had recruited, Radcliffe gave up publishing fiction in the last 25 years of her life—possibly, it is speculated, on her husband's instruction. Her lasting reputation has been as the novelist whom Jane Austen wrote *against*.

Walter Scott (1771–1832): Scott was born in Edinburgh, the son of a "Writer to the Signet" (attorney at law). In his very early childhood, he was lamed by polio: A malady for which he, along with doctors of the period, never knew the name. During his childhood, which was sickly, he was subjected to various remedies: all doomed to fail, some agonizing. Among the most successful remedies (although not at all in the way his doctors intended) was a long sojourn with farming relatives at Sandyknowe, in the borders between England and Scotland, where young Walter was steeped in oral song and balladry—a culture going back hundreds of years, to the prehistory of the country. This experience, and the dialect of the Lowlands which he heard around him at Sandyknowe, left an indelible mark on him. After a very early stint at Edinburgh University (he enrolled when he was just 12), Walter went to work in his father's law firm. But he was clearly too gifted, too intellectual, and—above all—too ambitious to remain a scrivener, or clerk. He enjoyed a second spell at university more than he had the first. Edinburgh was, at this period, a center of European enlightenment. On graduating, Scott qualified as an advocate (i.e. a lawyer entitled to argue cases in court). He was also active in literary circles in Edinburgh, avidly collecting ballads from the Borders, where oral traditions were dying out. These ballads would eventually be published, in 1701, as *The Minstrelsy of the Scottish Border*. Always interested in the business of books, Scott had formed friendships with, among others, the Ballantyne brothers, two printers who would work with and for him, and later be financially ruined along with Scott. Scott's first published works were ballads, in the German style. He had assured his professional security with what was, effectively, a sinecure in being appointed, in perpetuity, a "sheriff" (i.e. legal officer) in the border area of Selkirk. In 1797, he married the illegitimate child of an English nobleman, Charlotte Charpentier. She brought money to the marriage. Scott—a scholar by temperament, with an insatiable historical curiosity—was able to indulge his antiquarian and scholarly interests to the full. He wrote, published, and undertook research labors enough for 10 men. Scott and the Ballantyne brothers had their first great commercial success with the long poem, *The Lay of the Last Minstrel*, in 1805. The book-length, historical narrative in verse, was sensationally popular. Scott followed with other poems until 1812—when the arrival of Byron on the scene convinced him that he could not compete with this new rival. He, and his printing friends, together with the enterprising publisher, Archibald Constable, moved into prose fiction, with *Waverley*, a romance set in the 1745 Rebellion (the uprising in which Bonnie Prince Charlie came to grief). The work was published anonymously, as were its successors (Scott's poetry, a more "respectable" line of work, had been signed). The novel was sensationally popular. The "author of *Waverley*" was crowned "the wizard of the North." Scott, the most fluent of writers (his first novel took him only a few weeks to dash off), turned out a dozen more historical novels during the next 10 years, moving in 1819 from Scottish to medieval English settings with *Ivanhoe*. His success extended well beyond the merely literary. Scotland became, as a result of Scott's fame, a "romantic" country in the public mind, creating Britain's first tourist industry. Scott was also largely responsible for lifting the obloquy that had hung over his country since the 1715 and 1745 Jacobite uprisings (the second of which had come close to toppling the English monarchy). He was a favorite of the Prince Regent, later George IV, who confirmed his favor with a royal visit to Edinburgh (stage managed by Scott) in 1822. Scott, over-confident in his earning power, came to grief in 1825, when a catastrophic crash in the London banking system ruined him, the Ballantynes, and his publisher Constable. Much of his financial difficulty arose from the expense of the baronial castle he had built for himself, Abbotsford. Courageously, Scott undertook to pay of all his debtors with his pen. He came within creditable distance of doing so by the time of his death, accelerated by his heroic labors, in 1832. He changed the whole course of 19th-century literature.

Mary Shelley (1797–1851): Mary's mother was the feminist Mary Wollstonecraft and her father the radical philosopher, William Godwin. It was, for a novelist of ideas, the most propitious pedigree imaginable. Her mother, however, died shortly after Mary's birth—robbing her of what would have been a powerful intellectual influence. Nonetheless, Mary grew up in a stimulating domestic environment, somewhat blighted with Godwin's remarriage to Mary Jane Clairmont, a widow. Mary Godwin would have a difficult relationship with both her step-mother and her step-sister, Claire Clairmont. Mary grew up, surrounded by books, and was unusually well instructed in how to read them. Poets were frequent guests in the Godwin household. They included Coleridge and—momentously—the young radical poet, Percy Bysshe Shelley. In 1812, Shelley fell madly in love with the 15-year-old Mary. He was married at the time, and a father. In defiance of public morality (and Godwin's disapproval), Percy and Mary traveled extensively over the following two years. Their first child died, prematurely, in February 1815. A second child was born a year later. The couple married in December 1816, shortly after Percy's wife drowned, in tragic circumstances for which Percy cannot be entirely absolved. Earlier that year, in Switzerland, in the company of Byron and John Polidori, *Frankenstein* was composed. Godwin—who had been estranged from the couple—was reconciled by their belated marriage. Eventually the Shelleys settled in Italy. Mary's later life was attended by tragedy—notably the death of children and the death of her husband by drowning, sailing off the coast of Italy, in July 1822. Over the next 30 years, Mary Shelley wrote a number of works of fiction, which can be regarded as precursors of the genre we know as science fiction. None has enjoyed the perennial success of her juvenile masterpiece, *Frankenstein*.

Alfred Tennyson (1809–1892): Tennyson was born in Lincolnshire, a large, flat, coastal county in the dead center of England. Its landscapes would permeate his poetry. His father was a clergyman, and Alfred had 11 siblings. Both his parents were well born, highly cultivated, and took a keen interest in their children's education. Alfred was writing poetry in his early teens, and was encouraged to do so and even to publish his juvenile efforts. After attending various local schools, he went up to Cambridge in 1828. His experiences at the university were formative. Here it was he met his closest friend in life, Arthur Henry Hallam. The friendship was passionate. He also won the university's premier prize for verse. In 1830, he published a volume of his verse whose melancholy, mellifluous, Keatsian, lyricism attracted some scorn, although it contained what would prove to be some of his most enduringly loved poems. Melancholy would be the constant mood of Tennyson's manhood—a mood which he was capable of distilling into exquisite verse. He left the university in 1831, without taking a degree (not unusual at the time) on the death of his father. In 1833, Hallam, who had been intending to marry one of Tennyson's sisters, died. It prostrated Tennyson, utterly, and would lead, 17 years later, to his long meditation on bereavement and the meaning of life, *In Memoriam* (hugely popular, it was Queen Victoria's favorite poem and, as she said, consoled her on the death of her husband, Albert, in 1861). During the 1840s, Tennyson established his unchallenged status as the leading poet of the day, and the most popular. His narrative poems (*Enoch Arden, Maud*) sold as successfully as Dickens's fiction. In 1850, on the death of Wordsworth, Tennyson was appointed Poet Laureate. In the same year, he was able, after a long engagement, to marry. In 1854, he wrote the most famous poem on the Crimean War, "The Charge of the Light Brigade." It qualifies as the best public poem ever written by a laureate. In 1884, Victoria created him Lord Tennyson. His death, in 1892, was commemorated in London with what was, effectively, a state funeral. He is buried in Westminster Cathedral, although his religious views, shot through with the "doubt" so common among Victorian writers, may make his rest less than easy.

William Makepeace Thackeray (1811–1863): Thackeray was born in India, where his father was a senior civil servant, before dying in 1816. His mother remarried and William was sent back to England, to be educated, aged seven. He had his school education at Charterhouse and went on to Cambridge, which he left without a degree, in 1830. He also lost much of his inherited wealth, gambling. Prodigiously gifted—in art as well as writing—Thackeray was, as he readily admitted, "idle" by nature. His idleness, however, was compensated for by the quickest of wits. After false starts in law and art (he studied for a while in Paris) he settled on journalism, in which quick wits and a ready pen were principal assets. For 10 years in Paris and London, Thackeray "wrote for his life." His output was vast, and entirely anonymous. He compounded his financial difficulties by marrying, "imprudently." Having borne him two surviving daughters, Isabella Thackeray went incurably insane, in 1840. Thackeray was condemned to a clubman's and bachelor's life (with the addition of two children) for the remainder of his life. Having made his name as a satirist—particularly of the English middle classes (Thackeray invented the word "snob")—he finally realized his potential as a writer with the serialized novel, *Vanity Fair* (1847–1848). He was middle-aged when this work (the first to have his name attached) was published. A panoramic satire, with broad streaks of sentiment and worldly wisdom, this portrait of

512

the 19th century was a huge hit. Thackeray notably mellowed in his later work. As a novelist he was second only to Dickens in public reputation. His energies (always prone to dissipation) were lessened by his falling victim, in 1850, to the cholera epidemic which was sweeping London—it is pleasant to record that Dickens saved his life, by dispatching his personal physician to his great rival. Thackeray's later fiction is less vibrant than *Vanity Fair*, although his 18th-century historical romance, *Henry Esmond* (1852), has its admirers. Thackeray's last years were enriched by lucrative editorial work, and enabled him to build a fine "Queen Anne" period house in Kensington (it is now the Israeli Embassy). He died, prematurely, his health never having been strong. His daughter, Anne, went on to become a successful novelist in her own right.

William Wordsworth (1770–1850): The leader, and principal theorist, of the English Romantic Movement, Wordsworth was born in the mountainous "Lake District," in North West England, with which his career was later intertwined. "My native Alps," he called them. His "seedtime," and his quasi-religious views about "Nature," as he recalls in his great autobiographical poem, *The Prelude*, were profoundly influenced by the region. His mother and father—a lawyer, with whom he had a difficult relationship—both died early in his life. After going to school locally, the 17-year-old William attended Cambridge University. In 1790, he spent time in Revolutionary France, where he had an affair with and had a child by a French woman, Annette Vallon. The circumstances have always been mysterious. An inheritance at this period of his life enabled him to concentrate on poetry, which he always knew was his destiny. Although he had been writing, and publishing, poems from the early 1790s, Wordsworth's literary career took its destined direction with his meeting Coleridge in 1795. The result was the collaborative volume, *Lyrical Ballads*, in 1798. This volume and its revised editions over the next few years revolutionized English poetry, moving it definitively away from the Augustanism of the 18th century. As the 1790s came to a close, Wordsworth set up home with his sister Dorothy, in Grasmere, in the Lake District. A coterie (the "Lakers," as Byron dismissively called them) formed around him. Further inheritances enabled him to pursue his literary career, undisturbed. In 1802, he married, and can be said to have settled down in life. Over the next half century, it is sometimes felt, some of the fire went out of his poetry. Settling down is not always good for poets. The relationship with Coleridge, always intense, broke down, although another major poet, Robert Southey (a fellow "Laker"), took his place in Wordsworth's orbit. Over many years, he had been working on his most ambitious work, an autobiography in verse, *The Prelude*. It would not be published in its complete form until the time of his death. In 1843, he was appointed Poet Laureate—although he published, and wrote, little in the last decade of his life. He died and is buried in the Lake District. Few literary resting places are more appropriate.

Lectures 37-48

W. H. Auden (1907–1973): Auden was born in the Midlands, the son of a doctor (his father had strong interests in literature, and in Freud—interests his son inherited). At Oxford University, Auden established himself as a leading figure among what would later be known as "the thirties poets"—principally himself, Louis MacNeice, Stephen Spender, and C. Day-Lewis. They were enthusiasts for T. S. Eliot—who published much of their poetry—but, unlike him, they inclined towards political radicalism and, in their early years, politically agitating poetry. The 1930s was a decade in which ugly totalitarianism was ascendant in Germany, Italy, and Russia. Auden and his comrades were pro-Moscow until the Spanish Civil War disillusioned them. Auden had supported himself as a schoolteacher in his early professional life, although poetry always remained his principal interest. His first volume of verse was published in 1928. It, and its successors, established him as the leading young poet of the time, although his poetry was found even more difficult by lay readers than Eliot's. In January 1939, with war in Europe clearly imminent, Auden—disillusioned with the old world—immigrated to America, with his close friend, the novelist Christopher Isherwood. Both men were homosexual, and England's intolerance had made permanent residence impossible for them. Auden became an American citizen in 1946. The poetry of his maturity merges his extraordinary virtuosity and mastery of the techniques of verse with more personal and, increasingly, religious concerns. In his last years, he returned to England, now more morally relaxed than it had been, to live in his old Oxford college.

Samuel Beckett (1906–1989): Beckett was born in Dublin, into the city's lower middle classes. He went to school and to university in Dublin—manifesting an early enthusiasm for literature and (oddly) cricket. He graduated with a degree in modern languages—useful for a writer most of whose career would be spent in France. In Paris, in the late 1920s, Beckett made the acquaintance of James Joyce. The friendship (or, more properly, master—pupil relationship) would be formative on Beckett's literary development. After drifting between Paris, Dublin, and London, and a false start in university teaching, Beckett began writing on his own account in the 1930s. He settled at the same period in Paris. His first publications were novels (e.g., *Murphy*, 1938) which were both comic and experimental. Beckett, from the first, was doing new things. During the war, in France, he worked with the French Underground, for which gallantry he was later decorated. Beckett's reputation as a leading playwright in England was forged by the performance of his play (translated from the French) *Waiting for Godot*, in 1955. This absurdist drama, in which two tramps do nothing, while nothing happens to them, had a revolutionary impact on British theater. With successive works, which were increasingly enigmatic and minimalist, Beckett's fame grew. It was sealed with the award of the Nobel Prize, in 1969. *Breath*, a work performed that same year, has no characters, lasts 35 seconds, and the only "action" is the sound of breathing. This was as far as even Beckett could take his art. As his novels testify, he could, when it was required, be as copious, fluent, and verbose (in the highest sense) as James Joyce himself—the writer with whom he shares the very highest place in Irish literature. Whether Beckett truly belongs to that country, to France, or to Britain is still a matter of hot contention. This course appropriates him for Britain.

Rupert Brooke (1887–1915): Brooke was born at Rugby, where his father was a teacher at the famous public (i.e., highly selective) school. Precociously brilliant, Brooke was a luminary at Cambridge University and seemed destined for a glittering career in poetry. He volunteered for the armed forces, on the outbreak of war, in 1914. He died, in the Dardanelles, of blood poisoning in 1915. His war sonnet, "The Soldier," was adopted as a patriotic anthem by his country in their arduous struggle against Germany, although the poem's patriotism had come to seem offensively facile by the conclusion of that most bloody conflict.

Joseph Conrad (1857–1924): The most cosmopolitan of great English novelists, Jozef Teodor Konrad Korzeniowski was born, of Polish parents, in the Russian dominated Ukraine. Poland too was under the Russian heel and Conrad's father was a prominent revolutionary. Both his parents died early and Conrad (under the care of an uncle) migrated to France, where he embarked on a career as an officer in the merchant marine. As a mariner, rising eventually to the command of his own vessel, Conrad saw much of the world. It would feed his later fiction (particularly formative was a trip to the Congo, in the early 1890s). In 1886, he became a British citizen. After 20 years at sea, settled in England, married, and turned to writing. He was close on 40 years old before doing so—and doing so in what was, effectively, his third language. His influences were uniquely mixed: They included sturdy nautical novelists, spinners of seafaring yarns, and, much more ambitiously, Henry James (a personal friend of Conrad's). In the years that followed, with novels such as *Lord Jim* (1900), *Nostromo* (1904), and *Victory* (1915) he established himself as a great English novelist, and the greatest ever to take the sea as his subject.

Noël Coward (1899–1973): The consummately stylish showman of the 20th century, Coward was born the son of a piano salesman, and a mother who encouraged his early enthusiasm for theater. He had his first play put on the stage before he was 20, and enjoyed huge success with his modishly decadent psychological drama, *The Vortex* (1924), in which he himself took the leading role. Gay—something that the English theater could accept, and England outside the theater couldn't—Coward always had a keen eye for those who could not, quite, fit. He also had a fine ear for the nuances of English speech. He went on to cultivate a highly remunerative line of sophisticated "drawing room" comedy, increasingly light in manner, which audiences loved. His most enduring work is the screenplay he did for the perennially popular film, *Brief Encounters* (1944). He was knighted in 1970.

Arthur Conan Doyle (1859–1930): The creator of Sherlock Holmes was born in Edinburgh, into an Irish Catholic family. He qualified as a doctor at Edinburgh University, and took up his first practice in southern England. Inspired by a hawk-eyed instructor from his university days, Joseph Bell—who diagnosed his patients via "clues," not declared symptoms—Doyle introduced his amateur detective to the world in 1887, with the novella *A Study in Scarlet*. The Baker Street sleuth became sensationally popular—along with his assistant, Dr. Watson—with a series of short stories in the

Strand Magazine in the 1890s. A new "Holmes" could drive the circulation of the journal up to half a million. Doyle wrote much else—historical novels, which he himself thought very highly of, and science fiction—notably, *The Lost World*, 1912. After the First World War, he became a public advocate for spiritualism. But it is Holmes that Conan Doyle is principally remembered for.

George Eliot (1819–1880): Born Mary Ann Evans, the writer later known as George Eliot was brought up in Warwickshire, near Coventry—the Midlands setting of much of her subsequent fiction. The family background was nonconformist (another interest in her later novels) and, given access to a good library in her young girlhood (thanks to her father's position as land agent to a wealthy employer), she went on to finish her education among free-thinking, intellectual circles in Coventry. A firm-minded woman, she broke away from the devout religious orthodoxy of her father and closest brother, Isaac—a crisis dramatized in *The Mill on the Floss*. She moved, inevitably, to London where, initially, she picked up work in higher journalism, and as a translator from the German. This work served to sharpen her remarkable intellect still further. In the early 1850s, she formed the most important relationship of her life with George Henry Lewes. They would be partners until his death, in 1878. He could not marry her, however, being already married and having, according to his freethinking principles, condoned his wife's adultery. It was Lewes, along with the publisher John Blackwood, who encouraged her to write fiction. She did so with the declared aim of "raising" the literary form, making it a vehicle for important ideas and intellectual debate. After some experimental short stories, her first novel, *Adam Bede*, written under the male pseudonym, "George Eliot," appeared in 1859. Despite its challenging subject matter—the impact of the Methodist religious movement on rural life, at the turn of the century—the novel enjoyed a runaway success. Other works of fiction followed, culminating in what is generally agreed to be Eliot's masterpiece: *Middlemarch* (serialized 1871–1872), a study of the provincial world in which she grew up, and the impact of political "reform." After Lewes's death, which prostrated her, she wrote no more fiction: although by this stage of her life "George Eliot" was recognized as the leading woman of letters in England, and by some the leading "person of letters," irrespective of gender. She herself died two years after Lewes, having married a young disciple, John Cross, who tended her posthumous flame assiduously. Posterity recognizes her not as Mary Anne Evans, nor Mrs. Lewes (the title she preferred, socially), not as Mrs. Cross but—in tribute to her genius—"George Eliot." Because of the "immorality" of her relationship with Lewes no place could be found for her among the respectable writers of England in Westminster Abbey until the 1970s, when a commemorative stone was belatedly laid in the consecrated ground.

T. S. Eliot (1888–1965): Thomas Stearns Eliot was born in Saint Louis, Missouri—which has always rendered him ambiguously British or American literary property. His education was extensive: at the universities of Harvard, the Sorbonne in Paris, and Oxford in England. His early interests were in philosophy as much as in poetry, to which he was turned by Ezra Pound, in 1914. He settled in England and married, disastrously. The breakdown of his marriage, and the eventual madness of his wife, blighted his life over the following decade. During this decade, while working at a bank—until a subscription among his friends yielded financial independence—he worked on his epochal poem, *The Waste Land*. Published in 1922, it was recognized from the first as the primal work of literary modernism, along with Joyce's *Ulysses* (published the same year). In 1927 Eliot became a British subject. He was, in the second half of his life, as he proclaimed, a fervent royalist, conservative, and an Anglo-Catholic—anything but American. His interest moved into drama, and he wrote a number of verse plays of which the most often performed is *Murder in the Cathedral* (1935). Now a director at Faber, the most influential literary publisher in England, Eliot brought on the careers of a coterie of younger poets—including Auden and Larkin. His second great poetic project, *Four Quartets*, was completed in 1943. Although Eliot's published output was small, his influence as a poet, a critic, and a patron was immense. He was awarded the Nobel Prize for literature in 1948.

E. M. Forster (1879–1970): An only child, Edwin Morgan Forster was the son of an architect father, who died shortly after his son's birth, and a dedicated mother. He was brought up surrounded by women and, thanks to inheritances, comfortable financial circumstances which he would enjoy all his life. Forster was one of those fortunate authors who was never obliged to sacrifice his literary ambitions to the crude requirement of earning a living. Forster was unhappy at school, but blissfully happy at Cambridge University where his being intellectually brilliant, highly cultivated, and gay were no barriers to success. Indeed, they could be thought to promote it. At Cambridge, through the philosopher G. E. Moore—a thinker who had a profound influence on what came to be called the "Bloomsbury group"—Forster developed his conviction that the most important things in life were personal relationships. At a period when England was convulsing with patriotism and nationalism in World War I, this was a highly radical sentiment. Having left Cambridge, in the early years of the new century, Forster traveled widely in Europe and in India—something which would inspire his last, and finest, novel, *A Passage to India*, 1924. He began publishing fiction in 1905. His characteristic themes revolve around the motto to his 1910 novel, *Howards End* (1910), "Only Connect." For him as for the other members of the Bloomsbury group, the massive disconnections of WWI were traumatic. Forster effectively gave up writing fiction (or much else) in the last half century of his life. He remained a powerful force, however, always on the side of liberalism, tolerance, and the personal values which he extols in his fiction. His last published novel, *Maurice*, which came out only after his death (having been judged unpublishable when written, 70 years earlier) is a frank proclamation of his homosexuality.

William Golding (1911–1993): Golding was educated at one of Britain's best public schools and at Oxford University. On leaving university, he worked, variously, as a journalist, an actor, and a theater producer. He served in the Royal Navy in World War II, and was profoundly influenced by the total breakdown of civilization and the irrepressible rise of savagery, which he conceived that global conflict to represent. On demobilization, he took up work as a schoolteacher. His first novel, *Lord of the Flies,* had great difficulty finding a publisher and did not see print until 1954. It was recognized as a classic, if profoundly pessimistic, narrative—a work which, in its depiction of English schoolboys on a desert island reverting to primitive violence, overset a line of native optimism which can be traced back as far as *Robinson Crusoe*. The success of the novel allowed Golding to concentrate full time on his writing. It led to the award of a Nobel Prize in 1983, and a knighthood in 1988.

Graham Greene (1904–1991): Joseph Conrad's most distinguished disciple, Greene was educated in the public school, Berkhamsted, where his father was headmaster. While at Oxford University, he was impelled to convert to

Catholicism—something that would influence his subsequent fiction, much of which revolves around dilemmas of conscience and topical reformulations of "sin." Greene (who at one period of his life was a film reviewer) was fascinated by cinematic technique. He also believed that, as did the movies, the novel should have a broad popular appeal. He divided his own fictional output into what he called "Entertainments" (e.g., *A Gun for Sale*, 1936) and "Novels." Like Conrad, Greene was a nomadic novelist. Few writers have used as many foreign settings in their fiction (every one being a version of hell). Like Conrad, he even made his journey up the Congo, commemorated in *A Burnt-Out Case* (1961). During the Second World War, Greene was involved with espionage, which is a frequent theme in his postwar fiction (e.g., *The Human Factor*, 1978). A commercially successful writer, Greene spent his last years in the south coast of France—a pleasingly marginal location for a novelist always on the edge of what he wrote about.

Thomas Hardy (1840–1928): The writer who most clearly bridges the Victorian and modern literary eras, Hardy was born, the son of a stone-cutter and a woman who had been in service, in rural Dorsetshire (the region he would later call "Wessex"). He would never attend university—something that he would turn into angry fiction in his later masterpiece, *Jude the Obscure*. But he had an excellent school education, locally, and followed his father's trade. His clear intellectual ability allowed him to move upwards in the construction industry, into architecture. The great turn in his life came when he moved to London. Hardy's love life, in his 20s, has long fascinated, and eluded, biographers. But throughout life his relationships with women were complicated. His first marriage, to Emma Gifford, in 1874 (at the time when he was giving up architecture for writing) was passionate and unhappy. He would celebrate the relationship in some of the finest love poems in the English language—written, ironically, after her death in 1912. Hardy was a writer who always looked backward, and was always most inspired by events in his, and England's past. Elegy is his characteristic mode. Hardy began writing in the early 1870s, but it was not until the first of his great Wessex novels, *Far from the Madding Crowd*, in 1874, that he achieved success. Thereafter his progress was rapid. But his works, while they greatly entertained, also offended. Like the French realists of the time, Hardy was not prepared to avert his eyes from the realities of life, as he saw them and as many of his contemporaries preferred not to see them. Protest at his work climaxed with *Jude the Obscure*, in 1895. Thereafter, comfortably well off, and settled in a fine house which he had designed himself near his native Dorchester, Hardy turned his attention to poetry, most of it lyric, most of it infused with Hardyan gloom (exquisitely articulated). At the time of his death, in 1928, he was the Grand Old Man of English Letters, and much loved. His funeral was almost as spectacular a public event as Tennyson's had been. The prime minister insisted his remains be buried (against Hardy's wishes) in Westminster Abbey. His heart, however, was buried in Wessex, where it had always been.

Seamus Heaney (1939–): Heaney was born just over the northern border of Ireland, in Protestant Ulster, although his family was Catholic. This marginality, being between the Irish and English worlds, was formative on his later poetic stance. His father was a farmer—something often alluded to in his poetry. Heaney attended university in Belfast (Northern Ireland) and, on graduation, took up academic work. He would work in a number of British, Irish, and American universities over the following decades. His first collection of poetry appeared in his mid-20s. Other volumes followed as his reputation grew. In 1989, he was appointed professor of poetry at Oxford and in 1995 he was awarded the Nobel Prize for Literature. Since then, he has won virtually every major poetry prize in the English-speaking world. Immensely energetic, Heaney suffered a stroke in 2006, from which he happily made a swift recovery.

Henry James (1843–1916): The most influential practitioner and theorist of prose narrative in the 20th century, Henry James was born an American, in New York. His family was one of high intellectual distinction (a brother, William, was the leading philosopher of his time). James settled in Europe, in 1875, absorbing the new ideas about literature which were fermenting, particularly in France. He made it his mission to "raise" the novel to the level of an "art." He began writing novels on his great "international" theme in the 1870s. In the last twenty years of his life, England would be his base (he became an English citizen, shortly before his death, in 1915, as the Europe he loved was being torn apart by war). Relatively little of James's fiction is set in Britain, but his influence (particularly via the critical introductions he wrote to his "New York" collected editions of his work) is found everywhere in the English novel of the 20th century.

James Joyce (1882–1941): Joyce was born in Dublin, into a shiftless, Catholic family background which he immortalizes in his autobiographical novel, *A Portrait of the Artist as a Young Man* (1916). He was educated at Jesuit institution—something that left an indelible mark on his literary personality. Joyce came of age as Irish nationalism was in the ascendant, and with it a new literary aspiration. Joyce, however, found Ireland (specifically Dublin) both all-absorbing and impossible to live in—given his increasingly skeptical and "modernist" ideas. His subsequent career would be one of "silence, exile, and cunning." Having married his first love, he eventually settled for several years in Trieste, a place whose marginality suited his temperament. Here he taught and developed his increasingly experimental line of fiction. His first published work of fiction was the linked short-story collection, *Dubliners* (1914)—a title which would have been appropriate for everything he wrote. He moved well away from this early, French-realistic style, in *Portrait*, particularly in its opening and concluding sections. In this novel Joyce articulated his sense of what the modernist writer should be: aloof, like a god paring his nails above the hurly-burly of life. The full-blown practice of his artistic theory emerged with *Ulysses*, in 1922, the most playfully experimental novel in English (with much Irish in it) since *Tristram Shandy*. The novel, inevitably, encountered censorship obstruction in the English-speaking world. It was a decade before the English- or American-reading publics had full access to this most innovative of novels. Joyce's work was never commercial and he depended on patrons which, luckily, he never had difficulty finding. His sight failed in later years; his family situation was often difficult, a daughter, Lucia, fell mentally ill; and with Europe in upheaval his "exile" was increasingly difficult. He left behind what is generally regarded as the most difficult novel in the language, *Finnegans Wake* (1939).

Philip Larkin (1922–1985): Larkin was born in Coventry where, as he joked in one of his poems, his early years were "unspent." His father was a senior administrator in the city—which was heavily bombed during World War II. Philip was the Larkins' only child. He went to Oxford during the war, having been rejected for service on account of poor eyesight. At university he formed what would be a lifelong friendship with the novelist and poet, Kingsley Amis. On graduating, in 1943, Larkin took up a series of posts as a university librarian. He also wrote poetry and fiction. Two of his novels were published. They both throw a revealing light on the author. But it was his poetry which gained him a growing reputation. Larkin went against the violent, "apocalyptic" style of currently admired poets such as Dylan Thomas. His achievement is contained in half a dozen slim volumes—all of which express complex thought under what sometimes looks like a post-Hardyan superficial simplicity. Larkin moved the main current of English poetry away from international modernism to insular, English, traditionalism. His later poetry was increasingly somber in tone (he hated what England had become, over his lifetime). In his last years, as he liked to say, he had not given up poetry, but "poetry gave up me."

D. H. Lawrence (1885–1930): David Herbert Lawrence was born in the industrial Midlands of England, the son of a coal miner father and a former schoolteacher mother. The parental clash is commemorated in his most personal novel, *Sons and Lovers* (1913), although the tensions of his childhood may be tracked through to his last, and most scandalous, work, *Lady Chatterley's Lover* (1930). "Love" would be his great theme. His most complex notion of what this "shimmering rainbow" was is expressed most sensitively in the novels which are generally considered his best: *The Rainbow* (1915) and *Women in Love* (1920). Constitutionally frail, and jealously protected by his mother, young "Bert" Lawrence was spared hard labor in the pits. By dint of self improvement, and native intelligence, he qualified as a schoolteacher. But tame professional life in the classroom was not for him. He eloped with the wife of one of his college teachers, Frieda Weekley (*née* von Richthofen) in 1912. Thereafter, the couple's life was one of "passionate pilgrimage." After the First World War (difficult by virtue of her background, and his hatred of the conflict) they lived abroad. Lawrence's fiction, which constantly pushed against the limitations of censorship, reached its peak of unpublishability in the English-speaking world with *Lady Chatterley's Lover* in which, quixotically, he attempted to "hygienize" the Anglo-Saxon four-letter vocabulary of sexual relationships. Always prey to pulmonary weakness, Lawrence died of consumption in Venice. His reputation rose meteorically during the 20th century but, with the turn of the century, is somewhat depressed.

George Orwell (1903–1950): The author known to posterity by this name was born Eric Blair. He was born in India, the son of a British civil servant (administrator). His childhood was unsettled, apart from his school years at Eton. His family could not afford university, and he joined the Indian Imperial Police as an officer. The experience is recollected in an early novel, *Burmese Days* (1934) and many of his essays (notably that on shooting an elephant, which allegorizes the intrinsic weakness of British imperial rule). His early life, as a member of Britain's elite, did not indoctrinate Orwell: it made him an inveterate critic of Englishness. He attempted various experiments with the country's class system, chronicled in *Down and Out in Paris and London* (1933). His political views were given practical expression when he enlisted, to fight with the Anarchist forces (POUM), against the fascist Nationalists, in the Spanish Civil War. It was a deeply disillusioning experience. In the Second World War, Orwell worked in broadcasting and wrote voluminously for papers and magazines. His disillusionment with Communism found expression in his bitter Aesopian fable *Animal Farm* (1945), and his equal disillusionment with the postwar English welfare state, and superpower totalitarianism, was scathingly expressed in his dystopia, *1984* (1949). Both have had a profound effect not merely on subsequent literature, but on political thought and action in the English-speaking world.

John Osborne (1929–1994): John Osborne had a troubled childhood—which some might say contributed to his lifelong penchant for "anger." He (along with his fictional creation, Jimmy Porter) was the archetypal Angry Young Man—from birth. Born into the lower middle classes, his father died early in his boyhood. He cordially hated his mother (a former barmaid). Osborne left school early (and angrily), with no worthwhile qualifications. He drifted into the theater, first as an actor in provincial repertory companies, then as a writer. The first serious play written entirely by him, *Look Back in Anger,* was produced in London, in 1956. It was a low point in English drama (dominated by the vacuousness of Terence Rattigan's plays) and in English history (the empire effectively collapsed that year, in which Britain and France invaded Egypt in a futile attempt to recover the Suez Canal). The mood of the country was furious. Osborne's play expressed that fury, with blazing eloquence. Osborne followed up with *The Entertainer* (whose lead role was taken by the country's leading actor, Laurence Olivier), an elegy for the dying music hall tradition and, indirectly, the working class communities that supported it. Thereafter Osborne's career (not helped by a tempestuous personality) was distinguished, but less focused. He ceased being the spokesman for his time, and became one among a number of playwrights combining to create what posterity has seen as a second golden age of English theater.

Wilfred Owen (1893–1918): Owen was born into the lower middle class, his father being a railway station master in western England. Wilfred had his higher education at a technical college, but he was already drawn to literature, and was writing precociously clever and innovative poetry. After a period teaching English in France, he volunteered for the army in 1915. Here he formed a friendship with a fellow poet, Siegfried Sassoon. Different as their styles were—Owen's derived, quite clearly, from the Keatsian romantic tradition—they would establish themselves as the two leading poets of World War I. Owen experienced the bloodiest of trench warfare, was decorated for gallantry, and died on Armistice Day. His best poems were written in the last year of his short life. Like Sassoon, Owen was probably homosexual. How he would have developed as a poet, had he survived, can only be surmised— but given the promise of what he achieved, he would surely have established himself as one of the very greatest poets in the language.

Harold Pinter (1930–): Pinter was born in the East End of London, into the respectable Jewish middle classes who had a vibrant community there. His father was a gentleman's tailor. Young Harold was evacuated from London during the war, to escape the German bombs which rained down on London in the Blitz. The disorienting experience had a profound effect on him. Once returned to his home, Pinter had an excellent school education. On leaving school (and refusing national military service, on conscientious grounds) Pinter went into the theater, initially as an actor, under the stage name, David Baron. His style of acting was notably different from that current in provincial repertory theater at the time, making emphatic use of silence and unusual vocal stress. Some years into his acting career, Pinter began writing. His first notable work, *The Birthday Party* (1958) introduced all the elements of what would later be famous as "Pinteresque": namely enigmatic settings, fragmentary dialogue whose effect is cumulative rather than sequential, and—most strikingly—a looming atmosphere of "silent menace." *The Caretaker* (1960) certified him as one of the group of playwrights (with Osborne and Beckett) who were revolutionizing English theater. Over the next four decades, Pinter wrote for the theater, did film scripts, directed plays, and occasionally acted. He was awarded the Nobel Prize for Literature in 2005; the award coincided with his most furious attacks on America, for the "imperial" (as he saw it) invasion on Iraq, and the iniquities of U.S. foreign policy. He remains the angriest of the formerly Angry Young Men.

Terence Rattigan (1911–1977): The son of a diplomat, Rattigan followed the usual course of upper-class education, at Harrow School and Oxford University. On graduation, he devoted himself to writing popular drama for the London stage—at which he was, from the beginning, outstandingly successful. He adopted the Victorian "problem play" for modern settings; "light melodrama" was the presiding tone. His most popular work, *The Winslow Boy* (1946) centers on a court case, called to decide (preposterously) whether a public school boy has stolen a tiny money order or not. Some of Rattigan's plays, notably *Separate Tables* (1954) hint at more serious issues, notably the playwright's own sexuality. The revolution which wholly changed English theater in the 1960s—with anger, absurdity, and "kitchen sink" realism—frequently defined itself as virulently anti-Rattigan and his drawing-room melodrama. He himself defended his style, vigorously, but posterity has sided with the modernists.

Isaac Rosenberg (1890–1918): Rosenberg was brought up in the (then) Jewish quarter of East End London, the son of a peddler and trader. It was a scholarly and aspirant background and the young Isaac was able to develop precocious talent in poetry and painting. He was accepted to study at the country's best art school, the Slade, in the University of London. In 1912, he published his first volume of verse, which attracted a favorable response from discriminating critics such as, notably, Ezra Pound. Although his family background was pacifist, and although he was physically unfit for active service, Rosenberg volunteered for the army in 1916. He refused all promotion and was killed, a private soldier, in the last year of the war, having produced, during his two years in the trenches, his best poetry.

Salman Rushdie (1947–): Rushdie was born in Bombay, in the year of Indian independence; a coincidence which furnishes the theme of his novel, *Midnight's Children* (1981). The family background was prosperous and Muslim, but relaxed on religious matters. Rushdie was educated at one of England's best schools, Rugby (which he hated) and Cambridge University, where he was happy. After graduating, he worked as an advertising copywriter and occasionally an actor. The least insular of authors, he absorbed the innovative techniques of "magic realism." *Midnight's Children* used these to fine effect. The novel won Britain's premier fiction prize, the Booker. Thereafter, Rushdie's career bloomed. It received a harsh check, in February 1989, when the Ayatollah Khomeini, the supreme leader in the Islamic Republic of Iran, declared Rushdie's novel *The Satanic Verses* (1988) blasphemous, and imposed a *fatwa*. For many years Rushdie was obliged to go into protective custody—under the wing, ironically, of a Britain about which his novel had been fully as satirical as it had been about Muslim fundamentalism. He continued to write in these straitened circumstances, establishing himself as the most brilliant of the postcolonial school of novelists.

Siegfried Sassoon (1886–1967): Sassoon was born into the moneyed English upper classes. His mother encouraged him to be a poet. After leaving Cambridge University, he devoted himself to the activities of a member of the landed gentry—particularly fox hunting (something recalled in his postwar book, *Memoirs of a Fox-Hunting Man*, 1928). He volunteered for service when World War I broke out, and served with great gallantry, being awarded a Military Cross—which he later threw away in disgust. Sassoon was sickened by the carnage of trench warfare—brilliant as he was at it— and composed bitterly satirical poems which he was brave enough to publish during the war. Unlike his comrade, Wilfred Owen, Sassoon survived. His poetry thereafter lost its bite, as he returned to his gentlemanly prewar mode of existence. His later, religious poetry has been found largely uninteresting and he is remembered, and respected, as the most forcefully direct of the First World War poets.

George Bernard Shaw (1856–1950): Shaw was born in Dublin, into a family which he records as having been unusually frigid in its personal relationships. He was largely self-educated. Aged twenty, he moved to London. From his mother he inherited a passionate love of music. His most successful early writing was music criticism for the newspapers and magazines which teemed in the capital at the time. Less successfully, Shaw (who believed in writing 5,000 words a day) turned out five novels which were variously unpublishable and, if published, unreadable. He was, meanwhile, taking a keen interest in the theater, currently at a low ebb. He perceived, very early, that comedy (in a tradition extending as far back as Ben Jonson) could be the vehicle of "ideas." From the Norwegian dramatist, Ibsen, he also realized that drama could be used to assault, and overturn, bourgeois philistinism—even though bourgeois philistines made up the bulk of the audiences. Fusing his extraordinary comic gift (quite as brilliant as that of his Irish contemporary, Wilde) with the advanced thinking of Wagner, and Nietzsche, Shaw began writing plays. They were paradoxical in manner, and powerfully ideological. Shaw pulled off the virtuosic trick of entertaining the British public, while undermining their prejudices. His first play, *Widower's Houses*, examined the real source of middle-class wealth—working-class exploitation. Prostitution, he argued in *Mrs. Warren's Profession* (1898) was as rational as marriage—given the intrinsic irrationality of marriage. He himself was ultra-rational in his lifestyle: a socialist, a Darwinist, a secularist, a vegetarian, and a lifelong abstainer from alcohol (and sex). In his mid-career masterpiece, *Pygmalion* (1913), he anatomized the hierarchy of British class, in terms of accent. In his later career (the longest literary career in English literature) Shaw became increasingly religio-philosophical. His utopian adherence to the doctrine of "Life Force" is expounded, at vast length, in his five part "biological Pentateuch" *Back to Methuselah* (1921). He died, still writing, festooned with honors. He is the only writer to have won both the Nobel Prize and an Oscar.

Tom Stoppard (1937–): Stoppard was born Tomáš Straussler in Czechoslovakia. The family fled the country, to escape the Nazi invasion, in 1939. As Jews, they would probably not have survived the war. His father did not. Stoppard's surviving family settled in England, where the boy received a thoroughly English upbringing. He left school at the age of 17, and although clearly brilliant (with a natural gift for philosophy) he never attended university. He worked as a journalist, but was attracted to the theater, where he had friends who encouraged his writing. His first stage success, *Rosencrantz and Guildenstern are Dead* (1967), established him overnight as the wittiest of dramatists currently writing. The play is clearly a recycling of Beckett's *Waiting for Godot*, with the difference that Stoppard's characters talk at express train speed, and a dauntingly high intellectual level. His drama has since moved in various directions—although critics sometimes complain that there is no single masterpiece. He returns to his personal roots in *Rock 'n' Roll* (2006), in which the fall of Communism is chronicled via a "deviant" (i.e., Western-influenced) Czech musical group in Prague. Stoppard won an Oscar for the script of the film *Shakespeare in Love* (1998), and was knighted in 1997.

Evelyn Waugh (1903–1966): The son of a leading London publisher, Waugh was educated at public school and Oxford. He was notably idle at university and intended to become an artist. An unsuccessful spell of school-teaching and equally unsuccessful marriage (which was dissolved in 1930) was followed by conversion to Catholicism (in the same fashion as his contemporary, and friend, Graham Greene). Thereafter Waugh devoted himself to a literature, establishing himself in the 1930s as a ruthless satirist of the nihilistic barbarism, as he saw it, of the modern age. Waugh saw active service in the Second World War, and out of it, and his intensifying devotion to his church, he wrote what is considered his finest work, the "Sword of Honor" trilogy (1952–1961). Not only the most deeply felt, it is the most personal of his works—with the possible exception of *The Ordeal of Gilbert Pinfold* (1957), which playfully chronicles Waugh's mid-life nervous breakdown. Waugh was archetypally English, but incorrigibly antagonistic to what, in an early novel, he calls the "decline and fall" of his country. He and Greene (along with Anthony Burgess, Muriel Spark, and David Lodge) embody that principle, enunciated by George Orwell, that there are no good Catholic novels in the 20th century, but some excellent novels written by Catholics.

H. G. Wells (1866–1946): The Godfather of British science fiction (who always preferred to be known as a novelist of ideas, and popular philosopher), Herbert George Wells was born in Kent, into the lower classes. His father was a professional cricketer turned shopkeeper; his mother had been in service (i.e., a servant). After school education, the young Wells was put to work in a draper's shop (commemorated in his later comic novel, *Kipps*, 1905). By dint of heroic self-education, he gained entrance to the Normal School of Science, in London, where he came under the influence of the leading Darwinist of the day, T. H. Huxley. Not sufficiently gifted to be a scientist proper, the young Wells embarked on a series of "scientific romances," of daring novelty, for popular readership. They included *The Time Machine* (1895), *The Invisible Man* (1897), *The War of the Worlds* (1898). Having made a name for himself, and infected with the new socialist doctrines abroad at the time, Wells's later work—in fiction, journalism, and social commentary—is more "serious." He wanted to be a "sage," writing, for example, a preposterously ambitious *Short History of the World* (1922). He returned, brilliantly, to science fiction with the utopian *The Shape of Things to Come*, in 1933.

Oscar Wilde (1854–1900): Wilde was born in Dublin, into a well-off family, established as members of the "Ascendancy" (i.e., Protestant and loyal to England, rather than Catholic Ireland). His father was a surgeon. Wilde went to school and university in Dublin before completing his education (brilliantly) at Oxford University. Already his brilliance as a poet and a conversational wit were clear to his contemporaries, as was also his personal flamboyance. From the first, Wilde dedicated himself to the French "Art for Art's Sake" doctrine. Life, he liked to say, imitated art. The highest art was the highest artifice. At the same time he embraced "Hellenic" ideals of beauty and human relationship. It both fascinated, and appalled, the English middle classes. Wilde was famous before he had produced anything which would justify that fame. He wrote higher journalism, delicate fairy stories and fables, and decadent verse. It was not until he began writing high-society comedies for the London stage that his career took off, with *Lady Windermere's Fan* (1892), *A Woman of No Importance* (1893) and his one undisputed masterpiece, *The Importance of Being Earnest* (1895). Wilde was married (happily) with children, but bisexual, and recklessly adventurous. The highpoint of his theatrical career coincided with a vindictive prosecution for "indecent practices" (homosexuality) which led to him being imprisoned for two years. On his release he took refuge in France, where he died, a disgraced, once celebrated, author shortly after. His most famous poem, *The Ballad of Reading Gaol*, vividly commemorates his suffering, as does the spiritual memoir, *De Profundis*, not published until long after his death. It was not Oscar Wilde, but England, which—posterity has concluded—was disgraced by his prosecution.

Virginia Woolf (1882–1941): Virginia Stephen was born into a literary family. Her father, Leslie Stephen, was a leading liberal man of letters. But he was also Victorian, and Virginia's life would be a crusade against what her fellow "Bloomsberry," Lytton Strachey, called "Eminent Victorians." Early in her family life the Stephens moved to the north London area of

Bloomsbury. Virginia, a brilliant young girl, had no opportunity to go to university—something about which she is wittily furious, in her essay, "A Room of One's Own." She did, however, have that room. And she did have access to the leading literary paper in London, the *Times Literary Supplement* (whose reviews and articles were anonymous—disguising the sex of the contributor). She and like-minded intellectuals (Strachey, E. M. Forster, Maynard Keynes), all of a progressive and antiestablishment cast of mind, founded the "Bloomsbury group." In 1912, she married the author and social commentator Leonard Woolf. Rigorously antiromantic (and lesbian by preference), Virginia had none the less found a stable and loving partner. The two of them would, following one of her recurrent nervous breakdowns, and as a kind of therapy, founded the Hogarth Press, in 1917. Having an outlet for her creative fiction enabled her to pursue an experimental line of fiction which flowered with *Mrs. Dalloway* (1925), *To the Lighthouse* (1927), *Orlando* (1928), and *The Waves* (1931). In them she explored the potential of her "stream of consciousness" method, which broke away from the old rigidities of fictional narrative. Throughout her writing life, Woolf also published trenchant criticism and wrote lively personal diaries and letters which rank as among the best private correspondence of the century. Always prey to mental disturbance, she drowned herself, in her country house, in 1941 believing—as her last novel *Between the Acts* testifies—that England would quite likely lose the war. Posthumously, and particularly after the feminist energy brought to literary criticism in the 1960s, she has been recognized as one of the two or three most important novelists of the century.

W. B. Yeats (1865–1939): William Butler Yeats was born in Dublin into a cultivated, artistically inclined, Protestant family. His early circumstances were comfortable. His first ambition was to be an artist, like his father and brother, Jack. But in his early 20s he turned to literature. The nationalist revival of Irish ("Celtic") literature was in full flow. So too was the renaissance of Irish drama—notably at Dublin's Abbey Theatre. Yeats threw himself enthusiastically into both movements. At the same period, he developed a hopeless love for the woman who was both his muse and his siren, Maud Gonne. He adored and devoted himself to her for years, but she would never be his. He married—happily, as it would transpire—another woman in 1917. Yeats's poetry, much of which was dreamily expressive of the "Celtic Twilight" hardened, and matured, under the influence of Modernist writers such as Ezra Pound. It is a feature of Yeats's work that it was in constant evolution: His poetry never stood still, stylistically. In the first decades of the 20th century, now a leading Modernist, he produced his most enduring work, with the crises of Irish nationalist struggle leading to independence in the early 1920s. Yeats combined politics with poetry over the next decade—as what he called "a smiling public man." He was awarded the Nobel Prize in 1923.

Bibliography

Ackroyd, Peter. *Dickens: Public Life and Private Passion.* New York: Hylas Publishing, 2006. The best of many biographies.

Akers, Geoff. *Beating for Light: The Story of Isaac Rosenberg.* Boulder, CO: Juniper Books, 2001.

Allen, Michael. *Seamus Heaney.* London: Macmillan, 1997. Collects representative critical views.

Anonymous. *Beowulf.* Translated by Seamus Heaney. Norton Critical Editions. New York: Norton, 2001. Admirable, communicates the essence of the poem.

Anonymous. *Everyman and Other Miracle and Morality Plays.* Dover Thrift Editions. New York: Dover Publications. 1995. A useful accessible text.

Anonymous. *Everyman, with Other Interludes, Including Eight Miracle Plays by Anonymous.* Edited by Ernest Rhys. Project Gutenberg, 2006. http://www.gutenberg.org/catalog/world/readfile?fk_files=258723. Convenient and free.

Anonymous. *The Seafarer.* Translated by Ezra Pound. In *The Norton Anthology of Poetry.* 4th ed. New York and London: Norton, 1996.

Aristotle, *Poetics.* Translated by Malcolm Heath. Penguin Classics. London and New York: Penguin, 1997. Helpful for the first lecture.

Armstrong, Isobel, ed. *The Major Victorian Poets: Reconsiderations.* New York and London: Routledge, 1969. An overview of the topic.

Ashton, Rosemary. *George Eliot.* Very Interesting People Series. London and New York: Oxford University Press, 2007. An attractive pithy volume.

———. *George Eliot: A Life.* New York and London: Penguin, 1998.

————. *The Life of Samuel Taylor Coleridge*. Oxford: Blackwell, 1995.

Attridge, Derek, ed. *The Cambridge Companion to James Joyce*. Cambridge, United Kingdom: Cambridge University Press, 2004. A useful survey of what the Joyce industry is doing.

Auden, W. H. *Collected Poems by W. H. Auden*. Edited by Edward Mendelson. New York: Modern Library, 2007. The definitive edition.

Austen, Jane. *Pride and Prejudice, Emma, Persuasion, Northanger Abbey, Sense and Sensibility, Mansfield Park*. Austen's six major novels are available at budget price, well-annotated, in a number of imprints. The Oxford World's Classics and Penguin Classics volumes are both reliable and have good annotation.

————. *Pride and Prejudice*. Edited by Claudia Johnson and Susan Wolfson. Longman Critical Edition. London: Longman, 2002. Has the fullest critical apparatus.

Bate, W. Jackson. *Samuel Johnson*. New York: Counterpoint, 1998. The standard "life."

Baugh, Alfred C., and T. Cable. *A History of the English Language* 5th ed. New York: Prentice Hall, 2001. Anglo-Saxon is, for the vast majority of English readers, a foreign tongue. The first three chapters will help.

Beadle, Richard, ed. *The Cambridge Companion to Medieval English Theatre*. Cambridge, United Kingdom: Cambridge University Press, 1994. Comprehensive and straightforward.

Behn, Aphra. *Oroonoko, The Rover, and Other Works*. Edited by Janet Todd. Penguin Classics. London and New York: Penguin, 1999. Budget-priced and authoritative.

Bergonzi, Bernard. *H. G. Wells: A Collection of Critical Essays*. Twentieth Century Views. United States: Prentice-Hall, 1976. The pioneering critic of

Wells's scientific romances offers a good overview of serious criticism of Wells in this collection.

Blake, William. *Blake, The Complete Poems*. Edited by Alice Ostriker. Penguin Classics. New York and London: Penguin, 1978.

Boswell, James. *The Life of Samuel Johnson*. Edited by Christopher Hibbert. Penguin Classics. London and New York: Penguin, 1979. Well-indexed. There are other budget-priced paperback editions.

Bradshaw, David, ed. *The Cambridge Companion to E. M. Forster.* Cambridge, United Kingdom: Cambridge University Press, 2007.

Bristow, Joseph, ed. *The Cambridge Companion to Victorian Poetry*. Cambridge, United Kingdom. Cambridge University Press, 2000. An overview of the topic.

Brontë, Charlotte. *Jane Eyre*. Edited by Richard J. Dunn. Norton Critical Editions. New York: Norton, 2000.

Brontë, Emily. *Wuthering Heights*. Edited by Richard J. Dunn. Norton Critical Editions. New York: Norton, 2002.

Browning, Robert. *Robert Browning: Selected Poems*. Edited by Daniel Karlin. Penguin Classics. New York and London: Penguin, 2001. Has the latest, most authoritative annotation in an easily accessible form.

Buchan, James. *Crowded with Genius*. New York and London: HarperCollins, 2003. A useful survey of Scottish literature and its distinct differences from English literature.

Buchan, John. *Sir Walter Scott*. London: Cassell, 1932. A fellow Scottish novelist's insights.

Bunyan, John. *The Pilgrim's Progress*. Oxford World's Classics. London and New York: Oxford University Press, 1984.

Burns, Robert. *The Canongate Burns: The Complete Poems and Songs of Robert Burns*. Edited by Andrew Noble and Patrick Scott Hogg. Edinburgh: Canongate, 2003.

Butler, Marilyn. *Jane Austen and the War of Ideas*. London and New York: Oxford University Press, 1975.

―――. *Romantics, Rebels, and Reactionaries*. New York and Oxford: Oxford University Press, 1981. A useful exposition of the political, social and historical background to the *Lyrical Ballads*.

Byron, George Gordon. *Lord Byron: The Major Works*. Edited by Jerome J. McGann. Oxford World's Classics. New York and London: Oxford University Press, 2000. The best selection of the work, introduced and annotated by a leading Byronist.

Carey, John. *John Donne: Life, Mind, and Art*. London: Faber, 1991.

―――, ed. *Marvell: A Critical Anthology*. London and New York: Penguin, 1960.

Chaucer, Geoffrey. *The Canterbury Tales*. (original-spelling edition). Edited by Jill Mann. Penguin Classics. London and New York: Penguin, 2005. A little easier on the wallet, and very sound.

―――. *The Riverside Chaucer*. Edited by Larry Benson et al. London and New York: Oxford University Press, 1988. The best edition currently available, it has excellent notes, summarizing everything we can know, at this stage in history, about the author and his work.

Chickering, Howell D. *Beowulf: A Dual-Language Edition*. New York: Anchor, 2006. A taste of the original, with a helpful literal accompanying translation.

Conan Doyle, Arthur. *The Annotated Sherlock Holmes: 2 Vols. in One*. Edited by William S. Baring-Gould. New York: Random House, 2002. Huge entertainment and instruction are to be found in this edition.

Conrad, Joseph. *Heart of Darkness and the Congo Diary.* Edited by Owen Knowles, Robert Hampson, and J. H. Stape. Penguin Classics. New York and London: Penguin, 2007. The "Congo Diary" makes an attractive supplement to the novel in this edition.

———. *Heart of Darkness.* Edited by Paul B. Armstrong. Norton Critical Editions. New York: Norton, 2005.

Cooper, Helen. *Oxford Guides to Chaucer: The Canterbury Tales.* London and New York: Oxford University Press, 1996. Very useful.

Copeland, Edward, and Juliet McMaster, eds. *The Cambridge Companion to Jane Austen.* Cambridge, United Kingdom: Cambridge University Press, 1997. Covers the whole field.

Corcoran, Neil, ed. *The Cambridge Companion to Twentieth-Century English Poetry.* Cambridge, United Kingdom: Cambridge University Press, 2008. A good overview.

Craciun, A. *Mary Wollstonecraft's A Vindication of the Rights of Woman: A Sourcebook.* New York: Routledge, 2002.

Crystal, David. *The Stories of English.* New York: Overlook, 2005. See the first four chapters.

Daiches, David. *Sir Walter Scott and His World.* London: Thames & Hudson, 1971. An entertaining pictorial account of the Wizard of the North's life and times.

Daniell, David. *The Bible in English: Its History and Influence.* New Haven: Yale University Press, 2003.

———. *William Tyndale: A Biography.* New Haven: Yale University Press, 2000. The authoritative biography.

David, Dierdre, ed. *The Cambridge Companion to the Victorian Novel.* Cambridge, United Kingdom: Cambridge University Press, 2001. More accessible than the Tillotson's *Novels of the 1840s.*

Defoe, Daniel. *Robinson Crusoe.* Edited by James Kelly and Thomas Keymer. New York and London: Oxford University Press, 2007.

Dickens, Charles. *Dombey and Son.* Edited by Andrew Sanders. Penguin Classics. New York and London: Penguin, 2006.

———. *Oliver Twist.* Edited by Fred Kaplan. Norton Critical Editions. New York: Norton, 1993.

Disraeli, Benjamin. *Sibyl: or the Two Nations.* New York: Hard Press, 2006.

Dobson, Michael, and Stanley Wells, eds. *The Oxford Companion to Shakespeare.* Oxford: Oxford University Press, 2001. A handy and reliable guide.

Donne, John. *John Donne: The Major Works.* Edited by John Carey. Oxford Authors. London and New York: Oxford University Press, 2000.

Douglas, Hugh. *Robert Burns: The Tinder Heart.* New York: Sutton Publishing, 2003. A sympathetic recent biography.

Drabble, Margaret, ed. *The Oxford Companion to English Literature.* London and New York: Oxford University Press, 2000. Of vital use, throughout this course, will be a good, succinct reference book. Strongly recommended for this purpose.

Dryden, John. *John Dryden: The Major Works.* Edited by Keith Walker. Oxford World's Classics. London and New York: Oxford World's Classics, 2003. A comprehensive and scholarly edition.

Earle, Peter. *The World of Defoe.* New York: Atheneum, 1977. A good introduction to the novelist.

Eaves, Morris, ed. *The Cambridge Companion to William Blake*. Cambridge, United Kingdom: Cambridge University Press, 2003.

Edel, Leon. *Henry James: A Life*. New York and London: HarperCollins, 1985. The standard biography of "The Master."

Egremont, Max. *Siegfried Sassoon: A Life*. New York: Farrar Strauss Giroux, 2005.

Eliot, George. *Middlemarch*. Edited by Bert G. Hornback. Norton Critical Editions. New York: Norton, 1999. Kind to the eyes and fully annotated, and contains a wealth of critical commentary and factual material.

Eliot, T. S. *T. S. Eliot Collected Poems 1909–1962*. New York: Harcourt, 1991. The standard edition.

———. *The Waste Land: A Facsimile and Transcript of the Original Drafts Including the Annotations of Ezra Pound*. Edited by Valerie Eliot. London: Faber, 1986.

Ellmann, Richard. *James Joyce*. New York and London: Oxford University Press, 1983. The definitive life of Joyce.

———. *Oscar Wilde*. New York: Vintage, 1988. The authoritative life.

Equiano, Olaudah. *The Interesting Narrative of the Life of Olaudah Equiano: Written by Himself*. New York: St. Martins, 2006.

Evans, G. Blakemore, and J. J. M. Tobin, eds. *The Riverside Complete Shakespeare*. New York: Houghton Mifflin, 1997. The best starting point, it has superb introductions and annotations.

Ferguson, Margaret, Mary Jo Salter, and Jon Stallworthy, eds., *The Norton Anthology of Poetry*. New York: W. W. Norton & Company, 1996.

Fernihough, Anne, ed. *The Cambridge Companion to D. H. Lawrence*. Cambridge, United Kingdom: Cambridge University Press, 2001.

Fielding, Henry. *The History of Tom Jones, A Foundling*. Edited by Thomas Keymer and Alice Wakely. Penguin Classics. New York and London: Penguin, 2005.

———. *Joseph Andrews* and *Shamela*. Edited by Thomas Keymer. Oxford World's Classics. London and New York: Oxford University Press, 1999. Conveniently demonstrates the rivalry with Samuel Richardson.

Fletcher, M. D., ed. *Reading Rushdie: Perspectives on the Fiction of Salman Rushdie*. Amsterdam and Atlanta, GA: Editions Rodopi, 1994.

Forster, E. M. *Howards End*. New York and London: Penguin, 2000.

Foster, R. F. *The Apprentice Mage, 1865–1914*. New York and London: Oxford University Press, 1998. The first volume of the definitive two-volume life of W. B. Yeats.

———. *W. B. Yeats: A Life Volume II: The Arch-Poet, 1915–1939*. New York and London: Oxford University Press, 2003.

Fox, Christopher, ed. *The Cambridge Companion to Jonathan Swift*. Cambridge, United Kingdom: Cambridge University Press, 2003. Useful and wide-ranging.

Frank, Katherine. *A Chainless Soul: A Life of Emily Brontë*. New York: Ballantine, 1992. The best modern biography.

Furbank, P. N. *E. M. Forster: A Life*. London: Harvest Books, 1994.

Garner, Michael, Marilyn Butler, and James Chandler, eds. *Romanticism and the Gothic*. Cambridge, United Kingdom: Cambridge University Press, 2006. An introduction to the genre headed by Ann Radcliffe.

Gaskell, Elizabeth. *The Life of Charlotte Brontë*. Edited by Elisabeth Jay. Penguin Classics. New York and London: Penguin, 1998.

———. *Mary Barton*. Edited by Shirley Foster. Oxford World's Classics. New York and London: Oxford University Press, 2006. Best buy.

Gates, Henry Louis, ed. *The Classic Slave Narratives*. New York: NAL, 1987. Supplies excellent context to Olaudah Equiano's story and other slave narratives.

Gibbon, Edward. *The History of the Decline and Fall of the Roman Empire*. Edited by David Womersley. London: Allen Lane, 1996. This three-volume edition is highly recommended.

———. *The History of the Decline and Fall of the Roman Empire*. "Project Gutenberg." 1996. http://www.gutenberg.org/browse/authors/g#a375.

Gill, Stephen. *William Wordsworth: A Life*. New York and London: Oxford University Press, 1989.

Greer, Germaine, ed. *Kissing the Rod*. New York: Farrar, Straus and Giroux, 1989. A more frank tendentious selection of women poets.

Haight, Gordon S. *George Eliot*. New York and London: Penguin, 1985. The definitive biography.

Hardy, Thomas. *Jude the Obscure: An Authoritative Text : Backgrounds and Contexts*. Edited by Norman Page. New York: Norton, 1999.

———. *Selected Poems*. Edited by Robert Mezey. Penguin Classics. New York and London: Penguin, 1998.

Hastings, Selena. *Evelyn Waugh: A Biography*. New York: Houghton Mifflin, 1995. An admirable, straightforward account of a complex life.

Heaney, Seamus. *Beowulf: A New Verse Translation*. New York: Norton, 2001. Admirably communicates the essence of the poem.

———. *New Selected Poems, 1966–87 by Seamus Heaney*. London: Faber, 2002.

Heilpern, John. *John Osborne.* London: Chatto, 2006.

Herbert, George. *George Herbert: The Complete English Poems.* Edited by J. Tobin. Cambridge, United Kingdom: Cambridge University Press, 2007.

Hibberd, Dominic, ed. *Poetry of the First World War.* London: Palgrave Macmillan, 1981. A comprehensive overview.

———. *Wilfred Owen.* London: Phoenix Books, 2003.

Hill, Christopher. *Intellectual Origins of the English Revolution.* Oxford: Oxford University Press, 2001.

———. *Puritanism and Revolution.* London: Secker and Warburg, 1958.

———. *Society and Puritanism in Pre-Revolutionary England.* New York: Schocken Books, 1964.

———. *A Tinker and a Poor Man: John Bunyan and His Church, 1628–1688.* New York: Alfred A. Knopf, Inc., 1989. An excellent introduction to Bunyan.

Hitchens, Christopher. *Why Orwell Matters.* New York: Basic Books, 2003. Pugnacious and convincing.

Hobbes, Thomas. *Leviathan.* Edited by Michael Oakeshott. Oxford: Blackwell, 1946. Much reprinted and discussed.

Holmes, Richard. *Shelley: The Pursuit.* New York and London: HarperCollins, 1994. The authoritative biography.

Holroyd, Michael. *Bernard Shaw: The One-Volume Definitive Edition.* New York: Random House, 1998. A useful compact version of the three-volume work.

House, Humphry. *The Dickens World.* New York and London: Oxford University Press, 1960. Discusses the social background to *Oliver Twist.*

Howes, Marjorie, and John Kelly, eds. *The Cambridge Companion to W. B. Yeats*. Cambridge, United Kingdom: Cambridge University Press, 2006.

Hughes, Derek, and Janet Todd, eds. *The Cambridge Companion to Aphra Behn*. Cambridge, United Kingdom: Cambridge University Press, 2005. Contains, in a handy compressed form, most of what the modern reader of Behn will need.

Innes, Christopher, ed. *The Cambridge Companion to George Bernard Shaw*. Cambridge, United Kingdom: Cambridge University Press, 1998.

Johnson, Claudia L., ed. *The Cambridge Companion to Mary Wollstonecraft*. Cambridge, United Kingdom: Cambridge University Press, 2002.

Johnson, James William. *A Profane Wit: The Life of John Wilmot, Earl of Rochester*. New York: University of Rochester Press, 2004.

Johnson, Samuel. *A Dictionary of the English Language: An Anthology*. Edited by David Crystal. New York and London: Penguin, 2007. The most convenient and entertaining introduction to the lexicography.

————. *Samuel Johnson: The Major Works*. Edited by Donald Greene. London and New York: Oxford University Press, 2000. Good value and excellently annotated.

Jones, Nigel. *Rupert Brooke*. London: BBC Books, 2003.

Jonson, Ben. *Five Plays*. Edited by G. A. Wilkes. Oxford World's Classics. London and New York: Oxford University Press, 1999. Admirable, scholarly, and budget-priced.

Jordan, John O., ed. *The Cambridge Companion to Charles Dickens*. Cambridge, United Kingdom: Cambridge University Press, 2001.

Joyce, James. *A Portrait of the Artist as a Young Man*. Edited by Jeri Johnson. Oxford World's Classics. New York and London: Oxford University Press, 2001. Best buy.

————. *Ulysses*. Edited by Declan Kiberd. Penguin Modern Classics. New York and London: Penguin, 2000. Best buy.

Kastan, David Scott. *Companion to Shakespeare*. Oxford and New York: Wiley-Blackwell, 1999. Also handy and reliable.

Keats, John. *John Keats: Selected Poems*. Edited by John Barnard. Penguin Classics. New York and London: Penguin, 2007.

Kelly, Katherine E., ed. *The Cambridge Companion to Tom Stoppard*. Cambridge, United Kingdom: Cambridge University Press, 2001.

Kinkead-Weekes, Mark. *Samuel Richardson*. London: Methuen, 1973. The best critical introduction to the fiction and to what is known of the novelist's life.

————, and Ian Gregor. *William Golding*. London: Faber, 2002. The best critical introduction.

Knights, L. C. *Drama and Society in the Age of Jonson*. London and New York: Penguin, 1962. A good overview of the Jacobean situation, as it affects drama.

Kramer, Dale, ed. *The Cambridge Companion to Thomas Hardy*. Cambridge, United Kingdom: Cambridge University Press, 1999.

Larkin, Philip. *Collected Poems by Philip Larkin*. Edited by Anthony Thwaite. New York: Farrar Straus Giroux, 2004.

Leavis, F. R. *The Great Tradition*. London: Penguin, 1954. A fiercely opinionated reading of modern English fiction.

Lee, Hermione. *Virginia Woolf*. New York and London: Vintage, 1999.

Levin, Harry. *The Overreacher*. New York: Beacon Press, 1964. First published in 1952 and still the best way in to Marlowe's drama.

Lonsdale, Roger, ed. *Eighteenth-Century Women Poets: An Oxford Anthology*. New York and London: Oxford University Press, 1990. A comprehensive and annotated period selection.

Lycett, Andrew. *The Man Who Created Sherlock Holmes: The Life and Times of Sir Arthur Conan Doyle*. New York: Free Press, 2007. The first biography to use recently released papers of Conan Doyle.

MacCarthy, Fiona. *Byron: Life and Legend*. New York: Farrar, Straus and Giroux, 2004. A biography that judiciously separates Byronic myth from fact.

Mack, Maynard. *Alexander Pope*. New York: Norton, 1986. The standard biography.

Mackenzie, Norman and Jeanne. *H. G. Wells: A Biography*. New York: Simon and Schuster, 1973. The most comprehensive life of Wells.

Marlowe, Christopher. *Complete Poems and Translations*. Edited by Stephen Orgel. Penguin Classics. London and New York: Penguin, 2007. Wholeheartedly recommended, and easy on the pocket.

Marvell, Andrew. *Andrew Marvell: The Complete Poems*. Edited by Elizabeth Story Donno. London and New York: Penguin, 2005.

McKitterick, Rosamund, and Roland Quinault. *Edward Gibbon and Empire*. Cambridge, United Kingdom: Cambridge University Press, 2002. Necessary background.

Mellor, Anne K. *Mary Shelley: Her Life, Her Fiction, Her Monsters*. New York and London: Routledge, 1989.

Mendelson, Edward. *The English Auden*. London: Faber, 2001.

Meyers, Jeffrey. *Joseph Conrad: A Biography*. New York: Cooper Square Press, 2001. Highly readable.

Miles, Robert. *Ann Radcliffe: The Great Enchantress*. Manchester United Kingdom: Manchester University Press, 1995.

Milton, John. *John Milton: The Complete Poems*. Edited by John Leonard. Penguin Classics. London and New York: Penguin, 1999. Easier on the pocket and perfectly adequate.

———. *John Milton: The Major Works*. Edited by Stephen Orgel and J. Goldberg. Oxford World's Classics. London and New York: Oxford University Press, 2003.

———. *Paradise Lost*. Edited by Alistair Fowler. Longman Annotated Poets. London: Longman, 2006. The best and most comprehensively annotated edition: The notes are both explanatory and "variorum" (that is, they discuss various critical interpretations of crucial passages).

Moody, A. David, ed. *The Cambridge Companion to T. S. Eliot*. Cambridge, United Kingdom: Cambridge University Press, 1995.

Morrison, Blake. *The Movement: English Poetry and Fiction of the 1950s*. London: Oxford University Press, 1971. A good account of the movement to which Larson belongs.

Motion, Andrew. *Keats*. Chicago: University of Chicago, 1999. The best recent biography.

———. *Philip Larkin: A Writer's Life*. New York: Farrar Straus Giroux, 1993. The best biography.

Neale, John E. *Elizabeth the First*. New York: Doubleday, 1957. A readable background to Spenser's career as author, diplomat, and warrior.

Nicolson, Nigel, and Stephen Colover. *The World of Jane Austen*. London: Weidenfeld, 1997.

Nokes, David. *Raillery and Rage*. London: Palgrave Macmillan, 1987. A good overview of Augustan satire.

Norbrook, D., and H. R. Woudhuysen, eds. *The Penguin Book of Renaissance Verse, 1509–1659*. London and New York: Penguin, 1993.

Pearsall, Derek. *The Canterbury Tales*. A sound entry point into the vast commentary on Chaucer. London and New York: Routledge, 1985.

———. *The Life of Chaucer*. Oxford: Blackwell, 1992. Most recent biography.

Pilling, John, ed. *The Cambridge Companion to Beckett*. Cambridge, United Kingdom: Cambridge University Press, 1994.

Pope, Alexander. *The Poems of Alexander Pope: A Reduced Version of the Twickenham Text*. Edited by John Butt. New Haven, CT: Yale University Press, 1966.

Prickett, Stephen, and Robert Carroll, eds. *The Bible: Authorized King James Version with Apocrypha*. Oxford World's Classics. London and New York: Oxford University Press, 1998. The King James Bible is the most easily purloinable book in the Western world, but a useful version, from the point of view of this course, is this "literary" annotated edition.

Prose, Francine, ed. *The Mrs. Dalloway Reader*. New York: Harcourt, 2003.

Raby, Peter, ed. *The Cambridge Companion to Harold Pinter*. Cambridge, United Kingdom: Cambridge University Press, 2001.

———, ed. *The Cambridge Companion to Oscar Wilde*. Cambridge, United Kingdom: Cambridge University Press, 1997.

Radcliffe, Ann. *The Mysteries of Udolpho*. Edited by Jacqueline Howard. Penguin Classics. New York and London: Penguin, 2001. Usefully annotated and introduced.

Raine, Craig. *T. S. Eliot*. London and New York: Oxford University Press, 2006.

Rawson, Claude, ed. *The Cambridge Companion to Henry Fielding.* Cambridge, United Kingdom: Cambridge University Press, 2007. Current critical commentary is well represented.

Richardson, Samuel. *Pamela: Or, Virtue Rewarded.* Edited by Thomas Keymer and Alice Wakely. Oxford World's Classics. Oxford and New York: Oxford University Press, 2001. A good edition of a bulky text.

Richetti, John, ed. *The Cambridge History of English Literature, 1660–1780.* Cambridge, United Kingdom: Cambridge University Press, 2005. Less specifically directed to satire than the Nokes overview.

————. *Defoe's Narratives.* London and New York: Oxford University Press, 1975. Good introduction to the novelist.

Ricks, Christopher. *Tennyson.* London: Macmillan, 1989. The finest volume of critical commentary on Tennyson.

Rivero, Albert J., ed. *New Essays on Samuel Richardson.* London: Palgrave Macmillan, 1996. Offers a good selection of critical interpretations.

Rochester, John Wilmot. *Rochester: Complete Poems and Plays.* Edited by Paddy Lyons. Everyman's Paperback Classics. United Kingdom: Everyman's Library, 1993. A scholarly and easy-on-the pocket collection of the primary work.

Roe, Nicholas. *Romanticism: An Oxford Guide.* New York and London: Oxford University Press, 2005. An up-to-date survey of the critical field.

Roe, Sue, and Susan Sellers, eds. *The Cambridge Companion to Virginia Woolf.* Cambridge, United Kingdom: Cambridge University Press, 2000.

Rogers, Pat. *The Alexander Pope Encyclopedia.* New York: Greenwood Press, 2004. Too expensive to buy, but usefully consulted.

————, ed. *The Cambridge Companion to Alexander Pope.* Cambridge, United Kingdom: Cambridge University Press, 2008.

Bibliography

Ryals, Clyde De L. *The Life of Robert Browning*. Oxford: Wiley Blackwell, 1996. The most recent biography.

Schlicke, Paul, ed. *The Oxford Reader's Companion to Dickens*. New York and London: OUP, 1999. Compendious information on Dickens.

Scott, Sir Walter. *Waverley*. Edited by Andrew Hook. Penguin English Library. London and New York: Penguin, 1985. Has the most useful introduction and notes.

Selden, Michael. *Graham Greene: The Enemy Within*. New York: Random House, 1995. Readable and tendentious.

Shapiro, James. *A Year in the Life of William Shakespeare, 1599*. New York: HarperCollins Publishers, 2005. Highly recommended, as making the best of the tantalizing little we know of our greatest author's life. Inserts the dramatist into his *annus mirabilis*, 1599.

Sharrock, Roger. *John Bunyan*. London: Macmillan, 1968. A useful and straightforward introduction.

Shaw, Bernard. *Pygmalion*. Edited by Dan H. Laurence and Nicholas Grene. Penguin Classics. New York and London: Penguin, 2003. Best and handiest edition of the play.

Shelley, Mary. *Frankenstein*. Edited by J. Paul Hunter. Norton Critical Edition. New York: Norton, 1995.

Spenser, Edmund. *The Faerie Queene*. Edited by T. P. Roche and C. P. O'Donnell. Penguin Classics. London and New York: Penguin, 1979.

———. *Spenser: The Faerie Queene*. 2nd ed. Edited by A. C. Hamilton et al. London: Longman, 2006. Best buy.

Stape, J. H., ed. *The Cambridge Companion to Joseph Conrad*. Cambridge, United Kingdom: Cambridge University Press, 1996. A more comprehensive survey of the author's life and work.

Stenton, Frank M. *Anglo-Saxon England*. Oxford: Oxford University Press, 1971. An excellent introduction to the world that produced *Beowulf*.

Sterne, Laurence. *The Life and Opinions of Tristram Shandy, Gentleman*. Edited by Joan and Melvyn New. Penguin Classics. New York and London: Penguin, 2003.

Strachan, John. *John Keats: A Sourcebook*. New York and London: Routledge, 2003. Comprehensive.

Sutherland, John. *The Life of Sir Walter Scott: A Critical Biography*. Oxford: Blackwell, 1995.

————. *So You Think You Know Thomas Hardy?* London and New York: Oxford University Press, 2001. May tempt those of a fanciful disposition.

————, and Dierdre le Faye. *So You Think You Know Jane Austen?: A Literary Quizbook*. New York and London: Oxford University Press, 2005.

Swift, Jonathan. *Gulliver's Travels*. Edited by Robert DeMaria. Penguin Classics. New York and London: Penguin, 2003. Sound and good value.

————. *The Writings of Jonathan Swift*. Edited by Robert Greenberg and William Piper. New York: Norton, 1973.

Tanner, Tony. *Jane Austen*. London: Palgrave Macmillan, 2007. Specialist interpretations.

Taylor, Barbara. *Mary Wollstonecraft and the Feminist Imagination* Cambridge, United Kingdom: Cambridge University Press, 2003.

Taylor, D. J. *Orwell: The Life*. New York: Holt, 2004. An admirable straightforward account of a complex life.

Taylor, John Russell. *Anger and After: A Guide to the New British Drama*. London: Penguin, 1963. Still the best guide to the late 20th-century revolution in English theater.

Tennyson, Alfred. *Alfred Tennyson.* Edited by Adam Roberts. Oxford Authors. New York and London: Oxford University Press, 2000. Offers the best comprehensive collection of the poetry.

Thackeray, William Makepeace. *Vanity Fair.* Edited by John Sutherland. Oxford World's Classics. New York and London: Oxford University Press, 1992. Recommended, for immodest reasons.

Tillotson, Kathleen. *Novels of the 1840s.* Oxford: Clarendon Press, 1954. The best introduction, though hard to come by.

Todd, Janet, ed. *Be Good, Sweet Maid: An Anthology of Women and Literature.* New York: Holmes and Meier, 1981.

Tomalin, Claire. *The Life and Death of Mary Wollstonecraft.* New York and London: Penguin, 1974.

———. *Thomas Hardy: The Time-Torn Man.* New York and London: Viking, 2006.

Tyndale, William, trans. *Tyndale's New Testament.* Edited by David Daniell. New Haven, CT: Yale University Press, 1996. A superb modern-spelling edition.

Vendler, Helen. *The Poetry of George Herbert.* Cambridge, MA: Harvard University Press, 1975.

———. *Seamus Heaney.* Cambridge, MA: Harvard University Press, 1998. An authoritative verdict.

Waldock, A. J. A., *Paradise Lost and Its Critics.* Cambridge, United Kingdom: Cambridge University Press, 1962. The most useful first work of commentary, it pugnaciously confronts what the critic sees as "contradictions" in Milton's project.

Walter, George, ed. *The Penguin Book of First World War Poetry.* New York and London: Penguin, 2007. A comprehensive selection.

Webster, John. *The Duchess of Malfi and Other Plays*. Edited by Rene Weis. Oxford World's Classics. London and New York: Oxford University Press, 1998. Admirable, scholarly, and budget-priced.

Weis, Rene. *Shakespeare Revealed*. London: John Murray, 2007. Brilliantly reconstructs the Stratford, the Warwickshire, and the England, from which Shakespeare sprang, and whose highest aspirations he articulated.

Wells, H. G. *The Complete Short Stories of H. G. Wells*. Edited by John Hammond. London: Orion, 2001.

Wells, Stanley. *Shakespeare and Co.* London and New York: Pantheon, 2007. Places him in the theatrical world of Elizabethan London.

Wilde, Oscar. *The Complete Works of Oscar Wilde*. Edited by Merlin Holland. New York and London: HarperCollins, 2003. A compendious and budget-priced edition of the primary texts, edited by a descendant of the author.

"The William Blake Archive." www.blakearchive.org. An unusually stimulating, informative, and interactive source of information and scholarly exchange.

Wolfson, Susan J., ed. *The Cambridge Companion to Keats*. Cambridge, United Kingdom: Cambridge University Press, 2001. Comprehensive.

Woolf, Rosemary. *The English Mystery Plays*. Berkeley, CA: University of California Press, 1980. A good general introduction.

Woolf, Virginia. *Mrs. Dalloway*. Edited by Oliver Stallybrass. London: Harvest Books, 2005.

Wordsworth, William, and Samuel Taylor Coleridge. *Lyrical Ballads*. Edited by Michael Mason. London: Longman, 2007.

Wu, Duncan, ed. *Romanticism: An Anthology*. Oxford: Blackwell, 2005. Offers a generous selection of primary work.

Bibliography

Yeats, W. B. *The Collected Poems of W. B. Yeats*. Edited by Richard J. Finneran. New York: Scribner, 1996.

Zwicker, John, ed. *The Cambridge Companion to John Dryden*. Cambridge, United Kingdom: Cambridge University Press, 2004. Covers the critical consensus on the poet.

Zwicker, Steven N., ed. *The Cambridge Companion to English Literature, 1650–1740*. Cambridge, United Kingdom: Cambridge University Press, 1998. An excellent overview to this lecture's literature and its larger contexts.

Notes

Notes

Notes

Notes

Notes

Notes

Notes